SPENSER STUDIES

XX

SPENSER STUDIES

A Renaissance Poetry Annual

XX

EDITED BY
William A. Oram
Anne Lake Prescott
Thomas P. Roche, Jr.

AMS PRESS
NEW YORK

SPENSER STUDIES
A RENAISSANCE POETRY ANNUAL

edited by Anne Lake Prescott, William A. Oram, and Thomas P. Roche, Jr.

is published annually by AMS Press, Inc. as a forum for Spenser scholarship and criticism and related Renaissance subjects. Manuscripts must be double-spaced, including notes, which should be grouped at the end and should be prepared according to *The Chicago Manual of Style*. Authors of essay-length manuscripts should include an abstract of 100–150 words and provide a disk version of the article, preferably in a Windows-compatible format. One copy of each manuscript should be sent to Thomas P. Roche, Jr., Department of English, Princeton University, Princeton, NJ 08544, one copy to Anne Lake Prescott, Department of English, Barnard College, Columbia University, 3009 Broadway, New York, NY 10027–6598, and one copy to William A. Oram, Department of English, Smith College, Northampton, MA 01063.

Please send inquiries concerning subscriptions or the availability of earlier volumes to AMS Press, Inc., Brooklyn Navy Yard, 63 Flushing Ave.—Unit 221, Bldg. 292, Suite 417, Brooklyn, NY 11205–1054, USA.

ISSN 0195–9468
Volume XX, ISBN 0–404–19220–3

Contents

Illustrations
118, 119, 121, 231, 238, 244

Index
291

ROBERT ELLRODT

Fundamental Modes of Thought, Imagination, and Sensibility in the Poetry of Edmund Spenser

A survey of Spenser's modes of thought and sensibility may bring out some individual characteristics despite his self-conscious use of rhetoric. His favorite stanza form reflects his vision of the world. His eclecticism in his philosophical and religious views rests on the coexistence of contraries without reconciliation, yet without tension. His wandering reverie, focused on isolated figures, associates static and dynamic elements. His praise of action is always undercut by a yearning for repose. A conjunction of contraries without discord may be traced in his conception of change and in his reconciliation of the active with the contemplative life. Apparent contradictions in his treatment of human and divine love are accounted for through a parallel with the *Trattato dell' amore humano* of Flaminio de Nobili.

*I*N THREE VOLUMES on *L'Inspiration personnelle et l'esprit du temps chez les poètes métaphysiques anglais*[1] and in a recent English version, at once condensed and expanded, *Seven Metaphysical Poets: A Structural Study of the Unchanging Self,*[2] I have called attention to the permanence of individual modes of thought, imagination and sensibility in each author despite all changes in his life and convictions, his choice of themes and stylistic variations. After the publication of my book, *Neoplatonism in the Poetry of Spenser,*[3] I had also attempted to outline several aspects of authorial constancy in the much narrower compass

Spenser Studies: A Renaissance Poetry Annual, Volume XX, Copyright © 2005 by AMS Press, Inc. All rights reserved.

of an essay in French, published in a little known and now extinct periodical.[4] It probably remained unread and, not to disperse my attention overmuch in my research, I parted company with the Prince of Poets. Since this article on Spenser, though very different in its generality from my detailed studies on the Metaphysicals, may lend some support to my views on literary creation, it may be appropriate to reshape and revive it now in English. Besides, my incidental parallel between Spenser and Flaminio Nobili has attracted no attention and may still have some interest for the study of Renaissance Platonism at large. I have updated and enlarged the original text, mainly through references to more recent studies which either support or contradict my former assertions.[5]

The poetry of Spenser does not lend itself readily to the same type of scrutiny as the lyrics of the Metaphysicals, for the author of *The Shepheardes Calendar* and *The Faerie Queene* took the pose of a professional author.[6] He is, of course, intensely present in his poems, but I am not concerned with his "self-presentation,"[7] or his self-advertisement.[8] My present interest is not in his conception of his role or his opinions, but in the unchanging structures of his mind. Nor am I trying to explore the relationship between his writings and his life, as in *Spenser's Life and the Subject of Biography*, for I agree that this can only lead to a "hypothetical construction."[9] My own hypothesis, much more precisely illustrated in *Seven Metaphysical Poets*, is that the works of an author disclose some constant characteristics of an individual mind.[10] These are more easily discerned when a poet is not "consciously and continuously constructing a literary life for himself" as "a self-declared national poet."[11] Poetic composition with Spenser was inseparable from this ambition and always attended by a claim to learning. He was not "over-mastred by some thoughts" compelling him to yield "an inckie tribute" to them, as Sidney confessed.[12] He sought to become master of an instrument when he translated or paraphrased earlier works. Even in his pastorals he served an apprenticeship for a higher design: Renaissance poets were urged to cultivate minor genres before attempting the epic.

Spenser, however, must have been genuinely attracted to the pastoral vein since it emerged again in the Sixth Book of *The Faerie Queene*.[13] It allowed him to express a personal longing, a genuine love of rustic simplicity and the nostalgic yearning for the Golden Age, or edenic life, so prominent in the Proem to Book V and in the story of Calidore. Furthermore, even when he takes up one of the most traditional forms, the Complaint, and meditates on the *Ruines of Time* or *Visions of the Worlds Vanitie*, he betrays a tendency to a rumination over the past and a sensitivity to the emotional power of decay which suggest deeper affinities with du Bellay than a mere thematic and stylistic interest in the *Antiquités de Rome*.

An attempt to discern the dominant traits of Spenser's personality, however, may be defeated at times by his self-conscious use of rhetoric, so insistently pointed out, probably by the author himself, in *The Shepheardes Calendar*.[14] This makes it almost impossible to distinguish between figures chosen only for their rhetorical appeal and those that, even when deliberate, seem in deep harmony with the poet's cast of mind—a distinction drawn in my study of the Metaphysical Poets. In the case of Spenser I can only assume tentatively that we may be guided by the criterion of excellence. The true nature and inclinations of an artist are best revealed in his best work.[15] Now, obviously, close-packed figures in which the meaning is compressed or sharpened, as in the conceits of the Metaphysicals or some sonneteers, did not suit the genius of Spenser, which called for spaciousness in the period and the stanza. He was a Ciceronian at a time when Cicero was still the model; but I very much doubt he might have turned to Seneca a few years later when the fashion changed. Even when writing sonnets, he usually imparted to the poem the movement of an expansive single stanza. In *The Faerie Queene*, the celebrated Spenserian stanza is characterized by its amplitude, its *rallentando* rhythm, and the final outstretching of the line into an hexameter. It does seem to espouse the very rhythm of his mind. Emile Legouis likened it to the majesty of a deep river flowing evenly. A more accurate image may be offered by the unceasing unfurling of waves in the ocean, each of them rising in a renewed effort and culminating before subsiding in a vast and solitary expiration, immediately followed by a new swelling aspiration. The final hexameter, however, suggests at once the breaking of a wave splashing out on a shore, and the very firmness of the shore, the steadfastness of a solid base. One may observe the same movement in the longer stanzas of the *Epithalamion*, the only poem that may rival the *Faerie Queene* in excellence.[16] Spenser's distinctive apprehension of time was obviously very different from Donne's emphasis on the instant; but very different too from Crashaw's or Marvell's fluid and slippery present or Vaughan's rumination.[17] It seems closest to Shakespeare's, but Shakespeare offers no final repose and no leap from the world of change to eternity.[18] The Spenserian stanza reflects the poet's vision of a world in which every being is born, exalted and destroyed, yet whose innumerable, ephemeral, yet ever-reviving existence firmly rests on the pillars of eternity. It is in harmony with the philosophy of the *Mutabilitie Cantos*.[19]

Throughout the *Faerie Queene* the philosophical vision of Spenser is all-embracing. His mind welcomed the Neoplatonism of Ficino and Castiglione while retaining many Aristotelian notions; he could echo the stoicism of Seneca and at times the epicureanism of Lucretius.[20] In 1960 I had reacted to the current tendency to read into the *Faerie Queene* metaphysical allegories based on the elaborate Neoplatonic systems of Ficino and Pico with their hierarchy of emanations and graded worlds. My intention was not, as later critics sometimes assumed,[21] to oppose Christianity and Platonism, but to make a clear distinction between the more sophisticated Neoplatonism of the Italian Renaissance—carefully, though at times dubiously, reconciled with Christian dogma—and the Platonic notions, often of Augustinian origin, current and even at times "popular," through the Middle Ages.[22] I came to the conclusion that Spenser was less interested in metaphysics than in mythography and moral, historical, and political issues,[23] which, after all, is perhaps more in tune with present concerns, neohistoricist or not. I had acknowledged the poet's "syncretism," but again introduced a distinction between the carefully constructed syncretism of some Renaissance Neoplatonist thinkers and the "wide and undiscriminating sympathies of a Renaissance mind."[24]

In the 1972 article, analyzing only the poet's cast of mind (or "habits of thought" in Deborah Shuger's phrase[25]), I acknowledged it might be misleading to call it "syncretic" in the absence of any effort at synthesis, and characterized it as "eclectic." Eclecticism was, of course, a common trait in the Renaissance; yet Spenser seems to have shown a personal accessibility and an unparalleled readiness of response to heterogeneous ideas. His mind obviously indulged their coexistence and was not eager to build up a consistent system. This, however, does not lead to disharmony since "romantic poetics," as Northrop Frye argued, "resolves ethical discord into the unity of an aesthetic response to fiction."[26] In the verse of the *Faerie Queene* diverse elements seem to be suspended in the melodious homogeneity of a fluid element. This is the more remarkable since the poet usually expressed emotions and moral values through simple and unmitigated antitheses. In the *Shepheardes Calendar,* the *Complaints, Amoretti* and *Prothalamion,* as well as in the *Faerie Queene,* joy and grief, fear and hope, fair and foul, true and false, natural and artificial are bluntly contrasted. Two main contrasts, however, are presented in a particular way. Human love and heavenly love, as well as action and contemplation, are clearly in opposition, yet in a way which preserves the worth of each and allows a combination of both. This will be discussed later.

In my original article my assertions were only based on a few illustrations; I have fortunately discovered that Professor Carol Kaske has offered a far more elaborate and precise demonstration of what I had intimated. I need only subscribe from my own perspective—the poet's constant modes of thought—to her richly documented survey of "Spenser's pluralistic universe."[27] Spotting "contradictions between his world views, sometimes within a single passage"(123), she proved that the author of the *Faerie Queene* wrote *sententiae* "constructed to sound contradictory" (124), that "nothing is done to allay this and other contrasts" since "Spenser refuses to take sides" (128), and that the epic "is to some extent really about two or three different pictures of man and his world" (130). An effect of "ambiguity" is achieved "by the alternative causes, divine or human, and the alternative motivations, Christian or secular, assigned to so many of its events or actions" (143). She conceded that this pluralism has boundaries: in some instances Spenser resolves the contraries he has set up and is therefore rather a syncretist (146), notably in Book II, where he is a Christian humanist, a label with which my analysis of his modes of thought and sensibility is easily reconciled. She also admitted (147) that "syncretic imagery," distinguished from "syncretism of thought," pervaded *The Faerie Queene*, which creates the unity of aesthetic response I have earlier alluded to.[28] In her later study, *Spenser and Biblical Poetics*,[29] Kaske's close reading pointed out further contradictions and conflicting images which disclose an adiaphoristic point of view. When the contradictions seem to be used deliberately by the author, perhaps to promote an attitude of toleration, one moves beyond the mere acceptance of diversity and closer to a kind of conscious syncretism, but this does not seem to be always the case.

In my original argument, I had called attention to the contrast between statements which seem to imply an allegiance to a Calvinistic doctrine and the true nature of the emotions, religious or merely human, expressed in various episodes.[30] The most striking instance is the temptation of Redcrosse in the Cave of Despair. The poet juxtaposes various motives. The insistence on the prospect of inevitable damnation (I.ix.49–51) is in the tradition of Calvinism: Redcrosse has allowed himself to be convinced he is among the reprobate. The temptation of suicide may then seem illogical, but it was common and psychologically understandable: the man who has no hope of redemption may choose to go to hell immediately rather than live longer in "anguish"(49.4). Yet one hardly feels in the "trembling horror" of Redcrosse (49.3) the genuine terror of Bunyan or Cowper. In fact, Despair had initially resorted to a very different argument in favor of suicide: the *taedium vitae* of one who "trauels by the wearie wandring way "(39.1). The lure of death had been first evoked by the poet as an invitation to repose and the beautiful cadence of the stanza suggests an emotion more deeply felt than in the following menace of "fire and brimstone":

> He there does now enioy eternall rest
>> And happie ease, which thou doest want and crave,
>> And further from it daily wanderest;
>> What if some little paine the passage haue,
>> That makes fraile flesh to feare the bitter wave?
>> Is not short paine well borne that brings long ease,
>> And layes the soule to sleepe in quiet graue?
>> Sleepe after toyle, port after stormie seas,
> Ease after warre, death after life does greatly please.
>
> (I.ix.40)

When Redcrosse is saved by Una's intervention, the "heauenly mercies" in which he has "a part" also suggest Calvinistic predestination (I.ix.53), but once more a "humanistic" argument is urged first, as a call to action in this world:

> Fie, fie, faint-harted knight!
> What meanest thou by this reprochfull strife?
> Is this the battell, which thou vauntst to fight
> With that fire-mouthed Dragon, horrible and bright?
>
> (I.ix.52)

The fight against the Dragon is not primarily a fight against Hell or sin, but the war to be waged against Rome and the Catholic rulers. In Una's adjuration as in Despair's solicitation, the deeper motive precedes its theological justification; the call for action is directed against the attraction of repose.

Entertaining whatever suggestion came to his mind from profane or religious sources, Spenser allows contraries to emerge, but he keeps his attention—and the reader's—focused on each isolated instance or argument in succession, without attempting either to relate and reconcile them, or to point out and sharpen their opposition.[31] Such contrasts, I admit, are not uncommon nor surprising; they are probably experienced by many men and proceed from our nature. What I am inclined to consider as distinctly Spenserian is the apparent unawareness, or deliberate disregard, of the contradictions, which is

perhaps only possible because the conflicting impulses may be tolerated and appeased in a state of poetic reverie.[32] Spenser was inclined
to contemplativeness in the aesthetic as in the religious sphere.

In the play of the poet's imagination over scenes and characters the
association of static and dynamic elements is a characteristic feature.
Attention is often focused on a single object or figure, and therefore
is not roving, but its object is usually in motion, like "the Gentle
Knight . . . pricking on the Plaine" (*Faerie Queene*, I.i.1), followed
by a Lady riding on an ass and a dwarf lagging behind. Hence a
delight in processions in which solitary figures seem to move toward
the reader in turn, allowing a momentary contemplation almost in
stasis. The influence of Elizabethan pageants is, of course, noticeable;
but it does not preclude a personal inclination, since this descriptive
method is not so frequent, nor so impressive, in the works of other
contemporary poets. Besides, there is in the narrative poetry of
Spenser an anticipation of some aspects of modern cinematographic
technique. In Book II of *The Faerie Queene* Guyon's progress along
the corridors of the subterranean empire of Mammon seems to be
followed by a camera eye, as a continuous travelling, interspersed
with pauses before successive doors (II.vii.24 ff.). When he emerges
from "a darksom narrow strait" (40), a "broad gate" suddenly dis-
closes "a rowme . . . large and wyde"(43), and among a crowd the
"wondrous faire" face of Philotime is foregrounded. In a similar way
when the hero looks down into the river Cocytus he is brought face
to face with Tantalus "drenched to the vpmost chin" as in a close-
up (58).[33]

Though the poet's imagination always follows some kind of action,
often violent, his descriptions and the slow rhythm of the verse may
create the impression of indolence which later Spenserians have
tended to exaggerate. Spenser, however, was sincere and in line with
the Protestant spirit as well as Renaissance humanism when praising
action. He himself led a fairly active life and was anxious for prefer-
ment, but he repeatedly expressed a longing for rest which I am
inclined to consider as a constant trait, not as a result of his "trying
years under Grey."[34] He was acutely conscious of living in a changing,
ever-moving universe, yet he always had a yearning for stability and
quietude.[35] He acknowledged the value of action, but felt its necessity
as a constraint. Redcrosse experienced the temptation of repose; Guyon is invited by Mammon to sit down on a silver stool and "rest
[his] wearie person, in the shadow coole" (II.vii.63). Calidore will
also ask old Melibee "To giue leaue awhyle, good Father, in this
shore/To rest my barcke, which hath bene beaten late/With stormes
of fortune and tempestuous fate . . . ."(VI.ix.31).

Spenser, however, despite recurrent expressions of disenchantment, was capable of an intense enjoyment of life, not only in the contemplation of the world's splendor, but in his sympathy with the fertility of Nature and the infinite variety of forms it produces.[36] The Garden of Adonis (*Faerie Queene* III.vi), as the meeting place of form and substance, immortality and transience, is the efflorescence of a life with deep roots in the mystery of primordial being. This life has its rhythms, its cycles of destruction and rebirth. Spenser's poetry is the image of a temporal flux which is a source of energy, beauty, expansion, and even the mainspring of moral and spiritual progress. This is the philosophical lesson taught in the last cantos of the *Faerie Queene*. Mutability seeks to extend her reign beyond the earthly sphere of mortality. The solemn judgment of Nature reminds her that all things "changed be," yet "by their change their being doe dilate"(VII.vii.58). This concept of permanence in change was, of course, borrowed, from the *De Consolatione Philosophiae* of Boethius. Yet, as I have pointed out,[37] Spenser is not really concerned here, as a Platonist would be, with tracing the expression of the timeless and the stable through the temporal and the mutable, nor with bringing multiplicity to unity. When he claims that mutable things "Do worke their own perfection so by change"(58), time no longer appears as a degraded image of eternity—the Platonic conception— but as a teleological process designed by God to bring all created beings to their mature perfection, material or spiritual. Though I have called this idea "Christian," there are so many strands of thought in Christianity that it may be considered as distinctly Spenserian, though not original.

For a Christian poet time, of course, will have an end. No Platonic Great Year, no cyclical return is ever envisaged. The moment will come for a leap from the temporal succession into a timeless eternity. Unlike the mystics, but also unlike the poets who, like Donne, or Browning in "By the Fire-Side," celebrate a "moment one and infinite!", Spenser never seeks the transcendence of ecstasy as an immediate experience. In an ultimate stanza which is a fitting close, he only waits for "that same time when no more *Change* shall be,/But stedfast rest of all things firmely stayd/Vpon the pillours of Eternity,/That is contrayr to *Mutabilitie.*"

A philosophical synthesis is not achieved in the *Mutabilitie Cantos*. Two opposite ideas and longings have been expressed in succession; but they are not harmonized. Nor are they felt to be mutually exclusive, though the second might imply a rejection of the first.[38] Beyond a "perfection" reached through time in the world, the poet yearns for a timeless otherworldly perfection. A Christian philosopher would attempt to show how perfection in this world proceeds from a higher perfection, or may open a path to it. Spenser is content with encompassing two different prospects in what purposes to be a final vision.[39]

The epic poet had earlier combined and disjoined the claims of the active life and the contemplative life. Action will ensure the accomplishment of the divine will in this world; contemplation will give access to an intemporal mode of being. This duality is reflected in the Hermit's address to Redcrosse (I.x.57 ff.). At first sight Spenser adopts the familiar chronological distinction: action belongs to youth, contemplation is reserved for old age. The Knight is urged to do his "seruice" for "that soueraigne Dame," the ruler of Cleopolis, that is Queen Elizabeth, then "peaceably" bend his "painefull pilgrimage" to the celestial city, *Hierusalem* (59–61). I have shown, however, that Spenser, unlike Landino and other Renaissance writers, does not seek to harmonize and relate the claims of action and contemplation.[40] As Carol Kaske also pointed out, the service of Gloriana will not bring Redcrosse any nearer Heaven; "Cleopolis is not even on the 'path' to the New Jerusalem."[41] The hermit firmly asserts the superiority of contemplation while proclaiming the imperious necessity of action. He states the needs separately, urges action, yet declares it inseparable from sin : the warrior will have to "wash (his) hands from guilt of bloody field,/For blood can naught but sin, and wars, but sorrows yield"(60).[42] Yet he does not propose to substitute an immediate otherworldly quest of the "blessed end" for a worldly action which, though tainted with sin, will lead God's design to its fulfilment in time. I have rejected the assumption that Spenser's views here are "common to Calvinism and neo-Platonism."[43] Again I may have unnecessarily invoked a "medieval duality" to account for these seemingly incoherent pronouncements. The duality was in Spenser's mind.

The same duality accounts for the apparent palinode in the *Fowre Hymnes*. In the Hymns of "Heavenly Love" and "Heavenly Beauty" the poet gives up the world when turning to God, and yet human love, which he now utterly rejects, does not appear contemptible when the *Fowre Hymnes* are considered as a whole. In their dedication to the Countesses of Cumberland and Warwick it is even claimed that these "honorable and vertuous Ladies" are the "ornaments of true love and beautie, both in the one and the other kinde", which suppresses the opposition between the humanist and the religious hymns so emphatically stated in the latter. This contradiction, no doubt, could have been dictated by courtesy and convention, but it does seem to answer the deeper needs of Spenser's sensibility.[44]

Earthly love and earthly beauty are first praised as "heavenly"[45] just as the Queen of earthly Cleopolis, Gloriana, is praised as "heavenly borne" (*Faerie Queene*, I.x.59.9). But when the poet rises to a contemplation of God, the beauty which formerly awoke love "Thenceforth seemes fowle, & full of sinfull blame" ("Hymne of Heavenly Beauty," 276). Yet, as I have already argued, Spenser is unlikely to reject the human love he celebrates as holy when sanctified by marriage in his *Amoretti* and *Epithalamion*. His philosophy of love sought to answer two different needs of his sensibility when associating Platonic notions with an apology of the physical union of married lovers.[46] Yet "ambivalence" is present and "the unity thus created is felt to be very low indeed."[47] The poet thus steered clear of the purely aesthetic or intellectual pretense of Platonic gallantry. What is lost, however, is the genuine mystical *élan* of Renaissance Platonism in Ficino's or Pico's conception of love and beauty.[48] What they considered a degree on a scale leading to the divine becomes a self-sufficient experience in which the senses and the soul are engaged. Spenser asserts, as Giamatti notes, "that in married sexuality all duality will cease and wholeness, that human kind of holiness, will be ours."[49]

At first sight this may not seem surprising since Renaissance treatises on the philosophy of love often maintained that Platonic idealism did not prohibit an enjoyment of the pleasures offered by the senses. Yet in 1960 the only example I had found of a full identification of "l'honneste Amour" with married love and a praise of generation occurred in Louis Le Roy's commentary on *Le Sympose de Platon* (1558).[50] The historian of ideas may therefore take an interest in the association of the Platonic and the Christian ideal offered by Flaminio Nobili's *Trattato dell'amore humano* published in 1567.[51] Spenser could have read it in Italian or in a French translation published in 1588,[52] but I make no claim for a direct influence in the absence of verbal echoes. Nobili's conception of human love illustrates modes of thought and sensibility which were probably widespread. In their expression through the poetry of Spenser, however, they take on an individual character and account for some of the contradictions spotted.

Nobili starts from the idea that love is a desire of generation. He sets the authority of Plato against the Renaissance Neoplatonists who defined love as a desire of beauty whereas Diotima in the *Banquet* declared it "desio di parto nel bello,"[53] a desire of "generation in beauty." He shows that Diotima's opinion is supported by Aristotle (which would not have displeased Spenser) when the Philosopher claims that "Natura di niuna cosa vedesi prendere cura maggiore, &

niuna con più sollecitudine procurare, che la saluezza delle spetie."[54] He reminds us that Aristotle also maintained that each perfect living being has a natural propensity to engender something similar to itself, "figliuoli corporali, & spirituali"—including such spiritual creations as "virtù, Scienze, Leggi, Poemi, Orationi . . . ."(f. 15 v°. Through this generation one may participate of divinity and eternity: "Perche da Aristotele anchora fu giudicato, di tutti i viventi perfetti essere sopra tutte l'altre naturale, il generar cosa a se simigliante, percioche in questa guisa della diuinità, & eternità vengono a participare."[55]

According to Nobili a beautiful body lodges a beautiful soul and excites a desire which is "human love." Unlike Plato, he claims that male beauty cannot arouse the "carnal concupiscence excited by a woman, since the latter was ordained to awake in us a desire of corporeal generation."[56] The consequence is that the Platonic progression from the sight of corporeal beauty to the contemplation of intellectual beauty cannot be conceived in the same way as it was by Ficino or even by Leone Ebreo:

A me certamente non è mai auuenuto di conoscere alcun Lauinello [in Bembo' s *Gli Asolani*], il quale si contentatesse di goder la belleza in quel modo, nel quale propriamente si gode la bellezza, dico col vedere, coll' vdire, col pensare, anzi ho veduto, che tutti (se non forse nel principio dell'Amore, quando non si è anchora intieramente scoperto) vorrebbono sodisfare al tutto : & quel che dice Philone [in the *Dialoghi di Amore* of Leone Ebreo] esser fine dell'Amore, il goder la bellezza con vnione, a me non si lascia troppo ben comprendere : Imperoche, se della corporale fauelliamo, a goderla non si richiede unione, ma più tosto giusta distanza tra l'occhio, & lei : se della bellezza spirituale, cio è dell' animo della Donna amata, primieramente in questo mondo con tale bellezza unire non ci possiamo, ne puramente vederla, percioche ci si attrauersano nel mezzo questi corpi materiali, & grossi; & oltre a ciò, quando puramente la potremo vedere, non in lei appagheremo, ma nel Fonte della Diuina Bellezza, vera, & compiuta felicità nostra. Ora se queste cose da noi dette sono vere, come a mè certo pare, ragioneuolmente niegò Platone Amore esser desio di bellezza, non perche nell'Amore non si desideri di veder il bello, che ardentemente si desidera; ma perciò, che questo non era il principal fine del desiderio amoroso, ma bene l'immortalarsi, & propagarsi col partorire.[57]

If human love is a desire of generation in the beautiful, our longing for spiritual beauty cannot be satisfied in the contemplation of the beloved woman, but in "the Fount of Divine Beauty, our true and complete felicity." The difference in nature and orientation that Neoplatonism tended to blur is thus introduced between human love and divine love.

Nobili, however, went on to distinguish three forms of love. The beautiful is first descried by the eye, and it awakes a desire of conjunction and procreation (20 v°). But the understanding, stimulated by this emotion, may or may not intervene: "Se dall' intelleto non è seguito il senso, quel suo desio non merita in guisa alcuna il nome d'Amor humano, anzi è puro affetto sensuale."[58]

Like all Platonists he condemned a purely sensual passion, "Amore ferino, & bestiale"(21 r°), but also rejected a more refined love which has all the characteristics of courtly love. To the sensual desire excited in the lover is added the pleasure taken in the "value and noble perfections of the beloved lady" (21 v°). This lover will "break the rules, but do it prudently, with great regard for his own honor and for the lady's." Nobili will grant that this love "ha più dell'humano."[59] It is the kind of passion exposed by Spenser in the Mask of Cupid (*FQ*, III.xii). But according to Nobili, as in the eyes of Spenser, the only "honest" love is the love consecrated by marriage:

Hora se un Giouane essendosi messo ad amare vna bella, & ben costumata Giouinetta, & conueniente al grado suo s'ingegna di ottenerla per Moglie, & in questa guisa diuenir posseditore dell'animo & del corpo di lei, non violando le leggi, anzi obedienza prestando alla Natura, veramente humano & ragioneuole Amante se dirà, ne in questo Amore sarà peccato . . .

Per la qual cosa può apparire, quanto s'ingannino coloro, che ogni desio di congiugnersi chiamano bestiale, & ferino; la doue Platone non hauea per inconueniente, che come nelle Bestie da Natura, cos{{igrave}} in Noi da discorso di Ragione procedesse, poiche com mezzo suo si perpetua la nostra spetie. Et lasciamo stare, che la Donna, quasi altro testimonio non ha da assicurarti del suo Amore, laqual certezza è da se ardentemente disiderata, saluo il farti dono della sua persona . . . .[60]

Nobili finds a justification for this view in poems in which Petrarch and Bembo confessed they experienced a desire of physical union

(23 r°-v°). He also relies on the opinion of Aristotle: "che era usato di dire Amore non douer essere ne per lo congiugnimento de i corpi, ne senz' esso ; quasi volesse inferire, che principal fine douer essere l'unione de gli animi, ma pure etiandio quella de i corpi richiederuisi ; poiche quegli habitando in questi, tanto più pare che si uniscano, quanto più s'accostano i corpi."[61] Nobili, Spenser, and Donne achieved in the same way this transmutation of Platonic love with arguments borrowed from Aristotle.

This unifying concept of "human love" was bound to lead to a different kind of dualism when rising from human to heavenly love. Nobili, like Spenser, admits that human love will appear contemptible to a man rapt up in divine love. If such pleasure is found in the contemplation and enjoyment of the mortal beauty of a particular woman, "infinita felicità douere essere nella contemplatione, & vista della Diuina bellezza . . . " Man will then spurn all other delights: "& perciò à quella sola, sprezzando le creature, volge la mente, lei sola desidera, et desiderando arde, quasi nouello Seraphino, di Diuino Amore."[62]

The Platonic ladder, which led from the contemplation of the beauty of the beloved to Intellectual and Divine Beauty therefore seems of little use to Nobili:

A questo Diuino Amore non sò già quanto necessaria scala sia la bellezza donnesca; percioche il considerare i miracolosi, & pur ordinati effeti dalla Natura, i muouimenti stabili del Cielo, il vigor della luce, la perfettione dell' vniuerso, mi pare molto più sicura strada per condurci alla cognition della somma Bellezza, che il perdersi, & star fisso in un volto; nel quale si scorge la medesima arte del Creatore il secondo giorno, che il primo s'è scorta : & di questo parere auiso, che fosse il Bembo, il quale introducendo quel valente Romito a trattare dell'Amore Diuino, mentione giamai di Donna non fa, ma di quelle Bellezze eterne del Cielo, & sopra tutta della prima, & ultima cagione di tutte le cose, Oceano di bellezza, & di felicità; il che da i maggiori Philosophi togliendolo, il marauiglioso Dante ne gli ultimi Canti del Paradiso assai chiaramenle spiegò . . . ."[63]

I had already shown Spenser's agreement with Bembo on this point.[64] Man can only rise to a direct intuition of divine beauty through an Augustinian contemplation of the beauty of the created universe.

The relation between human love and divine love therefore can only be one of analogy or contrast, of inclusion or exclusion. The *Amoretti* exemplify the relation of analogy and inclusion. In the second Easter sonnet (LXVIII) the poet celebrates divine love, the Redeemer's love for mankind, but in the closing lines he tells the woman who will become his wife: "So let us love, deare love, lyke as we ought,/Love is the lesson which the Lord us taught." Divine love will justify their loving union. Platonism refined human love through abstraction; Christianity sanctifies it by consecration. All love proceeds from God and the desire of generation obeys the Biblical injunction. The will of God operates in the Garden of Adonis as in the House of Holiness. But human love is always apt to degenerate into bestial love when the lovers are not conscious of fulfilling God's intention.

Heavenly love, however, calls for a separation from human love and the rejection of Eros, though not of Agape: hence the invitation to turn away from "that faire lampe, which useth to enflame/The hearts of men with selfe consuming fyre"(*H.H.B.*, 275–76). One cannot rise to the love of God through the love of woman, but only through the love of *Sapience*, "The soveraine dearling of the *Deity*" (*H.H.B*, 183–84). In the same way Redcrosse, after doing his service for the "soveraigne dame" of Cleopolis, "The fairest peece, that eie beholden can," will have to seek "in Pilgrims poore estate" the path leading to the new *Hierusalem (Faerie Queene*, I.x.59, 64). It is noteworthy that this Protestant poet, who idealized celibacy,[65] commonly associated chastity with heavenly love. I believe him to have been sincere both in his praise of human love and in his exaltation of the contemplative life. But I am inclined to think he mainly expressed in the latter his deep human desire for rest.[66] In his final vision eternity seems to be identified with stability rather than a different mode of being or an apprehension of the *totum simul*. It is beyond time, and only accessible at the end of time, not in any rare moment of illumination.[67]

Sorbonne Nouvelle

NOTES

1. Paris: Corti, 1960. Henceforth cited as *Poètes métaphysiques*.
2. Oxford University Press, 2000.
3. Genève, Droz, 1960. Henceforth mentioned as *Neoplatonism*.

4. "Les structures fondamentales de la pensée et de la sensibilité dans l'oeuvre poétique de Spenser,"*Annales de la Faculté des Lettres de Nice* N°18, 1972, 5–16.

5. All quotations in my article will be taken from A.C. Hamilton's edition of *The Faerie Queene*: (London and New York : Longman, 1977). Quotations from the other poems are all from W. L. Renwick's editions for The Scholartis Press: *Complaints* (1928), *Daphnaïda* (1929), *The Shepherd's Calendar* (1930).

6. I have argued that amateur poets were more inclined to genuine self-expression in volume 3 of *Poètes métaphysiques*.

7. Noted by all critics, e. g., John D. Bernard in *Ceremonies of Innocence. Pastoralism in the Poetry of Spenser* (Cambridge University Press, 1989), 105, 171. Jon A. Quitslund sees in Spenser's self-presentation the "management of a persona" and admits "he never permits us to see through the mask."(*Spenser's Supreme Fiction: Platonic Natural Philosophy and the* Faerie Queene [Toronto University Press, 2001], p. 225.) I am not concerned either with the "selves" of the characters in the *Faerie Queene*, whether considered definite and stable (as in K.W. Gransden's "Allegory and Personality in Spenser's Heroes" [*Essays in Criticism* 20, 1970], 298–310), or "as unstable as language is," and "absorbed in structures of relationship, likenesses, identifications, indistinctions," as Jonathan Goldberg claims (*Endlesse Worke. Spenser and the Structures of Discourse* [Baltimore: Johns Hopkins University Press, 1981], 110, 119).

8. Studied by Derek B. Alves in "Who knowes not Colin Clout? Spenser's Self-Advertisement in the *Faerie Queene*, Book 6," *Modern Philology* 88 (1990–91), 26–42.

9. Judith H. Anderson, Donald Cheney, David A. Richardson eds., *Spenser's Life and the Subject of Biography*, (Amherst: University of Massachusetts Press, 1996), xiv.

10. One may argue that those who look for "Spenser" in Spenser's writings only discover "the instability—the fictive nature—-of the figure" (*Spenser's Life and the Subject of Biography*, xiii). I agree so far as this applies to a "personality," always multiple and elusive; my claim for constancy is limited to a number of "traits," or "structures," of the mind.

11. Gary Waller's words in *Edmund Spenser. A Literary Life* (Basingstoke: Macmillan, 1994) 5, 17, echoing Richard Helgerson's *Self-Crowned Laureate: Spenser, Jonson, Milton* (Berkeley: University of California Press, 1983).

12. G.G. Smith, ed., *An Apology for Poetry: Elizabethan Critical Essays* (Oxford: Oxford University Press, 1904), I.195.

13. This attraction may account also for his early translation of the *Culex*; see *Virgils Gnat*, 8–152.

14. Like Gary Waller I think it likely that E. K. is a pseudonym for Spenser himself: *Spenser. A Literary Life*, 87.

15. As I have repeatedly argued in *Poètes métaphysiques,* passim; cf. *Seven Metaphysical Poets*, 361–62.

16. The recurrence of "And" at the beginning of many lines is characteristic. The Derridean implications discerned by Goldberg in the "Ands" of the Proem to *The Faerie Queene* seem to me arbitrary: *Endlesse Worke*, 20–1.

17. As analyzed in *Seven Metaphysical Poets*; see my summary, 358.

18. Cf. R. Ellrodt "La perception du temps dans les Sonnets de Shakespeare," 35–46 in *Le Char ailé du Temps*, ed. Louis Roux (Publications de l'Université de Saint-Etienne, 2003), particularly 45. A complete analysis of Spenser's perception of time could not be attempted in the present article.

19.   In a pregnant essay, C.A. Patrides emphasized the important part played by the sound patterns in Spenser's so-called "poetry of reconciliation": "The Achievement of Spenser," *Yale Review* 69 (1980), 441–43.

20.   See the Index in *Neoplatonism*.

21.   Objections to my views are best represented by Elizabeth Bieman's balanced statement in *Plato Baptized: Towards the Interpretation of Spenser's Mimetic Fictions* (University of Toronto Press, 1989), 136 : "With incisive analytical scholarship Ellrodt demonstrates Spenser's familiarity with the neoplatonic lore available in the Renaissance. But he separates, as Spenser almost certainly did not [the separation, indeed, was mine, I never ascribed it to Spenser], elements in this lore into Jewish, pagan, Christian, Platonic, Neoplatonic, and so on [these subdivisions are an exaggeration of my single main distinction], and argues against the significance, for his reading of the Christian Spenser he admires [I admire Spenser for his poetry, not for his Christianity], of any element inconformable to his conception of Spenser's Christian orthodoxy [in this article as in my book I point out theological inconsistencies in Spenser's religious thought, and find these inconsistencies significant]." I readily admit I have at times, for the sake of brevity, opposed "Christian" and "Platonic" in a phrasing open to misinterpretation, but I did define Spenser as a "Platonizing Christian" rather than a "Christian Platonist" (*Neoplatonism*, 213).

22.   See Chapters III to V in *Neoplatonism*. I maintain my claim for the medieval sources of Spenser's Platonism in the *Faerie Queene* (64, 67–70, 74, etc.) without excluding other influences. The continuity between Medieval and Renaissance Platonism, which I have been supposed to ignore or belittle, was, in fact, stressed in *Neoplatonism*, 109, 122–24, 158, 212.

23.   See *Neoplatonism*, 51–52, 58–59. Metaphysical interpretations of the first two *Hymnes* were also rejected, e. g., 125, 133.

24.   *Neoplatonism*, 109.

25.   *Habits of Thought in the English Renaissance*, Berkeley, 1990.

26.   D.H. Radcliffe's summary of Northrop Frye's argument in *Edmund Spenser. A Reception History*. (Columbia: Camden House, 1996), 182–84.

27.   Richard C. Frushell and Bernard J. Vondersmith, eds., *Contemporary Thought on Edmund Spenser* (Carbondale and Edwardville: Southern Illinois University Press, 1975), 121–49. Other contradictions have been spotted by different critics, e.g. Laurence Goldstein in "Immortal Longings and 'The Ruines of Time,' " *JEGP* 75 (1976), 360: "Spenser has entangled himself in two myths of contradictory powers." Patrick Cheney discerned contradictions even in *Prothalamion: Spenser's Famous Flight : A Renaissance Idea of a Literary Career* (University of Toronto Press, 1993), 245.

28.   When John H. King writes that "Spenser's reformation of *literary genres* [my italics] is an example of his pervasive syncretism (*Spenser's Poetry and the Reformation Tradition*, Princeton University Press, 1990, 230), the claim is, indeed, justified from the point of view of "aesthetic syncretism"; a point of view chosen, too, by those who spoke like C. A. Patrides of a "harmony of atmosphere" and "unity arising from multeity" in "The Achievement of Spenser," *Yale Review* 69 (1980), 439. One, however, may not be convinced that the poet had achieved a philosophical and theological syncretism within the "Protestant tradition," which is itself so diverse. Another view of Spenser as a "Protestant poet" had been offered by Anthea Hume;

when speaking of his "synthesis of divergent materials," she admitted that "ambivalence lies at the center of his work." This, she assumed, "does not make him a pluralist or a relativist" since he "unites a wide-ranging eclecticism with a strong sense of direction" (*Edmund Spenser: Protestant Poet* [Cambridge: Cambridge University Press, 1964], p. 184). A strong sense of *moral* direction precluding "relativism" is undoubtedly present but, from a philosophical or psychological point of view, is there any difference between "pluralism" and "a wide-ranging eclecticism"? One may always choose to find a unifying principle in contradictions as Greg Kucick claimed in *Spenser Studies* VIII (1987): "we have come today, as Paul Alpers, Leigh De Neef, David Miller, Jonathan Goldberg, and A. Bartlett Giamatti among others have been recently arguing, to think of the tensions and contraries and dualities in Spenser's poetry as one of the great unifying and energizing principles of his art." I readily admit tensions are "energizing," but the kind of "unity" achieved is not revealed.

29. Ithaca: Cornell University Press, 1999.

30. See *Neoplatonism*, 198–204.

31. I agree with A. Bartlett Giamatti when he claims that Spenser offers "a double perspective on life," but seldom seems to "strive to reconcile them": *Play of Double Senses: Spenser's Faerie Queene* (Englewood Cliffs: Prentice Hall, 1975), 106. In some cases (but not in all) he may have intended the reader to achieve this reconciliation, as Carol Kaske suggested in *Spenser and Biblical Poetics*.

32. C. A. Patrides later also noted "the absence of tension" in the *Faerie Queene* ("The Achievement of Spenser," *Yale Review* 69, 1980, 427–43), but thought it "premeditated," which I doubt (437). I agree, however, that contradictory impulses were felt violently by Spenser when his moral precepts imposed a repression of his instincts. As Greenblatt points out, the destruction of the Bower of Bliss may signal his "violent resistance to a sensuous release for which it [his culture] nevertheless yearned with overwhelming intensity": *Renaissance Self-fashioning: From More to Shakespeare* (University of Chicago Press, 1980), 157–92. I am aware A. Kent Hieatt dismissed this assumption ("The Alleged Early Modern Origins of the Self and History" in *Spenser Studies* X, 29) but I am here inclined to side with Greenblatt, though I do not accept all his parallels for Guyon's actions.

33. Patrides also called attention to "the filmic fourth dimension," as Eisenstein called it, in Spenser's poetry: op. cit., 439.

34. In "Spenser's Lives, Spenser's Careers" Richard Rambuss dismisses this biographical assumption: *Spenser's Life and the Subject of Biography*, 7–9.

35. As many critics acknowledged, e.g., John Bernard in *Ceremonies of Innocence*: "The central motive in these poems is the desire for rest" (164). In the *Amoretti* "love is thus conceived as a kind of haven from the storms of life", *ibid.*, 173.

36. His insistence on generation in *Epithalamion* (383 ff.) and in the Garden of Adonis is characteristic: *Neoplatonism*, 56, 85; cf. J. N. King, *Spenser's Poetry and the Protestant Tradition*, 176–77. In *Short Time's Endless Monument* (New York: Columbia University Press, 1960) A. Kent Hieatt noted that human marriage in Spenser's poems makes its contribution to the cosmic renewal of life.

37. See *Neoplatonism*, 69.

38. A. Bartlett Giamatti claimed that Spenser in the Garden of Adonis (III.vi.47) as in the *Cantos* "demonstrates how mutability can be fashioned into an image of

eternity": *Play of Double Senses: Spenser's Faerie Queene* (Englewood Cliffs : Prentice Hall, 1975), 129. Yes, but only an "image," which is not even an "aeviternity" for a Christian poet.

39. These statements are based on my earlier analysis in *Neoplatonism* (1960), 68–70. Donald Cheney also admits that *Mutabilitie* is viewed with "a mixture of opposing attitudes" (*Spenser's Image of Nature*, New Haven: Yale University Press, 1965, 246–47), and Carol Kaske has pointed out that "what distinguishes Spenser" from other "pluralists" is "his dwelling on the contradictions as much as he does and, more important, his shifting back and forth several times between the more and the less worldy values . . . ." ("Spenser's Pluralistic Universe," 143). William A. Oram also concludes that "The Cantos end with a final formulation of ambivalence": ("Spenserian Paralysis, *SEL* 41 [2001], 67), echoing Sean Kane's conclusion: "the two attitudes are ambivalent, and it is difficult to see where Spenser actually stands": (*Spenser's Moral Allegory* [University of Toronto Press, 1989], 219). Elizabeth Bieman has attempted to reconcile the notion of perfection attained in a temporal cyle with the vision of "final quietude" by arguing ingeniously, but unconvincingly to my mind, that "pillars" need not be static, that "stefast rest" can apply to "the centredness of a top", and that the prayer to the Sabbaoth God is "a plea for an ongoing renewal of trust in the goodness of God's cosmos" (*Plato Baptized*, 278–42).

40. *Neoplatonism*, 208. See also Carol Kaske, op. cit., 136 ff.

41. "Spenser's pluralistic universe," 139.

42. This may be compared with the "pragmatic recognition of the inevitable imperfection of those who pursue good ends" ascribed to Spenser by Paul Suttie in "Spenser's Political Pragmatism," *Studies in Philology* 95 (1998), 76.

43. *Neoplatonism*, 208, note 65.

44. In *Spenser's Famous Flight* Patrick Cheney offered a summary of the "theories" concerning the poet's retractation: "progressive, dialectical [including mine], typological", but argued that "a careeric lens best views a text that openly advertises its disunity" (196–98). A more usual way of removing, or at least explaining, the contradictions is to assume that Spenser merely adopted the contemporary Neoplatonic compromise popularized by Bembo and Castiglione; it admitted a progress from "sensuall coveting" in youth to "true [spiritual] love" in age: cf. Thomas Hyde: *The Poetic Theology of Love: Cupid in Renaissance Literature* (Newark : University of Delaware Press, 1986), 139. But though the author of *Fowre Hymnes* insists (perhaps disingenuously) that the first two were written in his "greener times" (cf. *H.H.L.* 8–21), he never implies that the readers he addresses should wait until age to be inspired with "heavenly thoughts" (218–87).

45. Human Love is praised in "An Heavenly Hymne" (*H.L.* 302) and Beauty, which is not "an outward shew," proceeds from a "celestiall ray" (*H.B.,* 90–99).

46. I find I am in agreement with the conclusion of Dona Gibbes in *Spenser's Amoretti: A Critical Study* (Aldershot: Scolar Press, 1990): "Spenser does not endorse neo-Platonism as a philosophy in the *Amoretti*, but uses it in a witty and complicated way" (166). Carol Kaske had traced the "progress from Christian conflict to Christian-humanist resolution" in "Spenser's *Amoretti* and *Epithalamion* of 1595," *English Literary Renaissance* 8 (1978), 271–95.

47. Gibbs, op. cit., 122; Kaske, op. cit., 272.

48. On the absence of mysticism in Spenser see *Neoplatonism*, 69–70, 214.

49. A. Bartlett Giamatti, *Play of Double Senses: Spenser's Faerie Queene* (Englewood Cliffs : Prentice Hall, 1975), 133.

50. See *Neoplatonism*, 145 ff. In 1992 Lisa M. Klein still offered no further instance of the "overwriting" of the convention of Petrarchism "by the ideals of sixteenth-century marriage": "Protestant Marriage and the Revision of Petrarchan Loving in Spenser's *Amoretti*," *Spenser Studies* X, 109–37.

51. *Trattato dell'Amore Humano* Composto, & donato ha già molti anni da M. Flaminio Nobili. Stampato appresso Vincentio Busdraghi, in Lucca nell'anno MD LXVII.

52. *Traité de l'amour humain*. Traduit par I. de Lavardin, escuyer Seigneur du Plessis Aurouer & de Bourrot. De l'Italien du Seigneur Flaminio de Nobili Gentilhomme Lucquois. A Paris, chez Lucas Breyel . . . MDLXXXVIII. I quoted from the French version in the article I published in 1972.

53. *Trattato*, fol. 14 v°. I quote from a facsimile reprint which is a testimony to the interest taken in this treatise by an Italian poet Spenser admired, Tasso : *Il trattato dell'Amore Humano di Flaminio Nobili*, con le postille autografe di Torquato Tasso. Roma, Ermanno Loescher, E.C., 1895. In my quotations the *v*/*u* graphs have been retained but the modern form of *s* is used throughout. The translation into English is mine.

54. *Trattato*, fol. 15 r°: "Nature is never seen to be more attentive to any other thing, nor more mindful of its accomplishment, than she is of the perpetuation of the species."

55. Ibid., fol.15 v°-16 r°: "For Aristotle has also judged that for all perfect living beings it is a thing most natural to give birth to beings similar to them, the more so since they thus partake of divinity and eternity."

56. Ibid., fol. 16 v°: "concupiscenza carnale, come quella della Donna, la quale a questo fine fu ordinata di accendere in noi desio di generare corporalmente."

57. Ibid., fol. 17 r°-v°:

It certainly never happened to me to know any Lavinello [in Bembo's *Gli Asolani*] fully satisfied with enjoying beauty in the proper way in which it is enjoyed, that is with the eye, the ear, the intellect; but I usually see (with a possible exception at the beginning of enamoration, before the growth and full manifestation of love) that all lovers would have all; and I cannot understand what Philo says [in the *Dialoghi di Amore* of Leone Ebreo] when he claims that the aim of love is to enjoy beauty with union. For, if we speak of corporal beauty, union is unnecessary to enjoy it: what is rather requred is an appropriate distance between it and the eye. If spiritual beauty is meant, that is the beauty of the mind of the woman loved, we cannot in this world be united to this beauty, nor see it in its purity, for it can only be reached through material and gross bodies; besides, when we shall be able to see it purely, we shall not find our enjoyment in it, but in the Fount of Divine Beauty, our true and complete felicity. If what I have said is true, as it seems to me, Plato is right when he denies that Love is a desire of beauty, not because Love does not desire to contemplate beauty, for it is his ardent wish, but because this is not the main end of our amorous desire, which truly seeks immortality and perpetuation through generation.

58. Ibid., fol. 20 v°-21 r°: "If the understanding does not go beyond the sense, this desire does not deserve in any way to be called human Love, but only a sexual urge."

59. Ibid., 21 v°: "Questo Amore è d'huomo non giàvirtuoso intieramente, ma pure men difformato, che non era il primo, & più tosto d'incontinente, come sogliono dire i Philosophi, che di stemperato, onde per conseguente ha più dell'humano."

60. Ibid., 22 r°-v°:

> "Now, if a young man has fallen in love with a beautiful and well-behaved young lady and, in accordance with his social condition, exercises his wits to have her for his wife, and in this way take possession of her mind and her body without violating the laws, but obeying nature, his love will certainly be considered truly human and rational and there will be no sin in it . . . ." Accordingly one clearly sees how wrong are those who call any desire of conjunction bestial and brutish since Plato did not think it un-fitting that, just as this desire proceeds from nature with animals, in us too it should result from the discourse of reason forasmuch as our species is perpetuated through this means. Besides, as I need not tell you, the beloved has, as it were, no other means of giving us assurance of her love, which assurance is eagerly desired, than by this gift of her person.

61. 23 v°: "who used to say that Love should not be either for the conjunction of bodies nor without it; as if he wanted to intimate that its main end should be the union of the souls, but that the union of the bodies was also required, for, the former residing in the latter, the nearer the bodies are to each other, the closer the souls are united."

62. 24 v°: "and that is why, spurning the creatures, his mind will turn to it [the Divine Beauty] only, will desire it only, and will burn with Divine Love like a new Seraphim."

63. 25 r°-v°:

> To rise to this Divine Love, of course, I do not know how far womanly beauty is a necessary ladder, for the consideration of the miraculous, yet orderly effects of nature, of the regular movements of the celestial spheres, the splendor of light, the perfection of the universe seem to me a safer way to lead us to the knowledge of the supreme beauty rather than losing oneself in the constant contemplation of a face on which one descries on the second day the same art of the Creator as in the first day. And of this Bembo seems to have been conscious, for, when he introduces that talented Romito to treat of Divine Love, he makes no mention of women at any time, but calls attention to the eternal Beauties of Heaven, and chiefly to the First Cause of all things, that Ocean of beauty and felicity, which the marvellous Dante displays clearly enough in the last Cantos of his *Paradiso* . . . .

64. *Neoplatonism*, 150–51, 176.

65. As John King, admits in *Spenser's Poetry and the Protestant Tradition* (148–50, 155–59) though he finds no evidence for the "stubborn belief" in his opposition to clerical marriage (157).

66. In *Ceremonies of Innocence* John D. Bernard also seems to assume that the desire for rest repeatedly expressed in the poems (82–84) is Spenser's own when he insists on Colin Clout's inclination to withdraw from the active world (163), or on Spenser's "self-representation as a heroic agent yearning for respite from his own poetic labors" (171). See also note 40 above.

67. When speaking of poetic immortality Spenser uses the term "eternity" almost constantly : *Ruines of Time*, 367, *Teares of the Muses*, 582, *Ruines of Rome*, L'Envoy, etc. Shakespeare did so in Sonnet 122, but immediately corrected himself (lines 4–7). Spenser seems insensitive to the difference.

WILLIAM A. ORAM

Spenser in Search of an Audience: The Kathleen Williams Lecture for 2004[1]

This essay gives an overview of Spenser's development after he realized, during his London trip in 1589–91, that neither the queen nor the court, of which he had hoped to become a member, was willing to accord him the respect that he saw as his due. But while he may have wished to turn his back on his court audience, there was, for an epic poet in the 1590s, no viable alternative. He reacted to his new awareness in several ways. He responded first with the *Complaints*, an angry attack on the court, which he nonetheless dedicated to court figures. In *Amoretti & Epithalamion* he experimented by reworking the court-centered forms of sonnet-sequence and epithalamion in bourgeois fashion, addressing himself to Elizabeth Boyle and a middle-class audience. Finally, in the second installment of *The Faerie Queene* he addressed the queen and his court audience with a new irony, staging himself for future readers as a poet-hero.

*I*N THIS ESSAY I WILL discuss three related subjects: Spenser's self-presentation in the poetry he wrote after 1590, his understanding of his vocation, and his changing sense of the audience for which he was writing. I will foreground the issue of audience because, in my view, that drives the others. Through it, I will examine the important shift that takes place in Spenser's career. My argument develops out of a recent essay in *Studies in Philology*, which claimed that Spenser's career divides into two parts with the hinge coming at his trip to Elizabeth's court in 1589–91.[2] Before that stay Spenser saw himself

Spenser Studies: A Renaissance Poetry Annual, Volume XX, Copyright © 2005 by AMS Press, Inc. All rights reserved.

as aiming to become a court poet with the queen as his principal audience. I think that he did not see himself, in Puttenham's words, as a "cunning Princepleaser," but as a learned man, qualified by his learning and by his Irish administrative experience to become a court counselor, and he hoped that when he presented his credentials in the form of his epic he would not only be rewarded but listened to. His counsel, I assumed, would have matched what we find in the *View* and in parts of *The Faerie Queene*—an internationalist Protestant position, taking a hard line about the treatment of the Irish.

While he was at court, however, Spenser discovered that nobody was listening. It was not, I would guess, so much that courtiers were antagonistic to him but that, more gallingly, that they didn't take his pretensions seriously. Thus, despite the award by Elizabeth of a pension of £50, his time in London forced on Spenser the dismaying realization that the court's vision of a laureate poet was not his own and that, in fact, "cunning Princepleasers" were just as likely to gain royal attention as he was. I argued that this shock made him start to reconsider the audience he was writing for and, with that, the functions of his own art.

I should make it clear from the start that I do not believe Spenser ever wrote exclusively for any single audience.[3] His poetry from *The Shepheardes Calender* on implicitly addresses a range of overlapping groups—convinced Protestants, university wits, aristocratic patrons, the New English in Ireland. Indeed, the goal of becoming a court poet, and perhaps joining the ranks of courtier poets was more than a plan for court success. It joined with an ambition to become, like Virgil, a national figure whose verse and whose counsels would benefit the English commonwealth.[4] The means to that end were the queen and her courtiers, who figure as the primary audience for Spenser's early poetry. After 1590 he would never again have the same sense of the court as an interested audience. Yet it has become increasingly clear to me how limited the alternatives were for an epic poet like Spenser. Shakespeare and the writers that Richard Helgerson has usefully called "professional" might earn a living or even make a fortune from the public theater, but for a poet with Spenser's laureate ambitions, the public theater offered no serious hope of advancement or reward.[5] Even twenty years later, as David Riggs has shown, Jonson structured the 1616 folio of his work to suggest a vocational growth from the public dramatist to a court-centered lyric poet.[6] For Spenser there were few alternatives to the court even after his hopes had faded. He was, thus, forced to recognize that the audience for which he was writing was not listening, but to recognize as well his dependence on that audience.

The issue is important not only because it illuminates Spenser's developing sense of his own vocation, but because it says something about his sense of the class to which he belonged. Recently John Huntington has sketched out the ways by which poor and humbly-born poets attempted to argue that their talents entitled them to special status; his book touches briefly on Spenser, whom he sees as somewhat more timid than Chapman or Marlowe.[7] In a distinctively different but concurring fashion, Louis Montrose has argued that Spenser used his poetry to show his right to a "domestic domain" apart from and ultimately superior to the court world.[8] My own view is that Spenser's sense of his "domain" was less secure than Montrose suggests, but that he was in his own way quite as aggressively assertive as Huntington's other examples of poetic ambitiousness. Whatever his parentage, Spenser had an MA from Cambridge, a pension from the queen, and an Irish estate of more than three thousand acres. He could call himself a gentleman. Yet, at the same time, he saw those lands threatened by the indigenous Irish, as well as by his Anglo-Norman neighbors. The anxiety voiced in the *View* about incipient rebellion suggests that he knew the estate he had built up might easily be lost and, with it, the status that he had gained for himself. In what follows I want to look in a preliminary way at the literary effects of this rethinking of his audience—and with it, his career—from its first expression in the *Complaints*, through his late shorter verse and the second installment of *The Faerie Queene*.

I. ATTACKING THE COURT

In a recent article in *Spenser Studies* Richard Peterson transcribes a gossipy letter from the recusant Sir Thomas Tresham to a Catholic friend in the country. Part of the letter gleefully details the calling in of a poem about Mother Hubberd and he comments:

> He that writt this discourse is a Catabrigian and of the blood of the Spencers. Yt is nott yet a yeare sence he writt his booke in the prayse of the queene, which he entitled the Fayrie Quene, and which was so well liked, that her Majestie gave him an hundred marks pencion forthe of the Eschequer: and so clerklie was yt penned, that he beareth the name of a Poett Laurall. Butt nowe in medlinge with his apes tayle he is gott

into Ireland: also in hazard to loose his forsayd annual reward: and finally hereby prove himself a Poett Lorrell.[9]

Several things are worth notice about this passage. One is the implicit chronology. If Tresham's gossip is accurate, Spenser published *The Faerie Queene*, gaining a "Laureate" reputation and the promise of a pension. He *then* published the *Complaints* volume containing "Mother Hubberds Tale" and, when the book caused a scandal, left England under a cloud—possibly even in danger of losing the pension he had just gained. The account contradicts Ponsonby's statement in his preface to the *Complaints* that he has, after Spenser's return to Ireland, gathered together whatever he can find of his poems.[10] It further stresses the contrast—in Tresham's eyes, at least—between the "Poett Laurall" or Laureate who published *The Faerie Queene* and the "poet lorrell" or fool who published Mother Hubberd and risked losing the rewards of his work.

The *Complaints* have never been anyone's favorite book of poetry, but I want to argue here that it has a pivotal place in Spenser's work. It is an explosion of frustration at the court that has refused to take his calling seriously and, despite the critics who have seen the book as a collection of poems connected only by its loose generic title, the poems develop common argument.[11] Indeed, I will suggest that Spenser's stubborn insistence on this argument limits the weaker poems in the book. It is the first book in which Spenser takes an explicitly anti-court stance, and his rhetoric here will return in the more famous diatribes of *Colin Clouts Come Home Againe*.

The most notorious aspect of this calling in—the one that Tresham comments on—is the attack that the poet makes on William Cecil, Lord Burleigh, under the character of the fox in the last section of "Mother Hubberds Tale." But the attack on Burleigh is not limited to that poem. In "The Ruines of Time" the poet comments that since Walsingham's death "learning lies unregarded,/And men of armes do wander unrewarded" (440–41) and goes on to comment ironically that "he that now welds all things at his will/ Scorns th'one and th'other in his deeper skill."

> O griefe of griefes, ô gall of all good heartes,
> To see that virtue should dispised bee
> Of him, that first was raisde for vertuous parts,
> And now broad spreading like an aged tree,
> Lets none shoot up, that nigh him planted bee . . . .
>
> (447–53)

The specificity of this charge appears in the censorship that occurs twenty years later. When Spenser's works were published in 1611, "Mother Hubberds Tale" was omitted, presumably to avoid antagonizing Burleigh's son, Robert Cecil, earl of Salisbury, who had succeeded his father as lord chancellor. In the same edition the accusatory singular version of these lines was made into a toothless plural: it was no longer "he" who wields all things at his will but "they" that wield things at their will. It is, in this context, worth note that an obituary epigram by John Weever mentions that it was "The Ruines of Time"—not "Mother Hubberds Tale"—that was called in.[12]

In "The Tears of the Muses," which follows "The Ruines of Time," Spenser uses the same image of a great tree shading out potential competition, although here he uses a discreet plural. Cleo laments that those to whom Jove has given honor now "Despise the brood of blessed Sapience" (72), adding that

. . . learned Impes that wont to shoote up still,
And grow to hight to kingdomes government
They underkeep, and with their spredding armes
Doo beat their buds, that perish through their harmes.

(75–78)

The word "learned" is important, for the Muses are patrons of learning and Spenser saw himself as a learned man. The learned Impes here are educated men like Spenser, who would like to "grow to hight of kingdomes government"—to join the ruling elite—but who are kept down by their jealous elders, of whom Burleigh is the type.

This attack is more, however, than the lament of a courtier denied employment by the lord chancellor. Burleigh is for Spenser only the most egregious representative of a court that has lost its moral bearings. All the poems of the volume develop the same coordinated criticisms—criticisms suggesting that its title, Complaints, is not only a gesture in the direction of genre but a specific indictment of the present state of affairs. Its clearest articulation comes in the pair of poems with which the book opens, "The Ruines of Time" and "The Teares of the Muses." The first is largely a lament for the Dudley family—the earl of Leicester, his brother the earl of Warwick and his nephew and sometime heir, Sir Philip Sidney. But in the early 1590s this stress on the Dudley house had an ideological dimension. Leicester had been the leader in the privy counsel of the faction arguing that England should support the Protestant cause in the religious wars of the Continent—the cause for which his nephew Sir

Philip Sidney became the martyr. With Leicester's death in 1588, the
internationalist faction was decisively weakened.

> His hope is faild, and come to passe his dread,
> And evill men now dead, his deeds upbraid:
> Spite bites the dead, that living never baid.
> He now is gone, the whiles the Foxe is crept
> Into the hole, the which the Badger swept.
>
>   (213–17)

The failed hope remains undefined, but it seems likely that it refers
to the Protestant hopes of the earl and their loss as the more cautious
Burleigh comes to dominate policy. Here the fox looks toward the
Burleigh-fox of "Mother Hubberds Tale." It is no accident that
Spenser revised "The Ruines of Time" at the last minute to include
a lament for the recently deceased Sir Francis Walsingham, for Walsingham was another strongly Protestant voice on the Privy Council.
The poem laments not only the Dudley family but the waning of
the internationalist Protestant faction at court.

Where "The Ruines of Time" focuses on politics, "The Teares
of the Muses" concerns itself with art. But in fact the two poems
show different aspects of the same deterioration. In the "Teares" the
Muses ostensibly lament the absence of patronage, but they also claim
that poetry is a spur to political and military action. Spenser takes
the Elizabethan commonplace that by their verse poets bestow immortality on deserving heroes, and develops it by insisting that, without the poets to chronicle it, heroism itself will cease. "Who would
ever care to doo brave deed," asks Calliope,

> Or strive in virtue others to excell;
> If none should yeeld him his deserved meed,
> Due praise, that is the spur of dooing well?
> For if good were not praised more than ill
> None would choose goodnes of his owne freewill.
>
>   (451–56)

This argument differs markedly from the Sidneyan stress on poetry
as a series of virtuous examples that move the reader to act virtuously.
Rather, it is expectation of *praise* that impels men to do good deeds.
The poet, seeing virtue, rewards it with poetic immortality, but
without the hope of that reward—or alternatively, in a culture where

false poets bestow underserved praise—aristocrats content themselves with reading their genealogies. They boast, says Clio, of "of Armes and Auncestrie:/But virtuous deeds, which did those Armes first give/To their Grandsyres, they care not to atchive" (94–96).

As a result, the court world of *The Teares of the Muses* is taxed for its neglect of poets and simultaneously for its neglect of arms. (Similarly in "Mother Hubberds Tale" the ape and the fox drive away "Desire of honor or brave thought of armes" [825].) The pairing of "poetry" and "arms" occurs repeatedly in the *Complaints* and in the context of this book I think that the idea of "armes" is quite specific: it is code for heroic military action in the Protestant cause, on the Continent or in Ireland. In a Protestant court operating functionally, the poet spurs the nobility to fight for the faith.

What of the queen in such a world? Bereft of the muses, the court becomes the haunt of "Blinde Error, scornefull Follie, and base Spight" (317) allegorical false counselors.

> The noble hearts to pleasure they allure,
> And tell their Prince that learning is but vaine,
> Faire Ladies loves they spot with thoughts impure,
> And gentle mindes with lewd delights disdaine:
> Clerks they to loathly idlenes entice,
> And fill their bookes with discipline of vice.
>
> (331–36)

These evil counselors all advise the prince to pay no attention to learning (the ape in "Mother Hubberds Tale" 815–38 is precisely this kind of counselor). Yet, as the poem repeats tirelessly, without learning both prince and court lack a compass. At the end of the poem the queen is herself invoked as the sole hope of the world, "The true Pandora of all heavenly graces." Spenser is, of course, playing with the etymology of the name as "all giving," but the sinister overtones of "Pandora" cannot help but be present here. The court—corruption and all—is the prince's and even her gifts may be suspect.

This is not the place for a full discussion of the *Complaints*, but an attack on a complacent court unwilling to listen occurs repeatedly in the poems that follow, in the extended satire of "Mother Hubberd," the warning flea of "Virgil's Gnat" killed by the shepherd he saves, and the court references of "Muiopotmos" discussed by Robert Brinkley and, more recently, Ayesha Ramachandran.[13] Even the poems concerned with mutability—"The Ruines of Rome," "Visions of Bellay" and "Visions of Petrarch"—add to the general bill of complaint. If the first part of *The Faerie Queene* praised England as a potential empire, heir to Rome, these poems insist that no empire, including Rome's, will last. Even what seem the most conventional of the *Complaints*—the three "Visions" sequences, two of which revise earlier translations of DuBellay and Petrarch—make their implicit criticism. As Richard Peterson has pointed out, the short original sequence, the "Visions of the Worlds Vanitie," that begins the series, repeatedly picture "tiny creatures [which] relentlessly bite and sting the great, delivering a jolt far out of proportion to their size and considerably reducing the complacency engendered by sheer bulk."[14] One might take this comment further, by noting the sonnet with which the sequence ends. After meditating on the various visions of worldly greatness tormented, killed, or stopped in its tracks by something small, the poet comments:

> Thenceforth I gan in my engrieved brest
> To scorne all difference of great and small,
> Sith that the greatest often are opprest,
> And unawares doe into daunger fall.
>
> (159–62)

If the poet were speaking *sub specie aeternitatis* this would be no more than traditional Christian wisdom, since great and small will both be judged equally after death. But in these lines he is speaking of *this* world, and implying something very subversive indeed. The sonnet ends:

> And ye, that read these ruines tragicall
> Learne by their losse to love the low degree,
> And if that fortune chaunce you up to call
> To honours seat, forget not what you be:
>   For he that of himselfe is most secure,
>   Shall finde his state most fickle and unsure.
>
> (163–68)

The language of this declaration is that of traditional stern moralism, counseling humility. It is only in the application that it becomes an attack. Burleigh is, after all, another of those who have risen to "honours seat" and forgotten his origins. "Lo," as Jove says to the eagle in one of the sonnets, "how the least the greatest may reprove" (56).

The *Complaints* include some of Spenser's least loved poetry, and for good reason. The "Visions of the Worlds Vanitie," when stripped of its immediate contemporary reference, seems a group of Renaissance clichés about the insubstantiality of power. But the weakest poems in the book also lack the characteristic of so much of Spenser's verse, the tendency to imply alternative truths that qualifies so many seemingly absolute statements in *The Faerie Queene*—the tendency epitomized by Guyon's destruction of Acrasia's garden. The most striking instance of this single-mindedness, in this respect, is "The Teares of the Muses," which almost entirely lacks irony. The nine muses let loose their diatribes, and that is that. I think that irony disappears in these poems because the *Complaints* is an unusually angry book, written out of a sense of personal and Protestant frustration. In its two unmistakably great poems—"Mother Hubberds Tale" and "Muiopotmos"—Spenser's fury issues in a more complexly mediated form.

What audience, then, is this condemnation of the court intended for? It has, as I have argued elsewhere, a strikingly narrower set of dedicatees from the broad spectrum of court figures addressed in the multiple dedications to *The Faerie Queene*.[15] The first and most important of these, and the only overlap with the dedicatory sonnets to *The Faerie Queene*, is Mary Sidney, countess of Pembroke. She is addressed at the head of the first poem in the volume, *The Ruines of Time*, the elegiac celebration of her house. Lady Mary, translator of Duplessis-Mornay, is rightly at the head of the volume since she was associated with her Protestant brother, and was herself an important patron of Protestant letters.[16] To dedicate the volume to her was to invoke a Sidneyan ideal. The subsequent three dedications—the book is divided into four parts, each with its dedication—are interesting in a different way. These are addressed to three women of the Northamptonshire Spencer family with whom the poet claimed kinship—presumably successfully, since he continues to connect himself to them in *Colin Clouts Come Home Again*, published four years later. Spenser looks to a family connection.

Yet while the dedicatees have changed, it is important to notice that this angry attack on court culture does not in fact turn away from the court. On the contrary, all four women will reappear in the praise of Cynthia's ladies in *Colin Clout*. Mary Sidney was the wife of the earl of Pembroke, one of Elizabeth's privy councilors. The three Spencer sisters were married—or had been married—to important court figures. The necessary audience for a diatribe against the court would seem to be select members of that same court—those most likely to be sympathetic to the poet's views. The court itself seems the inescapable audience for one's work.

II. Audiences for a Love Poet

As we know, *Complaints* was called in and Spenser's hand was slapped but his pension was not revoked, which suggests the esteem in which the queen must have held him. He published nothing more, however, for the next four years. A version of *Colin Clouts Come Home Againe* seems to have been finished in December of 1591, the date of its prefatory epistle, but the poem was not published until 1595. This deferral is usually explained as Spenser's need to suppress the poem until Sir Walter Ralegh, who figures prominently in it, had risen from the disgrace he suffered in mid-1592, but it's not really necessary to hunt so far afield. Spenser had incurred at least Burleigh's anger with the *Complaints* volume and he needed to pull in his horns. But something else may have contributed to the wait before publication. Until Spenser returned to London, he possessed a clear sense of whom he was writing for and, hence, what kind of a poet he was. With the *Complaints* he had attacked Burleigh and the court, for a court audience, and been silenced. What audience, then, was he to address?

The first book that Spenser published after his four years of silence was *Amoretti & Epithalamion*, the sonnet sequence built around his wooing of and marriage to Elizabeth Boyle in 1594. This sequence opens by explicitly addressing the problem of audience. Its first sonnet is an envoy in which the speaker imagines the book's welcoming reception by the Lady. It ends: "Leaves, lines and rhymes, seek her to please alone/ Whom if you please I care for other none." (I.1–2) The Lady will be a fit audience, though sole. One might think that this idea of the beloved as the audience for the poems is obvious, but I know of no other Renaissance sequence that begins in this way. A few sequences—like Shakespeare's or Daniel's—address the beloved in the opening sonnet, displaying the speaker in the act of persuasion. Petrarch's sequence famously begins by condemning everything that follows as evidence of a destructive wandering, driven by the madness of desire and the lust for fame. But by and large Renaissance sonnet sequences do not concern themselves seriously with the Lady as audience.[17] While keeping the beloved a blurred and distant object of desire, they tend instead to focus with great intensity on the erring mind of the speaker. Their *audience* is the gentle reader who follows the speaker's unhappy musings, presumably feeling sympathy for his misfortunes and admiration for his rhetoric.

By contrast Spenser's sequence plays to the lady. Spenser does many things to open the normally enclosed, narcissistic space of the sonnet sequence to include Elizabeth Boyle. He quotes her; he comments on her actions; and he dramatizes her in dialogue, in laughing opposition to his own posturing. Roughly a third of the sonnets address her. But most importantly, the sonnets embody a game in which the poet addresses her tongue-in-cheek, allowing himself to be caught with Petrarchan clichés in his mouth. As Louis Martz first pointed out, this is a sequence in which the poet is not a young blade but a forty-year-old widower, and the Petrarchan conventions are forced to look comic.[18] In the first sonnet, for instance, these clichés surface in the second quatrain, where they appear curiously out of place.

> And happy lines, on which with starry light
> those lamping eyes will deigne sometimes to look
> and reade the sorrowes of my dying spright,
> written with teares in harts close bleeding book.
>
> (I.5–8)

The overriding word of the poem is "happy"—both "fortunate," and "content"—and it contradicts the references to "The sorrows of my dying spright" and the "tears in harts close-bleeding book." During the sequence Spenser will occasional give vent to exasperation, but there's no danger of death in any but a sexual sense, and the idea of a *silent* heart ("harts close bleeding book") is ridiculous in the context of a sequence giving voice to his woes.[19] These are the melodramatic gestures of Petrarchan isolation, and they appear here as part of a quiet comedy—a comedy meant for the lady to appreciate.

My point is that *Amoretti & Epithalamion* speaks directly to the issue of audience. The sequence is *for* Elizabeth Boyle in a way that *Astrophil and Stella* is not *for* Penelope Rich. Its title is significant. Most English sequences take the pseudonym of the beloved, whether Stella or Diana or Idea, which emphasizes the lady as goddess or goal—the object that the poet is aiming at. Instead Spenser's sequence is named for the sonnets themselves, the *Amoretti* that act as go-betweens. We follow the poet's attempt to speak to the lady, rather than his report of his own condition. The *Epithalamion* ending the book concerns itself similarly with audience. The poet begins by singing to himself alone, but the final stanza makes the achieved song into a gift:

> SOng, made in lieu of many ornaments
> With which my love should duly have been dect . . . .
> Be unto her a goodly ornament,
> And for short time an endlesse monument.
>
> (427–28; 432–33)

Thus, the sequence opens and closes with the poet sending his book to the Lady who is its audience. This is an extraordinary sequence in many ways, but not least in its taking the problem of audience and using it to intensify the sense of domestic intimacy. If the lady likes the work, the poet cares for "other none." Unlike the *Complaints*, or indeed almost all the rest of Spenser's works, this book has no dedication from the poet to a patron. The lady is patron enough.

Elizabeth Boyle was not, of course, the only audience for *Amoretti and Epithalamion*. We have the sequence because Spenser chose to publish it and in publishing it he was looking beyond her for readers. Those readers would inevitably have included members of the court, but it seems to me no accident that the sonnet sequence and especially the *Epithalamion* with which it ends is Spenser's most emphatically middle-class work. "Tell me ye merchants daughters did ye see/ So fayre a creature in your towne before?" (167–68) the narrator asks. What Spenser does is to take the epithalamic form which was normally used for royal or aristocratic weddings, and to use it for his own, set (with classical decoration) in an Irish market town.[20]

Spenser's middle-class orientation here is the more striking because in the early 1590s the English sequence of amatory sonnets tended to be identified with the court.[21] The famous progenitors of the English sonnet were Wyatt and Surrey, courtiers both. Sir Philip Sidney set the model for the sonnet *sequence* in English and his poems are full of references to court matters—to politics, jousts, the comments of court lords and ladies. After Sidney, to write a sonnet sequence was to write as if one were a courtier, whether one was one or not. John Huntington's remarkable *Ambition, Rank and Poetry in 1590's England* argues that the intense hostility generated by Barnabe Barnes's sonnet sequence *Parthenophil and Parthenophe* (1593) was due primarily to the sequence's aristocratic pretensions.[22] This court association lessens in the later 1590s, but even those later sonneteers like Daniel, Drayton, or Shakespeare who are not courtiers, nonetheless address their sonnets to a beloved above them in rank, recapitulating the medieval dynamic of lowly wooer and high-born lady. By contrast, Spenser's sequence turns its back on the court milieu. Elizabeth Boyle's constancy and virtue may be admirable, and may mark her as a gentleman's future wife, but she is not a courtly lady. This is a sequence with only two references to the court, one that implicitly sets Elizabeth Boyle in competition with the queen, and another that gives priority to the love-sequence over his courtly epic.[23] This is thus a poem, like *Colin Clout*, in which the poet stresses the class out of which he arose and seems to reject his former audience.

In his fine essay, "Spenser's Domestic Domain," Louis Montrose illuminates this shift, showing how *Amoretti and Epithalamion* and *Colin Clouts Come Home Againe* quietly subordinate their praise of the queen to the poet's own history. These poems foreground for the first time in English literature "the publicly inconsequential subjects of the poet's autobiographical fictions and [invest] them with the rhetorical energies hitherto reserved for his encomia of the monarch; and furthermore [call] attention to this very process of displacement." (95) Montrose argues that Spenser is using the comparatively new medium of print to insist that *as poet* he has a source of authority that is not simply dependent on royal favor. In this context, Montrose argues, Spenser, who is often taken as backward-looking and who struggled to raise himself to the status of a gentleman, is in fact preparing the way for the triumph of the middle class.

> . . . our sage and serious Poet exploited the resources of an emergent commercial mode of cultural production so as to enhance his symbolic capital in ways that princely or aristocratic favor alone could not, and this enhancement led in turn to further possibilities for material advantage through the still dominant system of patron-client relations. Spenser's motives were undoubtedly to affirm his status as a gentleman rather than to assert his place in the vanguard of the bourgeoisie. Nevertheless we may see in some of the thematic preoccupations of his later poetry, adumbration of those values and aspirations that come increasingly to characterize the lives of the middling sort and the culture of mercantile capitalism. (97)

While, as I shall argue below, I feel some skepticism about Montrose's larger picture of Spenser, his stress on the poet's creation of a "domestic domain" in the space of his poetry and the literal space of his

Irish holdings seems to me borne out by the emphasis of this sequence. One of the commonplaces about the *Amoretti* is that it substi-
tutes a Protestant—and one might say bourgeois—stress on godly
marriage for the dramatic frustration with which the usual sonnet
sequence comes to a close. If he humbles the aristocratic epithalamion
for this purpose, he equally reshapes the Italianate sonnet sequence
to move it in the direction of Christian conversation.

The turn to the lady as audience is related to a more general shift
in Spenser's subject matter, with focuses increasingly on love. If we
leave the second half of *The Faerie Queene* aside, the later poetry
consists of *Amoretti and Epithalamion*, and then *Colin Clouts Come
Home Again*, an extended eclogue which transforms itself at the end
into a mythological Hymn to Love. The *Fowre Hymnes* set earthly
and heavenly love against one another, and even *Prothelamion* is a
betrothal poem mediating between love and war, marriage and politics. Like many of Spenser's critics, I think that Colin's assuming the
title of "Love's priest" at the end of *Colin Clout* represent a special
claim to authority on Spenser's part—a claim opposed to the worldly
authority that a courtly audience might grant him.

III. The Audiences of *the Faerie Queene*

But what of *The Faerie Queene*? This was the poem that was to have
made Spenser's name and fortune, assuring his place at court. Spenser
now had to continue it under different circumstances, and his ambivalence about its courtly audience helps to make the second half into
a very different poem from the first. This is a larger subject than I
can treat fully here, but I want to argue that Spenser's new antagonism
toward the court alters the mode of the second three books. That
second installment may not differ as much from the first as the second
half of *Don Quixote* does from its predecessor, but it similarly subjects
the values and beliefs of the earlier volume to ironic interrogation.
It remains a poem written for the court because there was no alternate
audience available for a great patriotic epic, but the treatment of
audience and ideals changes.

One can get a preliminary sense of the difference in a curious
moment in Book IV, Canto viii, when Arthur, Amoret, and Poena
stay the night with Sclaunder. The narrator breaks off this episode
to comment:

Here well I weene, when as these rimes be red

With misregard, that some rash witted wight,
Whose looser thought will lightly be misled,
These gentle Ladies will misdeeme too light
For thus conversing with this noble Knight,
Sith now of dayes such temperance is rare,
And hard to finde, that heat of youthfull spright
For ought will from his greedie pleasure spare,
More hard for hungry steed t'abstaine from pleasant lare.

(IV.viii.29)[24]

And the speaker goes on to argue that back then, in Faerie, the world was purer and knights more trustworthy than they are now. Several things are worth notice here. The first is the unnecessariness of this defense. Without this stanza few readers would dream of accusing the ladies: romance heroines are routinely escorted by Arthurian knights without endangering their chastity. Thus the audience—here, as elsewhere in the book—is itself placed in a problematic or satiric position. It is they who are accused of a cynical and perhaps salacious attitude toward Spenser's characters—a cynicism that is a projection of their own corrupt daily experience.

The second thing to notice is the intrusion of the narrator, whose own experience of court slander leads him to accuse this supposedly dirty-minded audience. How are we to relate this narrator to Spenser himself? It seems unlikely that the poet who has spent much of the previous poem describing disreputable actions on the part of many of his characters—including Amoret's and Poena's own wandering off to meet Lust a few cantos earlier—seriously identifies his narrative with a picture of an idealized golden age. And yet the unmistakable bitterness of the tone suggests a personal investment in defending the past and attacking the present. I would argue that as happens often in the later books, as in the late shorter poems, Spenser stages a single aspect of himself—in this case, a weary, embittered poet longing for an idealized past. These intrusions of poet into poem have been remarked ever since Harry Berger's famous essay on Book VI, and Judith Anderson's study of Spenser and Langland.[25] What seems to me partly to drive them is the new sense of isolation on the part of a poet who is writing an epic for an audience he distrusts. There are few moments in the first half of the poem where the audience is thus criticized and the poet made a hero. In the second half there are many.

This new, New Poet stands forth in sharpest relief in the proems to the last three books, and I want to develop Spenser's self-portraiture by looking carefully at the proem to Book IV. This is the introduction to the world of the second part, and the poet presents himself

here differently from the way he presents himself in the first installment. In the proems to the first three books, the poet foregrounds his
relation to the queen, addressing her, praising her, even sometimes
covertly chiding her.[26] The greatest intensity in the first three proems
comes at moments of apostrophe (at the end of the first proem, the
beginning and end of the second, and the center of the third), when
the poet turns to the queen, dramatizing his connection with her,
insisting that he is *her* poet and that she is his poem's primary audience.

The proem to the fourth book, instead of starting with the queen
or the muse, begins with the poet's endangered situation. It turns
immediately to the disapprobation of Burleigh, the "rugged forhead"
of the opening line.

> The rugged forhead that with grave foresight
>   Welds kingdomes causes, and affaires of state,
>   My looser rimes (I wote) doth sharply wite,
>   For praising love, as I have done of late,
>   And magnifying lovers deare debate;
>   By which fraile youth is oft to follie led,
>   Through false allurement of that pleasing baite,
>   That better were in vertues discipled,
> Then with vaine poemes weeds to have their fancies fed.
>   (IV.Proem.1)

This opening recalls the opening of the second proem, which also
deals with potential criticism. But, where in the second proem the
poet addresses the queen from the start, urging her to laugh at his
critics, here he presents himself as alone and vulnerable. There are
only two figures in this stanza, the poet and the "rugged forhead":
Elizabeth is neither addressed nor mentioned. And the attack on the
epic does not, as in the second proem, come from skepticism about
the truth of fiction; instead the poet faces a morals charge, an accusa-
tion that love poetry misleads youth. In the context of Spenser's later
poetry and the praise of love in *Faerie Queene* III, such an attack goes
to the heart of Spenser's mature poetic project.

In the next stanzas, however, the poet fights back, insisting on the
authority his vision gives him. While he seems in the opening verse
to yield to Burleigh's moral criticism, referring apologetically to his
"looser rimes," he rejects it outright in the second stanza with a
starchy ad hominem attack. "Such ones judge ill of love that cannot

love/ Ne in their frozen hearts feele kindly flame . . . ." The audacity of this defense is worth notice. Burleigh was the most powerful man in England, and Spenser's earlier attack on him had been met by the calling-in of the *Complaints* volume. Despite that, Spenser is playing here with the traditional image of the impotent old man, like Malbecco, whose "frosen" heart can't feel the natural fire that other mortal hearts feel. While Burleigh's disapproval had nothing to do with his age, Spenser's metaphors can't help but cast aspersions on Burleigh's virility as well as his understanding. Against the charges of immorality the poet insists that love is the root "of all honor and all vertue" (IV.Proem.2.6–7) and, again, that it is responsible for both heroic deeds and the works of "wise sages" (IV. Proem.3.3) including, of course, poets.

For the first three stanzas we watch the poet publicly oppose his attacker. But then he announces his audience and in turning away from Burleigh he seems, in a familiar gesture, to turn to the queen, the central figure of earlier proems:

> To such [as Burleigh] therefore I do not sing at all,
>   But to that sacred Saint my soveraigne Queene,
>   In whose chast breast all bountie naturall,
>   And treasures of true love enlocked beene,
>   Bove all her sexe that ever yet was seene;
>   To her I sing of love, that loveth best,
>   And best is lov'd of all alive I weene;
>   To her this song most fitly is addrest,
> The Queene of love, and prince of peace from heaven blest.
>
> (IV. Proem.4)

This is the hyperbolic rhetoric one can find in the earlier proems, as in Spenser's other praises of his queen and it now has the special function of self-defense. Spenser goes over Burleigh's head, making Elizabeth, their common mistress, the true image of a kindly flame, a model of how to love and be loved. She would seem to be the person to whom the proem is addressed, a life-giving source of "bountie naturall" and it is fitting the poet should now address her, as he has in all the earlier proems.

But this is not what now happens. The fifth stanza disappoints any expectation of a moment of apostrophe to the queen.

> Which that she may the better deigne to heare,

Do thou dred infant, *Venus* dearling dove,
From her high spirit chase imperious feare,
And use of awfull Majestie remove:
In sted thereof with drops of melting love
Deawd with ambrosiall kisses, by thee gotten
From thy sweete smyling mother from above,
Sprinckle her heart, and haughtie courage soften,
  That she may hearke to love, and reade this lesson often.

(IV. Proem. 5)

Instead of addressing Elizabeth the poet invokes Cupid. This substitution creates a mild shock: we watch the poet refusing his moment of apostrophe to the queen, appealing instead beyond her, just as he has appealed beyond Burleigh, to an allegorical figure that embodies more abstractly and more completely the capacity to love. Further, the language of the stanza allies the queen with Burleigh: the references to "imperious feare," "awfull Majestie" and "haughtie courage," along with the suggestion in the first line that the queen may *not* "deign to heare," all associate Elizabeth with the rugged forehead of the opening stanza.

It is important to notice how different the characterization of the queen here is from her portrait in the preceding stanza. *There* she is the one who "loveth best" where *here* she's become one who needs to go to school if she's to learn how. The final line, with its sense that the poem provides a "lesson" that the queen needs to read recalls the final line of the proem to the first book: again the poet is presenting the queen with his work: "The which to heare vouchsafe, O dearest dread, awhile." (I.Proem.iv.9) But here the offer differs greatly. The speaker doesn't, so to speak, look the queen in the face, which is the rhetorical effect of a moment of apostrophe. He merely insists, with the voice of Cupid's schoolmaster if not Cupid's priest, that she needs to pay attention and to "reade this lesson often."

In speaking *about* Elizabeth and not *to* her Spenser undercuts her status as the reader for whom the book is written. The proem addresses the God of Love, whoever he is, but the shift in address opens up the poem to an entirely different audience, which watches this dramatic refusal of allegiance. The poet, who offered himself as a devoted courtier in the proems to the earlier books, has now shaken off that identity, and stands forward as a figure of virtue under attack. He assumes, indeed, a kind of heroic stance, setting himself against the greatest powers of the kingdom.

But what, then, is the audience that will mark and approve the poet's action? I think that for Spenser the obvious well-wishers—friends and supporters like Ralegh or Bryskett—or possible patrons like the earl of Essex—would certainly have been part of that audience. But this rhetorical grandstanding goes beyond them: it includes the readers of the future who are not beholden to the queen, and who will see the implicit heroism of Spenser's stance. What Spenser gives us, in the proem to Book IV, as in the bleak ending to Book VI, is the portrait of a poet who is essentially alone. This figure claims authority, but he does not expect his immediate audience to acknowledge it. He looks instead to a set of future readers for his justification.

These moments of grandstanding for the future appear with increasing frequency in the later books of *The Faerie Queene*. One of the most notable of them occurs when Colin/Spenser addresses Gloriana, apologizing for praising the central figure of the dance on Mount Acidale.

> Sunne of the world, great glory of the sky,
>> That all the earth doest lighten with thy rayes,
>> Great *Gloriana*, greatest Majesty,
>> Pardon thy shepheard, mongst so many layes,
>> As he has sung of thee in all his dayes,
>> To make one minime of thy poore handmayd,
>> And underneath thy feete to place her prayse,
>> And when thy glory shall be farre displayd
> To future age of her this mention may be made.
>
> (VI.x.28)

The problem with the apology, which is as unnecessary as the apology for Amoret's chastity in Sclaunder's house, is that it raises more hackles than it smoothes. What reader, including the queen, would ever consider Colin's praise of his love an act of disloyalty? Even if one refrains from stressing the uncertainty of the relation between Colin and Spenser, poets are always praising their ladies. The needless apology thus has the effect of highlighting what its language of transcendent divinity pretends to hide, the all too human vanities of the historical Elizabeth I. It suggests that she *might* take offence at this praise of the poet's lady, reminding one of her well known jealousies. This was, after all, the Elizabeth who disliked the thought of her favorites' marrying, and who disgraced Spenser's friend and patron

Sir Walter Ralegh for his secret marriage by first imprisoning him and later banishing him from the court. Under the guise of apologizing to the queen, it indicts her: the gesture of submission conceals a gesture of defiance. Further, the demand for pardon invokes a "future age"—an age which will see the present in perspective. This gesture toward the supposed audience for his poem is actually a gesture *for* that audience, which will understand the situation better than the old queen to whom the speaker seems to appeal.

IV

In the passage that I quoted earlier from his essay on "Spenser's Domestic Domain," Louis Montrose highlights Spenser's quiet acts of resistance in the later poems, his storing up "symbolic capital" in the marking out of his domestic domain. The term "symbolic capital," however, is tricky. It carries the overtones of the term "cultural capital" invented by the late sociologist Pierre Bourdieu, who was interested in the way that nineteenth—and twentieth-century elites developed cultural institutions that would judge and reward achievement in what Bourdieu calls "the cultural field" with honor and authority.[27] But Early Modern England did not yet have the conditions that would permit the creation of "cultural capital" by the writing of poetry and so Spenser—like Jonson after him—was faced with the task of *claiming* cultural capital even while remaining aware that the idea would have been meaningless and or even ludicrous to those in power. "The Teares of the Muses" is an early attempt to assert such authority, appropriating as it does the voices of the classical guardians of human arts. But the main thing that the Muses bewail is that nobody pays them any attention. It is, I think, in response to the sense that the audience he needed did not yet exist that Spenser developed the peculiar art of his later poetry, an art which highlights the figure of the isolated poet against a backdrop of antagonism and neglect. Spenser created his symbolic capital, but the notes that he minted could not be redeemed until the cultural currency had changed.

Smith College

APPENDIX I: WHO IS RESPONSIBLE FOR SPENSER'S COMPLAINTS?

The dating of individual *Complaints* and the part that Spenser had in putting together his book has been the subject of much disagreement; in the absence of fresh information the debate may never be finally resolved. The most carefully reasoned attack on the idea that Spenser had a hand in the book's publication is Jean Brink's "Who Fashioned Edmund Spenser?: The Textual History of *Complaints.*" *Studies in Philology* 88 (1991), 153–68.

Brink makes the following arguments: (1) In late 1590 and early 1591 Spenser's pension had not been finally granted and he would not have wanted to jeopardize it by publishing the inflammatory "Mother Hubberds Tale" and "the Ruines of Time" (157–59). (2) Spenser wouldn't have gained anything by "earning profits for his printer and bookseller" (160) and stood to lose a great deal. (3) Ponsonby's preface should be taken at face value when it says clearly that he has put together the book in Spenser's absence (161). (4) The corrections made while the book was in press are obvious and need not be authorial. (5) The theory propounded by Francis R. Johnson that the *Complaints* was made up of four independent units, each with its own dedication, is weakened by the illogicality of the organization and the fact that the second poem of the second section ("The Tears of the Muses" and "Virgils Gnat") has its own dedicatory sonnet to the earl of Leicester. Further, the order of the dedications ignores the respective ranks of the three sisters and "no logical connections are made between any of the dedicatees and the poems included in the gathering dedicated to her"(166). Finally, "the innocuous poems most suitable for presentation to a noble patroness—'The Ruines of Rome,' 'Visions of the worlds Vanitie,' 'The Visions of Bellay' and 'The Visions of Petrarch'—are printed without any dedications" (166–67).

These are serious arguments and deserve reply. For (1) and (2): I agree that Spenser had much to lose and little to gain by publishing "Mother Hubberds Tale" and "The Ruines of Time." But, as Kent says, "anger hath his privilege." I see Spenser as a man whose peculiar stubbornness led him repeatedly to insist on his own point of view. This stubbornness appears, for instance, in the criticism of the English church, however indirect, in the "July" and "September" eclogues; in his support for the disgraced Sir Walter Ralegh in *Colin Clout* and especially *Faerie Queene* IV.vii-viii, and for Lord Grey in the *View* (if

we assume Spenser wrote it), and in his continued defiance of Burleigh in the proem to Book IV, discussed above.

(3) The trustworthiness of Ponsonby's preface seems to me crucial
in deciding whether Spenser had a hand in assembling the book. As
I argue above, Tresham's letter suggests that Ponsonby's chronology
is wrong, though we can't know how accurate Tresham's information was. If he were uncomfortable about the "Mother Hubberds
Tale" Spenser could have used Ponsonby to avoid responsibility for
assembling the book.

(4) Several corrections in the *Complaints* are not self-evident. I see
no reason why the printer should have amended "a treasure" to "our
treasure" in MHT 160: the shift seems to me a writerly attempt to
make meaning clearer. "Tuneful" for "fruitful" (TM 549) is not, in
my view the change "anyone listening to the poem being read aloud"
would be likely to make. The addition of "Dull" before "Poppie"
in Mui 196 intensifies the subtle music of the line, which can be
scanned without it.

(5) Most important, in my view, are the four dedications. The
first, to Lady Mary Sidney, is clearly connected with the poem that
follows, being an elegy for her brother and several of her relatives.
The other groups of poems, I would agree, have no direct connection, so far as we know, with the women to whom they are addressed.
But the addresses to the three Spenser sisters unify the dedications
and suggest that they are part of a common project. One needs, in
any case, to account for the presence of these dedications: how were
they penned and where did Ponsonby find them? The simplest hypothesis seems to me that Spenser wrote them for this book. Further,
the argument that the book is illogically organized depends on the
standard of logic with which one approaches it. After the first section,
which is made up entirely of the original poem, "The Ruines of
Time," each successive section is composed of one or more original
poems followed by one or more translations. Which poems are suitable for particular ladies and which are not depends on individual
standards of decorum. Spenser thought highly of the Spencer sisters
and, in keeping with his own exalted sense of his work, honored
them with his poems. While the absence of attention to rank in the
ordering of the dedications is curious, it remains unclear why Ponsonby was any more likely than Spenser to make such a mistake—if
it was a mistake.

Complaints is a book with its own characteristic emotional register
and its own agenda. It is striking that, alone of Spenser's works, it
avoids the subject of love, and so often, directly or by implication,
glances at the court. It brings together recent poems with revised

versions of earlier work—notably the translations of the *Theatre for Worldlings*. In my view—which largely follows the careful reasoning of Harold Stein in *Studies in Spenser's Complaints* (New York: Oxford University Press, 1934)—the old poems are "Virgil's Gnat," "Visions of Bellay" and "Visions of Petrarch" and probably the "Ruines of Rome." The new poems are "The Ruines of Time," "The Teares of the Muses," "Muiopotmos" and "Visions of the Worlds Vanitie." The difficult poem to date is "Mother Hubberds Tale" whose history has been the more confused by Greenlaw's 1932 argument that the poem was written in 1579 to protest Elizabeth's possible marriage to the Catholic duc D'Alençon and that its reception made Spenser flee to Ireland. (For the refutation of the argument see Judith Anderson et al., *Spenser and the Subject of Biography* [Amherst: University of Massachusetts Press], 31–64.) I follow Stein in thinking that the first three sections of the poem were originally drafted earlier but that the very different final section (lines 943–1388) with its unmistakable attack on Burleigh was added before the publication of the *Complaints*. At that time there may have been extensive revision of the earlier poem.

Notes

1. I would like to thank the Committee of Spenser at Kalamazoo for inviting me to give this paper as the Kathleen Williams Lecture and to the audience of the lecture for their useful suggestions. I would also like to thank Paul Alpers, Nora Crow, Sharon Seelig, and especially Anne Lake Prescott for their help.

2. "Spenser's Audiences, 1589–91," *Studies in Philology* 100, #4 (Fall, 2003): 514–33.

3. In discussing the middle-class audience for romance, Michael Murrin comments, "Spenser then tacitly assumed that he could direct his poem to the court and yet expect everyone to enjoy it . . . ." "The Audience of *The Faerie Queene*," *Explorations in Renaissance Culture* 23 (1997): 1–21. For the middle-class audiences of medieval romances, see Nancy Bradbury, *Writing Aloud: Storytelling in Late Medieval England* (Urbana: University of Illinois Press, 1998).

4. See Stephen May, *The Elizabethan Court Poets* (Asheville, N.C.: Pegasus Press, 1999), 9–40 for an account of the place of courtier poets in the court's social organization. Spenser never became a courtier poet in May's sense (there is, for instance, no evidence that he had easy access to the queen's privy chamber and he never, so far as we know, exchanged new year's gifts with the monarch) though he may at first have aspired to courtier status. In my view Spenser saw a place at court as an acknowledgement of the national importance of his epic. This dream could have been nurtured by the common belief that Virgil had occupied a similar place

as poet-counselor during the rule of Augustus Caesar. On this Virgilian myth see M. L. Donnelly, "The Life of Virgil and the Aspiration of the 'New Poet'," *Spenser Studies* XVII (2003), 1–36.

5.   Helgerson, *Self-Crowned Laureates: Spenser, Jonson and the Literary System* (Berkeley: University of California Press, 1983), 25, 36–38.

6.   David Riggs, *Ben Jonson* (Cambridge, MA: Harvard University Press, 1989), 220–39.

7.   John Huntington, *Ambition, Rank, and Poetry in 1590's England* (Urbana: University of Illinois Press, 2001). See especially pp.15–21.

8.   Louis Montrose, "Spenser's Domestic Domain: Poetry, Property and the Early Modern Subject" in *Subject and Object in Renaissance Culture* (Cambridge, England: University of Cambridge Press, 1996), 83–130.

9.   Richard Peterson, "Laurel Crown and Ape's Tale: New Light on Spenser's Career from Thomas Tresham," *Spenser Studies* 12 (1998): 8.

10.   "Since my late setting foorth of the *Faerie Queene*, finding that it hath found a favourable passage amongst you; I have sithence endevoured by all good meanes . . . to get into my handes such smale Poems of the same Authors; as I heard were disperst abroad in sundrie hands, and not easie to be come by, by himself; some of them having been diverslie imbeziled and purloyned from him, since his departure over Sea." As Ronald Bond remarks in *The Yale Edition of the Shorter Poems of Edmund Spenser*, ed. Oram et al. (New Haven: Yale University Press, 1989), the sentence is ambiguous, and may refer "to his original departure for Ireland in 1580." (p.223) All references to Spenser's shorter poems follow this edition.

11.   In '*The New Poet': Novelty and Tradition in Spenser's Complaints* (Liverpool: Liverpool University Press, 1999) Richard Danson Brown argues that the poems are united by a common concern with the nature of art. While the theme of art is important in the volume, as it is in much of Spenser's writing, I think that its overriding concern is with cultural politics.

12.   R. M. Cummings ed., *Spenser, The Critical Heritage* (New York; Barnes and Noble, 1971), 100.

13.   Robert Brinkley, "Spenser's *Muiopotmos* and the Politics of Metamorphosis," *ELH* 48 (1981), 668–76; Ayesha Ramachandran, "Clarion in the Bower of Bliss: Poetry and Politics in Spenser's *Muiopotmos*" *Spenser Studies* XX (2005), 77–106.

14.   "Laurel Crown and Ape's Tail,"19.

15.   "Spenser's Audiences," 523.

16.   See Margaret Hannay, *Philips Phoenix: Mary Sidney, Countess of Pembroke* (New York: Oxford University Press, 1990), 78–79

17.   Anne Lake Prescott reminds me that Ronsard's final great sequence, the two books of the *Sonnets pour Helene*, does concern itself with the lady as audience, although Helene is considerably less accommodating than Elizabeth Boyle. Ronsard's courtly sequence ends, unlike Spenser's, with a bitter farewell and a lament for the death of Charles IX.

18.   Louis L. Martz, "The Amoretti: Most Goodly Temperature" in *Form and Convention in the Poetry of Edmund Spenser* (New York: Columbia University Press, 1971), 155–58.

19.   This joke about the eloquence of love poets on their supposedly silent pain goes back at least to Chaucer. In his *Tale* the Franklin describes how the Squire

Aurelius creates "manye layes,/Songes, compleintes, roundels, virelayes/ How that he dorste nat his sorwe telle . . . ." (947–49) (Quoted from *The Riverside Chaucer* ed. Larry D. Benson et al., 3rd edition [Boston: Houghton Mifflin, 1987]).

20. On the aristocratic background of the epithalamion, see Thomas Greene, "Spenser and the Epithalamic Convention" *Comparative Literature* 9 (1957): 215–18.

21. The love sonnet's association with the court is not, of course, characteristic of other literatures or for that matter of English literature in the late 1590s. While the premiere French sonneteer was Pierre de Ronsard, a court poet, there were other, competing sequences and locales including the Lyons of the middle-class poets Maurice Scève and Louise Labé.

22. Huntington, *Ambition, Rank and Privilege in 1590's England*, 37–43.

23. See Donald Cheney, "Spenser's Fortieth Birthday," *Spenser Studies* IV (1983), 6–8, and Montrose, "Spenser's Domestic Domain," 112–14.

24. All quotations from Spenser's epic follow Edmund Spenser, *The Faerie Queene* ed. A.C. Hamilton et al., 2nd edition (London: Longman [Pearson Education], 2001).

25. Harry Berger, Jr. "A Secret Discipline: *The Faerie Queene,* Book VI" in *Form and Convention in the Poetry of Edmund Spenser*, and Judith Anderson, *The Growth of a Personal Voice: Piers Plowman and The Faerie Queene* (New Haven: Yale University Press, 1976).

26. The most insightful comments on Spenser in the proems occur in a series of essays by Judith Anderson. See: " 'In Living Colours and right hew': The Queen of Spenser's Central Books" in *Poetic Traditions of the English Renaissance*, ed. Maynard Mack and George de Forest Lord (New Haven: Yale University Press, 1982), 47–66; "What comes after Chaucer's But: Adversative Constructions in Spenser" in *Acts of Interpretation: The Text and Its Contexts 700–1600* (Norman, OK: Pilgrim Books, 1982), 105–18; and "Narrative Reflections: Re-envisaging the Poet in *The Canterbury Tales* and *The Faerie Queene*" in Theresa Krier, ed., *Refiguring Chaucer in the Renaissance* (Gainesville, FL: University Press of Florida, 1998), 87–105. See also the suggestive commentary of Judith Owens on the proem to Book III in *Enabling Engagements: Edmund Spenser and the Poetics of Patronage* (Montreal: McGill-Queens University Press, 2002), 110–16.

27. See Pierre Bourdieu, *The Rules of Art: Genesis and Structure of the Literary Field*, trans. Susan Emanual (Stanford, CA: Stanford University Press, 1995), 214–84.

The Trials of Art: Testing Temperance in the Bower of Bliss and Diana's Grove at Nonsuch

This essay reconstructs the experience of visiting Diana's Grove at Lord Lumley's Nonsuch, a celebrated sixteenth-century pleasure garden, to show how the period's real gardens prepared readers to engage the didactic architecture of Spenser's Bower of Bliss. By establishing the parallel structural schemes of Bower and Grove, it demonstrates that Spenser's garden setting would have impelled contemporary readers to measure their own reactions to the Bower's moral tests against Guyon's. The paper traces the shifting triangulation of reader, knight, and garden to reveal Guyon as a flawed exemplum, an inadequate model of the right relation of virtuous man to sensuous art.

*A*T THE END OF THE SECOND BOOK of the *Faerie Queene*, when Edmund Spenser is constructing a climactic final challenge for his Knight of Temperaunce, the setting he chooses is a garden—an Italianate garden in the contemporary Roman style.[1] Such gardens had only just begun to appear in England during Elizabeth's reign. We can gain a sense of what it was like to experience them from a later text, Henry Wotton's description of one of their Italian originals:

> the first Accesse was a high walke like a *Tarrace*, from whence might bee taken a generall view of the whole *Plott* below but

Spenser Studies: A Renaissance Poetry Annual, Volume XX, Copyright © 2005 by AMS Press, Inc. All rights reserved.

rather in a delightfull confusion, then with any plaine distinction of the pieces. From this the *Beholder* descending many
steps, was afterwards conueyed againe, by seuerall *mountings* and
valings, to various entertainements of his *sent,* and *sight:* which
I shall not neede to describe (for that were poeticall) let me
onely note this, that euery one of these diuersities, was as if
hee had beene *Magically* transported into a new Garden.[2]

Unlike the older formal knot gardens, designed to be viewed from
above, an Italianate garden denied the visitor a detailed distanced
overview, offering instead an immersive, sequential experience. Its
layout often required the visitor to move through it in a predictable
order, so it could stimulate particular senses at key moments, or
surprise the visitor with new perspectives. Most such gardens also
asked to be "read" as the visitor walked along, sometimes literally,
in the case of inscriptions or statues representing a narrative scene, and
sometimes iconically or figuratively. But even when they required
interpretation, Italianate gardens first seized a visitor's imagination
by stirring his senses and passions.

Although Wotton demurs from describing these pleasures, his ac-
knowledgment that to do so would be "poetical" reminds us that as
a discourse, poetry distinguished itself by its commitment to these
techniques. As George Puttenham describes it, poetry

is . . . a maner of vtterance more eloquent and rethoricall then
the ordinarie prose, which we vse in our daily talke: because it
is decked and set out with all maner of fresh colours and figures,
which maketh that it sooner inuegleth the iudgement of man,
and carieth his opinion this way and that, whither soeuer the
heart by impression of the eare shalbe most affectionatly bent
and directed.[3]

Like a visitor on a garden path, a reader of verse moved linearly
through delights that engaged his intellect from the bottom up, by
permeating what was known as his sensitive soul—his "eare" and
affections—to gain access to his rational soul, or "judgement."[4] For
Sidney this property of poetry made the poet "the right popular
philosopher," a writer who knew how to take advantage of man's
fallen nature to convey his virtuous truths. Yet even as this seductive
force gave poetry its unique discursive power, it also rendered the

art morally suspect, producing what Margaret Ferguson has called the art's erotic threat.[5] Detractors charged that it was "the nurse of abuse, infecting us with many pestilent desires; with a siren's sweetness drawing the mind to the serpent's tail of sinful fancies."[6] The same was true for pleasure gardens.[7]

The perception that poetry and pleasure gardens shared definitive characteristics was common after the middle of the sixteenth century.[8] The pairing offered a poet who wanted to write verse about the art of poetry—particularly, about the experience of *reading* poetry—a way to meet the topic's special challenge. Let us accept, with Sidney, that a poet's job was to yield "to the powers of the mind an image of that whereof the philosopher bestoweth but a wordish description," so that "we seem not to hear" of "all virtues, vices, and passions" but instead "clearly to see through them."[9] How might the poet portray the contemplative process of reading, showing his readers the experience of poetry by kindling that experience in their imaginations, rather than telling them how to understand it? Such a question goes to the heart of the difference between poetry and other discourses. Self-reflective poets could address this difference by using the image of the pleasure garden to represent poetry's perils and charms. The image was useful for two key reasons. First, the characteristics that poetry shared with pleasure gardens in the period enabled the image to materialize and spatialize the experience of reading poetry, thus aiding readers to share imaginatively in that experience. Second, the image of a contemporary pleasure garden imposed a setting that constantly required the reader/visitor to reposition himself in relation to both the art he was viewing and his fellow spectators.

Spenser takes advantage of this dynamic in the Bower of Bliss, where the reader moves with Guyon through a garden that is poetry reified. Even as Spenser's narrative focuses the reader's attention on Guyon's position, the conventions of visiting contemporary Italianate gardens would have encouraged the reader to pay attention to his own position. The didactic force of the canto hinges on the reader's willingness to measure his own reactions to the Bower's art against Guyon's. At every step, the triangulation of reader, knight, and garden shifts, obliging the reader to reassess Guyon's status as a model of the right relation of virtuous man to sensuous art. If we trace this triangulation through the canto, we find that the demands made by the garden setting on Guyon and the reader prompt qualitatively different responses to the Bower's art, a process that climaxes in the jarring violence of Guyon's destruction of the Bower in the canto's final stanzas. Whether the distance between reader and knight is the distance between master and novice, or rather the distance between extremist zeal and more flexible moderation, an awareness of this distance is crucial to understanding Guyon as a flawed exemplum, an inadequate ideal of the relationship between a man ruled by 'vertuous and gentle discipline' and the pleasures of art that is, as Spenser puts it, "delightfull . . . to commune sence."[10]

To show how the experience of visiting real Italianate gardens would have sensitized Spenser's original readers to the triangulation that generates this distance, the first half of this essay reconstructs one of the only sixteenth-century English gardens for which detailed descriptions remain: the Grove of Diana at the palace of Nonsuch, laid out by John, Lord Lumley between 1579 and 1591. Like Spenser's Bower, Lumley's Italianate Grove was an allegorical landscape that required visitors to interact with a series of tableaux enacting a sequence of aesthetic and moral tests. Inscriptions and physical layout impelled visitors to think critically about their responses to the challenges posed by the garden's art by comparing their reactions to those of a prototypic viewer (in this case Actaeon, an obviously negative prototype). The resulting triangulation blurred the bounds between observer and observed, art and life, engaging the visitor physically, as a sensible body in relation to sculpture, architecture, plantings, and other bodies, and also intellectually, as a mind compelled to interpret the significance of the body's position. For those of Spenser's readers who understood the dynamics of this sort of immersive, self-conscious contemporary pleasure garden, the setting of Guyon's test would have lent its canto a charge not easily recaptured today: a formal injunction to choose a position and experience its moral consequences.

1.

This view of an early modern English garden challenges recent studies that view gardens as sites of unproblematic pleasure. Ilva Beretta has argued, for instance, that the period's actual gardens differed from poetic gardens like Spenser's. Whereas "the poetical tradition often emphasized the Christian associations of corruption in its treatment of the earthly paradise," she contends, "the real garden was seen as positive, without temptation and without the postlapsarian stain of sin; it was the manifestation of man's understanding of God's universe."[11] While confident advice dispensed by contemporary gardening handbooks provides Beretta with some confirmation, such a bald distinction is belied by eyewitness accounts of thematically complex gardens, particularly those of great Italian estates that served as models for the English. The Grove of Diana, in fact, seems to have employed a very similar thematic scheme to that of Spenser's Bower. In both, we find a sensual, forbidden woman enclosed in a garden setting and a male voyeur who must decide how to respond to her charms. Both are described in verse that ponders the dangers of following sensual urgings at the same time that it appeals to the senses through poetic language.

The Grove of Diana was part of a much larger and older complex of gardens at Nonsuch, some features of which traced to the palace's origins under Henry VIII. During Lumley's residence the gardens were considered some of the "finest in the whole of England," both by foreign visitors like Baron Waldstein and by such domestic writers as William Harrison, who ranked them with those at Theobalds and Hampton Court.[12] In part, Nonsuch's reputation arose from the elaborate, well-established privy garden that lay around the exterior walls of the inner court. On the south and east fronts of the palace this was a typical Tudor knot garden, enclosed by a fourteen-foot brick wall, with "walks and covered alleys, seats painted green, blue and russet, loftier plants and trees and twelve arbours, each with its own flower-bed."[13] To the west lay a "maze or labyrinth surrounded by high shrubberies to prevent one passing over or through them,"[14] a very unusual feature in the sixteenth century, when the hedges of most labyrinths were carefully clipped low so that the patterns they formed could be viewed and admired.[15] The privy garden was ornamented by a variety of fountains, obelisks, and columns, many of which featured elements of the Lumley arms.

Roy Strong has demonstrated that this heraldic scheme was paired with a complementary emblematic program celebrating Queen Elizabeth. This was realized by statuary that employed her royal symbols, including an imposing central fountain of what Strong terms "the usual early Renaissance type" depicting the goddess Diana with streams of water spurting from her breasts.[16] Together, Lumley's extravagant heraldic display and allegorical praise of the queen may have been designed to offset his precarious position as a Catholic and a known conspirator in the Ridolfi plot, imprisoned in 1571 and released in 1573 at Elizabeth's command. The Nonsuch gardens would have been ideal sites for compensatory self-display, as Lumley was repeatedly made to demonstrate his loyalty by hosting Elizabeth and her court at the palace.

The Grove of Diana played a crucial role in his allegorical homage, although not as a component of the privy garden. To reach the Grove

a wandering visitor had to put the maze on his right hand and walk
west, through an opening in the privy garden wall that led into the
palace's wilderness. Like the wildernesses of other sixteenth—and
seventeenth-century estates, the one at Nonsuch was hardly "wild."
These typically consisted of a man-made forest of trees, often planted
in regular patterns, designed for peaceful shaded walks.[17] Three walking paths threaded the Nonsuch wilderness, "the middle one worn
and sandy and the others turfed," leading the visitor past such amuse-
ments as a "wire-fenced aviary" and cleared, partitioned alleys used
for ball games.[18] Ultimately the paths converged at an ornate two-
story banqueting house where palace guests might enjoy dessert or
even a full meal. Wilderness, aviary, alleys for games, banqueting
house—all these lavish features were characteristic of contemporary
English pleasure gardens.

Shortly before arriving at the banqueting house the visitor would
traverse the creation that set the Nonsuch estate apart from its peers
as what Strong identifies as "the first large-scale symbolic garden in
the Italian Mannerist style to have been attempted in England." This
was the famous Grove of Diana, where Lumley created his domestic
version of the *boschetti* he had seen in Italy, shady groves that sheltered
"sculptural or architectural groups, each with its symbolic or allegorical meaning."[19] Such gardens asked for more than simple recognition
of heraldic devices or royal emblems, demanding instead that the
visitor read at several levels. Lumley's Grove invited perception of
at least three layers of meaning in the central sculptural group: in the
lowest register, the Ovidian narrative of Diana and Actaeon; above
this, the moral application of the tale; and beyond this, the relevance
of both to a subject whose queen was represented as a latter-day
Cynthia. The Grove of Diana was widely visited; some of the best
descriptions come from the diaries of fascinated tourists. A detailed
account appears in the journal of the Polish nobleman Baron
Waldstein, who toured Nonsuch on Wednesday the 16th of July,
1600. By following in his steps, with additions and corrections from
other accounts, we can gain some idea of a male visitor's sequential
experience of the Grove, as each new architectural feature added its
part to the developing allegorical whole.[20]

Waldstein reports that he initially encountered a "small stone
building," what Swiss traveler Thomas Platter had earlier described
as a "vaulted temple," containing a black marble table and three Latin
inscriptions.[21] Like epigraphs in an emblem book, these offered a
sufficiently educated visitor a moral framework for interpreting the
Grove's succeeding tableaux.

The temptation to baseness comes not from the Goddess,
who is chastity itself; it arises only from an evil mind
and from an evil spirit.

Out of an unclean spring, water defiled.
Out of a graceless mind, a tainted view.

    Shade for the heated,
    A seat for the weary.
Though in the shade, be not obscured
Nor in repose acquire the serpent's view.[22]

The inscriptions challenge the reader/viewer to confront the moral
weakness that may inform his desire for sensual pleasure. The first
two accuse the reprobate gazer whose "evil mind" disgraces himself
and defiles the object of his view. The third is more cryptic and also
more personal, integrating the visitor into the allegorical landscape
with direct address that wavers between warning and welcome. At
once an invitation to indulge his body in the garden's comforts and
a reminder not to abandon himself to these pleasures, this inscription
cautions against becoming "obscured," or withdrawn from the
world, and possessor of "the serpent's view," a perverted gaze.

The visitor did well to heed these cautions as he proceeded, leaving
the small stone building behind. In the fountain at the heart of the
Grove the inscriptions' rhetorical warnings took material form.
Waldstein describes the fountain or grotto, designed to represent the
Vale of Gargaphie in the third book of Ovid's *Metamorphoses*:

This spring rises in a secluded glade at the foot of a little cliff.
The source was from a number of pipes hidden in the rock,
and from them a gentle flow of water bathed Diana and her
two nymphs; Actaeon had approached; he was leaning against
a nearby tree to hide himself and gazing lecherously at Diana;
she, with a slight gesture of her hand towards him, was slowly
changing his head to that of a stag; his 3 hounds were in
close pursuit.[23]

The relative positions of the polychrome statues and the wooden
rails that surrounded at least some of them are largely a matter of
conjecture, but a 1613 visitor tells us that Actaeon stood "fifteen

paces away" from Diana and her nymphs.[24] As any visitor to the
Grove approached the fountain, at some point he would suddenly
find himself at Actaeon's distance, sharing his gaze at the very moment punishment took effect. This triangulation of viewer, prototypic viewer, and goddess involved the reader/viewer to a depth that
no emblem could reach.[25] Although the Grove, like a conventional
emblem book, demanded that a series of moral injunctions in the
form of mottoes be applied to a physical scene, by locating the visitor
in the midst of its central tableau it transformed him into a participant
in that scene, an integral part of its art, a viewer in a drama about
what it meant to view and to be viewed. Engaged in both body and
mind, he was denied the safe detachment an emblem book might
provide. The inscriptions he had read only a few moments earlier
made his response into a test. Would he shame himself like Actaeon
by taking inappropriate pleasure in the sight of the bathing goddess?
Or would he find a way to check that part of his nature in order to
appreciate the delights of her hidden grove on more acceptable terms?
If so, what might those terms be? While the mottoes are chillingly
specific about the evils of an unchaste gaze, they fail to offer the
visitor any positive guidance.

Rather than resolving this perplexity, the section of the Grove
that lay beyond the Diana fountain can only have served to intensify
the visitor's unease. Waldstein tells us that the next feature was a
"fairly high arch which is hedged all round with a thicket of shrubs."
Although he mistook the birds that ornamented the arch for "3
eagles," we know from an English source that the arch bore one
eagle accompanied by a pelican and a phoenix. As Strong has noted,
these were the "personal emblems of Elizabeth Tudor,"[26] England's
own Diana, a queen who cultivated recognition for her generous
self-sacrifice and for her resilience in adversity. Latin inscriptions on
the arch celebrated the goddess/queen and denounced her insolent
admirer:

The fisherman who has been wounded, learns, though late,
   to beware;
But the unfortunate Actaeon always presses on.
   The chaste virgin naturally pitied:
But the powerful goddess revenged the wrong.
   Let Actaeon fall a prey to his dogs,
      An example to youth,
   A disgrace to those that belong to him!

> May Diana live the care of Heaven;
> The delight of mortals;
> The security of those that belong to her![27]

In contrast with the naturalistic fountain, this architectural group featured Diana only in abstract form, emblematized by a triumphal arch celebrating her alternately vengeful and protective power. Actaeon's physical absence from the scene de-emphasized the triangulation of goddess, voyeur, and visitor, but not to the relief of the visitor. He now found himself before an undistracted representation of the goddess. Would he, like Actaeon, suffer for his disgraceful gaze? The answer would come from another element of the architectural group: a "pyramid of marble full of concealed pipes, which spurt all who come within their reach," apparently located "in the centre" of the archway.[28] In an Ovidian context this trick fountain had ominous implications. Having just witnessed the scene of Actaeon's metamorphosis, a visitor sprayed by the marble pyramid while reading the arch's inscription could hardly avoid recalling those fatally transforming droplets flung by the angry goddess.

What was the visitor to make of this experience? Was he meant to emerge from the Grove chastened and ashamed of his base nature? The presence of a trick fountain should warn us against jumping to so grim a conclusion, for no matter how sinister its narrative implications, the mechanical joke was designed to elicit laughter from the visitor's companions and, perforce, from the visitor himself. While such laughter did not negate the serious warnings of the Grove's allegory, it must have tempered them somewhat with a sense that the Grove belonged to the realm of art and play. He could leave the fantasy behind by walking out of the garden. For all of the Grove's incitements to moral self-reflection, the joke also provided a counterpoint by encouraging him to recognize and accept some degree of human fallibility.

The Grove's parting verses ensured that the visitor would emerge with both imperatives in mind. Not far from the archway, Waldstein tells us, stood a "small building; on the front of it [was] 'Diana's Grove'," and four inscriptions.[29] Here, at last, the visitor was allowed to contemplate the Grove's allegorical scheme from a distance. He stood outside the building that represented the Grove, surveying didactic poems—verses that spoke to each other instead of directly advising the reader. Rather than finding himself an unwitting participant in an emblematic scene, the visitor was now allowed to define his own relation to the garden's allegory. And here he finally had moral space in which to do so. Countering the constricted ethical environment of the fountain and the arch, the first two verses redescribed the Grove as a space of super—and subhuman ethical extremes, thus implicitly opening a human gap for the visitor to inhabit. On the one hand, there was Diana's chastity, revealed (in compliment to Elizabeth) as divine detachment:

> O goddess who seeks out forests, springs, the shady place and the hunt, who rules the nymphs and rural spirits with your chaste power, why do the affairs of the world not affect you? Why do you not cling to the embraces of men? Why do you, suffused with snowy beauty, flee from Hymen's rites? Surely divine jewels do not suit the mortal sphere: thus the decree of the gods stands fixed.

On the other hand lay Actaeon's lust, the province of monsters and beasts:

> Whoever like Actaeon, with raging desire, places no reins on his eyes and the madness of his soul, he is transformed into a beast and a monster-man, and he gives his seed to his own dogs to be devoured, while fearing the fires of passion, he submits to his emotions and restrains his senses with no governance.[30]

Once again, these inscriptions fail to define fully an alternative to the moral extremes evoked, but here the poetic speaker's wonder at the goddess's unearthly coldness balances his condemnation of Actaeon's lack of self-control. He suggests that the two are not really alternatives. Instead they are opposite ends of a spectrum along which the visitor may locate an intermediate moral position.

The final two inscriptions of the Grove invited the reader to take one more mental step outside the garden's frame. Now the challenge is to perceive how this ideal of moral self-awareness relates not only to Diana and Actaeon, but also to the garden as a form of art. In the first verse we finally hear from the unfortunate hunter, who characterizes himself as a casualty of art gone awry:[31]

> You would take offence if a painter should wish to join horses' necks or a dog's face to a human head. Diana joined a stag's head to this neck of mine; I request just pity for this injustice.

By gazing at Diana, Actaeon implies, he has fallen subject to a kind of art that is not mimetic, as art is meant to be. Instead this kind of art imposes a monstrous identity on what it represents. However, another voice, perhaps Lumley's, counters Actaeon's claim in the final inscription:

> There is a need for a human mind, lest Parrhasius paint a wild disposition in a [human] body, or Praxiteles grieve [at sculpting such a thing]. Actaeon, your heart is that of a stag; why should you not have horns? As a prudent man I protest at foolish hearts.[32]

Art in the Grove is indeed mimetic, this verse insists, and even revelatory. What Diana's art represents to Actaeon is a sensible manifestation of what is hidden in his "heart." At another level this is exactly what the garden's art accomplished for the Grove's visitor. By exposing him to its concentrated sensual pleasures in an atmosphere charged with moral doubt, the art of the Grove simultaneously elicited a passionate response and invited him to reflect on that response. This dual process might enable him to glimpse what lay within his own heart. Or it might not, if like Actaeon failing to perceive the moral relevance of his horns, he refused to see how his status as a voyeur and a victim of the trick fountain related to his own moral character.

2.

Like the Grove at Nonsuch, Spenser's Bower of Bliss asks how a reader/visitor may engage with the sensual pleasures of a garden's art in an ethically responsible way. But whereas the Grove restricts its moral focus to the reader/visitor, the Bower puts poetic art on trial. For most students of early modern verse the perils of the Bower are thoroughly familiar, partly because critics have painstakingly identified and analyzed them, partly because these are the perils of poetry as detailed by the period's detractors. In the Bower's evil Genius we find the effeminization and idleness that Philip Sidney's opponents are reported as decrying in his *Defence*. Sidney's siren reappears in the Bower's sequence of seductresses, including the garden itself, decked out like a "pompous bride."[33] But other characteristics of the

Bower bear a more puzzling relationship to poetry. Stephen Greenblatt's influential analysis of the canto was early in noting that what previous critics identified as the Bower's unwholesome competition between nature and art, its insidious harmonies and deceptive artifice, actually bore a resemblance to the properties of poetry that contemporary theorists singled out for celebration.[34] The implications of this resemblance for Spenser's poetry are unsettling. As Greenblatt puts it, the fact that the knight of Temperaunce destroys a realm that is "lavishly described in just those terms which the defenders of poetry in the Renaissance reserved for imagination's noblest achievements" suggests the possibility that "art itself" may be "idolatrous" in *The Faerie Queene*[35]—in effect, that the poem betrays Spenser's deep ambivalence toward his chosen form of discourse.[36]

This impression is reinforced by Acrasia's use of poetry as one of the Bower's seductive charms. A carpe diem lyric with a dark edge, the lay of the rose invites the listener to participate in a specific type of reading: "Ah see, who so faire thing doest faine to see,/In springing flowre the image of thy day" (74.2–3). To appreciate the lay's poetry, the lines suggest, the listener must be driven by a desire for beauty (a delight in "so faire thing") and a will to perceive allegorical meaning in sensual images. This mode of reading concurs with the lifestyle the lay recommends. Yet it is also the type of reading Spenser demands of us. In enjoying his allegorical poem, then, are we unwittingly falling prey to the Bower's seductions?

The risk comes into sharper focus in Spenser's letter to Ralegh. The letter asserts that on one hand, Spenser perceives *The Faerie Queene* as a poem adding didactic depth to a literary genre usually read only for aesthetic pleasure. As he explains,

> The generall end therefore of all the booke is to fashion a gentleman or noble person in vertuous and gentle discipline: Which for that I conceiued shoulde be most plausible and pleasing, being coloured with an historicall fiction, the which the most part of men delight to read, rather for variety of matter, then for profite of the ensample: I chose the historye of king Arthure . . . [37]

On the other hand, he recognizes that by choosing poetry over a more straightforward rhetorical form he is pandering to modern readers' sensual proclivities:

To some I know this Methode will seeme displeasaunt, which had rather haue good discipline deliuered plainly in way of precepts, or sermoned at large, as they vse, then thus clowdily enwrapped in Allegoricall deuises. But such, me seeme, should be satisfide with the vse of these dayes, seeing all things accounted by their showes, and nothing esteemed of, that is not delightfull and pleasing to commune sence.[38]

By "commune sence," here Spenser denotes a specific faculty defined by Renaissance psychology: "an 'internal' sense which was regarded as the common bond or centre of the five senses, in which the various impressions received were reduced to the unity of a common consciousness" (OED). In Book II, the dangers of art designed to please the "commune sence" are fully manifest in the character of Verdant, lying prostrate at the source of the Bower's "Musick" (72), enervated by an excess of sensual pleasure.

Curiously, although Greenblatt's apprehension of Spenser's ambivalence towards art leads us to doubt about the relation between poetry and "commune sence," Greenblatt himself arrives at a different conclusion. For him, instead of the sensual temptations he analyzes so shrewdly, the ultimate problem of the Bower's artifice is its "concealment of art."[39] Early in the canto we read that the garden's art "appeared in no place" (58.9). But never do we see anyone in danger of being tricked by it. Acrasia's garden does not induce the visitor to mistake what is artificial for something natural, but presents the artificial as so full of "pleasure and delight" that it will make him "drunken mad" in spite of his intellect's objections (II.i.52.1,2), as Greenblatt earlier acknowledges.[40] Why, then, does he choose to focus on this one facet of the Bower's art, excluding all the others that contribute to its allure? This focus gives Greenblatt's Spenser a way out of the disorderliness of ambivalence—a way to distinguish his own art, which "constantly calls attention to its own processes,"[41] from the corrupt art of Acrasia's garden. Greenblatt's methodological commitment to viewing "every form of behavior" as a "strategy"[42] leaves little room for unresolved ambivalence in his readings, or for aesthetic considerations that cannot ultimately be shown to manipulate the reader to the author's benefit. When he obscures the Bower's troubling resemblances to Spenser's poetic art by privileging a single distinguishing difference, he exercises just the sort of "civilizing" power that he attributes to Spenser and to Guyon, a power "richly, essentially creative; . . . the guarantor of value, the shaper of all knowledge, the pledge of human redemption," even though it "inevitably entails [the] loss" of whatever threatens the power-holder's sense of "civilization."[43] Greenblatt's is certainly a creative reading of the Bower, and one that helped to define a historicist methodology that would assure professional value and shape the field of literary studies for a generation of scholars. But in the loss that it so grimly declares "inevitable"—in the suppression of all that is undeniably, problematically poetic in the Bower—his reading reproduces the violence of Guyon's wrath.

Before his discussion takes this turn, however, it offers a vital corrective to analyses that follow C. S. Lewis in denying the Bower's appeal.[44] Greenblatt's receptivity to the Bower sensitizes him to Spenser's "near-tragic sense of the cost" of its ruin, which consequently offers no more than a provisional resolution of the problem of pleasure.[45] Spenser produces and shares the reader's intuition that something is worth saving in the Bower's ravishing art, something that cannot be rejected as mere manipulation, something tied to the value of his own poetic art.[46] More sustained attention to this connection, in all of its inconsistencies, can lead to a more robust understanding of Spenser's reasons for writing poetry in the first place. After all, if sensuous art is as treacherous as the Bower suggests, why didn't he elect to write moral philosophy? His delight in language and the sheer volume of his verse attest to more than a grudging accommodation of the modern taste for things "pleasing to commune sence." Something about the aesthetic pleasure of poetry, either for writer or reader or both, compels him to embrace it as a discourse.

As a writer Spenser can escape detractors' charges of encouraging idleness or hedonistic abandon by working in allegory and national epic, modes that require intellectual and moral engagement. But even so, he cannot be sure of his reader. If his poetic surfaces capture his reader's attention, what will prevent them from enthralling the reader's sensitive soul and distracting him from higher rational considerations?[47] This is the question Sidney evades when he offers the soldier Alexander as a model reader who effortlessly draws from poetry the exempla that stir his courage and strengthen his wit.[48] Rather than taking Sidney's way out, Spenser uses the final canto of his book of temperance to test a possible answer to the question; he sends Guyon through a garden that represents poetry at its most erotic. Although the allegorical figures the soldier encounters in moving through the garden represent vices extending well beyond the bounds of art, Spenser encourages us to think about them in relation to art. He frames each of these encounters with stanzas reflecting on the nature of art in the garden and, by extension, in the poem. As we have seen, the Bower combines the most celebrated aspects of poetic art with its most vicious abuses, producing the powerful "bad mixture" embodied by Acrasia. Since temperance does not entail a rejection of poetry's pleasures, only a rejection of their overindulgence, Guyon's job as a model reader is to sort out this mixture in the garden, distinguishing harmless delights from wicked temptations.

Spenser obliges the reader to assess the paradigm Guyon offers by designing the garden to work like Diana's Grove. Much as the Grove subjected its visitors to a series of moral tests, the Bower requires Guyon to take a position relative to each new scene he encounters. His attitudes are conveyed in physical postures that are constantly before the reader's eye. At the same time, experiences of visiting gardens like the Grove condition the reader to consider his own position relative to the garden and the knight. Paul J. Alpers nicely captures the division of the reader's attention between self and fictional character: "An episode in *The Faerie Queene* . . . is best described as a developing psychological experience within the reader, rather than as an action to be observed by him." This means that "when we read about the Bower of Bliss, our interest is not in rendering a moral judgement, but in the depth and quality of our moral understanding."[49] Yet, as the garden setting bids the reader to weigh his response against the knight's, moral judgment must come into play, particularly when their responses diverge. And Spenser's design ensures that they do diverge, increasingly as the canto proceeds.

At the garden gate, in their encounter with Genius, Guyon and the reader begin on the same footing. After a vague account of Genius's "comely" appearance (46.4), Spenser elaborates the threat of delusion and enfeeblement represented by this emblematic figure of art, so that at the end of four stanzas we are more than ready to concur in Guyon's defiance of "his idle curtesie" (49.7). But the alignment of knight and reader in this encounter only serves to highlight the divergence that develops in the second garden tableau. Now the structure of Spenser's canto begins to distance Guyon by manipulating the reader's exposure to the pleasures of the garden's art and eliciting a different response. In many respects this second episode duplicates the first, but the imperfect doubling throws the distinctions into sharper relief. Again Guyon approaches a gate with a porch (which turns out to be "No gate, but like one"), and again he confronts an allegorical figure in "garments loose" who offers him wine (53–57). But here the order of the stanzas does not encourage the reader to emulate Guyon's progress from observation to comprehension to just rejection. Instead, as we emerge from the first intoxicating description of the garden, suffused with flowers and blessed with an everlasting summer, we are informed that the knight "Much wondred . . . at the faire aspect/Of that sweet place, yet suffred no delight/To sincke into his sence, nor mind affect" (53.1–3). What reader of Spenser's poem, however cautious, can echo this claim? What reader would want to? Certainly not the reader Spenser envisioned in his letter to Ralegh, who esteems what is "delightfull and pleasing to commune sence." Even before the second test, then, Guyon and the reader advance from different angles, the one deliberately hardened against potential pleasures, the other inevitably more receptive.

Once this initial divergence develops, what Guyon and the reader encounter at the gate can only propel them along their separate trajectories. The episode again begins with observation. But instead of a spare sketch of the allegorical figure and her setting, we are flooded with physical details. Three and a half stanzas luxuriate in the "wanton wreathings" of the vine-embraced porch, describing the "comely dame" and the overabundant grapes she "scruz[es]" (56.4). Like Genius, the lady seems only marginally human, better understood as an extension of the art of the porch than any sort of independent agent, for she exhibits no more volition or force than the grapes that "incline" themselves "As freely offering to be gathered" (54.4–6). Presumably Guyon remains impervious to these delights of the garden's art, but the reader is another matter. Nor do these stanzas compromise the tableau's sensual appeal by imposing the interpretive framework we find found in the Genius episode. At this later point, we have plenty of worrisome details to suggest that the "comely dame" is somehow treacherous (her "fowle disordered" clothes, for instance), but her allegorical identity is not divulged until *after* Guyon's assault. In consequence, his shattering of her cup seems much more jarring than his destruction of Genius's bowl, an effect reinforced by the comparatively lengthy description of his violence:

> So she to *Guyon* offred it to tast;
>> Who taking it out of her tender hond,
>> The cup to ground did violently cast,
>> That all in peeces it was broken fond,
>> And with the liquor stained all the lond:
>> Whereat *Excesse* exceedingly was wroth.
>
> (57.1–6)

As an extension of the garden's art, Excess is powerless under Guyon's aggression, almost as if he has assaulted a statue. His violence seems oddly crude, inappropriate in the garden setting. Since the garden is a figure for poetry, the reader's perception complicates Guyon's status as a model reader. On the one hand, his destruction may be understood as a symptom of Guyon's limitations as a reader. Unable to distinguish between the fundamentally evil Genius, "foe of life, that good enuyes to all" (48.4), and the more flexibly problematic principle of Excesse in art, he responds to both with equal rigor, failing to recognize the first as a problem of kind, the second as a problem of measure. On the other hand, Guyon may repudiate the garden's art because it is irredeemably corrupt. In the latter case, the shocking impact of Guyon's violence on the Bower's art works to disclose the reader's own moral weakness—he is shocked because he is susceptible to the garden's wicked charms.

The distance that now separates the actual reader from the model reader abruptly inverts its valence when the two approach the Bower's third tableau. Now the reader is thrust to the opposite end of the scale of moral caution as Guyon exchanges his rigid resistance for an equally excessive state of sensual indulgence. Once again we and Spenser's knight begin with observation, gazing at the artificial wonders of the garden's laurel-ringed fountain with its bathing "Damzelles." As in the Excesse episode we are given no analytical overlay. We need to rely on our intuition that these "wanton Maidens" represent a dangerous aspect of poetic art. But whereas Guyon's willed imperviousness enabled him to outpace the reader in his defiance of Excesse, here instead we find him lingering as we linger, to enjoy the damsels' games: "Whom such when *Guyon* saw, he drew him neare,/And somewhat gan relent his earnest pace,/His stubborne brest gan secret pleasaunce to embrace" (65.7–9). As veterans of the Bower's temptations we know that this is bad. It is one thing to take pleasure in the garden's beauties, and quite another to be immobilized by titillation. Spenser devotes three more stanzas to detailing Guyon as he surrenders to his lust, splitting our attention between the damsels' "wanton meriments" (68.7) and growing alarm for the hapless knight.

Nowhere in the first three episodes is the double nature of the Bower's art, its erotic appeal and its danger, so compellingly in view. Nowhere else does the juxtaposition of garden, knight, and reader more forcefully impel us to question Guyon's status as a model reader. We have to recognize his inability to address—or even to perceive—this duality of art. Although the Palmer ultimately steps in to draw the knight out of danger, his intervention shows that the reason

that enabled the knight to move safely through the garden's initial
threats is insufficient to help him here, where for the first time he
registers sensual pleasure. Rather than embodying any sort of temperate mean at this point in the canto, it seems that Guyon can only
choose between one extreme and another. When he faces what he
can recognize as conventional threats of sensuous art, like idleness
or excess, a rigid form of reason represses his senses and produces
correspondingly rigid violence against art. When he encounters art's
subtler temptations, like those represented by the damsels in the fountain, however, his senses overpower his reason until an intervention
from outside him rights the balance. Crucially, at no point do we
observe any struggle between the two souls in Guyon, or any attempt
to mediate their dictates.

But perhaps we look for this too soon. Perhaps the knight can
only achieve temperate balance after he synthesizes the lessons of the
Bower's first three tableaux into a composite model of right reading.
Much in Guyon's climactic encounter with Acrasia suggests that this
is the case. Rather than approaching the witch with the brash, aggressive rationality of the initial episodes (which, as the Palmer warns
him, would only enable Acrasia to "slip away" unchallenged [69.9],
her erotic threat deflected but not mastered), he cautiously opens his
senses to her charms as he advances obliquely, "creeping" through
"couert groves, and thickets close" (76.6–7). Nor does Guyon allow
his passions to overwhelm him, as at the fountain. Instead he and the
Palmer move to capture Acrasia in the Palmer's net, and then to
release Verdant from his bonds, distinguishing depraved pleasure
from pleasure receptive to reason.

Here at last we have what looks like a model of reading that
integrates the intellect with the passions. However, just after Verdant's release this integrative model takes a violent turn:

> But all those pleasant bowres and Pallace braue,
>   *Guyon* broke downe, with rigour pittilesse;
>   Ne ought their goodly workmanship might saue
>   Them from the tempest of his wrathfulnesse,
>   But that their blisse he turn'd to balefulnesse:
>   Their groues he feld, their gardins did deface,
>   Their arbers spoyle, their Cabinets suppresse,
>   Their banket houses burne, their buildings race,
> And of the fairest late, now made the fowlest place.

$$(83)$$

Guyon destroys a landscape that is familiar, but not from Spenser's earlier descriptions. Here we see none of the landmarks we might expect to recognize from other parts of the canto: no gates, no porches, not even the central fountain. What we see instead are the standard features of a contemporary English pleasure garden. This recognition puts an edge of hysteria on Guyon's attack, as he expends prodigious energy assaulting inanimate objects, themselves only tenuously associated with Acrasia's enchantments. To the rigid rationality of the *Excesse* episode Guyon here adds the force of passion, in a scene so shocking that many readers have found it the moment that distances them once and for all from Spenser's knight of Temperaunce.

What are we finally to make of this distance between Spenser's model reader and the actual readers of his poem? As in the *Excesse* episode, two contrary interpretations seem equally plausible, each with its ominous implications for the art of poetry. From one perspective, Guyon's frenzy may represent a supreme integration, where reason's rightful sovereignty enlists the passions in a temperate renunciation of corrupt and corrupting art.[50] In this interpretation, the distance the reader perceives between himself and the knight is the distance between master and pupil. What Guyon may teach us about reading, difficult as the lesson may be for fallen sensibilities to accept, is that the gorgeous trappings of art must be stripped away to expose the plain truth of "good discipline" beneath. From this perspective the experience of the Bower can be distilled into a bare moral question with an unambiguous answer. "[W]hat meant those beastes, which there did ly"? Guyon asks as he leaves the ravaged garden, prompting us to regard what has gone before as nothing more than a protracted exemplum, summed up in the Palmer's sententious response: "Sad end (quoth he) of life intemperate,/And mournefull meed of ioyes delicious" (84.9, 85.6–7). From another perspective, however, Guyon's fury may be perceived as disintegration of the tenuous balance between reason and passion established in the capture of Acrasia. Read thus, his attack on the garden functions cathartically to release the passions that Acrasia's art has stimulated, allowing a pure but aridly ascetic reason to reassert itself in the final stanzas. Such a break would signal Guyon's failure to sustain temperance as an approach to poetic art, making the knight's excesses the didactic displacement of a negative exemplum for the reader with his more moderate responses to the garden.[51] Whichever way we choose to interpret Guyon's destruction of the Bower, it is clear that the canto must end along with the garden, because his furious destructiveness leaves no space for Spenser's poetic art. Whether the reader construes the knight as the emblem of a transcendent ethical ideal or as the misguided champion of an unnatural asceticism, there remains the question of what it looks like for a gentleman to enjoy the art of a pleasure garden or a poem in a responsibly temperate way.[52]

Like the Grove of Diana, the Bower challenges its visitor to find his way between two moral extremes. Both sequential experiences highlight multi-leveled participation and dynamic self-awareness as crucial in approaching art. When Spenser imported an Italianate pleasure garden into his poem, he produced in sophisticated contemporary readers a set of generic expectations that lent his canto a historically specific, moral and aesthetic force that modern readers must work to recover.[53]

College of the Holy Cross

NOTES

1.   Michael Leslie distinguishes Roman-style gardens like the Bower and Diana's Grove at Nonsuch from gardens in the style of the Veneto in "Spenser, Sidney, and the Renaissance Garden," *ELR* 22.1 (1992).

2.   Sir Henry Wotton, *The Elements of Architecture*, 1624 (Farnborough: Gregg, 1969), 109–10.

3.   George Puttenham, *The Arte of English Poesie*, 1589, eds. Gladys Doidge Willcock and Alice Walker (Cambridge: Cambridge University Press, 1936), 8.

4.   Renaissance psychology tended to understand human experience in terms of the three "sub-souls" that governed it. Lowest on the scale was the vegetative soul, which animated all living organisms; next came the sensitive soul, shared only by animals and human beings; and uppermost was the rational soul, which set human beings apart from all other forms of life. The senses and passions that poetry or a pleasure garden appealed to were both considered faculties of the sensitive soul. Ideally, these were subject to the rational soul's control. According to such influential divines as Pererius and Calvin, this was the case in Paradise, where man existed in a state of virtuous natural balance. (Arnold Williams, *The Common Expositor: An Account of the Commentaries on Genesis 1527–1633* (Chapel Hill: The University of North Carolina Press, 1948), 89 and William J. Bouwsma, "The Two Faces of Humanism: Stoicism and Augustinianism in Renaissance Thought," in *Itinerarium Italicum: The Profile of The Italian Renaissance in the Mirror of its European Transformations,* eds. Heiko A. Oberman and Thomas A. Brady, Jr. [Leiden: Brill, 1975], 19). In the postlapsarian world, however, "the passions . . . are turbulently rebellious servants. Often they overrule reason and impel one into evil and misery" (Lawrence Babb, *The Elizabethan Malady: A Study of Melancholia in English Literature from 1580 to 1642* [East Lansing: Michigan State College Press, 1951], 17). When a man allows his passions to dominate, he falls to the level of the beasts, which are always ruled by the

sensitive soul's demands. Even though many believed that "the passions ha[d] both a divine origin and an important role to play in leading the individual to the good," this hazard ensured that "the Renaissance response to the emotions" was what Wayne Rebhorn has described as "more a grudging acceptance than an ecstatic embrace" ("Thomas More's Enclosed Garden: *Utopia* and Renaissance Humanism," *ELR* 6 [1976]: 89). For an overview of humanist and Reformation traditions that held the passions in higher esteem, see Richard Strier, "Against the Rule of Reason: Praise of Passion from Petrarch to Luther to Shakespeare to Herbert" in *Reading the Early Modern Passions: Essays in the Cultural History of Emotion*, eds. Gail Kern Paster, Katherine Rowe, and Mary Floyd-Wilson (Philadelphia: University of Pennsylvania Press, 2004), 23–42.

5.   Margaret W. Ferguson, *Trials of Desire: Renaissance Defenses of Poetry* (New Haven: Yale University Press, 1983), 146. Ferguson traces this characterization of poetry back to Book 10 of Plato's *Republic*, where "Socrates, after offering poetry a chance to defend herself against his attacks, says that if her defense fails, we must act like those 'who have once fallen in love with someone, and don't believe the love is beneficial'; such persons 'keep away from the beloved, even if they have to do violence to themselves' " (146).

6.   Philip Sidney, *A Defence of Poetry*, 1579–80, ed. Jan Van Dorsten (Oxford: Oxford University Press, 1966), 34, 51.

7.   See, for instance, the Stoic Justus Lipsius's *Two Bookes of Constancie* (1584; Englished 1594), where the wise Langius character reproves naive Lipsius for his doting on gardens:

> You commend gardens, but so as you seeme only to admire vain and out-
> ward things therin, neglecting the true & lawful delights therof. You poare
> only vpon collours, and borders, and are greedy of strange Flowers brought
> from all partes of the world. And to what end is all this? Except it be that
> I might account thee one of that sect which is risen vp in our dayes, of
> curious and idle persons, who haue made a thing that was in it self good
> and without al offence, to be the instrument of two foule vices, *Vanity*
> and *Slouthfulnes*.

[Ed. Rudolf Kirk, trans. Sir John Stradling (New Brunswick, NJ: Rutgers University Press, 1939], 133–34.)

8.   Familiar from a multitude of classical texts, the idea of the Muses' garden—or, in Sidney's version of the trope, "Apollo's garden" (20)—encouraged Renaissance writers to think of poetry and pleasure gardening together. This pairing was rein-forced by the rediscovery of the "flowers of rhetoric," a figure that influenced such volumes of verse and prose as George Gascoigne's *The Posies* (1575), divided into "Floures, Hearbes, and Weedes" (Dedicatory Epistle "To al yong Gentlemen . . . ", ed. G. W. Pigman III [Oxford: Clarendon, 2000], 364). For Gascoigne and others, the reader's experience of moving through a collection of ornamented fictions was analogous to that of a visitor walking through a garden, with the same attendant delights and responsibilities:

> If you (where you might gather wholesome hearbes to cure your sundrie
> infirmities) will spende the whole day in gathering of sweete smelling Posies,

much will be the time that you shal mispende, and much more the harme
that you shall heape upon my heade. Or if you will rather beblister your
handes with a Nettle, than comfort your senses by smelling to the pleasant
Marjoram, then wanton is your pastime, and small will be your profite.

(367)

Although either the frivolous charms of the lighter texts or the deceptive attractions
of the "weeds" may tempt him, the reader is admonished to seek out more "whole-
some" writings joining sensual pleasure with moral "profite."

9. Sidney, 32, 33.

10. Edmund Spenser, A Letter of the Authors . . . to the Right noble, and Valorous, Sir Walter Raleigh knight, 1590, *The Faerie Queene*, 1590, 1596, ed. A. C.
Hamilton (London: Longman, 1977), 737.

11. Ilva Beretta, *"The World's a Garden"*: *Garden Poetry of the English Renaissance*
(Stockholm: S. Academiae Upsaliensis, 1993), 12.

12. Zdenek Brtnicky z Valdstejna, *The Diary of Baron Waldstein: A Traveller in
Elizabethan England*, trans. G. W. Groos (London: Thames, 1981), 159; William
Harrison, *The Description of England*, 1587, Ed. Georges Edelen (Ithaca: Cornell
University Press, 1968), 270–71. Lumley inherited Nonsuch from his father-in-law,
Henry FitzAlan, 12th earl of Arundel, in 1579; in 1591 he repaid an old debt to the
Crown by turning the palace over to Queen Elizabeth, although he continued to
live there until his death in 1609. For the Nonsuch gardens, see especially John
Dent, *The Quest for Nonsuch* (London: Hutchinson, 1962), 112–33 and Roy Strong,
The Renaissance Garden in England (London: Thames, 1979), 39, 63–69. On pages
57–60 Dent paraphrases the "most important eye-witness account of Nonsuch,"
written by Anthony Watson, Rector of Cheam and later Bishop of Chichester,
probably sometime between 1582 and 1592: *Magnificae, et plane Regiae Domus, quae
vulgo vocatur Nonesuch, brevis, et vera Descriptio* (Trinity College, Cambridge, MS.
R.7.22). Watson's description can be supplemented by several foreign travelers'
accounts of the estate, including Paul Hentzner, *Travels in England During the Reign
of Queen Elizabeth*, c. 1597–98, this translation 1797, eds. Horace Walpole and
Henry Morley, trans. Richard Bentley, Cassell's National Library (London: Cassell,
1889), 77–78; Thomas Platter, *Thomas Platter's Travels in England, 1599*, trans. Clare
Williams (London: Cape, 1937), 195–97; and Waldstein, cited above, 159–63.

13. Dent, 113.

14. Platter, 197.

15. Strong, 39.

16. Ibid., 65–66.

17. Keith Thomas defines the "so-called 'wilderness' " of period gardens as "a
dense plantation of trees, which, despite its name, was laid out in an orderly and
geometrical fashion" (Keith Thomas, *Man and the Natural World: A History of the
Modern Sensibility* [New York: Pantheon, 1983], 207). Lacking conclusive evidence,
other garden historians have stopped short of claiming that all wildernesses were
so formal.

18. Dent paraphrases Watson's account of the paths and aviary (60); Platter describes the ball courts (197).

19. Strong, 66, 63–64.

20. The Grove's position relative to other parts of the estate suggests that visitors were meant to move through the Grove as Waldstein does, from east to west, palace to banqueting house. Watson's imaginary tour of the grounds, unconstrained by conditions that might affect a particular visitor on a particular day, proceeds in the same direction. The only account that moves through the Grove from west to east is Thomas Platter's. But Platter was visiting the palace under unusual circumstances, when Elizabeth was actually in residence. Forced to retire to a tent outside the palace for his luncheon, he began his tour of the gardens not from the palace itself, as visitors normally would, but from a spot on the palace grounds. Moreover, we know that when he retired for lunch the queen was in her chambers, which directly overlooked the privy garden. It seems likely that access to this garden would have been limited while the queen was in her rooms, compelling Platter's guide to lead him through the grounds backwards, beginning with the gardens furthest from the palace windows. It is interesting to consider how such a reversal would have affected a visitor's experience of the Grove's allegory.

21. Waldstein, 161; Platter, 196. Dent identifies this structure with what Watson calls the "statelye bower for Diana" apparently lying beneath the Grove's monumental arch (122). But in doing so he disregards the order of the sequence Platter describes, which in this respect matches Waldstein's account (to which Dent apparently did not have access). Given the available evidence, it seems likely that Watson did not include the small stone building in his description and that his "bower" is either the westernmost "small building" whose four inscriptions Waldstein records or not a building at all but instead the glade or clearing that housed the arch.

22. Waldstein, 160, Groos's translation from the Latin:

> Nil impudicum pudicitia Dea, nil turpe suadet, sceleris vindicta, sed mala mens, malus animus.

> Impuri fontis impuri rivuli;
> Ingratae mentis impuri oculi.

> Aestuanti umbra, languenti sedes. Noli in umbra umbratalis esse, nec sint sedenti serpentis oculi.

(161)

23. Ibid., 161.

24. Strong, 66 cites Johann Wilhelm Neumayr von Ramssla, *Des Durchlauchtigen hochgebornen Fürsten . . . Johann Ernsten des Jüngern, Hertzogen zu Sachsen . . . Reise in Frankreich, Engelland und Neiderland* (Leipzig, 1620).

25. Closer analogues to the Italianate pleasure garden include contemporary pageants and allegorical processions, but even these three-dimensional forms perpetuated a spatial separation of audience and tableaux that prevented the kind of direct, individual interaction of viewer and art habitually experienced in a garden setting.

26. Waldstein, 161–63; Strong, 68–69. Strong cites Watson for the correct identifications of the three birds.

27.   Hentzner, 33–34, Bentley's translation. Waldstein records the Latin:

> Ictus piscator sapit: sed infelix Actaeon semper praeceps. Casta virgo facile
> miseretur: sed potens Diana scelus ulciscitur. Praeda canibus, exemplum
> juvenibus, suis dedecus pereat Actaeon. Cura coelitibus, chara mortalibus,
> suis securitas vivat Diana. (161)

Hentzner, who visited England in 1598, claims to have seen this inscription "at the
entrance into the park from Whitehall" (33). Waldstein's editor G. W. Groos suggests that "probably it had been moved from there as being so much more suitable
to Diana's Grove" (160). But given that at least six years earlier Watson had described
an elevated inscription set up by Lumley "in praise of the goddess and as a warning
to youths to avoid the fate of Actaeon" (Dent, 60), Strong's contention that Hentzner
simply erred in attaching the poem to Whitehall seems more likely (226, n. 50).
28.   Waldstein, 163; Hentzner, 78. This trick fountain was probably operated by a
gardener who turned a cock to release a stream of water when a visitor came within
range. The order of Platter's account suggests that the pyramid was located near the
entrance to the Grove, between the small stone building and the wilderness proper.
Unlike Waldstein, however, Platter does not directly describe the pyramid's position
relative to any of the Grove's architectural groups; nor does his account include any
mention of the triumphal arch. Waldstein's specificity and comparative thoroughness
mark his as the more reliable description.
29.   Waldstein, 163.
30.   My translation from Waldstein's Latin. For invaluable help with the translations
of this and the following three inscriptions, I am grateful to Nancy Andrews and
Joshua Scodel. Given the state of Waldstein's transcriptions, parts of the translations
are necessarily speculative.

> O Dea qui sylvas, fontes, umbram atque venatum
> Expetis, et nymphas et rustica numina casto
> Dirigis imperio, cur te commercia Mundi
> Non tangunt? hominum cur non amplexibus haeres?
> Cur Hymaenea fugis niveo perfusa decore?
> Scilicet hominae divina monilia sorti
> Non bene conveniunt: sic stat sententia Divum.

> Quisquis ut Actaeon grassante libidine, nullos
> Imponit frenos, oculis animique furori,
> Bellua fit monstrumque hominum, semenque vorandum
> Dat canibus propriis, dum timens affectibus ignes
> Subiicit, et nullo retinet moderamine sensus.

(163)

31.   I am indebted to Joshua Scodel for pointing out an echo of the opening of
Horace's *Ars poetica* here. Scodel also notes that the inscriptions' attempt "to fit into
Horation mimeticism is interestingly different from Spenserian allegory, with its
disjunction between surface and meaning."

32. The third transcription appears in my translation from Waldstein's Latin:

Splen copes humano capiti si [p]ictor equinas
Iungere cervices, aut canis ora velit.
Cervinum Diana caput cervicibus istis
Addit in injustum viscera justa rogo.

(163)

For the final inscription, Groos quotes Hentzner's version of the Latin, which avoids Waldstein's "numerous inaccuracies," and which I use as the basis for my translation:

Mente opus humana, ne feros in corpore mores,
    Parrhasius pingat, Praxitilesve dolet.
Cervina Actaeon tua sunt praecordia; quidni
    Cornua sint? prudens pectora stulta queror.

(162)

33. Sidney, 51; Edmund Spenser, *The Faerie Queene*, 1590, 1596, ed. A. C. Hamilton (London: Longman, 1977), II.xii.50.7. Subsequent quotations from this canto will be cited parenthetically by stanza and line numbers.

34. In fact, when the theorists labor to characterize the poet's extraordinary power over nature, they often resort to analogies drawn from the domain of landscape and gardening. "In that [the poet] speaks figuratiuely, or argues subtillie, or perswades copiously and vehemently," maintains George Puttenham, "he doth as the cunning gardiner that vsing nature as a coadiutor, furders her conclusions & many times makes her effectes more absolute and straunge." Indeed, Puttenham insists, the poet actually surpasses the gardener in this respect, because rather than being limited to "aiding nature" he can function "even as nature her selfe working by her owne peculiar vertue and proper instinct and not by example or meditation or exercise as all other artificers do, [and] is then most admired when he is most naturall and least artificiall" (307). Like Acrasia's art in the Bower, poesy succeeds best when its artfulness "appear[s] in no place" (58.9). Although Puttenham stops well short of claiming that poesy strives *against* nature, by positioning poesy as nature's simulator and her equal he raises the specter of the rivalry that materializes in Spenser's false paradise. For Sidney, too, the art of poesy functions as nature's partner rather than as her competitor, but when he describes the superior "golden" world that poesy creates he does so in terms that might have served as a pattern for the Bower's artificial landscape. His poet

goeth hand in hand with nature, not enclosed within the narrow warrant of her gifts, but freely ranging only within the zodiac of his own wit. Nature never set forth the earth in so rich a tapestry as divers poets have done; neither with so many pleasant rivers, fruitful trees, sweet-smelling flowers, nor whatsoever else may make the too much loved earth more lovely. Her world is brazen, the poets only deliver a golden.

(23–24)

35. Stephen Greenblatt, "To Fashion a Gentleman: Spenser and the Destruction of the Bower of Bliss," *Renaissance Self-Fashioning* (Chicago: University of Chicago Press, 1980), 189. For a classic example of the earlier critics' view, see A. Bartlett Giamatti, *The Earthly Paradise and the Renaissance Epic* (Princeton: Princeton University Press, 1966), 275.

36. Many earlier critics examined the status of art in the Bower without directly relating it to Spenser's art of poetry. C. S. Lewis aligned the Bower's "artifice" with "sterility" and "death" (*The Allegory of Love* [Oxford: Oxford University Press, 1938], 326). Robert M. Durling noted that Spenser departs from Tasso in making the Bower's art the product of "human intellect" rather than magic, foregrounding the problem of artistic creation that "corrupt[s] the appetite" ("The Bower of Bliss and Armida's Palace," *Comparative Literature* 6.4 [1954]: 344, 346).

Patricia Parker modifies Greenblatt's generalizations about art and poetry to argue that the Bower more specifically manifests "a simultaneously aesthetic and moral uneasiness about the seductiveness of lyric "charm"—the "potentially paralyzing suspensions . . . of a lyric form adapted to the domination of a woman"—"even if that charm is an inseparable part of the attraction of his own poetry" ("Suspended Instruments: Lyric and Power in the Bower of Bliss," in *Cannibals, Witches, and Divorce: Estranging the Renaissance*, ed. Marjorie Garber [Baltimore: Johns Hopkins University Press, 1987]), 36.

37. Spenser, 737.

38. Ibid.

39. Greenblatt, "To Fashion a Gentleman," 189.

40. Ibid., 172.

41. Ibid., 190.

42. Stephen J. Greenblatt, "Resonance and Wonder," in *Learning to Curse: Essays in Early Modern Culture* (New York: Routledge, 1990), 164.

43. Greenblatt, "To Fashion a Gentleman," 173.

44. Lewis, 325–26, 331–32.

45. Greenblatt, "To Fashion a Gentleman," 173, 178.

46. Compare Giamatti's analysis of Alcina's garden, one of Spenser's primary sources for the Bower:

> Alcina's garden remains as the image of a way of life which man can never wholly reject. He cannot reject it because it is so much a part of himself; it represented something reprehensible but profoundly enjoyable. Its danger lay not in what it did to you, but in what it allowed you to do to yourself . . . The garden teaches us that all deception is largely a matter of self-deception, and that no matter how strenuously we try to disagree, the final illusion is to think life would be at all bearable without illusions.
>
> (164)

For other source texts see Giamatti, 266ff and Durling on Tasso's Armida, as well as James Nohrnberg, *The Analogy of The Faerie Queene* (Princeton: Princeton UP, 1976), 490–513.

47. Spenser faces a version of this charge in the Proem to Book IV, where "The rugged forhead," thought to be William Cecil, Lord Burghley, accuses him of corrupting "fraile youth," "That better were in vertues discipled,/Then with vaine poemes weeds to haue their fancies fed" (1.6, 9).

48. Sidney, 56–57. If Sidney sidesteps this difficult question, some of Spenser's recent critics have failed to recognize its force, producing what seems to me to be a fundamental misunderstanding of Spenser's mode. Jeff Dolven's recent essay on "Spenser and the Troubled Theaters" provides an example. In a useful effort to relate Spenser's poetic discourse to the shifting forms of contemporary theater, Dolven ends up aligning allegory most closely with pageant, another "pedagogical mode that emphasizes detachment and analysis." Both allegory and pageant he contrasts with the seductive discourse of the public theaters (*ELR* 29.2 [1999]: 179–200). But this account denies or at best ignores fully half of allegory's appeal (and also pageant's, for that matter) by failing to acknowledge the aesthetic pleasure that both entices the reader into analysis and at the same time pulls against any impulse toward intellectual detachment. One of the reasons allegory like Spenser's cannot simply be decoded is that part of its meaning resides within the code itself, the allegorical substance that produces in the reader an immediate emotional response.

49. Paul J. Alpers, *The Poetry of The Faerie Queene* (Princeton: Princeton University Press, 1967), 14, 304.

50. A recent dissertation by David Wilson-Okamura demonstrates, mainly with reference to the traditions of Aristotle, Luther, and Peter Martyr, that Guyon's wrath is consistent with the principle of temperance when perceived in the context of just revenge ("Spenser and the Renaissance *Aeneid*" [Ph.D. Diss., University of Chicago, 1998], 186–97). Earlier commentators trace the Christian roots of this idea. Harry Berger, Jr. divides Book II into classical and Christian halves (*The Allegorical Temper: Vision and Reality in Book II of Spenser's* Faerie Queene [New Haven: Yale University Press, 1957], 62–63). Peter D. Stambler expands his scheme to argue that the destruction of the Bower crowns the "supplantation of the Aristotelian or 'classical' ethical model and its replacement by a radical Christian standard." "Guyon learns that the temperance demanded of the Christian is unrelenting and at times savage action, passionate and all-possessing" ("The Development of Guyon's Christian Temperance," *ELR* 7 [1977]: 52, 89).

51. Readers have long debated Guyon's moral status in this scene. For a concise overview of many of the major arguments from 1929 through 1973, see Hamilton's edition of the poem, page 168. Recent critics remain divided. Stambler sees Guyon's virtue as "laudable but unobtainable" (52). A. Leigh Deneef concurs: "Guyon is an image of perfection . . . he is a virtue. His condition, therefore, is not available to the sinful Everyman who is reading the text" (*Spenser and the Motives of Metaphor* [Durham, NC: Duke University Press, 1982], 107). Greenblatt's Guyon, however, is much more human, modelling the process of civil self-fashioning. He must destroy the Bower to achieve "a just, coherent, stable identity anchored in the ardent worship of power." Even so, this destruction "suggests the extent to which each self-constituting act is haunted by inadequacy and loss" (179). Anthony Esolen arrives at similar conclusions from a different angle, emphasizing Guyon's reestablishment of "theological and social hierarchies" ("Spenser's 'Alma Venus': Energy and Economics in the Bower of Bliss," *ELR* 23.2 [1993]: 285). Roland Greene agrees that

"the fashioning of a gentleman takes place only against the backdrop of a singular, civilized, territorialized world" in the epic, despite the contrary "tug of immediate imaginative experience, where worlds are continually emerging out of one another" ("A Primer of Spenser's Worldmaking: Alterity in the Bower of Bliss," in *Worldmaking Spenser: Explorations in the Early Modern Age*, eds. Patrick Cheney and Lauren Silberman [Lexington: University Press of Kentucky, 2000], 30, 31). Susanne Lindgren Wofford argues that we should attend more seriously to this tug. For her, the reader inhabits two interpretive positions that destabilize one another. "The 'knowing' and distanced reader at whom the allegory is aimed learns to interpret [Guyon's] destructiveness as acceptable and, indeed, politically necessary, but the reader inscribed in the action condemns it, and the absoluteness of interpretation that seems to allow, and indeed require, such violence." The tension between the two viewpoints informs the poem's "ongoing fictional interrogation of the mode of allegory," a mode marked by "the imprisonment and containment of human difference" (*The Choice of Achilles: The Ideology of Figure in the Epic* [Stanford: Stanford University Press, 1992], 252, 272, 304). Lauren Silberman assumes the second viewpoint in "*The Faerie Queene*, Book II, and the Limitations of Temperance," protesting that Guyon's form of "Temperance offers no alternative to Acrasia's perverse sexuality, no creative engagement with the sensual, merely defense" (*Modern Language Studies* 17.4 [1987]: 20).

52.   If, unsatisfied, the reader leaves the Bower behind and moves ahead into the other gardens of *The Faerie Queene* to search for this elusive model, he will only be disappointed again. In the Garden of Adonis he will find great creating nature but nothing about creation on a human scale, either in terms of art or in terms of immediate sensuous experience (III.vi.29–50). The garden on the Island of Venus's Temple will tantalize him with a vision of art in harmony with nature, in a landscape where lovers indulge their senses in "spotlesse pleasures," but the only gentleman he will be allowed to follow through this place is Scudamour, who breaches its temperate peace by seizing Amoret (IV.x.21–58).

53.   It is a pleasure to thank all those who helped shape this essay by reading drafts and offering comments and suggestions. I am especially grateful to Joshua Scodel, Michael Murrin, Janel Mueller, Lisa Ruddick, Jamil Mustafa, Nancy Andrews, and John Dixon Hunt.

AYESHA RAMACHANDRAN

Clarion in the Bower of Bliss: Poetry and Politics in Spenser's "Muiopotmos"

This paper explores the often remarked analogy between Spenser's "Muiopotmos" and the Bower of Bliss. It argues that by returning to the vexed problem of female authority, "Muiopotmos" challenges the epic poetics of the second book of the *Faerie Queene*. Both poems explore the relationship of gender and genre through analogies between aesthetic, erotic, and political control, commonly associated with Elizabeth's strategies of maintaining authority. However, the generic and textual parallels between Clarion's garden and Acrasia's bower, both worlds of romance entrapment, suggest that Spenser identifies Elizabeth's court with *mêtis* or cunning intelligence, a distinctly female power that opposes the characteristic *bie* (martial valor) of epic action. With a series of striking gender inversions, Spenser rewrites Guyon's flagrantly masculine display of epic strength as the destruction of the mock-epic hero of "Muiopotmos," thereby raising a troubling question for the poetry and politics of the *Faerie Queene*: can epic—epic action, epic heroes and the writing of epic itself—thrive in a courtly world governed by the shifting illusions of *mêtis*? A sobering answer emerges from the death of Clarion, the epic hero, in the feminine web of romance.

*E*VERY EPIC HERO LOVES a good romance.[1] When Circe suggests seductively to Odysseus, "We two/ Shall mingle and make love upon our bed./ So mutual trust may come out of play and love,"

Spenser Studies: A Renaissance Poetry Annual, Volume XX, Copyright © 2005 by AMS Press, Inc. All rights reserved.

the wily hero welcomes the challenge. In an encounter that resonates through the literary history of epic, Odysseus becomes the first (and last) epic hero to master the enchantress of romance as he says:

> Now it is I myself you hold, enticing
> into your chamber, to your dangerous bed,
> to take my manhood when you have me stripped.
> I mount no bed of love with you upon it.
> Or swear me first a great oath, if I do,
> you'll work no more enchantment to my harm.
>
> (X.382–87)[2]

Confronting a sword against her throat and an epic hero fortified with *moly,* Circe has no choice. And Odysseus, Homer tells us, entered "Circe's flawless bed of love," inaugurating a tradition of erotic enjoyment that no subsequent epic hero will be able to resist. Odysseus, however, exerts control over the romance world in which he finds himself, converting its menace into pleasure and enlisting the assistance of the dangerous seductress for the completion of his epic task. From Vergil to Spenser, epic heroes succumb to the temptations of romance, but fail to establish the delicate balance that Odysseus achieves almost effortlessly—the balance between submission to and control of a powerful and alluring woman who offers great pleasure and great danger—a balance so difficult to acquire and maintain that it will prove to be the entrapment of several generations of wandering knights.[3] Aeneas must be ordered to renounce Dido; Ziliante, Ruggiero, Corsamonte, and Rinaldo must be rescued from the clutches of Boiardo's Morgana, Ariosto's Alcina, Trissino's Acratia, and Tasso's Armida respectively. Spenser's Guyon, however, is an exception to the rule.

Warned of Acrasia's dangerous Circe-like enchantments, Guyon—the Spenserian Odysseus—takes adequate precautions.[4] Armed with the Palmer and his own brute strength, he resists the luscious temptations on display and, in what is one of the great cruces of the *Faerie Queene,* proceeds rapidly to destroy the Bower of Bliss in the space of a single stanza. Nowhere else in the epic tradition does the hero systematically and brutally destroy the artistry of the romance bower, which stands, at least in part, for the art of the epic poet himself.[5] But as Teresa Krier astutely observes, "the literary history of romance . . . becomes one of the burdens Guyon bears and has to fight against," even though Spenser "destroys the Bower with considerable pain."[6] The glittering menace of Circe's literary daughter must be triumphantly overcome, if epic is to march on with unswerving single-mindedness; and where Guyon cannot match Odysseus' cunning, he makes up for it with armed might.

It is all the more surprising, then, that Spenser revisits the dangerous temptations of the romance bower, barely a year after the publication of the first installment of the *Faerie Queene,* in "Muiopotmos," published in the *Complaints* volume of 1591.[7] It has often been pointed out in passing that the butterfly Clarion "in his franke lustinesse" seems to flit about a miniature bower of bliss with its mock-epic catalogue of flowers.[8] But the analogy is more pervasive than casual resemblance: Spenser draws a systematic parallel between Clarion's pleasure garden and Acrasia's bower in Book II of the *Faerie Queene,* by describing the butterfly's flowerbed as the *locus amoenus* of romance, complete with a malignant entrapping witch at the center (in this case, the spider Aragnoll). The competition between Nature and Art, so characteristic of the Bower of Bliss, reappears in "Muiopotmos" along with the suggestions of sensual excess and erotic abandon (Clarion, we are told, "pastures on the pleasures of each place" much like Verdant and Acrasia, and Tasso's Rinaldo and Armida before them). More significantly, as James Nohrnberg has noted, the veil Acrasia wears is compared to the "subtile web" of Arachne, from whom Aragnoll descends.[9] There is, however, a crucial difference between the fates of Guyon and Clarion: while Guyon catches Acrasia in a "subtile net," Clarion, the hero of "Muiopotmos," is caught in Aragnoll's spiderweb. In the *Faerie Queene,* Guyon's destruction of the Bower marks the triumph of the epic imperative over the seductions of romance; the entrapping garden of "Muiopotmos," however, effectively negates and reverses that victory. By exploring these suggestive parallels and sharply contrasting conclusions, I want to suggest that "Muiopotmos" marks Spenser's return to the problem of romance embodied by the Bower of Bliss. But why does Spenser revisit the romance bower which he destroyed "with considerable pain"? And what does the triumph of the bower signify for Spenser's poetics? More important, perhaps, can the relationship between "Muiopotmos" and the Bower shed any light on the relationship between the *Faerie Queene* and the *Complaints*?

"Muiopotmos: or The Fate of the Butterflie," is one of the enduring mysteries of the Spenserian corpus. Despite a range of inventive interpretations—it has been described as an epyllion, a mock-epic, an Aesopian fable, a parable, an allegory of the fall of man, a roman-à-clef of court intrigue, a statement of Spenser's Protestant poetics, a satire on envy at court, a declaration of Spenserian aesthetics—the

poem's genre and its central themes are still widely disputed.[10] Sources
have been identified in the mythography of Comes, Cartari, and
Ovid, in the emblem tradition of Alciati, Simeoni, and Corrozet, in
mock-epic insect poems such as the Homeric *Batrachomyomachia* and
Lucian's *Muia Encomion,* in Chaucer's *Nun's Priest Tale,* and in moral
fables such as John Heywood's *The Spider and the Flie* and Spenser's
own "Virgils Gnat."[11] Epic allusions to the *Iliad* and the *Aeneid* have
been discerned. However, by arguing that the most important source
for "Muiopotmos" may be Spenser's own epic, the *Faerie Queene,* I
want to suggest that the poem does indeed encompass this entire
range of sources and allegorical meanings, and does so quite inten-
tionally.

"Muiopotmos" announces itself as an allegory by its very setting[12]
—a pleasure garden that conceals an unseen snare—and the heaping
up of allusions to classical and vernacular texts, myths and emblems,
only heightens this conviction. Accordingly, the critical tradition
around the poem falls into three major camps based on distinct practices of allegoresis: political or topical allegory, theological or moral
allegory, and finally, a kind of aesthetic allegory or an allegory of
mimesis and *poesis.* Thus, the poem either becomes a reflection on life
at court (envy, the triviality of courtiers, particular court intrigues), a
cautionary tale of intemperate self-indulgence, the transitoriness of
pleasure and the inevitability of mortality, or a commentary on the
beauty and aspirations of Spenser's own art.[13] When read in conjunction with Book II of the *Faerie Queene,* however, this diversity of
interpretation no longer seems strange or surprising; all three themes
are of great significance for the story of Guyon, and engage moral,
ethical, and aesthetic questions at the heart of a book which has been
described as an "epic *moralisé.*"[14]

In this context, the resemblance of "Muiopotmos" to the Bower
of Bliss places it at the center of a complex web of relationships in
the *Faerie Queene* involving Christian morality and classical ethics,
the political effectiveness of a male hero under a female sovereign,
and the competing aesthetic demands of epic and romance. Recog-
nizing the threat of Acrasia to the autonomy and progress of the epic
hero, Spenser presents Guyon's raging destruction of the Bower of
Bliss as an epic solution to the problems of erotic intemperance,
ethical dissimulation, and rhetorical artifice associated with the romance world.[15] But, in doing so, he also suppresses a figure of female
authority and artistic genius whose political control is manifested in
terms of erotic power—a figure reminiscent, as Patricia Parker and
Louis Montrose have argued, of Elizabeth's erotic and political control over her courtiers.[16] The characteristic evocation of the romance

garden subject to a powerful female figure points repeatedly to the vexed relationship between art, politics, and erotic domination, typical of Elizabeth's strategies of maintaining authority, a key concern of the *Faerie Queene* as a whole. The return to the bower in "Muiopotmos" thus becomes a reexamination of Guyon's flagrantly masculine reassertion of epic supremacy; it is a reevaluation in which romance deviance and the deviousness of the woman at the center eventually win out.[17]

This essay examines the relationship between "Muiopotmos" and the Bower of Bliss in some detail, illustrating how "Muiopotmos" revises and challenges the epic poetics of Book II. It suggests that the rich parallels between the two poems derive from a troubling problem that haunted Spenser after his visit to Elizabeth's court in 1590, following the publication of *The Faerie Queene*. Could epic—epic action, epic heroes, and the writing of epic itself—exist and thrive under the political conditions of the Elizabethan court? Or to put the question differently, could an early modern queen support (and did she even need) an epic hero?[18] Robert Brinkley has identified the Ovidian politics of metamorphosis in the "Muiopotmos" as a revelation of the political codes of the Elizabethan world where "the fate of the butterfly offers an appropriate image for one of the fates at Gloriana's court."[19] But the poem also argues that the reduction of would-be epic heroes to fluttering mock-heroic insects has a specific cause. By associating the Elizabethan court with the romance garden rather than the epic battlefield, Spenser reveals and redefines the power relations that are at stake: romance is the world of Circe's bed, of Acrasia's garden and Aragnoll's web, a world where the artfulness of *women*, the duplicity and dissimulation associated with female power, prevails over single-minded epic might; it is a world in which the stark tableaux of epic poetics must give way to the intricately woven tapestries of romance.

I

It has long been noted that the final canto of Book II is closely modeled on books 10 and 12 of the *Odyssey*.[20] Behind the Italian temptresses on whom Acrasia is most immediately modeled, stands Homer's Circe: the sexual pleasure and erotic self-indulgence of the Bower, along with the risk of being turned into a beast, looks back to her dangerous and flawless bed of love. What distinguishes Spenser's poem most clearly from its Homeric prototype, however, is the way in which its hero responds to the challenge of the enchantress's wiles: while Odysseus engages and enjoys the sorceress through a mixture of cunning and threatened force, Guyon firmly turns to ruthless violence. These contrasting responses represent a fundamental difference of genre: the clever tricks of Odyssean romance have no place in the sharply circumscribed ethical world of Vergilian and Spenserian epic.[21] More importantly, the difference here between Odysseus and Guyon, between romance and epic, participates in a broader contest between two styles of establishing and maintaining authority, identified in the Homeric epics as *mêtis* (cunning intelligence) and *bie* (brute force).[22]

In their classic study, Marcel Detienne and Jean-Pierre Vernant describe *mêtis* in terms that recall the generic turf of romance:

> The many-coloured, shimmering nature of *mêtis* is a mark of its kinship with the divided, shifting world of multiplicity in the midst of which it operates. It is this way of conniving with reality which ensures its efficacity. Its suppleness and malleability give it the victory in domains where there are no ready-made rules for success, no established methods, but where each new trial demands the invention of new ploys, the discovery of a way out that is hidden . . . *Mêtis* is itself a power of cunning and deceit . . . In order to dupe its victim it assumes a form which masks, instead of revealing, its true being. In *mêtis*, appearance and reality no longer correspond to one another, but stand in contrast, producing an effect of illusion, *apátē,* which beguiles the adversary in error and leaves him as bemused by his defeat as by the spells of a magician . . . Such is the "duplicity" of *mêtis* which, giving itself out to be other than it is, is like those misleading objects . . . the Trojan horse, the bed of love with its magic bonds, the fishing bait are all traps which conceal their inner deceit beneath a reassuring or seductive exterior.[23]

The embodiment of *mêtis* is, of course, Odysseus "of the many ways," an expert in tricks of all kinds, the most subtle and skillful rhetorician in Greek epic.[24] It is precisely this elusive shiftiness, this ability to cope with multiplicity and a changing play of appearances that places Odysseus at the center of the romance world, enabling his conquest of the marvelous landscapes, unpredictable monsters, and seductive enchantresses in the *Odyssey*.[25] Yet subsequent audiences—whether Vergil, cinquecento commentators on the Homeric epics, or Spenser and Milton—have been troubled by this quality of cunning which defines the hero. As Detienne and Vernant acknowledge, there is something less than honorable about the use of *mêtis*, particularly in cultures that valorize straightforward armed might, since certain aspects of this slippery wiliness resemble treachery and dissimulation, "the despised weapons of women and cowards."[26] From its mythical origin, in fact, *mêtis* is a female attribute, embodied in the shape-shifting goddess Metis, mother of Athena and first wife of Zeus, who was swallowed in the shape of a fly by the king of gods.[27] A quality associated not merely with mental craftiness and duplicity, but with the physical crafts of weaving and metallurgy, and with the psychology of seduction (it is an attribute of Hermes, Athena, Hephaestos, Prometheus, and Aphrodite), it is central to all the arts of making, to the creation of any artifice.[28] In other words, it is the element responsible for the kinship between poetic (or rhetorical) skill, political acumen, and erotic allure exemplified in romance temptresses from Circe to Acrasia; its subtle, elusive power underlies the danger and promise of the romance garden and the woman at its center.

This understanding of *mêtis* as a defining characteristic of the romance world, and its long association with female crafts and craftiness, is of particular importance for analyses of Spenser's Bower and "Muiopotmos." The sly *mêtis* with which the romance enchantress entraps her victims and establishes her erotic empire stands in sharp contrast to the clear martial valor with which the epic hero exerts and legitimates his authority. Thus, when the epic hero strays into a romance garden, he enters a realm where the rules of engagement are very different from the martial challenges in which he excels; unless he subjugates the enchantress, he enjoys the sensual pleasures on offer at his own peril. For Spenser, the alignment of these two distinct styles of enforcing authority (*mêtis* and *bie*) with generic codes of romance and epic reflected two styles of political and aesthetic representation which had an immediate counterpart in the relations between the queen and her powerful aristocratic courtiers.

It is a commonplace now to observe that the presence of a powerful female sovereign in the rigidly patriarchal culture of early modern Europe generated male fears of being stripped of power, variously expressed as effeminization, castration, or seduction.[29] The queen's court, in these analyses, is a literal version of Circe's dangerous bed, where even the wily Odysseus feared having his "manhood" taken away. Thus, Patricia Parker describes the menace of Acrasia—and the suspension of the lyric and romance modes more generally—as stemming from a male courtier-poet's fear of having his instruments (political, sexual, poetic) suspended by female authority.[30] I want to suggest, however, that Spenser's encoding of the romance garden as a dangerous place of female control does not only stem from the fact of subjection to a powerful female sovereign, but from her particular style of maintaining authority. The elaborately politicized Petrarchan games, the medieval tournaments that cast the queen as a lady of romance, the demand for political allegiance disguised as erotic devotion, the lavish entertainments in pastoral settings, all these Elizabethan strategies of exerting and consolidating power may be associated with the quality of *mêtis* that characterizes the romance world.[31] Indeed, as several scholars have suggested, the Bower of Bliss bears striking similarities to the language of romance which structured the queen's relations with her courtiers.[32]

From this perspective, the confrontation of Guyon and Acrasia dramatizes a conventional showdown between epic might and romance cunning, but in this case, the hero's victory has potentially subversive implications. Guyon's triumph asserts the epic values of armed strength, brute force, and the single-minded pursuit of a clear goal over the beguiling insinuations of romance with its hidden entrapments, shifting motives, and illusory pleasures.[33] However, the similarities between the exercise of power in Elizabeth's court and in the Bower suggest that Guyon's triumph is also a demand for strong epic action in a political climate rife with the intrigues, deceptions, and elaborate masquerades characteristic of romance digression.[34]

Against this complex backdrop of interwoven generic and political concerns, the return in "Muiopotmos" to a garden closely resembling the Bower of Bliss takes on considerable significance, particularly when the aspiring (mock) epic hero is ensnared in a web reminiscent of conventional romance entrapments. Far from presenting a superficial resemblance, the echoes of Book II in the later poem suggest that Spenser was quite deliberately revisiting and revising specific *topoi* that made the garden so emblematic of Elizabethan court politics as he had pictured them in his epic. If Acrasia's defeat by Guyon in the *Faerie Queene* marks the violent triumph of the epic imperative over the seductions of romance, in "Muiopotmos," romance entraps, binds, and ultimately kills even the possibility of epic action. Indeed, we may think of "Muiopotmos" as a strategic rewriting of the action in the Bower where *mêtis* now triumphs: the peculiar mixture of epic and romance tropes in a mocking key, the *locus amoenus* with its voyeuristic delight, erotic abandon, and evil creature at the center, the intimations of a moral and theological fall from grace, and the final, cruel twist as the epic hero meets his fatal end. More important, and perhaps more insidiously, the focus on the power of *mêtis* in "Muiopotmos" creates an inversion of the gender hierarchy defended so decisively by Guyon by systematically effeminizing its protagonists. While the action of the poem seems to concern a male spider and male butterfly, the powerful inset mythological narratives suggest otherwise: the real control over the poem's action lies in the hands of Venus and Minerva, powerful female figures distinguished by their artfulness.

In this respect, "Muiopotmos" offers a means of reexamining Harry Berger's provocative claim that the demonization of Acrasia and "the gynephobic representation of woman is a target rather than a donnée" of Book II.[35] Berger's argument, which denies the historical specificity of Acrasia and returns her to the allegorical matrix of the Book of Temperance, insightfully demonstrates how the misogynistic representations of women typical of epic are an inevitable by-product of the rectilinear repressiveness of the discourse of temperance itself: "Romance and pleasure are its creations, its scapegoats, its necessary others."[36] However, while Berger's understanding of Acrasia reveals her to be nothing other than a *male* fear of impotence and weakness, it also has the effect of stripping her (and the other female figures in Book II) of any genuine agency or ability distinct from their authors (whether Spenser, or the male characters of which they are allegorical displacements). The careful interest in female power and agency evident in "Muiopotmos," however, suggests that, in addition to the allegorical texture of his plot in Book II of the *Faerie Queene,* Spenser may have been interested in the nature of female power on its own terms as well. Acrasia may be demonized not merely because she is a displacement of male *akrasia,* but because the epic world of the *Faerie Queene* valorizes strength (*bie*) rather than cunning intelligence (*mêtis*). In "Muiopotmos," however, these values are crucially reversed.

II

The most striking similarity between the Bower of Bliss and Clarion's pleasure garden is the description of the *locus amoenus* itself, which introduces the key themes of artistry and artifice through the characteristic interplay of Nature and Art.[37] Spenser develops this theme at length in the final canto of Book II, and it is worth examining two representative stanzas:

A place pickt out by choice of best alyue,
That nature's worke by art can imitate:
In which what ever in this worldly state
Is sweet, and pleasing unto living sense,
Or that may daintiest fantasie aggrate,
Was poured forth with plentifull dispence,
And made there to abound with lavish affluence.

. . .

One would have thought, (so cunningly, the rude
And scorned partes were mingled with the fine,)
That nature had for wantonesse ensude
Art, and that Art at nature did repine;
So striving each th'other to undermine,
Each did the others work more beautify;
So diff'ring both in willes, agreed in fine:
So all agreed through sweete diuersity,
This Gardin to adorne with all variety.

(FQ II.xii.42, 59)[38]

Nohrnberg's description of the relationship between nature and art in the Bower encapsulates the general critical consensus on these lines succinctly, as he observes that the Bower suggests "a host of related aesthetic issues, both in the area of artistic imitation and illusion, and in the area of artistic balance and proportion."[39] Excess, even an excess of beauty, cannot be tolerated in the Book of Temperance, and the garden's extravagant pleasures and delight in its own aesthetic perfection are not to be celebrated but condemned for their lack of decorum.[40] Similarly, it has been argued that Clarion intemperately enjoys his flowerbed, indulging his "glutton sense," and allowing his "wavering wit" to luxuriate in sensuous satisfaction.[41] However, the recurrent trope of Nature and Art contending with each other to produce an ideal *copia*—a favorite figure used by classical writers on poetics to praise (rather than to condemn) extraordinary artistry—suggests that Spenser may be concerned with more than just unseemly artistic striving.[42]

If the romance world is characterized by *mêtis*-mental craftiness as well as physical craftsmanship—we must expect to find it manifested in the garden which metonymically stands for the genre. And it is precisely in the contention of Nature and Art, in the shimmering illusions of beautiful harmony, that we encounter the Spenserian version of *mêtis*. The artistry of the Bower reveals the basis of Acrasia's power. Its subtle entwining of art and nature, which cannot be distinguished from each other, hints at an intelligence which asserts its supremacy by creating conditions in which "appearance and reality no longer correspond to one another, but stand in contrast, producing an effect of illusion."[43] Significantly, *mêtis,* "the power of cunning and deceit," has both an aesthetic and political function in the Bower. Spenser describes the production of the wondrous aesthetic effects of the garden in terms that are distinctly political—"nature had for wantonesse ensude/ Art, and Art at nature did repine;/ So striving each th'other to undermine/ Each did the others work more beautify." The image recalls the courtiers gathered at the court of Philotime, where "everyone did strive his fellow downe to throw" (II.vii.47) and at the court of Lucifera where "a noble crew/ Of Lordes and Ladies stood on every side,/ Which with their presence faire, the place much beautified" (I.iv.7). These descriptions serve as a useful gloss on activities of nature and art and suggest that the Bower is itself a court where the appearance of beauty masks a constant struggle to capture the attention of the queen/enchantress and gain political/sexual advancement.

This identification of Bower-as-Court is in fact hinted at as early as the third canto, where Braggadocchio catalogues the joys of court-life for Belphoebe:

> But what art thou, O Ladie, which doest raunge
>   In this wilde forrest, where no pleasure is,
>   And doest not it for ioyous court exchaunge,
>   Emongst thine equall peres, where happie blis
>   And all delight does raigne, and dearely loued bee,
>   There thou maist love, and dearly loved be,
>   And swim in pleasure, which thou here doest mis;
>   There maist thou best be seene, and best maist see:
> The wood is fit for beasts, the court is fit for thee.
>
> (*FQ* II.iii.39)

There is perhaps no more obvious counterpart to the "wilde forrest" than the elaborately cultivated Bower with its specular delights. Braggadocchio uses the language of sexual pleasure to describe the political world of the court, a metaphor that will be literalized in the sensual excesses of the Acrasia's garden. Indeed, the episode is striking because it explicitly directs anti-court satire against places like the Bower, where courtesans lure knights away from the pursuit of honor only to enmesh them in the "happie blis" of "court exchaunge."

Moreover, by using Belphoebe—the figure explicitly associated with Elizabeth in the *Letter to Ralegh*—to condemn the excesses of courtly life, Spenser slyly implies that the court in question (and by extension, the Bower of Bliss as well) is that of Elizabeth herself.[44] The nightmarish version of court politics is thus displaced onto Acrasia, while Belphoebe maintains the queen's moral integrity for the purposes of the poem.

The careful evocation of the political relationship between art and nature in the Bower also suggests that Spenser may well have been thinking of the central, well-established importance of the garden in Elizabethan iconography.[45] The image of such a garden, with its temptations to wealth, ease, and the good life of privilege, comfort, and sexual enjoyment, bore an obvious resemblance to the court itself, populated by languishing courtiers seeking to gain favors both political and personal in the language of romantic courtship.[46] The extent to which this analogy between the garden, the queen, and her court, was embedded in Elizabethan culture is further revealed by the actual spectacles of power that took place in the great English Renaissance gardens at Kenilworth, Hampton Court, Nonsuch, Theobalds, and Pymms.[47] Not only were lavish entertainments and recreations of idyllic pastoral or romance settings staged in these gardens, literally combining elaborate artifice and natural splendor, but the plan of the garden itself served as a monument in praise of the queen.[48]

Consequently, the evocation of a garden in "Muiopotmos," characterized by the identical tropes of variety, excess, and cunning artistry in the interweaving of nature and art, cannot possibly avoid the burden of romance invested in that other garden, the Bower of Bliss, with *its* strongly charged fabric of literary and political significance:

> And all the champion he soared light,
> And all the country he did possesse,
> Feeding upon their pleasures bounteouslie,
> That none gainsaid, nor none did him envie.
>
> The woods, the rivers the meadows green,
> With his aire-cutting wings he measured wide,
> Ne did he leave the mountains bare unseene,
> Nor the ranke grassie fennes delights untride.
> . . . .
>
> To the gay gardens his unstaid desire

Him wholly carried, to refresh his sprights:
There lavish Nature in her best attire,
Powres forth sweete odors, and alluring sights;
And Arte with her contending, doth aspire
T'excell the naturall, with made delights:
And all that faire or pleasant may be found,
In riotous excess doth there abound.
                    ("Muiopotmos," 149–56; 161–168)[49]

Clarion's "journey" to the "gay gardins" is a mock-epic quest, and
his wandering, adventurous journey, which culminates in the fatal
garden, resembles the careers of the many epic heroes lost in the
digressive pleasures of romance. But if Clarion's progress is modeled
on a distinguished literary tradition, it also has unmistakable political
overtones: he is heir to a throne and his long flight across a vast
landscape is akin to a sovereign's survey of his possessions; his entry
into the garden simultaneously suggests the epic hero's delighted discovery of a *locus amoenus,* and a political trespassing on another's
territory. Subtle as these gestures are, they gain weight by the associa-
tive relation of "Muiopotmos" to the other poems in the *Complaints*
volume. "Muiopotmos" belongs to the central set of beast fables
including "Virgils Gnat" and "Prosopopoia, or Mother Hubberds
Tale," which are explicitly concerned with court politics; moreover,
the poem itself is set off from the other two fables by two lyric
sequences ("Ruines of Rome" and "Visions of the Worlds Vanitie")
that mourn the decaying grandeur of civilization, for which the court
is a particularly appropriate emblem. In the immediate context of the
Complaints poems that refer to court life and politics in allegorical
or emblematic style, we cannot avoid the iconographic and literary
implications of Clarion, a well-armed (mock) epic hero journeying
through a vast landscape and entering an enchanting garden, reminiscent of Elizabeth and her court.

Clarion, in fact, seems to be beautifully dressed, much in the manner of a courtier. Here again, the analogy with Braggadocchio is revealing:

Lastly his shinie wings as silver bright,
Painted with a thousand colours, passing farre
All Painters skill, he did about him dight:
Not half so manie sundrie colours arre
In *Iris* bowe . . .

Nor *Iunoes* Bird in her ey-spotted traine
So manie goodly colours doth containe.

                              ("Muiopotmos," 89–95)

But for in court gay portaunce he perceiu'd,
    And gallant shew to be in greatest gree,
Eftsoones to court he ast t'auaunce his first degree.

And by the way he chaunced to espy
    One sitting idle on a sunny bancke,
    To whom auaunting in great brauery,
    As Peacocke, that his painted plumes doth prancke . . .

                              (*FQ* II.iii.5–6)

The repeated peacock simile suggests that Clarion, for all his elaborate
arming, may be a vaunting courtier like Braggadocchio, one who
has appropriately put on "gay portaunce" in preparation to visit the
"gay gardins." The artistry of Clarion's wings, whose variety and
subtlety of color rival the greatest painters' skill, parallels the artistry
of the gardens that he will visit, where Art aspires "t'excell the naturall, with made delights." But it is precisely this similarity which
condemns Clarion almost before he has even ventured forth. Like
Braggadocchio, he is taken in by the *appearance* of "gallant shew" and
is easily seduced by the gleaming illusions of *mêtis*. His gorgeous
wings are, after all, envied and desired by ladies at court who will be
gratified if their loves will "steale them privily away."

III

Though the Bower's extended *paragone* of nature and art is limited
to a single stanza early in "Muiopotmos," it contains all the characteristic elements of the earlier garden: the "riotous excess" of flowers,
the cunning artistry which produces an ideal harmony and *copia* of
sensual pleasure, a catalogue of flowers. These early intimations of a
hidden *mêtis* are developed pointedly in the tapestry contest between
Arachne and Minerva, which, in an extraordinary twist, depends on
the image of a butterfly in a garden. Spenser creates a moment of
dizzying meta-poetic insight as the poem collapses in on itself at
this point:

Emongst those leaves she made a Butterflie,
With excellent device and wondrous slight,
Fluttering among the Olives wantonly,
That seem'd to live, so like it was in sight:
The velvet nap on which his wings doth lie,
The silken downe with which his back is dight,
His broad outstretched hornes, his hayrie thies,
His glorious colours and his glistering eies.

(329–36)

Minerva's handiwork with its "excellent device and wondrous slight" slyly alludes to the earlier stanza describing the mimetic contention of art and nature within Clarion's flowerbed, and, in fact, her image of the butterfly is exactly how Clarion has last appeared in the poem, resting in the warm sun in "riotous suffisaunce" (ll.207). Here, the ostensibly "real" (or "natural") plot of butterfly and spider merges into its mythic ("artificial" or artistic) parallel. In effect, Minerva's portrayal of a butterfly in her web-like tapestry is proleptic: it foreshadows the fate of another butterfly, Clarion, who also will end the poem caught in a web. The tapestry thus reveals the fate of Clarion *and* its cause; it becomes a sophisticated gloss on the main plot of the poem as it offers a glimpse into the *métis*, the subtle, exquisite craft that will entrap the guileless butterfly.

Not surprisingly, much criticism has focused on the Ovidian tapestry contest, as readers instinctively sense that its action contains the key to the poem's significance. However, the importance of the contest may lie less in its etiological power as a myth, than in its celebration of the triumphant craftsmanship which becomes the cause of Clarion's entrapment. If the mimetic complicity of nature and art in the Bower reveals the *métis* behind Acrasia's power, then the tapestry contest in "Muiopotmos," as an extension of the nature/art theme, shows how Clarion's death is due to the same *métis*, manifested first in Minerva's tapestry and then in Aragnoll's web. In both cases, questions of aesthetic representation allude to problems of political representation, and this is made explicit by Minerva's victory. While Arachne sets out an image of successful *male* sexual domination emphasizing brute force, Minerva weaves a tale of *female* political domination emphasizing strategic natural bounty, with obvious parallels to Elizabeth's reign.[50] Significantly, the contest of Neptune and Minerva stages the showdown between violent military force and the civilizing, peace-making arts symbolized by the olive, pointedly depicting the goddess's mastery of the arts of making rather than

commemorating her martial valor. In effect, the tapestry dramatizes
the collision of battlefield (Neptune's "warlike steed") and garden
(Minerva's "fruitfull Olive tree" and "wreathe of Olyves hoarie"),
of epic might and romance craft. It celebrates Minerva as the embodiment of *mêtis* in *both* aesthetic and political terms as she weaves her
tapestry with a subtle artistry analogous to her astute defeat of
Neptune.

Indeed, Arachne's recognition of Minerva's superior skill, which
constitutes Spenser's main departure from his Ovidian source, may
also owe something to the fact that Minerva was the daughter of
Metis and thus the embodiment of supreme handicraft and craftiness.
It is only fitting then that Arachne is transfixed by the sight of the
woven butterfly "that seem'd to live"—the artist is herself outwitted
by the power of mimetic illusion crafted with a *mêtis* greater than
her own. More importantly, by conceding defeat through her silence
and subsequent metamorphosis, she dooms her descendents to repro-
duce endlessly this original image of supreme artistic skill. Arachne's
defeat, which is also implicitly a defeat of the male force and sexual
domination depicted in her tapestry, reinforces Minerva's style of
maintaining authority, a style associated with romance cunning and
the political acumen of the queen. By replicating Minerva's artistry
(both political and aesthetic) in the natural world every time a spider
entraps a butterfly in its web, Arachne's metamorphosis symbolically
brings us back to the story of Clarion and the action of the Bower
of Bliss.

The opposition of armed force (synonymous with epic) versus
cunning artistry (characteristic of romance) in Minerva's tapestry thus
both frames and explains the main plot of Clarion, whose image is,
after all, woven into the border of olive leaves. As a (mock) epic hero
equipped for battle, with arms compared to those of Achilles and
Hercules, Clarion is doomed to be trapped and outwitted in the
romance garden with its hidden, tapestry-like webs. Aragnoll's web,
a by-product (in mythological terms) of Minerva's artistry, is also an
image of art in nature (or, quite literally, of "natural art") and thus
becomes an imitation *in malo* of an ideal *mêtis;* in this, it functions
as an emblematic parallel to the Bower itself. The entrapping web
points back to Acrasia, another predator who also lurks at the center
of a romance garden:

> And was arrayd, or rather disarrayd,
> All in a vele of silke and silver thin,
> That hid no whit of her alabaster skin,

But rather shewd more white, if more might bee:
More subtile web *Arachne* cannot spin,
Nor the fine nets, which oft we woven see
Of scorched deaw, do not in th'aire more lightly flee.

(*FQ* II.xii.77)

The "subtile web" of Arachne has the extraordinary effect of referring
to *both* her tapestry and subsequent spiderweb with the same associa-
tive logic that we see at work in "Muiopotmos": the comparison of
the veil to exquisitely woven fabric (Arachne's "web") leads the
narrator to think of Arachne's fate and the resultant spiderwebs ("fine
nets"). In a deft gesture, Acrasia's cunning becomes associated with
the subtle artistry of weaving and the malignant snares of the spider;
like Aragnoll, she is rapacious in her artistry. The stanza also emphasizes the extent to which the tapestry contest in "Muiopotmos" may
be read as an extended gloss on Acrasia's entrapping tactics in the
Bower: the shining butterfly locked in Minerva's tapestry and the
dying Clarion caught in Aragnoll's web parody the condition of
Verdant entangled in the titillating charms of Arcasia's veil.

More interestingly, Louis Montrose suggests that the identification
of Acrasia with a spider may have been prompted by Elizabeth's own
courtly self-presentation.[51] A description of the queen by Johann
Jacob Breuning von Buchenbach in 1595 suggests that she may have
seen herself as an Aragnoll-figure: "Over her breast, which was bare,
she wore a long filigree lace shawl, on which sat a hideous large black
spider that looked as if it were natural and alive. Many might have
been deceived by it."[52] This unforgettable image of the queen embodies all the key themes of "Muiopotmos" and the Bower with
unmistakable clarity: the association of artifice (particularly weaving)
with political control through the symbol of the spider, the invocation of mimetic illusion (the trick spider), the sexualized presentation
of political control (the bare breast) that marks the sovereign's authority as distinctly female. The cunning artistry of the Bower thus finds
a powerfully revisionist counterpart in "Muiopotmos" as Spenser
interrogates Elizabethan strategies of enforcing political control
through strategies of aesthetic representation.

In this context, the gender inversions in "Muiopotmos" are of
particular interest. While the aesthetic, sexual, and finally political
control in the Bower of Bliss is retained by a powerful woman whose
resemblance to Elizabeth is primarily based on her gender, the spider
Aragnoll in "Muiopotmos" is identified as male, and his function as
a political predator is more fully symbolic. That this change of gender

is far from incidental becomes evident in the peculiar but pointed gender segregation at work in the poem: all the amplifying mythological action (the inset tales of Venus/ Astery and Minerva/ Arachne) is controlled *by* and enacted *upon* female figures, so that the main characters, Clarion and Aragnoll, are reduced to male inversions and extensions of a cosmic battle played out among powerful female forces. There is, in fact, some doubt about the gender of Clarion. In a crucial slip at the end of the Astery tale, the metamorphosed butterfly, clearly identified with Clarion, is still distinctly gendered female: "She turn'd into a winged Butterflie,/ In the wide aire to make *her* wandering flight;/ And all those flowers . . . / that bred her spight,/ She placed in *her* wings, for memorie" (138–42; my emphases).[53] The effects of this segregation are quite striking. As generations of readers attest, the poetic power of "Muiopotmos" seems to reside most fully in the inset tales which, though incidental to the ostensible plot of the poem, seem to be more central to its meaning. This suggests that Spenser may have deliberately set up an apparent aesthetic imbalance within the poem in order to demonstrate poetically the kinds of political effects induced by the queen's covert exercise of power. Thus, the actual power of the poem (aesthetically and in terms of plot-action) lies in the seemingly incidental female myths, and *not* in the ostensible main plot between the male actors; the inverse relationship between the parts of the poem itself becomes a sophisticated demonstration of the idea of *mêtis,* where appearance repeatedly belies reality.

IV

The relationship between the two poems and the drama of court politics on which they comment is further underscored by Clarion's resemblance to the many would-be epic heroes seduced by the delights of the Bower. Like Mortdant, Cymochles, and Verdant before him, Clarion, too, succumbs to "the pleasures of that Paradise" with sensual, unrestrained glee:

> There he arriving, round about doth flie,
> From bed to bed, from one to other border,
> And takes survey with curious busie eye,
> Of everie flower and herbe there set in order;
> Now this, now that he tasteth tenderly,
> Yet none of them he rudely doth disorder,

Ne with his feete their silken leaves deface;
But pastures on the pleasures of each place.

Of everie one he takes, and tastes at will,
And on their pleasures greedily doth pray.
And when he hath both plaid, and fed his fill,
In the warm Sunne he doth himselfe embay,
And there him rests in riotous suffisaunce
Of all his gladfulnes, and kingly joyaunce.

(169–76, 203–08)

The ubiquitous underlying image of a young woman as a flower infuses this scene with a comic eroticism, but it also recalls Cymochles's voyeuristic enjoyment in the Bower of Bliss:[54]

His wandring thought in deepe desire does steepe,
And his fraile eye with spoyle of beautie feedes;
Sometimes he falsely faines himself to sleepe,
While through their lids his wanton eies do peepe,
To steale a snatch of amorous conceipt . . .

(FQ II.v.34)

Cymochles's "wandring thought" and "wanton eies" find their equivalents in Clarion's "wavering wit" and "curious busie eye," suggesting that the gorgeous butterfly is an image for the knight in the grip of concupiscent passions, wandering through the romance bower with amazed enjoyment. However, the sexualized image of feeding ("pastures on the pleasures of each place"), appropriate to a butterfly sucking on the nectar of flowers, also recalls the insatiable sexual hunger of Acrasia who feeds on Verdant:

And all that while, right over him she hong,
    With her false eyes fast fixed in his sight,
    As seeking medicine, whence she was stong,
    Or greedily depasturing delight:

(FQ II.xii.73)

The image of pasturing or depasturing locates Clarion within a long tradition of epic heroes detained in the lap of a romance enchantress. It is a direct translation of a similar moment in Tasso's *Gerusalemme*

liberata where Rinaldo is described as feeding or pasturing avidly on
Armida's face: "i famelici sguardi avidamente/ in lei pascendo si
consuma e strugge" ("and avidly feeding on her his ravenous gaze,
[he] is consumed and destroyed"). Narcissistic and self-indulgent,
such self-consuming erotic feasting occurs when the hero submits to
the instant gratification of the romance world without seeking to
control or understand it. It is in this moment of unbridled sensual
indulgence that the epic hero becomes most fully enmeshed in the
web of romance. But such an effacement of epic selfhood in the
erotic excesses of the romance world is also a covert gesture back
toward to complex erotic-political games of courtship in which Elizabeth engaged her courtiers, as she offered the illusion of success even
when she may have stripped them of effective power. The erotic
action *in* the gardens of both poems is in fact only another aspect of
the *mêtis* which informs their exterior aesthetic appearance and hidden political style.

Clarion, like the legions of unfortunate knights before him, also
gets enmeshed precisely when he has fully surrendered himself to
erotic enjoyment. Significantly, his fate hovers between that of Mortdant and Verdant, the two knights whose capitulation to Acrasia
frame Guyon's quest, and links "Muiopotmos" to the showdown
between epic and romance in the Bower. In the second book of the
Faerie Queene, the book closest to classical epic, Acrasia represents
both romance digression and epic telos. This is an important and
unique innovation in the convention of contrasting the conflicting
impulses of epic and romance: Spenser makes the conflict between
the genres itself the focus of his plot. Acrasia is responsible for the
erotic deviance and deaths of Mortdant and Amavia, whose suicide,
in turn, precipitates Guyon's epic quest. The menace of the romance
world thus frames the second book of the *Faerie Queene*, and the
lament of Amavia, a hapless victim of romance intrigue, also echoes
in "Muiopotmos" where it is *her* vision of the world, rather than
that of Guyon, which comes to fruition. Amavia's lament in the first
canto of Book II is usually interpreted in the context of despair:

> But if that carelesse hevens (quoth she) despise
>   The doome of just revenge, and take delight
>   To see sad pageants of mens miseries,
>   As bound by them to live in lives despight,
>   Yet can they not warne death from wretched wight.
>
> (FQ II.i.36)

In the context of the *Complaints,* however, these lines are simply typical—a lament for the mutability and mortality of the sentient world. Indeed, while Clarion happily "rests in riotous suffisaunce," the narrator reflects on his fate in language strikingly reminiscent of Amavia and the fate of Mortdant:

And whatso heavens in their secret doome
Ordained have, how can fraile fleshly wight
Forecast, but it must needs to issue come?

(225–27)

Both moments have been associated with laments for the condition of fallen man and the loss of Eden (the original *locus amoenus*), but the parallels between Amavia's lament for Mortdant's death at the hands of Acrasia, and the narrator's lament for Clarion's impending death at the hands of Aragnoll, suggests a link between sexual excess, romance entrapment, and the destruction of the would-be epic hero in a world where the female power of *métis* reigns supreme. At the end of Book II, Guyon's brutal triumph powerfully eliminates the menace of romance with its labyrinthine sexual politics, avenges the death of Amavia, and reclaims its imaginative power for decidedly masculine epic action. In the gardens of "Muiopotmos," however, romance consistently entraps and destroys pretensions to epic success as Aragnoll, the descendent of Arachne, destroys Clarion in his web; female dissimulation trumps martial male valor.

Both *The Faerie Queene* and "Muiopotmos" are eventually concerned with investigating the nature of female authority—its fascination, its menace, its pleasure. Both portray the relations of power within the Elizabethan court as the challenges of the romance world, ruled by powerful enchantresses who threaten the epic hero with emasculation and destruction. But their dramatically different conclusions suggest equally different answers to a central question: does the epic hero and the epic poem have a place in a world where only the rules of romance apply? Is there a place for heroic action in the court of an early modern queen? To have a chance of survival, the unsuspecting epic hero must encounter these shifting, changing, ultimately female worlds with either the *metis* of Odysseus or the exterminating drive of Guyon. But Spenser also seems to suggest that these two responses are no longer adequate, and perhaps, no longer possible.

The pointed rewriting of Acrasia's defeat in Clarion's death suggests an unsettling response to the fate of epic poetics and politics. If the final canto of Book II is framed by allusions to Odyssean temptations which must be overcome, Spenser returns once again to the same poem at the end of "Muiopotmos," but this time, he signals a decisive shift of focus *away* from the epic action of the *Iliad* and the *Aeneid*. This change is all the more striking because "Muio-potmos," unlike Book II, is framed not by the danger of romance deviance, but by allusions to epic battles. The opening lines of the poem ("I sing of deadly dolorous debate/ . . . Betwixt two mightie ones of great estate") clearly allude to the invocation of the *Iliad* ("Sing, goddess, the anger of Peleus' son Achilleus/ . . . since that time when first there stood in division of conflict/ Atreus' son the lord of men and brilliant Achilleus"), and suggest a poem of epic amplitude.[55] There are, of course, many requisite epic conventions in the course of the poem—the arming of the hero, the cosmic politics of gods and mortals, the intimations of a great battle—but these gestures remain poetic decorations and never crystallize into the grandeur of epic action, even mock-epic action. As if to acknowl-edge this failure of epic purpose, the poem turns to another unmistak-able epic allusion at its end: Clarion's death ("his deepe groaning spright/ In bloodie streames foorth fled into the aire/ His bodie left the spectacle of care") mimics the death of Turnus in the *Aeneid* ("Then all the body slackened in death's chill,/ And with a groan for that indignity/ His spirit fled into the gloom below").[56] Ironically, if Aeneas's triumph over Turnus crystallizes the imperial tone of Vergil-ian epic, then Spenser's transformation of his hero (Clarion) into the epic adversary (Turnus), who is inevitably destroyed, marks a decisive moment of revision. Epic is no longer the genre defining the politics of empire; it is no match for the guile of romance intrigue.[57]

In a final twist that reasserts the relationship between the Bower of Bliss and "Muiopotmos," Spenser folds into both poems an allu-sion to the famous golden net of Vulcan: in Book II, the Palmer's "subtile net" recalls Vulcan's capture of Mars and Venus, while in "Muiopotmos," Vulcan's net becomes Aragnoll's web:

> The noble Elfe, and carefull Palmer drew
> So nigh them, minding nought, but lustfull game,
> That suddein forth they on them rusht, and threw
> A subtile net, which only for that same
> The skilful Palmer formally did frame.
>
> (FQ II.xii.81)

> Ne doo I thinke, that that same subtil gin,
> The which the *Lemnian* God framed craftily,

Mars sleeping with his wife to compasse in,
That all the Gods with common mockerie
Might laugh at them, and scorne their shamefull sin,
Was like to this.

                    ("Muiopotmos," 369–74)

The echoes of "subtile net" in "subtile gin" and the emphasis on
the skilful workmanship of the device highlight the relationship between the two texts, as well as their source. Significantly, the allusion
is drawn from the two major classical texts that stand against the
totalizing voice of martial epic—Homer's *Odyssey* and Ovid's *Metamorphoses*—and in both texts, the net symbolizes the triumph of *mêtis*
(the artistic craft of the net itself and the craftiness of the ploy):

Those shackles fashioned hot in wrath Hephaistos
climbed to the bower and the bed of love . . .
light as a cobweb even gods in bliss
could not perceive, so wonderful his cunning.
Seeing his bed now made a snare, he feigned . . .

                    (*Odyssey,* VIII. 292–98)

And Vulcan dropped whatever he was doing,
And made a net, with such fine links of bronze
No eye could see the mesh: no woolen thread
Was ever so delicate, no spider ever
Spun filament so frail from any rafter.

                    (*Metamorphoses,* IV. 175–79)[58]

By inverting the original comparison of Vulcan's net to a spider's web
in both his poems, Spenser aligns the god's trick with the cunning of
Acrasia and Aragnoll, and reveals his Bower and flowerbed for what
they are—romance worlds where even the golden war god Mars is
entangled and unmanned.[59] We can now recognize Guyon's destruction of the Bower of Bliss as an epic mask for the real, rather unheroic
and sly triumph of the Palmer, who catches the dangerous enchantress
with a net symbolic of her own craftiness; it is the Palmer who
manifests the necessary Odyssean *mêtis* which Guyon lacks. Clarion,
on the other hand, has no such guide, and with the weight of this
literary tradition bearing down upon him, has no chance of survival:
his Iliadic epic future is ruthlessly annihilated in the Odyssean web
of romance.

Yale University

Notes

1.   An earlier version of this essay was presented at the Spenser at Kalamazoo sessions of the International Congress for Medieval Studies, May 2004. I would like to thank William Oram, Anne Prescott, and David Quint for their invaluable help with transforming earlier thoughts into the present essay.

2.   Homer, *Odyssey,* trans. Robert Fitzgerald (New York: Vintage Classics, 1990). All citations are from this edition.

3.   On the romance *topos* of a hero detained by an enchantress and diverted from his task (with particular reference to Spenser) see A. Bartlett Giamatti, *The Earthly Paradise and the Renaissance Epic* (Princeton: Princeton University Press, 1966), 250–54; Patricia Parker, "Suspended Instruments: Lyric and Power in the Bower of Bliss," in *Literary Fat Ladies: Rhetoric, Gender, Property* (New York: Methuen, 1987); David Quint, "The Anatomy of Epic in Book 2 of *The Faerie Queene,*" *The Spenser Review* 34, no 1 (2003); and John Watkins, *The Specter of Dido: Spenser and Virgilian Epic* (New Haven: Yale University Press, 1995), 2–8.

4.   Guyon most closely resembles Vergil's Aeneas for most of Book II, but in Spenser's imitation of the Odyssey in the final cantos, Guyon is more akin to Odysseus. Of course, Vergil too draws on Homer's Odysseus for Aeneas's interlude in Carthage (the so-called "odyssean" half of the *Aeneid*). On the models for Guyon in classical epic, see Theresa M. Krier, *Gazing on Secret Sight: Spenser, Classical Imitation, and the Decorums of Vision* (Ithaca: Cornell University Press, 1990), 99–112; and Quint, "The Anatomy of Epic."

5.   In previous epics, it is the enchantress—rather than then epic hero—who destroys either herself or the bower. Dido commits suicide, Alcina would commit suicide if she could but destroys her army instead, and Armida dissolves her island after Rinaldo leaves and tries (rather half-heartedly) to commit suicide at the end of the poem.

6.   Krier, 104, 112.

7.   On the dating of "Muiopotmos" and the *Complaints,* see the classic studies by Francis Johnson, *A Critical Bibliography of the Works of Edmund Spenser Printed before 1700* (Baltimore: The Johns Hopkins Press, 1933; facsim. rpt. 1966), 24–28, and Harold Leo Stein, *Studies in Spenser's Complaints* (New York: Oxford University Press, 1934), especially 1–33, 65–67. In a recent essay, Jean Brink has called attention to dating problems with the *Daphnaida* and the *Complaints* volume, because of the discrepancies between dates of entries, dedications, and imprints in the Stationer's Register. The crux of these questions rests on whether the 1591 date refers to the Old Style or New Style Julian Calendar and Brink argues that New Style dating should be applied consistently, a practice which raises problems given the "1590" imprint of "Muiopotmos" and the "1591" imprint of other poems in the *Complaints* volume (see Jean R. Brink, "Dating Spenser's Letter to Ralegh," *The Library: Transactions of the Bibliographical Society* 16:3 [1994]). This problem seems to be resolved by Adrian Weiss who uses watermark evidence to argue that the imprint is indeed in the New Style, which means that the *Complaints* volume can be dated as being published in 1591; see "Watermark Evidence and Inference: New Style Dates of

Edmund Spenser's *Complaints* and *Daphnaida,*" *Studies in Bibliography: Papers of the Bibliographical Society of the University of Virginia* 52, (1999).

8.   Similarities between "Muiopotmos" and the Bower have been remarked upon by Don Cameron Allen, *Image and Meaning: Metaphoric Traditions in Renaissance Poetry* (Baltimore: Johns Hopkins Press, 1968), 34–35; Richard Danson Brown, *'The New Poet': Novelty and Tradition in Spenser's Complaints* (Liverpool: Liverpool University Press, 1999), 213–14; Judith Dundas, *The Spider and the Bee: The Artistry of Spenser's Faerie Queene* (Urbana: University of Illinois Press, 1985), 6–7; James Nohrnberg, *The Analogy of the Faerie Queene* (Princeton: Princeton University Press, 1976), 512–13.

9.   Nohrnberg, 512–13.

10.   For a thorough review of the critical traditions around "Muiopotmos" see Eric C. Brown, "The Allegory of Small Things: Insect Eschatology in Spenser's Muiopotmos," *Studies in Philology* 99, no. 3 (2002) and Franklin E. Court, "The Theme and Structure of Spenser's Muiopotmos," *Studies in English Literature 1500–1900* 10, no. 1 (1970).

11.   On the mythographic traditions see Allen, 20–41. On the emblematic tradition see Eric Brown; Judith Dundas, "Muiopotmos: A World of Art," *Yearbook of English Studies* 5 (1975); and Henry Green, *Shakespeare and the Emblem Writers: An Exposition of Their Similarities of Thought and Expression. Preceded by a View of Emblem-Literature Down to A.D. 1616. With Numerous Illustrative Devices from the Original Authors* (New York: B. Franklin, 1966). On the mock epic tradition of poems with animal or insect protagonists see Isabel Rathborne, "Another Interpretation of Muiopotmos," *PMLA* 49, no. 4 (1934). On the Chaucerian analogues see Judith Anderson, "Nat Worth a Boterflye": Muiopotmos and the Nun's Priest's Tale," *Journal of Medieval and Renaissance Studies* 1 (1971) and James H. Morey, "Spenser's Mythic Adaptations in Muiopotmos," *Spenser Studies* 9 (1988).

12.   On the allegorical import of a beautiful garden or *locus amoenus* see C. S. Lewis, *The Allegory of Love: A Study in Medieval Tradition* (London: Oxford University Press, 1973), 119–20, 50–53 and Giamatti, 83–86. For an alternate view that strongly argues against allegorical or quasi-allegorical readings of "Muiopotmos," see Andrew Weiner, "Spenser's 'Muiopotmos' and the Fates of Butterflies and Men," *Journal of English and Germanic Philology* 84, no. 2 (1985).

13.   The interpretations of the political allegory in "Muiopotmos" range from an attempt to identify Clarion and Aragnoll with various court figures to more sophisticated analyses of the poem in terms of court politics more generally. For representative examples of the former, see C. W. Lemmi, "The Allegorical Meaning of Spenser's Muiopotmos," *PMLA* 45, no. 3 (1930) and Elizabeth Mazzola, "Spenser, Sidney, and Second Thoughts: Mythology and Misgiving in Muiopotmos," *Sidney Journal* 18, no. 1 (2000). Court, 1–3, notes 9–16, offers a concise survey of the various "identifications." Ronald Bond, "Invidia and the Allegory of Spenser's 'Muiopotmos'," *English Studies in Canada* 2 (1976) discusses the poem as an allegory of envy and the desire for fame, while Robert A. Brinkley, "Spenser's Muiopotmos and the Politics of Metamorphosis," *English Literary History* 48, no. 4 (1981) presents an illuminating reading of the poem in terms of court politics. For representative theological and moral analyses see Allen, 20–41, Eric Brown and Court. Analyses

that discuss the poem in terms of Spenserian aesthetics include Richard Danson Brown, 213–54; Dundas, "Muiopotmos: A World of Art"; and Craig Rustici, "Muiopotmos: Spenser's 'Complaint' against Aesthetics," *Spenser Studies* 13 (1999).

14. Quint, "The Anatomy of Epic," 28.

15. For a concise and useful discussion of the danger and attraction of the romance world, particularly as it was theorized in sixteenth-century Italian treatises, see Melinda Gough, "Tasso's Enchantress, Tasso's Captive Woman," *Renaissance Quarterly* 54, no. 2 (2001): 526–29.

16. Louis Montrose, "Spenser and the Elizabethan Political Imaginary," *English Literary History* 69, no. 4 (2002) and Parker.

17. On epic as a quintessentially masculine genre and romance as the realm of prominent female characters and domestic concerns, see Mihoko Suzuki, *Metamorphoses of Helen: Authority, Difference, and the Epic* (Ithaca: Cornell University Press, 1989), 1, 57–59.

18. It is worth noting that this is a common problem for male poets with female patrons, particularly in the sixteenth century where women were powerful patrons of the arts; epic poetry was usually written in the (ostensible) praise of a male patron, while erotic poetry was typically written to celebrate a woman. There are several examples of this phenomenon: Castiglione's *Il libro del cortegiano* is concerned with the question of female rule and influence over men (it is set in the court of Urbino ruled by Elisabetta Gonzaga); patronage at the French court was often the province of women, and artists such as Marot, Cellini, and Ronsard both profited and chafed under the patronage of Renée de France, the Duchesse d'Estampes, and Catherine de' Medici. The situation of English poets under Elizabeth was thus not unique. I am grateful to Anne Prescott for bringing this point to my attention.

19. Brinkley, 668.

20. For discussions of the Odyssean elements in Book II see Krier, 99–112, and Quint, "The Anatomy of Epic."

21. On the generic contrast of epic and romance see Erich Auerbach, *Mimesis: The Representation of Reality in Western Literature,* trans. Willard Trask (Garden City, N.Y.: Doubleday Anchor, 1957), 83–124; Colin Burrow, *Epic Romance: Homer to Milton* (Oxford: Oxford University Press, 1993), 2–7; W. P. Ker, *Epic and Romance: Essays on Medieval Literature* (New York: Dover Publications, 1957), 16–35; Nohrnberg, 5–22; and David Quint, *Epic and Empire: Politics and Generic Form from Virgil to Milton* (Princeton: Princeton University Press, 1993), 9–10, 248–53. The debate between the relative merits of Homer and Vergil with regard to epic style was one of the key issues in sixteenth-century poetic theory; see Bernard Weinberg, *A History of Literary Criticism in the Italian Renaissance,* 2 vols. (Chicago: University of Chicago Press, 1961). On Renaissance interpretations of the Homeric poems, particularly the tendency toward allegorization see also Howard W. Clarke, *Homer's Readers: A Historical Introduction to the Iliad and the Odyssey* (Newark: University of Delaware Press, 1981), 62–107.

22. On the contrast of force and cunning in the Homeric epics see Marcel Detienne and Jean Pierre Vernant, *Cunning Intelligence in Greek Culture and Society* (Atlantic Highlands, N.J.: Humanities Press, 1978), 11–23. In writing of force and fraud as the two great organizing principles of imaginative literature, Northrop Frye locates

the dichotomy in the contrast between the Homeric epics, "the story of *forza* in the *Iliad,* the story of wrath (*menis*) of Achilles, of *froda* in the *Odyssey,* the story of the guile (*dolos*) of Ulysses" (Northrop Frye, *The Secular Scripture: A Study of the Structure of Romance* [Cambridge: Harvard University Press, 1976], 65–66).

23.   Detienne and Vernant, 21, 23.

24.   On the association of Odysseus with *mêtis* see Detienne and Vernant, 18–19, 227–29; Pietro Pucci, *Odysseus Polutropos: Intertextual Readings in the Odyssey and the Iliad* (Ithaca: Cornell University Press, 1987), 14–17, 56–62, 98–109; Suzuki, 90–91; John J. Winkler, *The Constraints of Desire: The Anthropology of Sex and Gender in Ancient Greece* (New York: Routledge, 1990), 129–61; and Froma I. Zeitlin, *Playing the Other: Gender and Society in Classical Greek Literature* (Chicago: University of Chicago Press, 1995), 35–38. In the *Odyssey,* the likemindedness between Odysseus and Penelope stems from their shared *mêtis,* which explains the hero's homecoming and ensures domestic tranquility; moreover, the reigning goddess Athena is herself the daughter of Metis.

25.   The *Odyssey* has long been identified as the "beginning" of romance; see for instance, Northrop Frye, 68. Writing in defense of the *romanzi* in the sixteenth century, Giraldi Cinzio argues that "one should realize that in make-up Romances are much more like Homer's *Odyssey* than the *Iliad*" (*Giraldi Cinzio on Romances: Being a Translation of the Discorso intorno al comporre dei romanzi,* trans. Henry L. Snuggs [Lexington: University of Kentucky Press, 1968], 57). Of the Homeric poems, the *Odyssey* contains elements of both epic and romance, as the teleological progress of the hero's homecoming coexists with the adventure and marvelous typical of romance. On Odysseus as a romance hero, see Pucci, 56. On the association of guile and craft with the genre of romance, particularly in the context of the *Odyssey* see Northrop Frye, 67–70, and Pucci, 98–109.

26.   Detienne and Vernant, 13. In *The Rhetoric of Concealment: Figuring Gender and Class in Renaissance Literature* (Ithaca: Cornell University Press, 1994), Rosemary Kegl describes the similarities between rhetorical and political strategies of dissemblance and dissimulation in late Elizabethan literature in terms that suggest the Greek concept of *mêtis.*

27.   The myth of Metis and Zeus is told in Hesiod's *Theogony* lines 886–906 (Hesiod, *The Works and Days, Theogony, the Shield of Herakles,* trans. Richmond Lattimore [Ann Arbor: University of Michigan Press, 1959], 176–77) and in Apollodorus's *Bibliotheke,* I.3.6 (Apollodorus, *The Library of Greek Mythology,* trans. Robin Hard [Oxford: Oxford University Press, 1997], 31.) The story is retold by Conti: see Natale Conti, *Mythologie,* trans. Jean de Montlyard (A. Lyon: Chez Paul Frelon, 1600), 294. For theoretical reflections on the feminists on the feminist implications of the myth of Metis see Lillian Eileen Doherty, *Siren Songs: Gender, Audiences, and Narrators in the Odyssey* (Ann Arbor: University of Michigan Press, 1995), 1–8.

28.   The concept of *mêtis,* and the distinction between the gods in the Greek pantheon who are distinguished by *mêtis* and those who are not, are discussed in Norman Oliver Brown, *Hermes the Thief: The Evolution of a Myth* (Madison: University of Wisconsin Press, 1947), 62–65 and in Detienne and Vernant, 1–23, 279–318.

29.   The relationship between the queen and the literature of the late sixteenth century, particularly Spenser's poetry, is variously and influentially discussed by

Parker; Phillippa Berry, *Of Chastity and Power: Elizabethan Literature and the Unmarried Queen* (New York: Routledge, 1989), 134–65; Katherine Eggert, *Showing Like a Queen: Female Authority and Literary Experiment in Spenser, Shakespeare, and Milton* (Philadelphia: University of Pennsylvania Press, 2000), 1–50; Susan Frye, *Elizabeth I: The Competition for Representation* (New York: Oxford University Press, 1993), 97–147; and a series of articles by Louis Montrose, particularly, "Spenser and the Elizabethan Political Imaginary," " 'Eliza, Queene of Shepheardes,' and the Pastoral of Power," *English Literary Renaissance* 10 (1980), and "The Elizabethan Subject and the Spenserian Text," in *Literary Theory/Renaissance Texts,* ed. Patricia Parker and David Quint (Baltimore: Johns Hopkins University Press, 1986).

30. Parker, 60.

31. On Elizabethan court spectacle and ceremony as strategies of maintaining power, see Berry, 61–110; Susan Frye, 22–96; Richard Helgerson, "Tasso on Spenser: The Politics of Chivalric Romance," *Yearbook of English Studies* 21 (1991); and Frances Yates, *Astraea: The Imperial Theme in the Sixteenth Century* (London: Routledge & Kegan Paul, 1975).

32. See especially Parker and Montrose, "Spenser and the Elizabethan Political Imaginary," 927–33.

33. The classic discussion of Guyon's destruction of the Bower is Stephen Greenblatt, *Renaissance Self-Fashioning: From More to Shakespeare* (Chicago: University of Chicago Press, 1980), 157–92.

34. On the collision of epic and romance in the Bower, see Watkins, 135–43, and Krier, 99–112. Montrose discusses the political implications of Guyon's destruction in terms of anti-court satire (see Montrose, "Spenser and the Elizabethan Political Imaginary," 929).

35. Harry Berger, Jr., "Wring Out the Old: Squeezing the Text, 1951–2001," *Spenser Studies* 18 (2003), 89.

36. Berger, 87.

37. On the characteristics of romance gardens see Giamatti and Nohrnberg, 490–519.

38. All citations are from *The Faerie Queene,* ed. A. C. Hamilton (New York: Longman, 2001).

39. Nohrnberg, 507. For a thorough treatment of the *paragone* of art and nature, along with the problem of mimetic illusion, see Dundas, *The Spider and the Bee,* 34–63.

40. Condemnations of the aesthetic excess in the Bower of Bliss are traditional: see for instance Giamatti, 258–90; Lewis, 324–33; and Nohrnberg, 504–12. More recently, scholars have been inclined to acknowledge Spenser's uneasiness in destroying his aesthetically gorgeous Bower; see for instance Krier, 112 and Madelon Sprengnether Gohlke, "Embattles Allegory: Book II of *The Faerie Queene,*" *English Literary Renaissance* 8 (1978).

41. Allen, 32–35; Eric Brown, 262–63; and Court, 7–8.

42. The striving of human art to imitate and surpass nature is a commonplace of classical poetics—see for instance, Horace's *Ars poetica* lines 408–11; in the *Ars Amatoria,* Ovid famously writes, "ars est celare artem" (II.313), a concept that will find its courtly analogue in Castiglione's ideal of *sprezzatura,* also an attempt to make art look natural.

43.   Detienne and Vernant, 21.

44.   Montrose comments on Belphoebe's critique of the court, which he argues, is a critique of Elizabeth's court—see "Spenser and the Elizabethan Political Imaginary," pp. 924, 927; for the argument that the Bower of Bliss is a representation of Elizabeth's court see pp. 927–29. More interestingly, he also notes Timaeus's reference to Belphoebe's "bowre of blis" in Book III.v (927), which retrospectively links Belphoebe with Acrasia.

45.   Parker suggests that the Bower, as a *hortus conclusus,* alludes to the female body itself—and this is especially true of the Gardens of Adonis in Book III (59–59). A traditional symbol of the Virgin Mary, the *hortus conclusus* was transformed into one of the iconographical attributes of Elizabeth, the Virgin Queen, by the mid-1580s (see Stanley Stewart, *The Enclosed Garden: The Tradition and the Image in Seventeenth Century Poetry* [Madison: University of Wisconsin Press, 1966], 31–59, Roy Strong, *The Renaissance Garden in England* [London: Thames and Hudson, 1979], 32 and Sarah Van der Laan, "Treading the Maze: The Labyrinth as an Image of Court and Courtiership in Elizabethan England" [Unpublished MA Thesis, Queen Mary College, University of London, 2002], 10–11).

46.   Van der Laan, 11. On the rhetoric of courtship and courtiership in the Elizabethan court, see Catherine Bates, *The Rhetoric of Courtship in Elizabethan Language and Literature* (Cambridge: Cambridge University Press, 1992).

47.   For a discussion of the symbolic political function of these gardens see Strong, *The Renaissance Garden in England* and Van der Laan, 19–37. See also Michael Leslie, "Spenser, Sidney, and the Renaissance Garden," *English Literary Renaissance* 22, no. 1 (1992).

48.   Montrose emphasizes the resemblance between Theobalds and the Bower of Bliss, particularly in terms of the contention between art and nature in "Spenser and the Elizabethan Political Imaginary," 927–29. See also Strong, *The Renaissance Garden in England,* 56, and Van der Laan, 26–27.

49.   All citations from *Muiopotmos* are from Edmund Spenser, *The Yale Edition of the Shorter Poems of Edmund Spenser,* ed. William A. Oram et al. (New Haven: Yale University Press, 1989).

50.   In Ovid's *Metamorphoses,* the tapestry contest between Minerva and Arachne is also a political allegory: Arachne depicts the crimes of the gods, while Minerva shows the gods punishing mortals who overreach themselves. On the parallels for Elizabethan politics see Brinkley, 670–74.

51.   Montrose, "Spenser and the Elizabethan Political Imaginary," 930.

52.   Victor Klarwill, ed., *Queen Elizabeth and Some Foreigners Being a Series of Hitherto Unpublished Letters from the Archives of the Hapsburg Family* (London: John Lane, 1928), 394. Montrose discusses this passage in the context of Acrasia; see note 51 above.

53.   I am grateful to David Quint for bringing this point to my attention. Significantly, there is no such slippage in the transition from Arachne's metamorphosis into a spider to Aragnoll's rage (see lines 353–55).

54.   The sexualized analogy between flowers and women is underlined by the inset myth of Astery who has been collecting flowers when she is transformed into a butterfly by Venus on the suspicion that Cupid "did lend her secret aid."

55.   "Muiopotmos," lines 1–3; *Iliad,* I.1–7. Citations from the *Iliad* are from Homer, *Iliad,* trans. Richmond Lattimore (Chicago: University of Chicago Press, 1962).

56. "Muiopotmos," lines 438–40; *Aeneid* XII.1296–98. Citations from the *Aeneid* are from Virgil, *Aenied,* trans. Robert Fitzgerald (New York: Random House, 1983).

57. Such an analysis of the conflicting pressures of epic and romance as they are parodied in "Muiopotmos" suggests a deliberate inversion of traditional epic practice, where epic teleology overcomes romance deviance; on the political uses of epic and romance, see Quint, *Epic and Empire,* especially pp. 9–10, 248–53, 302–08.

58. Citations from the *Metamorphoses* are from Ovid, *Metamorphoses,* trans. Rolfe Humphries (Bloomington: Indiana University Press, 1955).

59. Within the *Odyssey* itself, the entrapping bed of Aphrodite overlaid with the golden net is emblematic of the many dangerous beds in the poem—those of Calypso, Circe, Helen and finally the test of the bed with which Penelope will satisfactorily establish the identity of Odysseus. On the symbol of the bed in the *Odyssey,* see Zeitlin, 19–52.

EMILY A. BERNHARD JACKSON

"Ah, who can love the worker of her smart?": Anatomy, Religion, and the Puzzle of Amoret's Heart

Amoret participates in the Masque of Cupid with her heart removed from her chest, pierced, and held in a basin before her. The apparent cruelty of this treatment is, in fact, based in Early Modern beliefs about the role of the heart as seat of the emotions, the notion of bleeding as a way of correcting humoral imbalances, and the heart as religious symbol. When Amoret's plight is reconsidered in light of these beliefs, both Busirane's cruelty and the masque itself take on new meaning Contemporaries would have found Busirane's machinations comprehensible, indeed plausible. In light of these historical considerations, the masque deserves reassessment. This reassessment in its turn sheds light upon the masque's relationship to the larger theme of the cantos that surround it.

*A*MORET IS PERHAPS the most abused of all the women in *The Faerie Queene*. Taken captive not once, nor twice, but three times, narrowly escaping rape, she is repeatedly wounded both physically and emotionally: her sufferings are so complete that they endanger even "her tender toes" (IV, vii, 21, 9).[1] None of her travails, however, rivals the sadism and strangeness of her captivity in Castle Busirane. Her chest cracked open and her pierced heart displayed in a basin before her, Amoret remains a mystery. But Amoret's heart and Busirane's

---

Spenser Studies: A Renaissance Poetry Annual, Volume XX, Copyright © 2005 by AMS Press, Inc. All rights reserved.

abuse of it have their bases in canonical Renaissance medical and religious beliefs. Placing Amoret's heart in its historical context begins to solve the riddle of the Masque of Cupid and the perverse puzzles lodged in Castle Busirane.

Both the masque and Amoret's role in it have been the subjects of intense ongoing critical investigation. The more canonical explanation is a psychoanalytic one, which posits the entire performance as a projection of Amoret's own psyche. More recent work uses feminist and other theoretical approaches.[2] Few if any critics, however, pay sufficient attention to Amoret's actual physical heart, its presentation and possible deeper significance. Recent works on Renaissance medicine and anatomy as well as Christian iconography and anatomical symbolism open the way to a full examination of what meanings Amoret's exposed heart would have held for Spenser and his audience, and how this most puzzling episode ties into the larger theme of the cantos that surround it.[3] Busirane, like all the objects and figures produced in his castle, is a representation not of fear rooted in a specific mind, as critics have argued,[4] but of the general threat at the heart of Book III, that of love distorted or abused.

The human heart attained a position of great importance in the Galenic medical beliefs that predominated during the late sixteenth century.[5] Along with the brain and the liver, it was one of the three controlling loci of the body and emotions. While the brain governed intellect and motion and the liver the sexual impulses, the heart was responsible for regulation of the emotions and passions. These "passions" should be understood as related to but different from physical desire: the lustful liver was responsible for the physical arousal that culminated in actual sexual intercourse, but the heart was certainly the seat of the originating *eros* that led to such arousal. Although not directly sexual, it was intimately necessary to sexual desire, because it was necessary to love in all its forms.[6] Timothy Bright, writing in 1586, calls it "the seate . . . of affections, and perturbations of love, or hate, like, or dislike; of such things as fall within the compasse of sense; either outward, or inward; in effect, or imagination onely (he describes the liver as the seat of lust of propagation)[7] Just as we identify the heart with love, loneliness, longing, and emotional pain—"matters of the heart"—so the Renaissance reader, conditioned by a long line of associations stretching backward to the medieval period and earlier, did the same.[8]

Furthermore, the heart was to a large extent considered the primum mobile, first among anatomical equals. In his *Profitable Treatise of the Anatomie of Mans Body* (1577), Thomas Vicary affirms that:

"[The] Hart . . . is the principal of al other members, and the beginning of life . . . .So are al other members of the body subjectes to the
Hart, for they receyve their living of him . . . [He] geveth to every
member of the body both blood of life, and spirite of breath and
heate." In *The Anatomy of Melancholy* (1621) Robert Burton concurs
with Vicary: "the *Heart* . . . is the seat and fountaine of life, of heat,
of spirits, of pulse and respiration, the Sonne of our body, the king
and sole commander of it: The seat and organe of all passions and
affections, a part worthy of admiration, that can yeeld such variety
of affections, by whose motion he is dilated or contracted, to stirre
and command the humours in the body."[9] As Robert Erickson puts it,

> By the early modern period, the word heart had come to mean
> a variety of things: the center of all vital functions, the source
> of one's inmost thoughts and secret feelings or one's inmost
> being, the seat of courage and the emotions generally, the essen-
> tial, innermost, or central part of anything, the source of desire,
> volition, truth, understanding, intellect, ethics, spirit. *It was the
> single most important word referring both to the body and the mind.*[10]

Thus, when Amoret appears in the Masque of Cupid, her
"trembling hart . . . drawne forth, and in a siluer basin layd,/Quite
through transfixed with a deadly dart" (III, xii, 21), Spenser's readers
would not have seen a woman unable to "reconcile an inborn and
inbred conception of love as 'chaste affectione' . . . with her own
experience of sexual passion in the real world."[11] They would have
seen a woman with the center of her being, or at the very least the
seat of her love and desire, evicted from her body, and would have
recognized the operation as an attempt at alterations firmly grounded
in legitimate medical philosophies.[12] Busirane has literalized Galenic
theory to serve his own purposes, for if the heart is the "principall
of al other members, and the beginning of life," what surer way to
eradicate the passions and emotions of the old self than by removing
the heart? Galenism taken to its furthest extent would see such a
procedure as precisely what was necessary in order to change something as firm as fixed affection; Spenser confirms this when he tells his
audience that Busirane's "thousand charmes could not her [Amoret's]
steadfast heart remoue" (III, xii, 31, 9).[13]

Yet even the most benighted Galenist would have known that
complete removal of the heart causes death. What Spenser makes
Busirane attempt, therefore, are two somewhat less radical solutions.

The first is simple, although perhaps as ill-advised as his foray into amateur surgery. Amoret's heart, as the poet describes, is "drawne forth, and in a siluer basin layd." This curious detail becomes clearer when viewed through the prism of etymology. The *Oxford English Dictionary* defines "basin" as a "hollow circular vessel," then specifies, "circular vessel of greater width than depth, with sloping or curving sides, used for holding water and other liquids, especially for washing purposes."[14] Given the particularity of the word, especially if one considers the number of other possible terms the rhythm would comfortably allow ("salver" or "platter," for example), "basin" seems intended to give rise to the image which it does, in fact, produce: that Amoret's heart is presented and prepared for an actual cleansing. Drawn from her body but not severed from it, placed in a vessel designed for the purpose, it awaits an alteration by lavage.

Whereas Busirane's attempt at heart-cleaning is implied, his second solution to Amoret's steadfastness is made obvious within the text. As she participates in the Masque of Cupid, Amoret's heart lies "in her blood yet steeming fresh embayd." Later, when Britomart enters the inner room, she sees Amoret "With liuing bloud . . . /Dreadfully dropping from her . . . " (III, xii, 21, 4; 31, 3–4). However clumsily or brutally, Busirane is bleeding Amoret dry. In so doing, he is following accurately, although perhaps not temperately, the tenets of humoral theory.

Humoral theory was the single most commonly employed component of Galenic medicine, integral to Renaissance understanding and treatment of the body and its workings. It offered a simple resolution for physical and emotional ailments: they were all caused by imbalances of the four humors. Although none of these humors (black bile, yellow bile, phlegm, and blood) was seen as bad in itself, excess of any one was thought to be the root cause of all disease, with different humoral excesses resulting in different illnesses. There were an array of possible cures for humoral imbalances, ranging from change of diet and/or ingestion of medicines and simples to what would now be thought of as more psychological remedies: sniffing perfume, listening to music, or changing one's situation (for example, one cure for melancholy was to expose the patient to mirth, often in the form of merry women). If the illness, and thus its generative imbalance, proved immune to such prescriptions or was judged extreme enough, the patient's blood had to be relieved of some of the offending humor: bloodletting was required.[15] Because blood was not yet thought to circulate (that would have to wait for another forty years and William Harvey), this extraction was understood to reduce humoral excess that would not be replaced, rather than to empty a vein or body part which would quickly fill with blood again.

Phlebotomy was a tense business at the best of times. Normally accomplished by venesection (slitting open a vein) in the arm, it could also be performed using leeches, or by the two in combination. Instructions for bleeding were often scrupulously precise; in *De vita libri tres* (1489), for example, Marsilio Ficino offers meticulous guidance for phlebotomizing "litteratis"—the learned:

> Solum vero ubi abundantiam sanguinis indicat vel profusior risus audaciaque et confidentia multa vel color rubens venarumque tumor, mittere sanguinem litteratis, quando res postulat, debemus e vena liensi sinistri brachii lata quadam incisione, quattuor uncias mane, vespere totidem. Deinde paucos post dies, saltem septem, ad sumum quattuordecim, tum frictione quadam asperiore, tum admotis hirudnibus, quas sanguisugas nominant, mariscas irritare, ut sanguinis unciae tres aut quattuor inde destilent. [16]

A skilled physician, taking all the particulars of the patient's condition and imbalance into account, could manage to draw blood painlessly. The intended end result was the siphoning off of the ill humors, with concomitant recovery of health and well-being. After oral medication, phlebotomy was the most popular form of medical treatment in the Renaissance (perhaps because the alternative was cauterization).[17]

Busirane, then, acts well within the limits of accepted medicine for his time, if not with the finesse of an accomplished doctor. Indeed, his procedure is close to perfectly logical. As Michael Schoenfeldt argues, "humoral theory encouraged . . . the careful maintenance of constitutional solubility . . . .Galenic medicine renders the obstructed body the source of mortal pathogens."[18] A body which was bled, and which was able to bleed freely, was a healthy body. Diagnosis was highly subjective, and treatment was at the physician's discretion (Indeed, Galen himself offers at least one piece of advice that, misconstrued, could have supported Busirane's actions: "Quod si vero aliquae illorum partes pravam sortitae sunt structuram, potissimum quae in thorace sunt, omnino eis celeriter sanguinem mittes[19]). Busirane, it can be argued, is simply attempting to bleed Amoret free of her excessive love for Scudamore. Certainly his strict adherence to medical logic makes him brutal to his patient (and does not excuse this brutality), but his action is grounded in contemporaneous medical practice. A fifteenth-century manuscript illustration actually depicts a physician, wielding what might well be called a "deadly" dart and bleeding a patient into a basin. Considering that there were "dire warnings about the damage unskilled phlebotomy could do, especially by inadvertently cutting an artery,"[20] it is worth taking a moment to see how different the Masque of Cupid might look if Busirane were an unskilled doctor rather than an evil sorcerer. His actions become not unfathomable tortures, but the canto's most immediate "ensamples" of love distorted and normality perverted.

In addition to bloodletting for specific medical purposes, general purifactory purging was recommended by Renaissance medical texts; bodies both male and female were thought to benefit from regular purges and "ventilation."[21] This emphasis on purging led to one of the contradictions so frequent in Renaissance medicine and thought. Because of menstruation, women were considered to have an advantage over men: their bad humors and other unpleasant physiological detritus were purged on a monthly basis, thus ensuring that they achieved by nature a cleanliness which men could only achieve by human intervention. Conversely, the very fact that menstruation occurred at all demonstrated that women were inherently fouler and more in need of such purification than men: their monthly purging was evidence that they were full of excess which needed to be purged. This inherent humoral imbalance meant that women were naturally emotionally unstable, their passions more in need of outside monitoring through male control. Not only this, but their physical softness and pliability meant that ill humors could travel faster and cause more, and more complete, damage.

> [A woman] cannot rule her passions, or bridle her disturbed affections, or stand against them with force of reason and judgement. . . . If any man desires a naturall reason for it, I answer him thus, that a womans flesh is loose, soft, and tender, so that the choler being kindled presently spreads all the body over, and causeth a sudden boyling of the blood about the heart. . . . I can find no neerer cause that can be imagined, than the venim and collection of humours that she every month heaps together and purgeth forth . . . ; For when she chanceth to be angry, as she will presently be, all that sink of humours being stirred fumeth, and runs through the body, so that the Heart and Brain are affected with . . . it, and the Spirits both vitall and animal, that serve those parts that are inflamed. . . . [Women] cannot rule their passions.[22]

This belief raises the fascinating possibility that Spenser, through Busirane, provides in his presentation of Amoret's bleeding heart a form of substitute or additional menstruation. Busirane attempts to regulate Amoret's unruly passion by purging her of "the venim and collection of humours" she unintentionally secretes within. By removing the "boyling of the blood about the heart," he seeks to relieve the "Heart and Brain . . . affected with . . . it, and the Spirits both vitall and animal, that serve those parts that are inflamed."

Equally plausible is the supposition that Busirane attempts his radical phlebotomy not as a substitute for menstruation but because of the condition menstruation presupposes. That is, he is aware that Amoret's femaleness puts her at the mercy of her emotions and seeks to regulate by phlebotomy what he sees as an imbalance in her passions (in this case, her love for Scudamore). Here again Busirane practices sound Galenic medicine, for the knowledgeable early modern physician was aware that, as Thomas Wright put it, "Passions cause many maladies, and wellnie all are increased by them." In fact, Wright himself warns of the possible dangers of too much love or pleasure: "if the Passion of pleasure be too vehement, questionlesse it causeth great infirmitie: for the heart being continually invironed with great abundance of spirit, becomes too hote and inflamed. . . . Besides, it dilateth and resolveth the substance of the heart too much; in such sort as the vertue and force thereof is greatly weakened."[23]

Of all the emotions that influenced the heart, however, none had so profound an effect as fear and sorrow. The fearful body drew its blood inward, gathering it to the heart in order to assist that beleaguered organ:

> fear . . . maketh the mind which conceiveth it to startle, and looking about for meanes of defence, it calleth al the bloud into the innermost parts, specially to the heart . . . ; whereby the exterior parts being abandoned and deprived of heate, and of that colour which it had from the bloud and the spirits, there remaineth nothing but palenesse. And hereof it cometh to passe that we see such men as are surprised with feare, to be not only pale, but to tremble also . . . [24]

Amoret, with her breast "as net iuory" and her "trembling hart" (III, xii, 20, 1; 21, 1), is the paradigm of fearfulness, and thus Busirane's medical intervention is both more logical and more brutal. Capitalizing on her heart's blood-suffused state, he can achieve the greatest extraction with the greatest efficiency. Interestingly, the question of how much blood to extract was a contested one. Although practitioners who bled patients profusely at one sitting were frowned upon by many medical writers (Simon Harward, for one, declared firmly that "it is dangerous to avoyd too much bloud at once," not least since it risked "swounings"[25]), copious purging, even of people who did not display the preferred ruddy plumpness, was often considered valid and could yield great success.[26] In this way too, then, Busirane's actions draw upon conventional Renaissance medicine.

This is by no means to be taken as a suggestion that Busirane should be viewed positively rather than negatively. Spenser labels him "vile" (III, xii, 31), and Busirane's brutality is apparent: he cares nothing for Amoret's comfort or wellbeing; indeed, the very notion of him doing so seems ludicrous. He is an exemplar of cruelty. What is now apparent, however, is that this cruelty is not arcane or even necessarily allegorical. It is based on sound contemporaneous medical belief, and Busirane's ruthlessness lies in his application of theoretical medical knowledge without regard for anything but achievement of his own goal. He will make Amoret love him, no matter how much pain he must inflict upon her.[27]

By using bloodletting to alter not only Amoret's humors but her very self, Busirane exploits another concept of Renaissance medicine, just as integral to the early modern concept of humanity: pneuma. Pneuma, variously described as or conflated with "innate heat," "breath of life," and "spirit," is the soul's emanation, and its chief instrument in the body.[28] Pneuma is not inherent in the body but results from a mysterious, almost mystical, mixing of matters gathered from both within and without the individual. It derives from matter infinitely refined, present in the outside air and inhaled into the lungs. This mixes in the heart with thin hot blood, producing "vital pneuma." This blood, now rich with "vital spirit," travels via the arteries to all parts of the body.

For the Renaissance subject life and self could not exist without pneuma. In *Mikrokosmographia* (1615), Helkiah Crooke explains that

> [t]his spirit whilest it shineth in his brightnes and spredeth it self through all the Theater of the body as the Sunne over the earth, it blesseth all partes with joy and jolitie and dies them with a Rosie colour . . . . . So wonderfull and almost so heavenly are the powers of the heat and spirit, that the divine *Senior Hippocrates* . . . calleth it the Soule.

If the presence of pneuma brought warmth and color, its absence or diminution produced exactly the opposite result. Crooke goes on to state that "when it is retracted intercepted or extinguished, all things become horred wanne and pale and finally doe utterly perish."[29] This explanation helps to elucidate Spenser's description of Amoret as she participates in the Masque of Cupid.

> She dolefull Lady, like a dreary Spright,
>> Cald by strong charmes out of eternall night,
>> Had deathes own image figurd in her face,
>> Full of sad signes, fearefull to liuing sight; . . . .

> Her breast all naked, as net iuory,
>> Without adorne of gold or siluer bright,
>> Wherewith the Craftesman wonts it beautify,
>> Of her dew honour was despoiled quight,
>> And a wide wound therein (O ruefull sight)
>> Entrenched deepe with knife accursed keene,
>> Yet freshly breeding forth her fainting spright,
>> (The work of a cruell hand) was to be sene,
> That dyde in sanguine red her skin all snowy cleene.
>
>   (III, xii, 19–20)

Amoret becomes a dark parodic version of that Petrarchan ideal, the "red and white" lady.[30] She is red and white not because of Petrarchan requirements, however, but because her pale skin, rendered thus by Busirane's bleedings, is being stained by the blood he is draining as it drips over her breast: "That dyde in sanguine red her skin all snowy cleene." She is being deprived of her vital pneuma, that blood so thin and refined that it can be used as ink when it bleeds from the heart which produces it. She has "deathes own image figurd in her face" because she is dying. Without the pneuma which Busirane is extracting she will, Spenser's contemporaries know, "utterly perish." The adorning craftsman here may be not only an artisan who supplies necklaces and other gewgaws, but "*the* Craftesman": God, who adorns the skin with bright color via pneuma.

Sly warlock that he is, Busirane knows that this pneumic blood, which Spenser so significantly describes as "living," is the blood to use to work his charms.

And her before the vile Enchaunter sate,

Figuring straunge characters of his art,
With liuing blood he those characters wrate,
Dreadfully dropping from her dying hart . . .

(III, xii, 31, 1–4)

Bleeding the essence out of Amoret, Busirane "figures" her a new "character" from that very essence—not "character" in our modern sense of "personality," but rather "characters" in the sense of writing: Busirane is attempting to write a new Amoret. He seeks to create her new life out of the vital force of her old life, manipulating and mastering that force to suit his needs. By writing her anew with her own pneuma he ensures that his enchanted Amoret will be the true one. In a curious way, Busirane may be the poem's most accurate representation of an allegorizing author, for his characters are literally alive.

The significant etymological vagaries inherent in the "spright" that Busirane extracts from Amoret should not be overlooked here. Although the *OED*'s primary definition of the word is indeed as a noun meaning "spirit," its secondary definition is as a verb meaning "to invest with spirit," a late medieval definition not lost by 1590.[31] Like a palimpsest, Spenser's word has shadowed beneath it the understanding that in his attempts to remove her present spirit Busirane also seeks to invest Amoret with a new one. With the loss of one spright he supplies another. Busirane does not attempt merely to enchant Amoret; he wants to devise an entirely new Amoret, the same in body but more amenable in spirit: a sort of truer False Florimell.

Notions of Busirane as man of letters as well as medical practitioner attain deeper resonance when one considers the heart's place in Renaissance (and contemporary) symbolism, as the representation of love ne plus ultra. Richard Mallette and a number of other scholars suggest that the fractious Scudamore may be seen as a parody of the Petrarchan lover, but that label need not be applied to him alone. Busirane can be seen as a more darkly parodic, extreme version of that lover, Petrarchan formality actualized in an anatomist (blazoner?) of brutal accuracy: "My true love hath my heart and I have his" made real. A. Kent Hieatt argues that Busirane is "an element in Scudamour himself," and, indeed, he is an element in any lover, insofar as all love, even love in the formalized world of courtly poetry and wooing, contains within it (as Hieatt also proposes) the potential for and seeds of domination.[32] In a neat conflation of the actual and the allegorical, Spenser has Busirane work that domination upon an organ that is itself both an actual medical metonymy and an allegorical metonymy for love.

In addition to the medical beliefs informing the masque, there is another possible cultural influence upon this episode, for connections between heart and blood and life and spirit did not affect Renaissance medicine alone. The concept of the heart as the seat of the passions, and of the blood it produced as an outpouring of the self, also informed early modern religious beliefs and iconography. Most simply, the heart was considered the source of all the religious passions and also the true measure of a human.[33] 1 Samuel 16:7 says, "for **God seeth** not as man seeth: for man looketh on the outward appearance, but the Lorde beholdeth the heart."[34] Just as the heart was able to be known, so was it able to know. In the Christian faiths the heart possessed the perceptive powers of a conscience: "The heart could on some level compete with the brain as a locus of perception through its ability to see things unseen."[35] Most significantly, the heart could be cleansed and cleared by religious faith. Jesus could enter a heart and literally expel all previous threats and enemies to spiritual life, a process that was figured concretely at this period. Anton Wiericx's *Cor Iesu amanti sacrum*, a religious emblem book published slightly later than *The Faerie Queene*, depicts just this process. The infant Jesus, armed with a broom and a cheerfully determined expression, brushes the heart clean of all its contaminating matter, which bleeds out in a cascade from the bottom (fig. 1).[36] In what is believed to be the first book of Protestant sacred emblems, Georgette de Montenay's *Emblemes, ou Devises Chrestiennes* (1571), emblem 81 displays a man proffering his heart heavenward in a dish, with God pouring liquid (Christ's blood, intended to act as "new blood" for the heart) over it (fig. 2). The similarity to Busirane's torture of Amoret is obvious.[37]

Indeed, Protestant doctrine in this period held that God could act upon the heart from without, grace alone working to alter the sinner without his or her cooperation. Barbara Lewalski draws attention to the speaker of Herbert's "Love Unknown" (admittedly a later work than *The Faerie Queene*), who is not a willing partner in working changes upon his heart, but rather is disturbed by the alterations worked by "a lord whose actions seem bizarre and even strange."[38] This vision of God as most powerful, a seemingly brutal force that in fact acts for the benefit of his "victim," resonates in Busirane's actions. As with his phlebotomy, for Spenser's audience the horror of what Busirane does would have lain not in the action itself, but in his distortion of the accepted thinking that lay behind it.

As well as the mortal heart, the iconic symbology of the divine heart, in the form of the Sacred Heart, may have significance here.

Fig. 1. "Jesus Purging a Heart," woodcut by Antonius Wiericx, from Peter Konig, *Das Hertz Jesu welches Liebhaber Heillig macht* (1625); Rare Book, Manuscript and Special Collections Library, Duke University.

Fig. 2. Emblem 81, from Georgette de Montenay, *Emblemes, ou De-vises Chrestiennes* (Lyons, 1571), f.Z[1ʳ]. The verse reads:

Not without reason the Lord bestows
Blessedness on one who is heart–pure,
But mark well that heaven spreads
The water that cleanses it, removing stain and foulness.
That which so cleanses is the spirit of the Lord
In the blood of Christ, which alone regenerates us,
Reforms, and make us to be of good odor
To God through Christ, which no other could have done.

Type 515 71.579, Department of Printing and Graphic Arts, Houghton Library, Harvard College Library.

This is, however, a more vexed issue. Although the icon was known during the sixteenth century, it is difficult to determine how widely its familiarity and veneration had spread. In the Catholic church, the introduction in 1354 of the Feast of the Lance led to a burgeoning cult surrounding Christ's five wounds and the Sacred Heart (Christ's heart having been pierced with the "holy lance"). Early English Protestant emblem books were frequently simply revisions of Catholic collections—same emblems, different text—and Jesuit meditation books, a product of the Counter-Reformation, began making their way into England by the end of the sixteenth century. Unquestionably, veneration of the Sacred Heart was common enough in seventeenth-century England for the symbol to be depicted in emblem books.[39] The Sacred Heart, then, would have been familiar to Spenser and also to his readers; adoration made inroads even among Protestants whose faith transcended the church to link with Christian mystical traditions, "par le mécanisme bien connu des visions inspirées plus ou moins inconsciemment par des images enregistrées dans la mémoire."[40]

While the Sacred Heart was primarily a Catholic emblem in this period, as it remains today, the boundary between Catholic and Protestant remained porous—indeed, in some cases Catholic traditions were simply kept alongside, or absorbed into, the Protestantism Elizabeth reinstated, taking decades to die out.[41] Moreover, Spenser's eclecticism in his symbolic and religious borrowings elsewhere means we cannot dismiss this symbol's significance here out of hand. Although it is unlikely that he intended any direct correspondence between Amoret and Christ, it is not unreasonable to suggest some undertones for this scene. Amoret's heart is not the Sacred Heart, but certainly the symbolic resonance of that Heart, figuration of Christ's supreme sacrifice and love for man, has bearing on her sufferings. To sixteenth-century Christians, Christ's heart was not simply a metaphor for his soul; it was a visceral reification of his fleshly, mortal body, and thus of his fleshly, mortal sufferings.[42] Amoret's perforated heart is the textual equivalent of the pierced Sacred Heart, in many cases rendered with an almost clinical physiological precision, that features in religious iconography of the period (fig. 3).[43] Spenser points up the relationship between Amoret's heart and the Sacred Heart when he has Scudamore explain to Britomart that

My Lady and my loue is cruelly pend
    In dolefull darkenesse from the vew of day,
    Whilest deadly torments do her chaste brest rend,

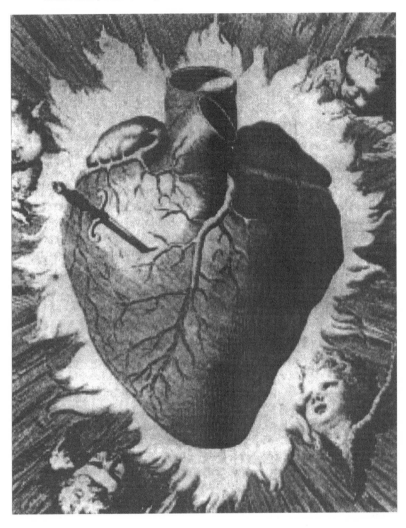

Fig. 3. Anonymous print (1685); Bibliothèque nationale de France.

And the sharpe steele doth riue her heart in tway,
All for she *Scudamore* will not denay.
Yet thou vile man, vile *Scudamore* art sound, . . .
For whome so faire a Lady feeles so sore a wound.

(III, ix, 11)[44]

Amoret's determination to remain steadfast in her faithful love for
Scudamore is indeed her primary motive for withstanding Busirane,
but one hears the ringing of church bells in the ambiguous phrase
"vile Scudamore . . . /For whome so faire a Lady feeles so sore a
wound." Amoret so loves Scudamore that she gives her only begotten
heart for that love, and her willingness to bear and withstand extreme
suffering is both a demonstration of her steadfast love and a means
of proving it.[45]

But another, less commonly known, religious image comes into
play here as well. Amidst the welter of symbols and significances
connected to the Madonna is The Immaculate Heart of Mary. This
heart traces its roots back to Luke 2:35, in which Simeon prophesies
to Mary that her "**childe** is appointed for the fal and rising againe
of many in Israel, and for a signe which shal be spoken against, (Yea
and a sworde shall pearce through thy soule) that the thoughtes of
many heartes may be opened.[46] It is usually pictured as a heart pierced
through by either one or seven swords. The prophecy, with its accompanying symbol, numbers among the Seven Sorrows of Mary
(hence the second number of swords). While it is tempting to figure
Amoret as linked to Christ, it is perhaps more plausible to connect
her with the Virgin.[47] This connection is strengthened by the number
of the sorrows, which of course coincides precisely with the months
of Amoret's captivity. This number can be explained, by analogy, as
The Seven Sorrows of Amoret: like Mary, Amoret suffers through
no will or desire of her own, but with no apparent regret for those
sufferings.[48] Again, one should be wary of reading one-to-one correspondence here, but, again, undertones sound loudly. Amoret is not
a parallel to the Virgin Mary, but the circumstances of her suffering,
her own chastity, and the length of her imprisonment strongly suggest
a link between the two.

Both the medical and religious significations of the heart achieve
greater import when considered in light of Busirane's own derivation
from an Egyptian priest named Busiris in the *Ars Amatoria*. Roche
gives the source story from Ovid:

Egypt is said to have lacked the rains that bless its fields, and to
have been parched for nine years, when Thrasius approached

Busiris, and showed that Jove could be propitiated by the out-
poured blood of a stranger. To him said Busiris, "Thou shalt be
Jove's first victim, and as a stranger give water to Egypt . . . ."[49]

Busirane's identity is based in a story in which the religious concept
of suffering for the good of others perversely mingles with the medical
concept of blood as conduit of life. Further, inherent in that story is
an understanding that the Gods may be propitiated, and circumstances may be changed for the better, by bloodshed that is intimate
and personal (as opposed to the impersonal slaughter of war).[50]

II.

With these historical underpinnings near to hand, it is worth reexamining the Masque of Cupid and its relationship to the larger themes
of Cantos xi and xii. Viewing Busirane and his enchantments not as
transcendentally maleficent but rather as firmly grounded in what
were accepted beliefs during the Renaissance, one may look over
the masque and its related occurrences from a different vantage point.
To begin with, one notices that Amoret's imprisonment in Castle
Busirane is only one of a number of her kidnappings by men. In
addition to Busirane, she is captured both by Lust in Book IV, Canto
vii, and by Scudamore himself (IV, x, 54–58). Indeed, in moving
from Scudamore to Busirane Amoret merely steps from one captivity
to another, albeit that when she is seized by Scudamore her tears at
least mingle with "witching smyles" (IV, x, 57, 3).[51] Kathleen Williams acknowledges this parallel when she writes that "Scudamore
sees his winning of Amoret as a conquest—the word is used in the
quotation prefacing Canto x and is implicit in the whole perilous
enterprise . . . .Scudamore is a devotee of the destructive Cupid of
the world," the same Cupid whose "warres" decorate Busirane's
tapestries (III, xi, 29, 5).[52] Busirane, one can argue, simply mirrors
Scudamore's successful capture in his own unsuccessful attempt, and
a mere change of connective prompts the reader's squeamishness:
where Scudamore captures Amoret's heart *and* her body, Busirane
tries to capture Amoret's heart *through* her body.

In fact, this brutality, and its asymptotic relationship to the delights
of love, is clearly prefigured in what Britomart beholds at Castle
Busirane before she sees the masque. Everything in this larger episode, from her encounter with Scudamore in mid-mourning to the

"warlike spoiles" on the walls of the inner antechamber (III, xi, 52, 2) emphasizes a perversion of love of which Busirane's machinations are the culmination. This warping, gradually but inexorably manifested, first shows itself, as Williams's remark suggests, in the figure of the wailing Scudamore. His "wallowing on the ground," as Mallette calls it, does indeed mark him out as a satire of the Petrarchan suitor,[53] but this inability to control his passion, as well as his cries to God for vengeance (III, xi, 9–11), also hint at the connection between violence and love that becomes progressively stronger, and progressively more real, as Cantos xi and xii proceed. Inside Castle Busirane, the "greedy will and enuious desire, . . . /threatfull pride" (III, xi, 26, 3–6) that keep Scudamore from penetrating its surrounding wall of fire find clearer expression.

Given the wealth of critical material on the subject, it seems redundant to chart the theme of love's brutality as presented in the antechambers Britomart moves through and examines in the Castle.[54] What does bear consideration, however, is the progression of the manifestations of that theme, a progression itself foreshadowed in Spenser's "introductory" stanza, with its smooth, swift movement from pleasure to destruction, from formal grace to vicious rout:

> And in those Tapets were fashioned
> Many faire pourtraicts, and many a faire feate,
> And all of loue, and all of lusty-hed,
> As seemed by their semblaunt did entreat;
> And eke all *Cupids* warres they did repeate,
> And cruell battles, which he whilome fought
> Gainst all the Gods, to make his empire great;
> Besides the huge massacres, which he wrought
> On mighty kings and kesars, into thraldome brought.
>
> (III, xi, 29)

What begins "faire"ly ends with massacre, a speedy progression from fashion and courtly feats to mayhem. In this Castle, love is about mastery, in all senses of that word, and the final form of love is "thraldome," an echo and a presage of Busirane's cruel penning of Amoret.

While the tapestries chart this progression in their depictions, moving through a series of ever-more violent kidnappings, deaths, and woundings to culminate in a "long bloudy river" (III, xi, 46, 8), the means of representation itself also progresses, first as the tapestries defy their form to depict changing time and circumstance (as when they show the Shepherds' "often" calling to Ganymede in III, xi, 34, 9), and then when the artistic medium itself changes from cloth to stone. The reification of perverted love takes yet another step forward with the golden statue of Cupid, both a symbol of brutal love with his "cruell fist/ . . . mortal bow and arrowes keene" and dominion over the blinded dragon of chastity,[55] and himself the object of perverted devotion: "And all the people in that ample hous/ Did to that image bow their humble knee/And oft committed fowle Idolatree" (III, xi, 48, 1–49 and 5). Spenser here presents an allegory, to be sure, but it is an allegory that marches closer and closer to the real world of the poem, love warped into mastery progressively moving from the realm of artistic representation to the realm of the actual. Furthermore, Spenser has again taken care to link Busirane's forthcoming abuses to the larger scene by repeated references not just to Cupid's own deadly darts but to the numerous breasts they have rent and pierced: "Therein [in the tapestries] was writ, how often thundering *Ioue*/Had felt the point of his heart-piercing dart"; "For priuy loue his [Neptune's] brest empierced had"; "There was he [Mars] painted full of burning darts,/And many wide woundes launched through his inner parts" (III, xi, 30, 1–2; 41, 8; 44, 8–9).[56] Thus, as love is represented as increasingly brutal, it is also continually knit to the culmination of that brutality, Busirane's manipulation of Amoret.

The final manifestation of this brutality preceding the masque is the inner antechamber with its gnomic lintel motto, "Be bold." In this room the outrage of warped love is laid out in all its destructive glory: "A thousand monstrous formes therein were made,/Such as false loue doth oft vpon him weare,/For loue in thousand monstrous formes doth oft appeare" (III, xi, 51, 7–9). Although these are forms "such as" false love often wears, it is significant that Spenser leaves unanswered the question of whether what Britomart beholds is false love or not; these are like the forms of false love, yet he reminds readers that love itself "doth oft appeare" in such guises. As with the actual manipulation of Amoret's heart, the suggestion here is that the line between sound and spurious is a fine one, and that the latter may well be a distorted version of the former, as false love is a dangerous twisting of true.

The masque itself abounds with images of captivity and mastery that echo those in the art and rooms that precede it. The first masquer after the prologue Ease, Fancy, "like a louely boy," is likened to both Ganymede and Hylas, each spirited away by a higher power (III, xii, 7).[57] Spenser thus subtly prefigures Amoret's fate even this early in the proceedings. Fancy is accompanied by "*Desyre,*/Who seemd of riper yeares, then th'other Swayne,/Yet was that other swayne this elders syre" (III, xii, 9, 1–3). The decline from light-hearted imagination and love to lust, depicted in the tapestries, is again emphasized here. Furthermore, "fancy['s]" alternate definitions during the period as "caprice, changeful mood," or "capricious or arbitrary preference,"[58] and Spenser's embedding of "sway" in "Swayne," give a hint both of the shaky nature of delight and of the hidden, but still threatening, might inherent in even the most ephemeral love. As if to emphasize this, the two figures are followed by Danger with his net, with which "he his friends ment to enwrap:/ For whom he could not kill he practizd to entrap" (thus is Busirane again foreshadowed). Later comes Dissemblance, peering from behind his lattice, and Grief with his heart-gripping pincers (III, xii, 11, 8–9; 15;16).

Just before Dissemblance, Hope and Fear appear together, she the very opposite of Amoret with "chearefulle look . . . louely to behold," but nonetheless suggestive of Amoret through the

> . . . holy water Sprinckle, dipt in deowe,
> With which she sprinckled fauours manifold,
> On whom she list, and did great liking sheowe,
> Great liking unto many, but true loue to feowe.
>
> (III, xii, 13, 6–9)

Like Amoret's blood, Hope's holy water favors those for whom she sheds it, and Hope, again like Amoret, is no cruel wanton but a courteous, chaste dame, willing to bestow her liking on many but withholding her love more carefully. She easily may be seen as a version of Amoret.

The appearance of Amoret herself, we now know, is not the appearance of a being undergoing preposterous tortures, but of a woman who is both medical patient and living religious icon. Equally, the two "villeins" who support her (III, xii, 19, 2) can be read as physician's assistants, or mourners at the cross, or—most temptingly, given Spenser's use of "villeins"—as two thieves. Busirane is a mockery of a doctor, consulting in his book "straunge characters of his art," or a priest. Like a doctor or priest, only he knows the secret lore which will return Amoret to her healthy state, and Spenser perhaps alludes to Amoret's heart and blood-as-ink when he tells readers not once but twice that Busirane "red" his enchantments from his book (III, xii, 36, 4,8).

This is not to say that Busirane should simply be reduced to a confused physician or an over-zealous curate. Spenser himself repeatedly tells readers that Busirane is an enchanter, and this fact cannot be written out of the text. What changes, however, is the view of his spells, and how they and Amoret's plight would have resounded in the ears of Spenser's audience. Contemporary readers would have recognized the references to phlebotomy, would have seen in Busirane's treatment of Amoret's heart and blood attempts to alter her life and self in ways that fit perfectly with then-current medical beliefs. Through the poet's suggestive connection of Amoret's sufferings with those of Mary and Christ, they would have understood not only the extent of her sacrifice but the depth of her love for and devotion to Scudamore. Busirane himself would not have been an irrational practitioner of incomprehensible acts, but rather a man attempting traditionally based procedures, albeit with cruelty and for selfish, indeed evil, purposes. This view links to and enhances the moral toward which the entire episode in Castle Busirane points: that false love such as Busirane's is not necessarily far from, or clearly distinct from, true love, and that the latter can easily tip and become the former. The similarities between Scudamore's Venus-sanctioned attainment of Amoret and Busirane's court-sanctioned capture of her—for he first makes off with her during the masque presented before the assembled guests on her wedding night (IV, I, 3)—stress this.[59]

The question not answered by this evidence, the situation not elucidated, is, For whom is the Masque of Cupid performed? Although Spenser does say about the castle's golden cupid, that "all the people in that ample house /Did to that image bow their humble knee" (III, xi, 49, 3–4), none of the putative inhabitants watch the masque, and even the curious mixture of singulars and plurals in the two lines suggest that there may be only one inhabitant. The show is performed while all in "silence and in sleepe themselues did shroud" (III, xii, 1, 4). Britomart herself observes from a hidden vantage point, "aside in sickernesse" (III, xi, 55, 8). Apparently Busirane performs the elaborate charade for no one, an aging impresario restaging his moment of glory to an empty house.

Yet there is someone who does not act in the masque, who views all of it, and who may well be the intended audience: Amoret. Coming as she does caught between the last of the two organized secondary characters, she can observe those who go before her, learning from their unpleasantness and poor alliances, given ample opportunity to rethink her own heart's choice. Bound to the pillar, she can see those who come after her and muse on the consequences of a poorly-considered union: "There were full many moe like maladies,/Whose names and natures I note readen well;/So many moe, as there be phantasies /In wavering wemens wit" (III, xii, 26, 1–4). Busirane has supplied her with a whirling cast of figures based on stock female fears.[60]

Significantly, the two allegorizations which precede Amoret in the Masque are Displeasure and Pleasance,

> He looking lompish and full sullein sad
> And hanging downe his heauy countenance;
> She chearefull fresh and full of ioyance glad,
> As if no sorrow she ne felt ne drad;
> That euill matched pair they seemd to be . . .
>
> (III, xii, 18, 2–6)

How better could an apparently ill-suited swain woo a maiden than by showing her such an unlikely success story? Spenser toys with the "seemd," leaving open the possibility that Displeasure and Pleasance are a successful match. To seem is not to be, and to say that a couple seems evil-matched is to suggest that appearance belies reality.

Finally, one should remember how Busirane first managed to kidnap Amoret. Plucking her from the audience, he installed her in the masque and spirited her away without attracting the notice of the crowd. The masque, then, is Busirane's one proven method for capturing Amoret: "By way of sport, as oft in maskes is knowen,/Conueyed quite away to liuing wight unknowen" (IV, I, 3, 8–9). His iterated performances of it are attempts to capture her more thoroughly and deeply by capturing her heart, as well. This final blandishment having failed, he moves on to his attempt to "refigure" her, this final cruelty aborted only by the arrival of Britomart, whose chastity and true love of Artegall are the antidote to Busirane's warped "maisterie."[61]

"Ah, who can love the worker of her smart?" Spenser asks near the end of Amoret's captivity (III, xii, 31, 8). The question is rhetorical, but any reader of the earlier cantos of Book III knows the answer: Britomart. She loves Artegall absent or present, unknown or known; she even "with self-pleasing thoughts her wound . . . fed" (III, iv, 6, 1). A Renaissance audience, steeped in Galenic medical tenets and practices and familiar with the religious iconography of a church not long abandoned, or not abandoned at all, would have known other answers as well. A patient whose humors needed to be balanced by her phlebotomist; a woman whose menstrual cycle, or lack of it, rendered her a sink of ill humors and iniquity desperately in need of forced purging; the Christ who died for man's sins; the Virgin who suffered for her Son: all loved the workers of their smarts. Such knowledge changes the tenor of the question, just as it changes the tenor of the episodes in Castle Busirane. Such a change, for its part, helps to unravel the most baffling episode in *The Faerie Queene*. Like the vile enchanter himself, readers can now begin to figure the strange characters of Busirane's art.[62]

Brandeis University

NOTES

1. All Spenser quotations are taken from the Penguin edition of *The Faerie Queene*, ed. Thomas P. Roche, Jr. (New York: Penguin, 1987). Subsequent reference is parenthetical.

2. See Thomas P. Roche, Jr.'s *The Kindly Flame* (Princeton: Princeton University Press, 1964). See also Mark Rose's *Heroic Love: Studies in Sidney and Spenser* (Cambridge: Harvard University Press, 1968), Helen Cheney Gilde, " 'The Sweet Lodge of Love and Deare Delight': The Problem of Amoret," *Philological Quarterly* 50 (1971): 63–74, Kathleen Williams, *Spenser's Faerie Queene: The World of Glass* (London: Routledge, 1966), and Gary Waller, *Edmund Spenser: A Literary Life* (New York: St. Martin's, 1994). More recent approaches, feminist and otherwise, of particular note are Lauren Silberman's *Transforming Desire: Erotic Knowledge in Books III and IV of* The Faerie Queene (Berkeley: University of California Press, 1996); Susanne Lindgren Wofford, "Gendering Allegory: Spenser's Bold Reader and the Emergence of Character in *The Faerie Queene* III," *Criticism* 30 (1988): 1–22; as well as relevant sections in Michael Schoenfeldt's *Bodies and Selves in Early Modern England: Physiology and Inwardness in Spenser, Shakespeare, Herbert, and Milton* (New York: Cambridge University Press, 1999), and Dorothy Stephens's *The Limits of Eroticism in Post-Petrarchan Narrative: Conditional Pleasure from Spenser to Marvell*, Cambridge Studies in Renaissance Literature and Culture 29 (New York: Cambridge University Press, 1998). Most of the earlier scholars follow a psychoanalytic interpretation, succinctly summed up by A. Leigh Deneef (who does not necessarily agree with it) in "Spenser's *Amor Fuggitivo* and the Transfixed Heart" *ELH* 46 (1979): "Busyrane is a psychic projection of Amoret's fear of male domination and the incident as a whole depicts the Triumph of Chastity succeeding the Triumph of Cupid" (20). I find this explanation unconvincing. While it would be reasonable to argue that Busirane and the Masque of Cupid are Amoret's projections if she alone views them, that is not the case here. Britomart watches the masque from her hiding place in Castle Busirane. Indeed, the masque is described from Britomart's point of view; Spenser states that "The noble Mayd . . . all this vewd" (III, xii, 5: 1). On the

question of who produces what in this episode, I throw in my interpretive lot with Judith Anderson, who argues that "Representation of this site [Castle Busirane] is finally the poet's, as are all the figures within it, though by now it goes almost without saying that the poet's control of the site, his agency with respect to it, is mediated, limited, and compromised by his own position in language and history" ("Busirane's Place: *The House of Rhetoric*," *Spenser Studies* 17 [2003]: 133–50).

3.   I refer here not only to Nancy Siraisi's *Medieval and Early Renaissance Medicine: An Introduction to Knowledge and Practice* (Chicago: University of Chicago Press, 1990), and F. David Hoeniger's *Medicine and Shakespeare in the English Renaissance* (Newark: University of Delaware Press, 1992), but also to the more recent *The Body in Parts: Fantasies of Corporeality in Early Modern Europe,* ed. David Hillman and Carla Mazzio. (New York: Routledge, 1997) and Robert Erickson's *The Language of the Heart, 1600–1750* (Philadelphia: University of Pennsylvania Press, 1997), which provides an excellent and thorough overview of the significance of the heart in the Renaissance.

4.   I refer here to the criticism I mentioned in note 2, but more specifically to the readings of Roche and Hieatt. Roche maintains that "[t]he mask that takes place at the House of Busyrane is Amoret's interpretation of the wedding mask," while Hieatt contends, "All, or almost all, the figures in the Masque exist in Amoret's imagination, but this imagination is one that bodies forth the real consequences of a certain course of action for a chaste woman to whom frivolous surrender has for the first time become a live option" (see Roche, *Kindly,* 72–95; Hieatt, *Chaucer,* 115–33).

5.   Although the ideas of Paracelsus had some impact during the sixteenth century, they never achieved parity with Galenism, which continued to be dominant. Galenism also continued to be widely re-disseminated: between 1500 and 1600, roughly 590 editions of Galen's works were published. See Hoeniger, *Medicine,* 71, and Andrew Wear, "Medicine in Early Modern Europe, 1500–1700," *The Western Medical Tradition 800 BC to AD 1800,* ed. Lawrence I. Conrad, et al. (New York: Cambridge University Press, 1995), 253.

6.   As Debora Shuger says, "[Renaissance] desire is . . . engendered in the eyes and dwells in the heart" ("Panel Discussion," *Renaissance Discourses of Desire,* ed. Ted-Larry Pebworth [Columbia: University of Missouri Press, 1993], 271–77). See also Erickson, *Language,* 4, as well as Scott Manning Stevens, "Sacred Heart and Secular Brain," *The Body in Parts: Fantasies of Corporeality in Early Modern Europe* (Cambridge: Harvard University Press), 263–82.

7.   Timothy Bright, *A Treatise of Melancholy* (London, 1586, rpt. New York: Columbia University Press, 1940), C[8[r]]. Here and elsewhere I normalize i, j, u, and v.

8.   Stevens, "Sacred," 271.

9.   Thomas Vicary, *Profitable Treatise of the Anatomie of Mans Body,* (London: 1577), H[4v]-I1[r]; Robert Burton, *The Anatomie of Melancholy* (Oxford: 1621), B6[r]. Burton and Vicary also offer similar, and similarly arresting, physical descriptions of the heart. Burton calls it, "of a paramadicall forme, and not much unlike to a Pineapple," while Vicary says it hath the shape and form of a Pyneapple, and the brode end thereof is upwards, and the sharpe ende is downewardes (I1[r]).

10.   Erickson, *Language,* 11 (authors italics).

11.   Gilde, "Sweet," 64.

12.   The difference between reading and seeing is an important and contentious point here. That is, Spenser's readers would not have been "seeing" anything: they would have been reading. Yet the line between the two is smudged in this instance, as much by what the text depicts as by what the text requires the reader to do with that depiction. A performed masque is neither clearly an entertainment to be seen nor clearly an allegory to be read; it is a delicate combination of the two. In this same way, the reader of the Masque of Cupid episode is not, and would not have been, simply reading it or seeing it; in this instance the two actions are all but conflated. In order to "see" the masque, the reader must read the text, but in order to interpret ("read") the text, that reader must become a kind of viewer, "seeing" the masque in his or her head as it would be seen if performed on a stage. Thus, a simple bifurcation of "read" and "see" is not possible here.

13.   Laurel Hendrix, examining Amoret's heart in detail ("Pulchritudo vincit?: Emblematic Reversals in Spenser's House of Busirane," *Spenser Studies* 16 [2002]: 23–54), poses the question, "Why . . . does Cupid make Amoret his bloodied 'spoile' when Amoret's only "transgression" is that she loves Scudamore chastely and stead-fastly?" (32). In Hendrix's allegorical interpretation of the masque, Cupid is its prime mover. My consideration of the incident, clearly not an allegorical one, posits Busirane, not Cupid, as the producer/director of the masque. In light of this, it is obvious why Amoret is bloodied and punished: for Busirane, her "only" transgression is the only transgression that matters, and the one he seeks to alter by any means necessary.

14.   *OED, s.v.* "Basin."

15.   Galen himself stressed the wisdom of using phlebotomy in combination with other cures in specific cases. He writes, for example, "in quibus igitur multa vacuatione estopus, vires autem sunt imbecilliores, in iis vacuationem recondere convenit. . . . Nam pauco sanguine vacuato. Proitnu mulam probe coctam cum extenuatium medicamentorum quopiam, aut hyssopo, aut oregano, & nonnunquam calamintha, aut pulegio exhibeo. . . . Deinceps rursum anguinem aufero, interdum quidem eodem die, interdum vero postero, in quo rursum similiter prædictorum medicamentorum quodpiam exhibens, iterum sanguinem detraho, ac teriot die similiter bis [in cases where extensive evacuation [of blood] is called for, but the faculties are not strong, it is appropriate to divide up evacuation . . . . After I have let a little blood I immediately give some melicratum [honey and water or milk], nicely cooked, with one of the attenuating drugs, hyssop or organy or even mint or pennyroyal . . . . After this I take blood again . . . ; at which time I again give one of the drugs mentioned, in the same way, and remove blood once more] (*De Curatione per sanguinis missionem Liber* [On Treatment by Venesection] *Claudii Galeni Pergameni . . . Comentariis illutsrata* [Paris, 1550], Yy5[r]; trans. Peter Brain, *Galen on Bloodletting* [New York: Cambridge University Press, 1986], 85). For a summary of remedies, isolated and combined, in this period, see Siraisi, *Medieval*, 136–52.

16.   "Only when rather excessive laughter and much boldness and confidence or a ruddy complexion and a swelling of the veins indicates an abundance of blood, should we bleed learned people, when the situation demands it, from the spleen-vein of the left arm with a wide incision, four ounces of blood in the morning and

four ounces in the evening. Then a few days afterwards—seven at the least, fourteen at the most—irritate the welts with a rather harsh rubbing and the application of leeches . . . in order that three or four ounces of blood may drip out" (trans. Carol V. Kaske and John R. Clark [Binghamton: Renaissance Society of America, 1989], 153).

17.   See Siraisi, *Medieval*, 136–51 for an excellent brief overview of the process of Early Modern phlebotomy and the concerns surrounding it. Bloodletting has experienced something of a popular resurgence recently. For a useful consideration of the medical legitimacy of Galen's theories of phlebotomy see Brain, "Galen's use of venesection as an evacuant: can it be justified? A medical digression," *Bloodletting*, 158–76.

18.   Schoenfeldt, *Bodies*, 15.

19.   "If they [patients] appear further to be deformed in some part, and in particular a part of the chest, you will phlebotomise them for certain, without delay" (*De Curatione*, Yy3[ʳ], trans. Brain, *Bloodletting*, 83).

20.   Siraisi, *Medieval*, 141.

21.   One sixteenth-century medical writer recommends that people sleep "rather open-mouthed then shut, which is a great help against internall obstructions, which more ensweeteneth the breath, recreateth the spirits, comforteth the braine, and more the [sic] cooleth the vehement heat of the heart" (Walkington, qtd. in Schoenfeldt, *Bodies*, 37, my brackets).

22.   Lemnius, *The Secret Miracles of Nature* (London, 1658), pp[1r-v].

23.   Thomas Wright. *The Passions of the Minde in Generall* (London: 1604), [E8ʳ]; [E6ᵛ]. In "On Treatment by Venesection," with reference to menstruation, Galen urges immediate treatment of women who experience irregularities: de mulieribus quibus menstrua est supressa purgatio. Neque enim . . . prorogare vacuationem oportet [in women whose menstrual purgation has been supressed. . . . . [e]vacuation should not be deferred] (*De Ratione*, Yy3[ᵛ]; trans. Brain, *Bloodletting*, 83).

24.   Lodowyck Bryskett, *Discourse of Civill Life* (London: 1606), Hh3[ʳ].

25.   *Harward's Phlebotomy: Or, a Treatise of Letting Bloud* (London, 1601; rpt. New York: Da Capo Press, 1973), H[1ᵛ].

26.   Galen tells of phlebotomizing an anorexic woman who had suffered from eight months of amenorrhea. During the first day's venesection he removed a pound and a half of blood, a pound during the second, and a half pound during the third (altogether, about one liter of blood, nearly a quarter of the total blood of a small adult). She was, he alleged, quickly restored to health (Brain, *Bloodletting*, 133).

27.   For an interesting interpretation which suggests that this episode represents the masculine adherence to "meaning" (which this adherence to logic and theory might be said to represent) and the feminine preference for understanding, see Wofford's "Gendering Allegory." Wofford, too, connects Spenser and Busirane, although her discussion centers on their shared use of imagery (16).

28.   Hoeniger, *Medicine*, 91–93. Burton calls pneuma "Spirit," and describes it as "a most subtile vapor, which is expressed from the *Blood*, and the Instrument of the Soule, to perform all his Actions, a common tye or *medium*, betwixt the Body and the Soule (*Anatomy*, B3[ʳ⁻ᵛ]). For a discussion of the difference between "soul" and "spirit" in writings of the period, and the difficulty in defining such differences, see

D.P. Walker, *Spiritual and Natural Magic: From Ficino to Campanella* (Notre Dame: University of Notre Dame, 1975), 113–15,189–92.

29.   Qtd. in Erickson, *Language*, 7.

30.   In making this observation I am indebted to the Nancy J. Vickers's discussion of the suppressive tactics inherent in the use of Petrarchan description in "Diana Described: Scattered Woman and Scattered Rhyme," *Critical Inquiry* 8 (1981): 265–79.

31.   *OED, s.v.* "Spright."

32.   Richard Mallette, *Spenser and the Discourses of Reformation England* (Lincoln: University of Nebraska Press, 1997), 109; A. Kent Hieatt, *Chaucer, Spenser, Milton: Mythopoeic Continuities and Transformations* (Montreal: McGill-Queen's University Press, 1975), 130. For a discussion of the role of rhetoric in these two cantos, and of Busirane as rhetorician/author, see Anderson, "Busirane's Place."

33.   Ferguson, George, "Heart," *Signs and Symbols in Christian Art* (New York: Oxford University Press, 1958), 27.

34.   *The Bible* (London: 1578), f.U1[ʳ]. Geneva translation.

35.   Stevens, "Sacred," 271.

36.   Mario Praz, *Studies in Seventeenth-Century Imagery,* Sussidi Eruditi 16 (Rome: Edizioni di Storia e Letteratura, 1964), 151–55.

37.   Montenay, *Emblemes, ou Devises Chrestiennes* (Lyons: 1571), f.Z[1ʳ]. See Barbara Lewalski, *Protestant Poetics and the Seventeenth-Century Religious Lyric* (Princeton: Princeton University Press, 1979), chap. 6, for background that informs much of my discussion here. Lewalski writes that sacred emblem books "were often produced by simple transformation of characteristic figures from the love emblem books" (184; see also Hendrix, "Pulchritudo"). Busirane is, perhaps, a too-literal reader of such books.

38.   Lewalski, *Protestant*, 206.

39.   Lewalski, *Protestant*, 185; Louis L. Martz, *The Poetry of Meditation: A Study in English Religious Literature of the Seventeenth Century* (New Haven: Yale University Press, 1954), 5–6; Praz, *Studies*, 152.

40.   Orest Ranum, "The Refuges of Intimacy," *A History of Private Life*, ed. Roger Chartier (Cambridge: Belknap Press, 1989), 239; Louis Réau, *Iconographie de L'Art Chrétien*, vol. 2 (Paris: Presse Universitaire de France, 1957), 47.

41.   As Doreen Rosman puts it, "Old beliefs and practices were not easily wiped out. For decades after Elizabeth came to the throne church bells were wrung on All Saints night to comfort souls in purgatory. The custom of reading the gospels over crops was preserved in some parishes, regardless of new orders . . . .Some pictures and images could still be seen in churches . . . long after Elizabeth's reign. A few parishes even failed to acquire the basic essentials of Protestant worship" (*The Evolution of the English Churches 1500–2000* [New York: Cambridge University Press], 43–44).

42.   Stevens, "Sacred," 263. One thinks here of *The Merchant of Venice*, where those same fleshly, mortal sufferings are made real to spectators via the potential sufferings of Antonio (*The Merchant of Venice*, ed. M.M. Mahood [New York: Cambridge University Press, 2003])

43.   Although Kurt Weitzman warns that a "distinction must be made between these images of the spear and the true fifteenth-century image of the Sacred Heart

that depicts not the wounded heart but the holy Child in the open heart of God"
(195), this distinction seems not to have been clear even during the early modern
period, and it is no clearer now. Most discussions of the Sacred Heart conflate it
with the pierced heart (see particularly Ranum).

44.   In "Singing Unsung Heroines: Androgynous Discourse in Book 3 of *The Faerie
Queene*," in *Rewriting the Renaissance: The Discourses of Sexual Difference in Early Modern
Europe*, ed. Margaret W. Ferguson, et al. (Chicago: University of Chicago Press,
1986), 264, Lauren Silberman points out that by "punning on the preposition *for*,
Spenser indicates the ambiguity of the relationship between Amoret's suffering and
Scudamore. She feels a wound for his sake—because she will not betray him—and
because of failure to protect her."

45.   Hendrix describes Spenser as "deftly employ[ing] 'word emblems'—what Peter
M. Daly defines as vivid literary images 'lacking only the visual *pictura* to be a *bona
fide* emblem' " ("Pulchritudo," 25).

46.   *Bible*, f.Ee1[ᵛ].

47.   As a Catholic country, England had entered wholeheartedly into veneration
of the Virgin. A later resurgence of it, encouraged by the Jesuits of the Counter-
Reformation, suggests that susceptibility to devotion to the Virgin lingered throughout the late sixteenth and early seventeenth centuries (Martz, *Poetry*, 96).

48.   The Seven Sorrows of Mary, as given by Linda Murray in *The Oxford Companion to Christian Art and Architecture* (New York: Oxford University Press, 1996), 500,
are Simeon's prophecy, the Flight into Egypt, the absence of Christ for three days
while disputing with the Doctors in the Temple, the Way to Calvary, the Crucifix-
ion, the Deposition, and the Entombment.

49.   Roche, *Kindly*, 82.

50.   See also the Garden of Adonis, in *FQ Book* III, Canto vi.

51.   As this quotation makes clear, Amoret is herself something of an enchantress,
and she is no more successful at her art than Busirane is at his, since she is captured,
rather than capturing.

52.   Williams, *Glass*, 105–06.

53.   Mallette, *Spenser*, 109.

54.   Hendrix's "Pulchritudo Vincit" offers a fine reading of the emblematic significance of these rooms; her reading, as well as that of Hieatt, in *Chaucer*, 115–33,
strongly influences my interpretation of this episode.

55.   For a more thorough description of the symbolic and allegorical significance
of the statue of Cupid, see Hieatt *Chaucer*, 127.

56.   Indeed, he may well have included a sly nod to Busirane himself, recast as the
least prepossessing of overmastering love's victims: "Next *Saturne* was, (but who
would euer weene,/The sullein *Saturne* euer weend to loue?/Yet loue is sullein,
and *Saturnlike* seene" (III, xi, 43, 1–3).

57.   Spenser may also intend an identification with Amoret in his description of
Fancy's attire—he is dressed "like as the sunburnt *Indians*" (8)—perhaps gently
drawing a parallel between the Indians' status as a colonized people and Amoret's
own captivity (England's first successful settlement in America, the soon-to-be-lost
colony of Roanoke, was undertaken in 1587). This possibility is complicated, however, by lack of clarity regarding Spenser's own opinions about overseas colonization.

His friendship with Ralegh and his own repressive actions in and writings about Ireland seem to indicate that he was an advocate (see Andrew Hadfield, *Edmund Spenser's Irish Experience: Wilde Fruit and Savage Soyl* [Oxford: Clarendon Press, 1997]); however, for an exploration of English and Spenserian ambivalence about overseas colonization (into which category, in Spenser's view, Ireland may not have fallen), see David Reed, *Temperate Conquests: Spenser and the Spanish New World* (Detroit: Wayne State University Press, 2000).

58.   *OED*, *s.v.* "Fancy."

59.   It is no accident that this kidnapping takes place "before the bride was bedded" (4, i, 3, 5). As long as Amoret remains a virgin she remains, technically, a maiden, and thus does not yet "belong" to Scudamore.

60.   It is worth bearing in mind that 26, line 4 makes no reference to Amoret's "wit," nor in fact to Amoret at all. Spenser's remark is a general one, its reference to the category of women, rather than to a specific woman. It is certainly more than plausible that Busirane has conjured these characters knowing them (as does the poet who conjured *him*) particular to "wemens wit." This stanza supports that reading far more sturdily than it supports the assertion that these figures are the products of Amoret's imagination.

61.   My thinking here both sprang from and agrees with Hieatt's reading, *Chaucer*, 133. For another, complementary, interpretation, see Hendrix.

62.   I am grateful for the help Dr. William Flesch, Dr. Gabriele Bernhard Jackson, and Roselyn Farren gave me as I formulated my ideas and wrote this article, and to Dr. Thomas H. Jackson for help with the translation of the verse accompanying fig. 2. I also wish to thank the two anonymous readers at *Spenser Studies* for their comments.

REBECCA YEARLING

Florimell's Girdle: Reconfiguring Chastity in *The Faerie Queene*

The minor crux in Book V, canto iii of *The Faerie Queene* in which the False Florimell is briefly seen to be wearing Florimell's magic girdle of chastity, has generally been viewed by critics as an authorial error or moment of inattention. The girdle, Spenser claims repeatedly, can only be worn by those who are "continent and chast," and the False Florimell hardly seems suitable as a representative of such virtues. However, it is possible to review this scene not as a mistake on Spenser's part, but as a pivotal moment in his continuing exploration of the meaning of "chastity" within the poem. *The Faerie Queene* contains two images of chastity—the simple state of fidelity and virginity (essentially, the refusal of illegitimate sex) that characterizes most of the book's early relationships, and the more complex, inclusive, and socially weighted virtue that the poem later comes to consider as the ideal—and the development between these concepts can be traced in the changing symbolic role of Florimell's girdle.

IN BOOK V, CANTO III of *The Faerie Queene,* the False Florimell, who has been intermittently present in the narrative since her creation in III.vii.6–8, is finally dispatched. When Artegall sets the imitation beside the original—the false image of beauty, who exists only in exterior, against the true, complete beauty of the real Florimell—the imitation cannot survive, and melts away like the snow from which it was created. As the narrator comments, "Ne of that goodly hew remayned ought, /But th'emptie girdle, which about her wast was wrought," and Artegall is described as picking up this girdle and

Spenser Studies: A Renaissance Poetry Annual, Volume XX, Copyright © 2005 by AMS Press, Inc. All rights reserved.

presenting it to the remaining lady (V.iii.27). The girdle, the symbol of chastity, has been restored to its rightful owner. However, there is a problem with the interpretation of this scene. The girdle, as has repeatedly been insisted, is a magical one, which can only be worn by the faithful and chaste. In Book IV, at Satyrane's tournament, it is won by the False Florimell, as the most beautiful lady present, but she cannot wear it: according to IV.v.16.3–5, "about her middle small/They thought to gird [it] . . ./ But by no meanes they could it thereto frame." By Book V, however, the False Florimell is wearing the girdle.

Those few critics who have remarked this problem are generally dismissive of its significance. The response of Alfred Gough in the Variorum edition is typical: he comments, "How she [the False Florimell] is able to wear it [the girdle] now is not explained, but such inconsistencies are frequent in the *F.Q.*"[1] However, the way in which the incident is presented serves, if anything, to make a point of the apparent inconsistency. The girdle's powers have been made plain in Book IV, and now, immediately after it is rescued from the waist of falsehood and restored to true virtue, the narrator reiterates the theme, with a flat denial of what has gone before:

> Full many Ladies often had assayd,
> About their middles that faire belt to knit;
> [. . .]
> Yet it to none of all their loynes would fit,
> Till *Florimell* about her fastned it.
>
> (V.iii.28.1–5)

The girdle, he claims again, can be worn only by those who are "continent and chast," and in his insistence in stanza 28 that only the true Florimell fits that description, the narrator contradicts both the end of the tournament in Book IV, where Amoret manages to wear it, and also stanza 24 of V.iii, in which it is described falling from the False Florimell's waist. The inconsistency of the girdle is not, therefore, a matter of the poet forgetting what he has written over the course of two books, but, apparently, forgetting over the course of five stanzas—a far less likely occurrence. A strange double-image is created by the passage, which raises the question of what exactly it means to wear the girdle of chastity.

From one perspective, the girdle seems to have changed its function briefly in stanza 24. From being a symbol of truth, it has become a deceptive sign that imputes a virtue to the False Florimell that she does not in fact possess, and is only restored to its full meaning by being given to the chaste real Florimell. The girdle therefore temporarily becomes another of the poem's misleading appearances, implying a virtue where there is none, only revealed as a fraud when it is tested and found wanting—an equivalent to the false St. George of Book I, who is revealed as the wicked magician Archimago only after entering into combat and losing (I.iii.33). This is A. C. Hamilton's reading in his Longman edition of the poem: "As Braggadochio's shield proclaims his bravery, the girdle displays the False Florimell's virginity, until both are uncased by justice."[2] There is, the poem implies, little real difference between true and false virtue when neither has yet been tested, and so the trials the knights undergo throughout the poem can be seen not merely as confirming them in valor, but in establishing their virtue in the first place: Virtue cannot exist passively, but must be proved in opposition.

However, from another perspective, the False Florimell is indeed tested within the poem, and found virtuous—albeit in a very limited sense. Despite Hamilton's claim, there is no evidence to suggest that her "virginity" is in question: the symbolically "snowy" False Florimell seems, like the untouchable lady of Petrarchan tradition, largely incapable of sexual desire.[3] Moreover, she does demonstrate a kind of fidelity in her amorous attachments: she is initially "won" from the witch's son in III.viii.13 by Braggadochio, and it is Braggadochio that she chooses again after the tournament:

> Sweete is the loue that comes alone with willingnesse . . .
> At last to *Braggadochio* selfe alone
> She came of her accord . . .
>
> (IV.v.25.9; IV.v.26.8–9)

Contrary to Roche, the False Florimell does not seem to find all men "indistinguishable,"[4] and this might explain why she is able to assume the girdle by Book V when she was unable to do so in IV.v.16: with her choice of Braggadochio in IV.v.26, the False Florimell seems to have in some sense earned her girdle, as a faithful lover.

The match between the False Florimell and Braggadochio can be seen as having uneasy implications for the unions of other lovers within the poem, and for the virtue of chastity itself. The pair do in fact make a good match, as William Oram points out: the false lady has picked the knight "whose worth most closely approximates her own."[5] Both are hollow characters, who have borrowed their exteriors from others—Braggadochio in Guyon's armor, and the False Florimell created to resemble the real Florimell—and this point is underlined when both are revealed for what they truly are in V.iii, and thereupon vanish from the poem. They display none of the other virtues that Spenser emphasizes in his poem—they are not holy, or just, or courteous in anything other than appearance—and nor are they even described as being in love. They show only a basic fidelity to their first choice of partner, and if such a union can be described as "chaste," the value of chastity in itself is brought seriously into question.

The relative worthlessness of their relationship and the limitations of the False Florimell's "virtue" immediately become obvious. Indeed, the lady is exposed as a fraud before it is even suggested that she may not be: the fact that the False Florimell was wearing the girdle becomes known only in retrospect, as it falls to the ground after she vanishes. At once, therefore, two incompatible views of chastity are offered. The False Florimell is both chaste and unchaste at the same time, able to assume the girdle in its most limited sense, that of simple fidelity, but unfit to stand beside the image of true chastity, symbolized, by this stage, by the real Florimell. The false couple is unworthy of love, whereas both Marinell and the true Florimell have undergone a series of trials in order to reach the state befitting matrimony. Marinell has overcome his resistance to love, after receiving his wound from Britomart, and has abandoned in his illness his proud and aggressive virginity—what Berger describes as his "too stern abstention"[6]—by realizing that he needs Florimell to be truly whole. She, meanwhile, has finally found a mutual relationship in which she is no longer fleeing from a pursuer, but rather willingly approaching her lover, as she is seen doing in IV.xii.34. Their relationship is all that marriage should be: the willing submission of virtuous equals to each other, who will complement each other's strengths and weaknesses and admit their mutual dependence.[7] The state of true chastity is found to overshadow the state of the False Florimell completely, and she melts away. The girdle changes the significance it has held in the poem up until this point and its history is rewritten: the False Florimell could never have worn a girdle that signifies chastity as ultimately embodied by Florimell and Marinell. With the girdle's changed significance, therefore, the reader retrospectively realizes its previous limitations as an indicator of virtue. Indeed, Florimell herself assumes the girdle of full chastity for the first time in V.iii: previously, she too was only chaste in the technical sense of fidelity, displaying what Brill describes as merely "a negative virtue" that "involves no more than a steadfast refusal to be seduced."[8]

History is also rewritten in the case of Amoret: V.iii.28 denies that she ever wore the girdle, seemingly forgetting that in IV.v.19, she found "it fit, withouten breach or let." Like the False Florimell, therefore, Amoret—a faithful virgin—was able to assume the girdle in its initial, more limited significance, but—V.iii suggests—may not be adequate as a model of chastity in its new sense, after the confrontation between the two Florimells.

In a consideration of Spenser's attitude towards Amoret in the later books of *The Faerie Queene,* it is necessary to look briefly at the notorious 1596 revision to the original conclusion of Book III, in which Spenser cancelled the hermaphroditic embrace between Amoret and Scudamore, preferring to keep the lovers apart. In his *The Kindly Flame,* Thomas Roche attempts to downplay the significance of this alteration: he argues that "the original ending of Book III provides the most simple, the most satisfactory conclusion for the allegorical education of Amoret." However, this remark raises the question, "satisfactory" for whom? Spenser did not ultimately consider it so; he chose, rather, to continue Amoret's "education" after the House of Busirane, and as Book IV proceeds, he sets her further trials in which it becomes clear that she is still somewhat deficient in true chastity. It is never suggested that she is any way "unchaste" in the sense of being unfaithful: once she has set her heart on Scudamore, after some initial resistance, she never wavers in her affections. However, while Britomart may have freed Amoret from immediate sexual fear, in her vanquishment of Busirane,[9] Amoret cannot be truly "chaste" while she remains a victim, unable to protect herself against masculine desire, as she does throughout her remaining appearances in Books IV and V. Sheila Cavanagh has protested the tendency among critics to "blame the victim" when discussing Amoret's further misfortunes, such as her abduction by the lustful "saluage man" in IV.411.4,[10] but in the poem's allegorical scheme, Amoret does seem at least partly culpable. If, as Cavanagh argues, chastity is presented as essentially a self-interested virtue, then Amoret needs to learn that she cannot wander freely, "of nought affeard" (IV.vii.4.1), but must be constantly vigilant in order to protect herself from lust—both her own and that of others.

Moreover, Scudamore himself seems, in *The Faerie Queen's* second half, not yet ready for a truly chaste union of the kind the poem has posited as the ideal. In his short essay, "Scudamore's Practice of *Maistrye* Upon Amoret," A. Kent Hieatt suggests that Spenser presents

Scudamore initially as an example of a lover who is not merely bold, but "too bold,"[11] and I would argue that this characterization is continued throughout Book IV. Scudamore remains an aggressive adolescent in outlook, unable to understand a love that involves positive surrender rather than violent conquest. The ideal presented in *Amoretti* LXVII, in which the lady is pictured as a "gentle deare," who willingly gives herself up to the huntsman, is alien to his way of thought. It is, of course, impossible to say what might have happened to the couple if the poem had been completed, but as the text stands, Amoret and Scudamore never develop fully into the ideal of marriage.

The initial alternative forms of chastity within the poem can be seen in the punning Argument which opens Canto i of Book III – "Guyon encountreth Britomart,/Fair Florimell is chaced." Britomart and Florimell here appear as contrary models of behavior. Both are faithful to their loves, but while Britomart is an aggressive figure in her virtue, as capable of defending herself against Guyon as any man, Florinell is a passive figure, continually being "chaced," pursued by various lustful figures. As the poem progresses, however, both initial models are shown to be flawed. Florimell's chastity is a fragile state, continually under threat. It brings out the domineering, aggressive side of the men of the poem. Britomart, on the other hand, is in danger of upsetting the sex-roles by effectively becoming a man, and of turning her chastity into a state where she, a woman, is "chacing" them—as seen by her pursuit of, and martial superiority to, her intended husband Artegall. As *The Faerie Queene* gradually makes clear, relationships which involve "chasing" are not truly "chaste," in that word's fullest sense, and Lauren Silberman provides an interesting analysis of how "the binary structure of winning and losing" that appears in Book IV works against the developing image of lovers as a balanced hermaphroditic unit, by reducing one-half of the couple to the status of a prize rather than a partner.[12] True chastity is the desire for a marriage in which each individual plays a complementary, if not an equal, role; and Britomart herself, though predominantly hunter rather than hunted, is at risk from both extremes of behavior, as can be seen from the fact that she must defend herself and the ideal of marriage against both Busirane and Radigund, the conquering man and the aggressive woman. She has her own equivalent to the dagger in Amoret's heart, in the fisherman's book that "hath infixed faster hold/Within my bleeding bowels" (III.ii.39.1–2), and must resist seeing herself as a passive victim. At the same time, she must recognize that for a true marriage, she must subdue her masculine aggression in order to restore Artegall to his proper place of authority, overcoming the elements of Radigund within herself, and returning women "to mens subiection"—not the masculine domination that Scudamore represents, but a relationship in which the woman is strong enough to choose to submit to the man.[13]

The concept of chastity in *The Faerie Queene* is therefore a complex one, which the poem continually develops, qualifies and refines. From Britomart's first act—the unhorsing of Guyon, in the opening of Book III—it becomes obvious that Guyon's simple rejection of sexuality is inadequate: sexual desire must be accepted and assimilated into human life. However, as the poem proceeds, it becomes clear that chastity involves more than merely dealing with desire. In Oram's words, "Chastity demands someone to whom one can be faithful and with whom sexuality can become more than just temptation."[14]: true marriage involves not just the hermaphroditic embrace of private sexual bliss, but a greater and more inclusive union of noble hearts and minds. However, as the poem's conception of marriage becomes more sophisticated and more inclusive, moving towards a view of marriage as an image of ideal human concord, the happy ending sought by so many of the characters becomes correspondingly more elusive, continually disrupted and postponed. As Berger points out in his essay, "The Spenserian Dynamics," concord in *The Faerie Queene* is presented as not in itself an end, but as the "continual tempering of opposites," a "sustained process of control that can never stop."[15] Like all the virtues of *The Faerie Queene*, chastity is not a static virtue but an ongoing process: the poem's lovers must continue in their quest for the right to wear Florimell's girdle.

Worcester College, Oxford

NOTES

1.   Alfred B. Gough (1918), quoted in *The Works of Edmund Spenser A Variorum Edition, The Faerie Queene,* Book V, ed. Ray Hefner (Baltimore: John Hopkins Press, 1936), 190.

2.   A. C. Hamilton, (ed), *The Faerie Queene,* (NY: Longman, 1977), Notes on V.iii.24, 547.

3.   Artegall, it is true, describes her as a "fayre Franion" (V.iii.22.7), but nevertheless, the False Florimell is never presented as behaving in a voluptuous or sexually provocative fashion, unlike, for example, Acrasia in Book II, or Hellenore in Book III.

4. Thomas P. Roche Jr., *The Kindly Flame: A Study of the Third and Fourth Books of Spenser's* Faerie Queene (Princeton, NJ: Princeton University Press, 1964), 162.

5. William Allan Oram, *Edmund Spenser* (NY: Twayne Publishers, 1997), 222.

6. Harry Berger Jr., "The Spenserian Dynamics," *Studies in English Literature (1500–1900),* 8 (1968), repr. *Revisionary Play: Studies in the Spenserian Dynamics* (Berkeley, LA: California University Press, 1988), 30.

7. The union between Florimell and Marinell also has considerable allegorical significance, given their roles as symbolic representatives of the land and the sea: an aspect discussed comprehensively by James Nohrnberg in *The Analogy of The Faerie Queene* (Princeton, NJ: Princeton University Press, 1976), 568–98.

8. Lesley W. Brill, "Chastity as Ideal Sexuality in the Third Book of *The Faerie Queene,*" *SEL* 11 (1971): 25.

9. This is Gilde's reading of Amoret's experience in the House of Busirane, which has become popular in recent years, and with which I largely concur. See Helen Cheney Gilde, " 'The Sweet Lodge of Love and Deare Delight': The Problem of Amoret," *Philological Quarterly* 50 (1971): 63–74; James Broaddus, *Spenser's Allegory of Love: Social Vision in Books III, IV, and V of* The Faerie Queene (London: Associated University Presses, 1995).

10. Sheila T. Cavanaugh, *Wanton Eyes and Chaste Desires: Female Sexuality in* The Faerie Queene (Bloomington, IN: Indiana University Press, 1994), 145.

11. A. Kent Hieatt, "Scudamore's Practice of *Maistrye* Upon Amoret,' *PMLA* 77.4 (1962): 509–10.

12. Lauren Silberman, *Transforming Desire: Erotic Knowledge in Books III and IV of* The Faerie Queene (Berkeley: University of California Press, 1995), 77.

13. For a fuller discussion of the theme of gender hierarchy within *The Faerie Queene,* see Broaddus, *Allegory of Love* 134–45; Julia Walker, "Spenser's Elizabeth Portrait and the Fictions of Dynastic Epic," *Modern Philology* 90.2 (1992), 172–99.

14. Oram, *Edmund Spenser* 110.

15. Berger, "Spenserian Dynamics," 21.

HOSSEIN PIRNAJMUDDIN

The "antique guize":
Persia in *The Faerie Queene*

As part of a larger project investigating the figurations of Persia in Renaissance English Literature, this essay traces the matter of Persia in *The Faerie Queene* and attempts to address some of the issues that compound any reading of the matter of the East in the light of Edward Said's notion of orientalist discourse. I suggest that whereas Persia figures as an imperial realm of pomp and glory in *The Faerie Queene,* the representation of Islam is adversarial in character. The paper addresses how and why it is so.

> The vast empires [of Asia] . . . give a further sublimity to the feeling associated with all oriental names and images.
> —Thomas De Quincey, *The Confessions of an English Opium-Eater*

*I*N BOOK IV CANTO 3 of *The Faerie Queene,* Spenser describes Cambina's chariot as decorated "After the Persian Monarks antique guize."[1] This essay will discuss the figurations of Persia in *The Faerie Queene,* suggesting that, though the Persian material is slight, its consideration lays bare the lineaments of an orientalist discourse that is heterogeneous in character, unlike what Edward Said's account of orientalism would imply. Persia figures as a monarchical realm of "antique guise," of pomp, power and glory, whereas the Islamic East figures as adversarial. Furthermore, whereas in Spenser the matter of Persia is mostly rhetorical in character, derived from the classical heritage and, to a lesser extent, contemporary accounts of the East, figurations of Islam are more crucial to the thematics of *The Faerie Queene.*

Spenser Studies: A Renaissance Poetry Annual, Volume XX, Copyright © 2005 by AMS Press, Inc. All rights reserved.

The Orient, says Said, is one of Europe's "deepest and most recur-
ring images of the other."[2] Said's vastly influential study of Western
representations of the East analyzes images of the Orient from classical
to modern times. Borrowing Foucault's concept of discursive forma-
tions and articulation of knowledge with power, Said has emphasized
the complicity of orientalism, as a form of "knowledge" about the
Orient, with European imperialism and colonialism. Said's pivotal
thesis in *Orientalism* is that orientalist texts "can *create* not only knowledge but also the very reality that they appear to describe."[3] As such,
orientalism is defined as "a kind of Western projection onto and will
to govern over the Orient."[4] "The relationship between Occident
and Orient," Said maintains, "is a relationship of power, of domination, of varying degrees of a complex hegemony."[5]

This model of orientalism has been subject to the criticism that it
is monolithic—that it oversimplifies what is heterogeneous and obscures many nuances. Though it remains immensely useful, the speci-
ficities of particular texts and contexts complicate the notion of
orientalism. Fascination with, and threat from, the East has been
central in western accounts of the Orient.[6] I would suggest that in
Spenser, Persia seems to have more to do with "fascination" and
Islam with "threat."

An analysis of the Persian material in the poem prompts a few
observations. First and foremost, it shows that the orientalism of the
poem is not uniform: the Persian references figure rather differently
from those to Muslim orientals.[7] The images of the Arabs, the Moors,
and especially the Turks (variously subsumed under the rubric "Muslim," "Mohametan," "Saracen") were laden with dread associations
as they embodied the ever-present menace of Islam—the current
notions about which were, in Said's words, that of "some necessarily
diminished version of those great dangerous forces that is symbolized
for Europe."[8] By contrast, the Persians pictured in the works of the
same period are mostly associated with sensuous luxury, wealth, and
opulence rather than dread. On this Anthony Parr writes:

> The animus against Islam joined with the notorious cruelty of
> Ottoman sultans to create an immovable stereotype of the rang-
> ing and expansionist Turk. Persia was a rather different case.
> Traditionally the land of wealth and luxury, with a glorious
> imperial past, it was for Western writers a genuinely exotic
> country, not a malign and unknowable neighbor but a fabulous
> resource. Like India or Japan, it was not so much Europe's

Other as its opposite or foil; and while the fascination with the glamorous east [sic] was later to become a disabling orientalism, arguably it was during the early modern period a positive alternative to views of Asia either as the home of barbarian hordes or of the hellish doctrine of Islam. . . .[9]

Parr's observations, by and large correct, need some modification. Persia is mostly associated with figures of "excess" and evil (Lucifera, Malecasta, Duessa, Radigund) in Spenser's poem. In other words, "the disabling orientalism" that Parr takes to have emerged after the early modern period is already there. Nonetheless, an analysis of the matter of Persia in Spenser bears out the fact that "Persia was a rather different case." To use Gayatri Spivak's distinction, Spenser's Persia is "the self-consolidating" rather than the "absolute" other, because it has some reassuring and desirable similarities with the same.[10] This simultaneous similarity and difference, I suggest, enables Spenser "to refashion its monarch under the pretext of praise rather than engaging in simple adulation or flattery."[11] Additionally, orientalism here intersects in a complex manner with imperialism. I will start with the relation between orientalism and imperialism and proceed to consider orientalist topoi of sensuality, pride and pomp, and finally to discuss Islamic figurations in *The Faerie Queene* as compared and contrasted with those of Persia.

★

In *Culture and Imperialism,* discussing the complicity between culture (orientalism) and imperialism and its disregard in literary studies, Said mentions Spenser as an outstanding example.[12] Though things had already begun to change some time before the publication of Said's book in 1993, little attention seems to have been paid to the relationship between the matter of the East in Spenser's magnum opus and imperialism. Nonetheless, this relationship is there, right from the outset. In his *Letter to Ralegh,* Spenser expresses his purpose in writing *The Faerie Queene:* "The general end therefore of all the booke is to fashion a gentleman or noble person in vertuous and gentle discipline." He goes on to refer to Xenophon's *Cyropaedia* which he deems preferable to Plato's *Republic* in "fashioning" a gentleman:

for that the one in the exquisite depth of his judgement, formed a commune welth such as it should be, but the other in the person of Cyrus and the Persians fashioned a gouernement as might best be: so much more profitable and gratious is doctrine by ensample, then by rule. So haue I laboured to doe in the person of Arthur.[13]

Significantly, *Cyropaedia* is the story of the *imperial* expeditions of an Eastern king. Xenophon's text with its "great potential for instruction about political power"[14] seems the perfect text to refer to in a poem intended to encourage Elizabeth's imperial and colonial ambitions. The passage testifies to Spenser's familiarity with things Persian through classical writers and a tradition of works on Persia which he draws on and reinforces.

For more than twenty-five centuries Persia has been known to the west. This "knowledge" about Persia was first produced by the writers of ancient Greece and then by their Roman inheritors. In the writings of Greek authors such as Aeschylus, Herodotus, and Xenophon and the Romans such as Lucan, Livy, and Plautus certain "orientalist" topoi appear, such as luxury and fabulous riches, pomp and pride, sensuality, despotism and degeneracy, which Renaissance writers and their successors later appropriated and developed in their Persian references.[15] These representations are part and parcel of Orientalism whose formation Edward Said locates as early as Aeschylus's *The Persians*.[6]

The writers describing Persia could not help being impressed by her might and wealth. These writers first transform the image of Persia "from a very far distant and often threatening Otherness into figures that are relatively familiar."[17] For instance Herodotus, the bulk of whose *History* dramatizes the confrontation of Persia and Greece as that of Asia and Europe, describes the Persians as hardy and valiant figures who nevertheless "as soon as they hear of any luxury . . . instantly make it their own," and who arrogantly "look upon themselves as very greatly superior in all respects to the rest of mankind."[18] Xenophon idealizes and romanticizes Cyrus and the Persian mode of life in his *Cyropaedia* only to wind up his work with a discourse on the Persians' degeneration after the death of Cyrus.[19] Orientalist topoi (pomp, pride, "oriental" degeneracy as well as sensuality and despotism) therefore have their origins mostly in early Greek thought about Persia, although even biblical mentions of Persia contain some of these motifs.[20]

Aeschylus's *The Persians* is the first extant Attic tragedy, and Said identifies it as the first, and paradigmatic, orientalist text in which "Europe . . . articulates the Orient."[21] The fabulous riches and luxury of Persia figure prominently. The Persians' Persia is the land "that enfolds great wealth,"[22] and its inhabitants have "rich/Estates laden with gold."[23] When the Persian women mourn, they do so with emotional excess, luxury, and sensuality:

> And the veils of many by tender hands
> Are torn through,
> Their breasts drenched with tears
> As they share in pain.
> With delicate sobs the women of Persia
> Are longing to see their newlywed men;
> The beds of their marriage with delicate covers,
> The luxurious pleasure of youth they have lost,
> And they grieve with long, insatiable sobs.[24]

The motif of "oriental" tyranny also suffuses the play. Xerxes is the proud despot par excellence (he even tries to "[Throw] a yoke on the neck of the sea"[25]) and the play depicts the Greek defiance of his tyranny. It celebrates Greek victory over "the army of Persians/With its proud display and mass of men."[26]

Unlike Aeschylus, Xenophon was a writer whose life and career were enmeshed with Greco-Persian relations. In his semi-fabulous *Cyropaedia,* he outlines the life of an exemplary man who united a nation and then founded the greatest empire of the time. In writing "the education or instruction of Cyrus" during a period of political turmoil and decline in his country, Xenophon wanted to "educate" and "instruct" his audience, as Spenser tried to do in composing *The Faerie Queene.* Though to Spenser, Xenophon may not have been as important as, say, Virgil or Ovid, one can feel the Greek's shadowy influence in *The Faerie Queene.* There are interesting parallels between the life of Cyrus and the Persians as a nation (both historically and as idealized in Xenophon) and the ideal emperor (or courtier or "gentleman"). For instance, one could consider Cyrus's simple, nomadic life as a child among the Persians; his dislike of the luxury of the court life; his generous treatment of the defeated king of the Medes, Astyage, who had risen against him; his wisdom and tolerance (routing the Babylonians, he called himself their liberator and not conqueror, and he restored the Babylonian temples and even participated in one of their religious ceremonies[27]); his venture of liberating the Jews from their Babylonian Captivity and creating a reformed state in Jerusalem,[28] like Elizabeth's intervening in Ireland or Britomart's reformation of the Amazonian state after beheading Radigund; his power and glory; even his handsomeness.

One more possible parallelism concerns the concept of justice.
Here again Spenser implicitly refers to one of Persia's "antique guize[s]" in the mention of the *Cyropaedia* as a model text. Xenophon
tells us from the very beginning about Cyrus's exemplary character,
stressing that it results from the Persian system of education. Cyrus
is a "just" emperor because as a boy he has been "fashioned" in ways
of justice.[29] By contrast, in the proem to Book V Spenser complains
of the impossibility of writing about justice in his era because men
have so degenerated since antiquity. The "antique" Persia stands for
a time and a land when and where the idea and the ideal of justice
were not yet corrupted. Britomart is "just," as Cyrus was. She acts
as a surrogate for the knight of Justice and "plays the part of Justice
better than Justice himself."[30] The Persian matter, then, is related to
this "fashioning" of a monarch, a gentleman or a nation and Persian
monarchs are imaged variously: Cyrus is a model ruler while other
Persian monarchs are figures of "excess."

Another mention of Cyrus is related to the idea of empire. In
"the teeming, often contradictory character of Spenser's repertory of
spaces, images, and worlds,"[31] the borders of the Persian empire
pushed outward by Cyrus appear as well. Hence another way of
approaching the matter of Persia in the poem is to view it as part of
an "imaginative geography."[32] Orientalism in Said's account is the
maintaining of geographical divisions within scholarly and aesthetic
texts in an attempt to create for Europe a "flexible positional superiority" over its others.[33] There is ample evidence of these "geographical divisions," of spatial mapping in Spenser's work. These concerns
are symptomatic of orientalism's endeavor to control, incorporate,
and domesticate "manifestly different" and novel worlds.[34] "England's nascent imperialist discourse," in Walter Lim's words, manifests itself in this concern with geography in Spenser's poem.[35]

The allusion whose context shows a merging of ideas taken from
classical writers and contemporary travel writings (here Ralegh's *Discoverie of Guiana*) occurs in Book IV. In his catalogue of rivers, Spenser
includes "Ooraxes," a river in the ancient Persian Empire, which,
according to Herodotus, Cyrus's decision to cross led to his death:
"Ooraxes, feared for Great Cyrus fate" (IV.xi.21). To appreciate fully
the significance of this allusion we need to elaborate on the colonialist
discourse of the poem subtending its orientalism here. The allusion
occurs in the final cantos of Book IV where the marriage of the rivers
Thames and Medway creates a vision of England as an imperial and
colonial power: "It fortun'd then, a solemne feast was there / To all
the Sea-gods and their fruitfull seede, / In honour of the spousalls,
which then were / Betwixt the Medway and the Thames agreed"

(IV.xi.8). Hamilton quotes Alistair Fowler on this stanza who argues that the marriage here intimates the marriage of England to Elizabeth; as the Medway was the center for naval operations, the event signifies "a visionary England—and Ireland—united in friendly alliance."[36] The vision continues in the catalogue of great ancient rivers:

> Great Ganges, and immortal Euphrates,
> Deep Indus, as Mœander intricate,
> Slow Peneus, and tempestuous Phasides,
> Swift Rhene, and Alpheus still immaculate:
> Ooraxes, feared for great Cyrus fate;
> Tybris, renowned for the Romaines fame,
> Rich Oranochy, though but knowen late;
> And the huge Riuer, which doth beare his name
> Of warlike Amazons, which do possesse the same.
>
> (IV.xi.21)

The cataloguing of the rivers mentioned in the Bible (Euphrates, see Genesis 2:1) and classical writings ("Ooraxes—see Herodotus, *History; 201–14*") leads to "Oranochy" ("mentioned by Ralegh in his *Discoverie of Guiana,* 1595") featuring in a contemporary exploration text.[37] All this leads to an overt articulation of English colonial aspirations in the next stanza:

> Joy on the warlike women, which so long
> Can from all men so rich a kingdome hold;
> And shame on you, O men, which boast your strong
> And ualiant hearts, in thoughts less hard and bold,
> Yet quaile in conquest of that land of gold.
> But this to you, O Britons, most pertaines,
> To whome the right hereof it selfe hath sold;
> The which for sparing litle cost or paines,
> Loose so immortal glory, and so endless gaines.
>
> (IV.xi.22)

"That land of gold" is "Guiana with the empire of Amazons on its southern borders" whose conquest Ralegh urges "in the *Discoverie of Guiana,*" so "Spenser's exhortation to his countrymen to plunder the land was topical."[38]

Spenser's allusion to Persia occurs in this context and is quite apt as Cyrus was known as a great empire-builder. Its significance with regard to the theme of empire can be further clarified if we consider it in a biblical context.[39] "The ancient Persian empire," Linda McJannet reminds us, "was understood to be one of the four divinely sanctioned 'monarchies' or empires (the Assyrian, the Persian, the Greco-Mace-donian, the Roman) featured in the Book of Daniel."[40] In the episode under discussion Spenser mentions all the four empires. Assyria is alluded to in stanza 15 ("Great Belus: the founder of Babylon"); Greece ("Peneus: a river in Greece"), Persia ("Ooraxes") and Rome ("Tybris, renowned for the Romaines fame") appear in stanza 21.[41] The implication is that the English, as Spenser's exhortatory rhetoric in stanza 22 indicates, should be the fifth great monarchy or empire, the inheritor of Rome. Elsewhere, Spenser expresses this idea more explicitly. *The Ruines of Time,* with its elegiac tone, catalogues the great empires of the past fallen to the ravages of time:

What nowe is of th' *Assyrian* Lyonesse,
Of whome no footing now on earth appears?
What of the *Persian* Beares outrageousnesse,
Whose memory is quite worn out with years,
Who of the *Grecian* Libbard now ought heares,
That ouerran the East with greedie powre,
And left his whelps their kingdomes to deuoure?

(64–71)[42]

Rome is then described as the crown and "Empresse" (87) of all nations. Of this imperial Rome the English are descendants and should be inheritors. The forlorn city of the poem is Verulamium, "That citie, which the garland wore/Of Britaines pride, delivered unto me/By Roman victors, which it wonne of yore" (37–39). The poem is not just a lamentation on the ruins of time but, among other things, a celebration of national and imperial aspiration. Time has ruined the great imperial powers of the past but now is the moment for England, Rome's inheritor, to become the "Empresse"—the feminine form is significant—of the world.

The enumeration of rivers and lands in *The Faerie Queene,* Helgerson proposes, "presents an image of royal and artistic power exercised in defiance of the very geographical differences that it seems intent on celebrating."[43] On the relationship between geographical figurations and the ideology of the poem Walter Lim notes: "The Other is identified in this poem as that uncharted space beyond England's geographical and political confines that the Queen should occupy through an extension of her literal and symbolic body."[44] In addition to this spatial mapping there is a temporal one. The whole of the poem is supposed to inhabit a world in a legendary past. Yet Persia is conceived of as predating that legendary time. It is an even more "antique guize"—a far-away land belonging to a long-ago past.

Apart from the positive representation of Cyrus as a model emperor and man, other Persian monarchs figure forth motifs of pomp, sensuality, and pride. Hence they mostly appear in places that the poem's allegory marks as evil. I will first discuss the idea of Persian "pomp" as a motif used to sharpen the imperialist imagery and thematics of the poem.

In Book III the warlike Britomart virtually kills Marinell whose mother is a sea nymph who: "Her Sea-god syre she dearely did perswade,/T'endow her sonne with threasure and rich store,/Bove all the sonnes that were of earthly wombes ybore" (III.iv.21). Her wish is granted and:

Shortly upon that shore there heaped was,
Exceeding riches and all pretious things,
The spoyle of all the world, that it did pas
The wealth of th' East, and pomp of Persian kings;
Gold, amber, yuorie, perles, owches, rings,
And all that else was pertious and deare,

(III.iv.23)

Marinell's treasures are the wealth of nations swallowed up by the sea but, after overcoming him, Britomart "would not stay/For gold, or perles, or pretious stones an howre/But them despised all; for all was in her powre" (III.iv.18.6–9). A religio-allegorical reading of these lines would suggest that the pious Britomart is not tempted by worldly riches. A politico-allegorical reading on the other hand would pinpoint the discourse of empire-building. First, there is the destruction of England's enemies; as critics have noted, the reference is specifically to the Armada and the defeat of Spain, England's daunting enemy of the time. Second, the association of the sea and the "spoyle of all the world" is apt here as "the sea and its treasures constitute an important metaphor in the discourse of colonialism and imperialism in early modern England."[45] Last, I would suggest, we have here, to use Homi K. Bhabha's phrase, the "ambivalent protocols of fantasy and desire" in Spenser's narrative.[46]

On the one hand there is the moral idea of resisting the mundane temptation of wealth ("But them despised all"), on the other there is the suggestion of Britomart's having the treasures in her control ("for all was in her powre"), the dream of England ruling the waves and hence having in its control the wealth of all the nations. A close look at the catalogue of goods here—gold, amber, ivory, pearl, jewels—shows them to be all those of the East and Africa, the commercial destinations and the would-be colonies. The "spoyle of all the world" are indeed the spoils of the would-be and actual colonies ("Guiana," "Peru") and the Orient captured in the symbolic register of "pompe of Persian kings." These spoils are enumerated and reiterated time and again. In psychological terms, there is a compulsive repetition betokening the return of the repressed, the spoils of the East, the object of desire, a desire that is denied fulfillment due to the particular workings of the politics and power relations of that time.[47] Orientalist discourse here underlines what is ostensibly disavowed but actually desired. The pomp and splendor of Persia and her kings and queens is also ostensibly disavowed but it is exactly that which is coveted and dreamed of for England and Elizabeth, the "Great Lady of the greatest Isle, whose light/Like Phoebus Lampe throughout the world doth shine" (I, proem, 4). Spenser's text with its fetishistic repetitions is trying to cover a felt lack—that of England's universal supremacy. There is here, then, a split in the ideological deep structure of the poem that is typical and symptomatic and its consideration, as the work of Homi K. Bhabha elaborates, suggests one of the major points of departure from a Saidian model of orientalism. Persia and the Persian comprise that "surrogate self" against which England and Queen Elizabeth are, in however refracted a way, set off to gain "in strength and identity."[48]

More can be said about this concept of power and its workings in the Elizabethan period. To grasp fully the implications and the ideological moorings of the poem we need, to quote Stephen Greenblatt, "a poetics of Elizabethan power" which is "inseparably bound up with the figure of Queen Elizabeth, a ruler without a standing army, without a highly developed bureaucracy, without an extensive police force, a ruler whose power is constituted in theatrical celebration of royal glory and theatrical violence visited upon the enemies of that glory."[49] Elizabethan authority still very much depended on the royal charisma associated with her. The matter of Persia in the poem can also be read in the context of this theatricalism, this display of power and glory, this augmenting of Elizabeth's charismatic figure. Generally speaking, the matter of the East in the poem, especially as regards Persia, is associated with this power and glory; the exoticized and "theatricalized" invocations of the glories of the past, the Persian monarchical pomp and display, well suited the literary creations of a "deeply theatrical" society and culture.[50] These topoi act as foils to the Elizabethan royal power which Spenser simultaneously idealizes and feels anxious about. They also show that in Spenser, as with orientalist discourse generally, the border between self and other is permeable. Regarding Persia, we have Spenser using the classical tradition, to "argue over the nature of the state he inhabited."[51]

Spenser's praise and defence of Queen Elizabeth in Book V, especially the Radigund episode, can further clarify the point. Radigund (whose name suggests possible Persian ancestry[52]) is, as Pamela Joseph Benson points out, "politically and sexually corrupt."[53] Spenser, Benson continues, "represents the rejection of the Amazonian model of queenship as praiseworthy . . . he . . . advises Elizabeth on how she ought to behave."[54]

Elsewhere Spenser associates the matter of the East, here Persia, with sensuality. When, in the first canto of Book III, Britomart and Redcrosse enter Malecasta's chambers, they find them "full of Damzels and of Squiares,/ Dancing and reveling both day and night,/ And swimming deepe in sensuall desires" (III.i.39). Malecasta is lust personified. Spenser emphasizes both sensuality and riches in describing Malecasta's own chamber:

> Thence they were brought to that great ladies uew
>   Whom they found sitting on a sumptuous bed,
>   That glistred all with gold and glorious shew,
>   As the proud Persian Queenes accustomed:
>   She seemed a woman of great bountihed,
>   And of rare beautie, sauing that askaunce
>   Her wanton eyes, ill signes of womanhed,
>   Did roll too tightly, and too often glaunce,
> Without regard of grace, or comely amenannce.
>
> (III.i.41)

Malecasta's excesses do not touch Britomart. Aesthetically, one could imagine that in order to provide figures, images, and pictorial details for so massive a poem as *The Faerie Queene,* Spenser had to resort to every available source including the bits and pieces of Orientalia in classical writers and the early travel writings about the East.[55] After all, to a Renaissance Englishman, Persia was something of a "faerie" land. In a romance references to the great monarchs of the past with their exotic aura are quite natural. As it does in this scene, orientalist discourse exoticizes Spenser's romance.

Oriental figures and images were useful both for the setting of the romance and its thematics, although, it is not easy—some would say wrong—to separate the two. From a formalist point of view, Spenser creates an archaic diction and style to produce the aura of antiquity suitable to his epic romance, hence the whole apparatus of myths and legends, exotic names and places including the oriental ones, which, apart from the thematic and allegorical aspects, help give the poem a sort of verbal sensuousness. The passage under discussion reproduces central orientalist motifs of pompous show, luxury, riches, sensuality and pride, specifically associated with Persia. In a book treating of chastity the allusions to Persia function to embellish a backdrop of seductive luxury, pomp, and sensuality—"luxurious corruption," to use C. S. Lewis's words—the better to make Malecasta a foil to chaste Britomart.[56]

There is only one instance in which this motif of Persian luxury is not used in association with an evil character. In canto 3 of Book IV Cambina's chariot is described: "The charet decked was in wondrous wize,/With gold and many a gorgeous ornament,/After the Persian Monarks antique guize" (IV.iii.38). Hamilton's gloss on Persian Monarks" is: "traditionally associated with wealth."[57] Aside from this example and the references to Cyprus, Persian images appear in places that the poem's allegory characterizes as evil, figuring forth "oriental" excess.

★

I have suggested that orientalism in Spenser has two main components—Persia and the Islamic East—which figure somehow differently. But they also converge, as in the following two passages where they are used to throw into relief an identical ideological purpose.

Duessa calling herself Fidessa beguiles the Knight of Redcrosse who has left Una and leads him to the House of Pride. They enter the hall of Lucifera:

> By them they passe, all gazing on them round,
>   And to the presence mount; whose glorious uew

Their frayle amazed senses did confound:
In liuing Princes court non euer knew
Such endlesse richesse, and so sumptuous shew;
Ne Persia selfe, the nourse of pompous pride
Like euer saw.

(I.iv.7)

The concept of pride is essential to the thematics of the poem. Critics have noted that Orgoglio, for instance, is meant to evoke associations with Rome and Catholicism. S. K. Heninger notes that "viewed in the light of contemporary history, the victory of Prince Arthur over Orgoglio becomes the victory of pious Protestantism over corrupt Catholicism."[58] But Orgoglio is also a "Saracen figure."[59] The motif of Persian pomp and pride makes the images associated with Persia fit material for the thematic structure of the poem. Elsewhere, two cantos earliler in the same book, we read:

He had a faire companion of his way,
A goodly Lady clad in scarlot red,
Purfled with gold and pearle of rich assay,
And like a Persian mitre on her hed
She wore, with crownes and owches garnished . . . .

(I.ii.13)

"Sarazin" Sansfoy is accompanied by Duessa, which intimates the similarity between or identity of Islam and Catholicism. Here we need to consider Spenser's representation of Islam to see how it differs from or resembles his representation of Persia.

The text needs to be considered in the wider context of the Renaissance world of Europe and its relation with Islam dating back to the Middle Ages. The poem shares the same context with works such as *The Song of Roland*, *Orlando Furioso*, and *Gerusalemme Liberata*, which are concerned with forging a national as well as a European identity. They are seminal texts that demonstrate "Europe's attempt to historicize and locate itself."[60] These texts as well as an array of non-literary ones helped construct an image of Islam—and the Orient—as "a monotheistic, culturally and militarily formidable competitor to Christianity"; in them "Islam . . . is viewed as belonging to a part of the world—the Orient—counterpoised imaginatively, geographically and historically *against* Europe and the West."[61] Hence, "in *The Faerie Queene*—as in so many poems of the Middle Ages and

Renaissance—the action in some sense turns on the defeat of Sar-ecens."[62]

The idea of nation permeates Spenser's poem. In Book III Merlin prophesies the future of Britomart's progeny chronicling the history of England up to the "sacred Peace" of Elizabeth's reign.[63] There Spenser expresses the aspirations for a powerful imperial nation rising out of a people enfeebled "with long warre" and "civil jarre" (III.iii.23). But this nation is defined against that perennial other of all nations, "that forreign foe that comes from farre" (III.iii.23). Else-where this "forrein foe" is more precisely specified: "To this [Arteg-all's] native soyle thou backe shall bring/Strongly to ayde his country to withstand/The powre of forreine Paynims which invade/Thy Land" (III.iii.27).

By Paynim here is meant both the Catholic powers, especially Spain, and the Turks, the enemies of true Christianity.[64] A look at the etymology of the word Paynim as it appears in the OED is revealing.

A. 1. Pagan or non-Christian lands collectively; pagandom, heathendom.
2. A pagan, a heathen; a non-Christian; esp. a Muslim, a saracen.
B. adj. of pagans; pagan, heathen; non-Christian, chiefly Mus-lim or saracen.

Here Paynim embodies a sort of undifferentiated, un-nuanced other. Orientals (the Turks representing the Islamic Orient) and Europeans (the Catholic) are commonly the "forreine foe." The term extends even to the Saxons who oppose the British in the "forreine foe." The term extends even to the Saxons who oppose the British in Merlin's history: "Then shall Britons, late dismayed and weake,/From their long vassalage gin to respire,/And on their Paynim foes avenge their ranckled ire" (III.iii.36).

In Book I, canto ii, the Knight of Redcrosse, beguiled by Archi-mago, is led astray and encounters Sansfoy accompanied by Duessa, whom he kills:

> At last him chaunst to meet upon the way
> A faithless Sarazin all arm'd to point,
> In whose great shield was writ with letters gay
> Sanfoy: full large of limbe and euery joint
> He was, and cared not for God or man a point.

(I.ii.12)

Sansfoy is a sarazin (Saracen). Again *OED*'s definition of the world:

> A 1.a Among the later Greeks and Romans, a name for the nomadic people of Syro-Arabian desert which harassed the Syrian confines of the Empire; hence, an Arab; by extension, a Muslim esp. with reference to the Crusades.
> 2.a Non-Christian, heathen, or pagan; an unbeliever, infidel.
> 2.b An ignorant and tasteless person, a "barbarian," "Goth," "Vandal."

These definitions, taken as indicators of a discourse, are telling ones. They show, among other things, how the East and Islam, as the ultimate alter ego of a Europe busy consolidating and enhancing its boundaries, merge. The Saracen is the oriental, the Arab, the Muslim, the barbarian, the pagan. The Sansfoy episode "in the most simplistic terms" says that "militant—and Protestant—Christianity (the Redcrosse Knight), separated from Truth (Una), will fall prey to the duplicity and pride of the Roman Catholic Church (personified by Duessa, daughter of the Pope.)"[65] Orientalist imagery is here subsumed in the allegorical apparatus of the poem. As we see, however, the Islamic figures constituting an important part of this imagery are adversarial while the Persian figures embody "excess."

One more example is the scene in which Prince Arthur and Artegall save Samient, servant of Mercilla, from two "paynim" knights who pursue her, knights sent by Adicia, the wife of the "souldan" (V.viii.24). Arthur and Artegall go on to kill the "proud souldan," a "paynim" of "fell tyranny" (V.viii.59, 28). The word "souldan" (sultan) with strong resonance of the Islamic Orient and its echo of despotism again exemplifies the merging of discourses on Islam and the Orient. Critics commonly take the allegorical figure of the "proud souldan" to represent Philip II of Spain and the Pope.[66] The oriental figure of "souldan" opens up a symbolic space of the alien other invoking paganism, pompous pride and despotism. Although the figure of sultan can refer to any oriental ruler, it is particularly associated with the Ottoman, and occasionally the Egyptian, sovereigns (as in Marlowe's *Tamburlaine*). For a Europe embattled against the Ottomans, the word sultan was evocative of menace. As such the poem easily associates the figure of sultan with its conceptions of the Spanish monarchy and the Pope.[67] By contrast the Persian monarchs were merely associated with opulence, and Cyrus himself appeared a model emperor.

The discourse on Islam is nowhere more explicit than in the three episodes in which the "paynim" knights swear by the prophet of Islam. In Book I, as we saw, Sansfoy (faithless) who fought the Red-crosse Knight (personifying militant Christianity) was a "sarazin." In Book II Prince Arthur (assuming the role of Christ), who "hath to paynim knights wrought great distresse,/And thousand sar'zins foully done to dye," saves Sir Guyon from "paynim brethren," Pyrochles and Cymochles (II.viii.18). Seeing his brother killed by Arthur, Cymochles: "fraught with great griefe/And wrath, he to him [Arthur] leaped furiously,/And fouly said, By Mahoune, cursed thief,/That direfull stroke thou dearely shalt aby" (II.viii.33).

In canto 8 of Book IV Prince Arthur fights and kills another "pagan," Corflambo. Struck by Arthur, "All full of rage he gan to curse and sweare,/And uow[68] by Mahoune that he [Arthur] should be slaine" (IV.viii.44). "Mahoune," as with its previous occurrence in Book II, is "Mohammed, god of Sarecens or pagans generally."[69] Corflambo conquers his victims by "casting secret flakes of lustfull Fire/From his false eyes, into their harts and parts entire" (IV.viii.48). He: "Of an huge Geauntesse whylome was bred;/And by his strength rule to himself did gaine/Of many nations into thraldome led,/And mighty kingdomes of his force adred;" (IV.viii.47). Allegorically, "nations into thraldome led" means that "nations enthralled by lust are ruled by Corflambo."[70] However, I suggest, also implicit in the imagery of conquest and slavery is the rapid spread of Islam after its advent. Further, the association of Islam and the East with sensuality and tyranny is characteristic. During the Renaissance "the European representation of the Muslim, Ottoman, or Arab," Said reminds us, "was always a way of controlling the redoubtable [Islamic] Orient."[71]

The last explicit reference to the figure of the Muslim and the prophet of Islam occurs in canto 7 of the Book VI in a rather curious context. Mirabella is tormented by Disdaine and Scorne. Disdaine "wore no armour, ne for none did care:"

> As no whit dreading any liuing wight;
> But in a Jacket quilted richly rare
> Upon checklaton he was strangely dight,
> And on his head a roll of linnen plight,
> Like to the Mores of Malaber he wore;
> With which his locks, as blacke as pitchy night,
> Were bound about, and uoyded from before,
> And in his hand a mighty yron club he bore.

(UI.uii.43)

Disdaine, fighting a Squire who tries to rescue Mirabella, "oftentimes by Turmagant and Mahound swore" (VI.vii.47). Representing one aspect of discourtesy in the Book of Courtesy, Disdaine is dressed like the Irish, wears his hair like the Muslim Moor and swears by the prophet of Islam. Here we see a good example of Spenser's synthetic powers. As critics have noted, here Spenser is trying to justify Lord Grey's brutal treatment of the Irish rebels. Anne Fogarty argues that colonial ideology subtends Book VI and suggests that "the text aims at educating and controlling our political responses."[72] Significantly, in order to evoke in his readers feelings of utmost dread and abhorrence about the Irish, Spenser couches his rhetoric in orientalist motifs and imagery. Again, we see that the figurations of the Islamic East are more important to the ideological orientation of the poem than those of Persia.

The Faerie Queene's orientalist discourse in treating the Islamic East is even more apparent when it is set against its important ideological intertext, the *Orlando Furioso,* which describes Charlemagne's defense of Europe against Islam, the apocalyptic beast emerging from the dark forest.[73] Englishness—a Protestant England—is defined, "fashioned," against both the European others (the Spanish, the Irish, the French, the Germans) and the non-European ones (the Arabs, the Moors, the Turks, the Indians, the Persians). The Orient with its vague contours appears both as the abode of heathens (Sarazins) and the realm of fabulous monarchs (of Persia).

Benedict Robinson has convincingly shown the importance of Islamic figurations in Spenser's allegory, and has demonstrated how we can read them as part of the way English poets and playwrights responded to "the roughly contemporary experiences of Ottoman expansion and Christian schism by adapting, rewriting, or resisting the conventions of 'Sarecen' romance."[74] Thus Spenser suggests "through allegory a holy war fought against multiple forms of faithlessness" and investigates "the sense of identity offered by this vision of embattled Protestant community."[75]

If in Spenser Persia figures as a non-Islamic, monarchical land (whether of a model emperor such as Cyrus or rulers marked by "excess"), Islam represents a contemporary formidable competitor to Christianity. Both, however, are in different ways related to the sense of identity that is so crucial to Spenser's poetry.

University of Isfahan

NOTES

1. Edmund Spenser, *The Faerie Queene*, ed. A. C. Hamilton (London: Longman, 1977), IV.iii.38. All further quotations are from this edition.

2. Edward W. Said, *Orientalism* [1978] (London: Penguin Books, 1995), 1.

3. Ibid., 94.

4. Ibid., 95, 5.

5. Ibid., 5.

6. Said is chiefly criticized for taking this experience to have been unified. As Dennis Porter puts it: "Unlike Foucault, who posits not a continuous discourse over time but epistemological breaks between different periods, Said asserts the unified character of Western discourse on the Orient over some two millennia, a unity derived from a common and continuous experience of fascination with and threat from the East, of its irreducible otherness." Francis Barker et al., eds., "*Orientalism* and its Problems," *Politics of Theory. Proceedings of Essex Sociology of Literature Conference* (Colchester: University of Essex, 1982), 181.

7. A long tradition in the Greek and Roman writing on Persia was available to the Renaissance writers, one that hardly existed in the case of other orientals, say the Arabs or the Turks. In the case of the latter, the memory of the Crusades and the later conflicts with Europe were still relatively fresh in the memory of the Renaissance writers. These Arabs, the Moors, and later, Turks became in a sense the embodiment of Islam in the European imagination of that time. The Turks were thus seen differently and more negatively than the Persians. John Hale writes that: "To those who saw the Ottoman Empire from the outside, they were, above all cruel . . . . Whenever a Turk featured in an English or French play of the sixteenth century, he appeared laden with dread" (*The Civilization of Europe in the Renaissance* [London: Fontana Press, 1993], 41). An angry Othello could cry out to his rowing companions: "Are we turn'd Turks, and to ourselves do that which heaven has forbid the Ottomites?" (*The Complete Works of William Shakespeare* [New York: C.M.C., 1989], II.iii. Or he could call himself a "malignant and a turban'd Turk" (IV.ii).

8. *Orientalism*, 60.

9. Anthony Parr, ed., "Introduction," *Three Renaissance Travel Plays* (Manchester: Manchester University Press, 1995), 11.

10. Gayatri C. Spivak, "The Rani of Sirmur," in *Europe and Its Others*, 2 vols. ed. Francis Barker et al., (Colchester: University of Essex, 1985), vol. 1, 131.

11. Colin Burrow, "Spenser and classical traditions" in *The Cambridge Companion to Spenser* (Cambridge: Cambridge University Press, 2001), 227.

12. Edward Said, *Culture and Imperialism* (London: Chatto & Windus, 1993), 5.

13. Hamilton, 737.

14. James Tatum, *Xenophon's Imperial Fiction* (Princeton, NJ: Princeton University Press, 1989), xiv.

15. There are many references to Persia in English Renaissance works. These passing allusions refer mostly to the monarchs of Persia, its history, and customs reproducing the common motifs of orientalism. In *The Advancement of Learning*, (ed., Arthur Johnston [Oxford: Clarendon Press, 1974]) for instance, Francis Bacon alludes

to the Persian history: "and it is of Xenophon the philosopher, who went from Socrates" school into Asia, in the expedition of Cyrus the younger against king Artaxerxes (The First Book, VII, 30); to its mythic splendor: "For your majesty had truly described, not a king of Assyria or Persia in their extern glory" (The Second Book, II, 8); and to "the Persian pride": "When one of Antipater's friends commended him of Alexander for his moderation that he did not degenerate into the Persian pride, in use of purple, but kept the ancient habit of Macedon, of black" (The First Book, VII, 17). There are also references pertaining to commerce, most probably inspired by contemporary travel accounts to the East: like Jonson's reference to "your best Persian carpets" (*The Magnetic Lady,* in *The Works of Ben Jonson,* ed. F. Cunningham, 9 vols. [London: Blackers And Son, 1875], vol. 6, IV.iii, 51). A writer like Sir Thomas Browne to give an exotic aura to his book about gardening could call it *The Garden of Cyrus* and write about the passion of Cyrus for gardening. Christopher Marlowe, Spenser's contemporary, makes extensive use of Persian settings and figures in his *Tamberlaine, the Great.* See also note 43.

16.   *Orientalism,* 21.

17.   Ibid.

18.   Herodotus, *Histories,* trans. A. G. Grant, 2 vols. (London: John Murrey, 1897), Book I, 81–82. Much of the whole tradition of classical Greek and Roman writings as concerned with the Orient "existed to prove that Romans and Greeks were superior to other kinds of people" (Said, *Orientalism,* 57). For the importance of Herodotus in this tradition, suffice it to say that from at least the second century B.C. on, the Orient was "subdivided into realms previously known, visited, conquered, by Herodotus and Alexander as well as their epigones, and those realms not previously known, visited, conquered" (*Orientalism,* 58). Persia was of course, as the bulk of Herodotus's writings indicates, the most "known" of these realms.

The Greek construction of Oriental otherness was not uniform. To the Greeks, Persia appeared an enemy more often than not, but it was not exhaustively and irrevocably antagonistic. There were inhabitants of the unknown territories to the northeast of Persia who could be far more demoniac (the Indians, for instance, who featured as a "monstrous race"). See Peter Childs, "Introduction," in *Post-Colonial Theory and English Literature: A Reader,* ed. Peter Childs (Edinburgh: Edinburgh University Press, 1999), 6. Here, where the consolidation of the Greek identity against its Oriental others is at issue, there are "known" others like the Persians and "unknown" ones like those inhabiting the realms beyond Persia. Gayatri Spivak's distinction between a "self-consolidating other" and an "absolute other" is applicable here. "The self-consolidating other" is no doubt in a subordinate position but it is "known" and has to some extent similarities with self which the "absolute other"—the unknown "barbarian"—does not ("Overdeterminations of Imperialism: David Ochterloney and the Ranee of Simoor," in *Europe and Its Others,* vol. 1, 131). See also John Barrell's introduction to his *The Infection of Thomas De Quincey: A Psychopathology of Imperialism* (New Haven: Yale University Press, 1991) where he offers a tripartite division in Western conceptions of the East instead of binary oppositions and exemplifies his case with Greco-Persian relations.

19.   See Xenophon, *The Cyropaedia or Instruction of Cyrus,* trans. J. S. Watson and Henry Dale (London: George Bell & Sons, 1876).

20. For instance, Ahasuerus, the Persian king, in a feast shows "the riches of his glorious kingdom and the honour of his excellent majesty" (Esther 1:4). For biblical allusions to Persia as a source of Western knowledge about her see A. J. Arberry, ed., *The Legacy of Persia* (London: Oxford University Press, 1953) and John D. Yohannan, *Persian Poetry in England and America. A 200 Hundred Year History* (New York: Caravan Books, 1977).

21. *Orientalism*, 1, 57.

22. Aeschylus, *The Persians,* trans. Anthony J. Podlecki (London: Bristol Classical Press, 1991), 250. References are given with line numbers.

23. Ibid., 1–5.

24. Ibid., 537–45.

25. Ibid., 65.

26. Ibid., 533–34. In *Virgils Gnat* Spenser also alludes to the Persian invasion of Greece (47–9; 54–5).

27. See R. Ghirshman, *L'Iran, des Origines à L'Islam* (Paris: Payot, 1951), ch. 3.

28. "Cyrus king of Persia" (2 Chronicles 36:22) "stirred up" by "the Lord" liberates and rebuilds Jerusalem (Ezra 1:1–10). One could also think of some parallels between Cyrus's life and that of Spenser. Cyrus starting from humble origins proceeding to become an emperor is perhaps comparable to Spenser's supposed projectile as a pastoral poet to one of epic poetry. Their dislike of the court and "courtly" manner of life could be another parallel.

29. See *Cyropaedia,* Book 1, chapter 1.

30. Linda Gregerson, "Sexual Politics," in *The Cambridge Companion to Spenser,* 187.

31. Roland Greene, "Spenser and contemporary vernacular poetry" in Andrew Hadfield, ed., *The Cambridge Companion to Spenser,* 241.

32. *Orientalism*, 73.

33. Idid., 7. For the importance of cartography, its reflections in the writings of the Renaissance writers including Spenser, and its ideological effects, see Richard Helgerson, "The Land Speaks: Cartography, Chorography, and Subversion in Renaissance England," in *Representing the Renaissance,* ed. Stephen Greenblatt (Berkeley: University of California Press, 1988). In his introduction to the book Greenblatt writes: "a heightened interest in boundaries emerged in Western Europe in the late sixteenth and early seventeenth centuries" (xiii).

34. *Orientalism*, 12.

35. Walter S. H. Lim, *The Arts of Empire: The Poetics of Colonialism from Raleigh to Milton* (New York: The University of Delaware Press, 1988), 158.

36. Hamilton, IV.xi.8–53n.

37. Ibid., IV.xi.21n. In general, there were three main sources of "knowledge" about Persia: classical writings, the Bible, and contemporary accounts of the East, mostly in the form of travelogues. They are best reflected in the following list of English Renaissance plays: 1527 *Godly Queen Hester* (Anon.); 1561 *Cambyses, King of Persia* (Thomas Preston); 1576–1580 *The wars of Cyrus;* 1578/88 *Tamburlaine, Parts 1 and 2;* 1600 *Alaham* (Fulke Greville); 1600 *The Four Prentices of London* (Heywood); 1603 *The Tragedy of Darius* (William Alexander); 1604 *The Tragedy of Croesus* (William Alexander); 1605 *The Tragedy of Philotas* (Samuel Daniel); 1607 *The Alexandrean*

Tragedy (William Alexander); 1607 *The Travels of Three English Brothers* (John Day, William Rowley and George Wilkins); 1614–15 *Abulmanzar* (Thomas Tomkis); 1622 *The Prophetesse* (Fletcher and Masinger); 1636 *The Royal Slave* (William Cartwright); 1637 *Aglaura* (Sir John Suckling); 1639 *The Phoenix in Her Flames* (William Lower); 1641 *The Sophy* (Sir John Denham); 1647 *Mirza* (Robert Baron). See Linda McJannet, "Bringing in a Persian," *Medieval and Renaissance Drama in England,* 12 (1999), 240.

38.   Hamilton, IV.xi.22n.

39.   Hamilton glosses the historical context: see the note to IV.xi.22.

40.   McJannet, "Bringing in a Persian," 244. McJannet points out that the Scottish nobleman William Alexander wrote a series of "Monarchick Tragedies" concerned with divinely sanctioned monarchies (*The Tragedy of Darius* [1603], *The Tragedy of Croesus* [1604], *The Alexandrian Tragedy* [1607]. See also 247–48.

41.   Hamilton's gloss, IV.xi.15.6–7n.

42.   *The Yale Edition of Shorter Poems of Edmund Spenser,* ed. William A. Oram et al. (New Haven: Yale University Press, 1989). All references to Spenser's shorter poems are to this edition.

43.   "The Land Speaks," 355.

44.   Lim, *The Arts of Empire,* 168.

45.   Ibid., 156.

46.   Homi K. Bhabha, "Signs taken for wonders," in *The Location of Culture* (London and New York: Routledge, 1994), 112.

47.   Maureen Quilligan comments that there is in Spenser "a kind of wordplay which by its subliminal fluidity, resembles Freud's theory that the truth of the unconscious can be revealed through word association" (*The Language of Allegory: Defining the Genre* [Ithaca: Cornell University Press, 1997], p. 33).

48.   *Orientalism,* 3.

49.   Stephen Greenblatt, "Invisible Bullets," in *Political Shakespeare: Essays in Cultural Materialism* [1984] (Manchester: Manchester University Press, 1994), 44.

50.   Stephen Greenblatt, *Renaissance Self-Fashioning from More to Shakespeare* (Chicago and London: The University of Chicago Press, 1980), 162.

51.   Colin Burrow, "Spenser and Classical Traditions," in *The Cambridge Companion to Spenser,* ed. Andrew Hadfield (Cambridge: Cambridge University Press, 2001), 217–37, 234.

52.   Radigund, Hamilton notes, "may derive from the valorous Persian princess, Rhodogune, in Plutarch, *Artaxerxes*" (V.iv.33.3n.).

53.   Pamela Joseph Benson, "Praise and Defence of the Queen in *The Faerie Queene,* Book V.", in *Edmund Spenser,* ed. Andrew Hadfield (London: Longman, 1996), 163.

54.   Ibid., 162. She concludes that: "Given the traditional and Calvinist arguments against woman rule, Spenser must admit that there can be bad female monarchs (just as there are bad male monarchs), if his praise of female monarchy is to be taken seriously instead of being discounted as mere courtier's flattery." Such contests account for the references to Persian monarchs (and orientalist motifs accompanying them) to characterize Malecasta, Lucifera, Duessa, and Radigund.

55.   This would be yet more highlighted if one would agree with Northrope Frye's view that Spenser has "limited conceptual powers" and in his poetry "imagery is

prior to allegory." Northrope Frye, "The Structure of Imagery in *The Faerie Queene*," in *Essential Articles for the Study of Edmund Spenser*, ed. A. C. Hamilton (Hamden, Conn.: The Shoe String Press, 1972), 155.

As regards travel writings about the East, accounts of Persia were available from the Medieval times whether in Sir John Mandeville's fabulous "Travels;" in Marco Polo's writings; or those of other travelers to the Orient such as the Franciscan friar Ordericus, Clavijo (the Spanish ambassador to Tamburlaine in 1404), and the Venetian Josafa Barbara (in 1474). See *The Legacy of Persia* and Riza-Zadeh Shafagh, *Iran as Seen By Iranologists* (Tehran: University of Tehran Press, 1956). A host of European travelers visited Persia after the foundation of the Safavid Dynasty in the early sixteenth century. The English were the first among Europeans to open up trading relations with Persia. The Muscovy Company sent many delegations to Persia headed by Anthony Jenkinson, who in 1561, accredited with letters from Queen Elizabeth, was received by Shah Tahmasp (Marlowe draws on Jenkinson's accounts in *Tamburlaine*), Thomas Barker, Geofrey Duckat, and many others. Commercial relations were followed by political contacts which brought the famous Shirley Brothers to the court of Shah Abbas I. See Samuel C. Chew, *The Crescent and the Rose, Islam and England During the Renaissance* (Oxford: Oxford University Press, 1937). See also note 75.

Accounts of travels to Persia were also available in Hakluyt's *Principall Navigations, Voiages, and Discoveries of the English Nation*, first issued in 1589 and much enlarged in 1598–1600. Many contemporary writers referred to Hakluyt including Spenser's friends Ralegh, who was associated with him from 1582, and Gabriel Harvey. See Richard Helgerson, "Writing empire and nation," in *The Cambridge Companion to English Literature 1500–1600*, ed. Arthur F. Kinney, (Cambridge: Cambridge University Press, 2000), 310–29. See also note 37.

56.   C. S. Lewis, "*The Faerie Queene*," in *The Essential Articles*, 7. This sensuality is of course, that of the East in general. When at the climax of his quest, Guyon, the Knight of Temperance, meets Arcasia in the Bower of Bliss, Spenser describes her "through langour of her late sweet toyle" as sweating a "few drops, more clear then nectar, forth distild,/That like pure Orient perles adowne it trild" (II.xii.78). In this particularly voluptuous scene the oriental motif of exoticism is invoked to portray intemperance personified. Spenser could well have read something about the pearl divers in the Persian Gulf and the pearl trade in Persia, say, in Marco Polo's *Travels* or the early travel writings about Persia. The "Orient perles" are in any case meant to evoke an ultimate exotic beauty.

The motif of Eastern sensuality culminates in Romantic orientalism, particularly in the works of Byron (most notably in "Turkish Tales"), Robert Southey, Landor, and Thomas Moore. In Moore's *Lalla Rookh* (an "oriental," or, more precisely, a Persian romance) even the landscape oozes sensuality. See Thomas Moore, *Lalla Rookh, An Oriental Romance* (London: Longman, 1846), "The Paradise and the Peri", 159. Moore laid on so thick the note of "oriental" eroticism that contemporary reviewers accused him of having a "licentious" imagination. See Javed Majeed, *Ungoverned Imaginings, James Mill's The History of British India and Orientalism* (Oxford: Clarendon Press, 1992), 105.

57.   IV.iii.38.8n. The notion of Persian opulence is even further supported in contemporary travel writings. See, for example, Anthony Jenkinson's descriptions

of the courts of Shah Tahmasp and the Prince of Shirvan in Richard Hakluyt, *Voyages*, ed. Ernst Rhys, 8 vols. (London: J. M. Dent & Sons, 1932), II, 22 and 14.

58.   S. K. Heninger, Jr., "The Orgoglio Episode in *The Faerie Queene*," in *Journal of English Literary History*, XXVI (1959), 178.

59.   Benedict Robinson, "The 'Secret Faith' of Spenser's Saracens," in *Spenser Studies* XVII (2003), 25.

60.   Jacqueline Kaye, "The Islamic Imperialism and the creation of some Ideas of 'Europe,' " in *Europe and Its Others*, vol. 1, 66.

61.   Said, "After-word to the 1995 Printing," *Orientalism*, 344. See also 59–73 for a discussion of Europe's representations of Islam.

62.   Robinson, "The 'Secret Faith' of Spenser's Saracens,' "2.

63.   Hamilton, III.iii.23n.

64.   John Hollander and Frank Kermode, eds., *The Literature of Renaissance England* (New York: Oxford University Press, 1973), 213.

65.   Russell S. Meyer, *The Faerie Queene: Educating the Reader* (Boston: Twayne Publishers, 1991), 43–44.

66.   Lim, *The Arts of Empire*, 153.

67.   Meyer points out that apart from Philip II of Spain the actual model for the souldan and his cruel wife in the souldan episode could well have been a "near-contemporary figure," Süleyman the Magnificent of the Ottoman Empire (reigning from 1520 to 1566). As such, he continues, "the victory of Artegall and Arthur is meant to represent not only the English defeat of the Spanish, but also the superiority of Christian warriors over the 'pagan' Süleyman as well" (*Educating the Reader*, 104–105). Compare this with Marlowe's representations of the Turks and the Persians in *Tamburlaine the Great* where the Turkish emperor is defeated and sadistically humiliated by a Tamburlaine who calls himself king of Persia. Whereas in Spenser the matter of Persia is mostly derived from the classical heritage, in Marlowe it betokens the conflation of classical elements and contemporary travels to and interest in the East. See Richard Wilson, "Visible Bullets: *Tamburlaine the Great* and Ivan the Terrible," *ELH*, 62 (1995), 48. In the case of Persia one source of this interest, apart from commercial contacts, was the Perso-Turkish hostility intensified with the rise of the Safavid dynasty in the early sixteenth century. We see this reflected, for instance, in John Day's play, *The Travels of Three English Brothers* (1607), based on the travel accounts of Anthony and Richard Shirley in Persia, which promotes the idea of a Perso-European alliance against the Ottomans, hence his positive image of the Persian rulers in sharp contrast to the cruel and violent Turkish potentates. So is it with Robert Baron's *Mirza* (1647).

69.   Hamilton, IV.viii.44.3n.

70.   Ibid., IV. viii.47n.

71.   Said, *Orientalism*, 60.

72.   Anne Fogarty, "The colonisation of language: narrative strategy in *The Faerie Queene*, Book VI," in *Edmund Spenser*, ed. Andrew Hadfield, 198.

73.   Lim, *The Arts of Empire*, 158–59.

74.   Robinson, "The 'Secret Faith' of Spenser's Saracens," 1.

75.   Ibid.

D. ALLEN CARROLL

The Meaning of "E. K."

If we *hear* these two characters together as a sounded word, and not as conventional initials standing directly for a name, then several fresh possibilities occur, one or more of which point to Gabriel Harvey himself or to Harvey and Spenser in collaboration as being responsible for the apparatus. There is *eke* or *eek*, that which is added on, lengthened "beyond its just dimensions, by some low artifice" (Dr. Johnson), a term also used back then for "a tag to a bell rope," that is, an add on, an extention, suggesting Harvey's father's occupation, and he the son of that father. Then there is the Latin *ecce*, in its classical pronunciation, for "Lo!," and "Behold," which points to something remarkable or wondrous (to *signa et prodigia*), here proclaiming the advent of "the new Poete." *Ecce* is *the* word voiced frequently by the angel herald and prophet, a Gabriel word that more than any other outside his real name would have identified Gabriel Harvey. "Ecce" is also in many contexts demonstrably ironic, meaning not, or not solely, "Look!," but rather "Look out!," "Don't be taken in!," here, in the case of the *Calender*, by the hoax. Finally, *ecce* may have suggested *"Ecce signum!,"* with Spenser's initials, one of the two phrases in this period (the other is *"Ecce homo!"*) regularly associated with *ecce*, according to the *OED,* with *signum* meaning "a sign in the heavens, a constellation" (as in the woodcuts) and also "surname." It is primarily through such aural associations with these paired characters "E. K." that we arrive at that cluster of verbal clues one or more of which help identify the annotator(s).

Spenser Studies: A Renaissance Poetry Annual, Volume XX, Copyright © 2005 by AMS Press, Inc. All rights reserved.

The identity of E. K., the annotator of the *Shepheardes Calender*, is one
of the darkest and most controversial mysteries in Spenser scholarship.

> Paul E. McLane (1961)

I must in hande with my familiar for a newe stratageme.

> Gabriel Harvey, *Letter-Book*[1]

*I*F WE MODIFY THE WAY WE HAVE interpreted the initials
that appear at the beginning and end of the *Calender's* Epistle to
Gabriel Harvey, several fresh possibilities emerge. Efforts to identify the annotator thus far, almost without exception, have fixed
on these initials, confident as to the kind of evidence they present.
When read conventionally, they have made the leading candidate
for years the unlikely **E**dward **K**irke, thereby giving elocution to
the otherwise mute and inglorious. Of late the case for Kirke seems
to have weakened before a growing sense, perhaps consensus, that
E. K.'s contribution is more likely to be by Spenser himself or
Harvey or the two in some kind of collaboration. In this view
the editorial apparatus exhibits that particular brand of jocularity,
a playing with irony, suggesting trickery and deceit and that blend
of self-promotion and -protection we find elsewhere in dealings
between these friends. If Spenser and Harvey, and not Kirke, then
what are we to make of the initials?[2]

One line of argument has been to accommodate Spenser's
name: there are early suggestions, "Edmund the Kalendarer" or
"Edmundus Kalendarius"; and recent ones, "Edmundus Kedemon," *kedemon* being the closest Greek equivalent to *spencer*, that
is, steward; and "Edmund (of) Kent," with reference to Spenser's
residence when much of the *Calender* was composed. None has
yet proved fully satisfying.[3] These two letters *E* and *K* can be read
in another, radically different way, such that other meanings reveal
themselves, rising out of that special context in the *Calender* and
reflecting the spirit and agenda of Spenser and Harvey, any one
or all of which meanings may have been intended. My approach
diminishes seriously or else eliminates altogether Kirke's place in
the story, gives Harvey a clear, perhaps dominant presence, and
may strengthen the case for Spenser's involvement. "Strange things
were done with initials [in] the period," W. L. Renwick had to
acknowledge in 1930, even as he sponsored the nomination of
Kirke.[4] These initials, at once evasive and revelatory, participate
fully in an apparatus Hugh MacLean called an "elaborate literary
game" and Bruce R. Smith "a kind of academic in-joke."[5]

Initials conventionally stand for letters in an actual name or pseudonym. But "E. K." is a case where they may stand for something
other than a name—they may stand for a *word*, that is, *be seen and
heard together as such,* which *word* then carries an appropriate meaning
in and of itself and also supplies a clue as to the identity of the
annotator(s). I offer three possibilities. The first is the word *eke,*
pronounced [i_k]. Most obviously, *eke* (or *eek*), according to the
OED (*n.*[1] 1.), meant "a piece added on, a supplement." *Ek* was a
spelling for the verb from the fourteenth to the sixteenth centuries
(*OED*). *To eke out* (**eke** *v.*3.b.) may already have meant "to prolong"
a composition (quotations begin with Milton in 1641), "to lengthen
it," as Dr. Johnson said, "beyond its just dimensions, by some low
artifice." E. K.'s contribution, some of it quite obtuse, in solemn
mockery of typical scholarly editions of the classics, amounts in bulk
to more than half the *Calender.* Moreover, the word *eke-name,* super-
ceded with us now by its corrupt descendant *nickname,* meant "an
additional name" (*OED*), not one's true name—and thereby suggested that "E. K." was not to stand for some real, formal name such
as *Edward Kirke.*

Another meaning of *eke,* specialized back then (*OED n.*[1] 2.; **eche**
n.[1]), points directly at Harvey—"a tag to a bell rope," that is, a piece
added, to repair a rope's end worn out or become untwisted from
use. That Harvey's father was a rope maker would become widely
known a few years later through Thomas Nashe's attacks and then
be, for Harvey, a source of great embarrassment and pain. It appears,
however, that for himself and Spenser and, he may have hoped, few
others, Harvey was willing through this sense of *eke* early on to glance
at his origins discreetly, perhaps proud of having transcended them,
as he led the celebration (helped ring the bell) proclaiming his friend's
accomplishment. It is with a rope metaphor that Nashe accuses Harvey of attributing to someone else the Epistle to *Three Proper Letters*
(1580), published a few months after the *Calender,* "when [in fact]
hee [Harvey] was the onely writer himselfe," and of falsely claiming
for Spenser a role in that publication: "*Gabriel,* thou canst play at fast
and loose as well as anie man in England."[6]

This image of the rope (the *eke*) would have prompted the notion
of the *ropery* (a place where *ekes* were made and from which they
were purchased) and may have suggested, in the *Calender* context,
such affiliate terms as *rope-tricks, ropercall,* and *roperipe*—a nexus that
then carried certain specific and apt connotations. In the fullest and
most useful scholarly discussion of this group of words, Richard Levin
shows that, more than to simple trickery, these words refer to *rhetoric,*
encouraged perhaps by aural associations, among which rhe*toric*

(-*trick*) and t*ropes* (-*ropes*) have been suggested. They refer in particular, Levin shows, to what is pretentious in rhetorical terms and speech, verbal affectation, the use of "straunge, ynkehorne termes" (Thomas Wilson's words), self-conscious and overly-elaborate language in general.[7] "E. K." thereby takes on the persona of the pedantic academician. It suggests an effort to caricature a role that, when in earnest, came easily to Harvey, a role he seems to have been incapable of suppressing. The list of technical terms from rhetoric in the *Calender*'s glosses, as Heninger notices, is "surprisingly long" (he gives sixteen).[8] In *Have With You to Saffron-Walden* (1596), Nashe ridicules Harvey's "rope-rethorique" for his "*strange untraffiqu't phrases new vented and unpackt,*" and calls him "*Archibald Rupenrope.*"[9]

Eke was a favorite word with Spenser, judging by how often he used it. The "partial list" in the concordance goes beyond a hundred.[10] It had the right resonance, being both ancient and Chaucerian ("Whan Zepherus eek . . . "), and, even while quaint and obsolescent, was still in use. He may in some way have linked it with it his own name—perhaps on grounds of initials in Latin or Greek versions of his surname such as those that have been proposed. It also seems likely, if I may speculate, that the Roman hand and font at that time allowed the letter **d** to separate into and be constructed out of, and therefore be on occasion perceived as, the two letters **c** and **l**; so that Spenser could have thought of **Ed**mund as beginning with and abbreviated to **Ec**. Two illustrations will have to serve here for what I am convinced was a widespread idea. First, there is only one way to explain the sign that hung outside the bookseller John Trundle's shop—the sign, as we know from commentary on a place in *The Tempest*, was a "picture of Nobody"—that is, a figure with head, arms, and legs but no body, no *trunk*. To get from *Trundles*, as in *Trundle's* Shop, to *Truncles(s)* or *Trunkles(s)*, one separates a **c** from the letter **d**. Second, when Will Kemp in *Nine Daies Wonder* (1600) refers to "a booke in Latine called *Mundus Furiosus*: printed at *Cullen*," he actually means at *Londen*. To get from *Cullen* to *London* (*Lunden*), one combines the **C** with one of the two **l**s to create a **d** and then rearranges the remaining letters.[11] We may, accordingly, be forgiven for recalling here very familiar lines from *Amoretti LXXV* (she to him): "for I my selve shall lyke to this decay,/and **eek my name** bee wyped out lykewize."

A very similar form of subterfuge Samuel Halkett describes in the introduction to his *Dictionary of Anonyms and Pseudonyms*. Through it, a pseudonym, that is, *word*, apparently a name, is meant to *sound like* (that is, *be heard as*) initials, which initials then provide conventional clues as to identities. His examples, all from the nineteenth century, include "Effessea" (=F. S. C.), "Arrelsee" (=R. L. C.), and "Aitiache" (=A. T. H.). Understanding "E. K." would seem to require the exact reverse of this procedure, that is, *seeing and/or hearing the initials as a word and then using it as a clue.*[12]

We should also hear, I believe, a second word in these initials, indeed are more likely to, as this one has two syllables, a word that gives us a second possible reading. It is the Latin *ecce*, meaning "Lo!" "Mark!" or "Behold!"—an interjection that can be followed by various grammatical forms. As an expression, *ecce* points to something remarkable, wondrous, prophetic, perhaps miraculous—to *signa et prodigia*—conditions or events taking place, or about to, that strike one with awe and amazement. *Ecce* fits exactly the spirit of the Epistle as it announces to the world the advent "of the new Poete" and introduces the evidence thereof through the commentary and poetry. Its pronunciation, out of the three listed in the Revised *OED*, would be, presumably, the classical ([_ekei]), not that we may call the English ([_eksi]) or that of the Church ([_etsei])—given the tastes and education of Spenser and Harvey and the effort with the *Calender* to imitate a classical edition.

In the Vulgate, the messenger angel Gabriel opens with "ecce" when he informs Zacharias that his aged wife Elizabeth will give birth to John the Baptist (Luke 1:20); and, a few verses later, when he informs Mary that she will conceive ("ecce concipies" [1:31]); and, still later, as the unnamed herald angel, himself introduced with "ecce" ("ecce angelus Domini" [2:9]), when he informs the shepherds of the birth of Christ ("ecce . . . natus est vobis hodie salvator" [10:11]). *Ecce* is *the word* of this angel/prophet, a Gabriel word that more than any other outside his real name would have identified Gabriel Harvey. And it suggests that Harvey had a great deal, if not everything, to do with this Epistle and commentary. Nashe, who had a nose for such things, in the opening sentence of *Strange Newes* (1592) ridicules Harvey without mercy for his role as messenger angel in purveying those obsequious *Foure Letters* (1592), and he may be thinking of the *Calender* as well: "*Gabriel*, and not onely *Gabriel*, but *Gabrielissime Gabriel*, no Angell but ANGELOS, id est, *Nuntius*, a Fawneguest Messenger . . . ."[13] To Spenser in a poetic moment of tenderness, we should remember, a few weeks before the *Calender* is published, he is "good Harvey, . . . both angel and Gabriel."[14]

Harvey's marginalia on astronomical and calendric learning in his copy of Dionysius Periegetes's *Survey of the World* (1572), which Louise Schleiner believes reflects "possibly the main source [that is, in Harvey's thinking] of Spenser's idea of a calendric framework for his

eclogues," three times in one brief space use "ecce" to praise particularly fine expressions—in Chaucer, in Textor, and in the *Book of
Common Prayer* (1559), the last especially for its elegance ("Ecce eleg-
ans . . . ") "De anno, et partibus eius" (concerning the year and its
parts).[15] In this same place, where he regrets that Spenser knows so
little astronomy, Harvey lists, with clear contempt, that other, popular "Shepherds Kalendar" among books inadequate for their astronomy (that is, their practical meteorology).

Are there examples of "E. K." used by others at the time as a
construction of "ecce" and therefore as something more than conventional initials? Here are a few possibilities. Franklin B. Williams,
Jr., who wrote the book on initials in this period, finding no appropriate knight, took to be a fiction the "*Sr* E. K." that appears above a
poem "*concerning the* Philosophers Stone," one preliminary to George
Ripley's *Compound of Alchemy* of 1591.[16] The "*E. C.* Esquier"
("Ece"?) who appears as the author of a curious 1595 sonnet sequence
called *Emaricdulfe*, which in part recounts a fantasy love affair between
a mortal and a fairy nymph, has never been identified despite a great
deal of effort.[17]

Of more complexity as a possibility is the pseudonym of Francis
Godwin, Bishop of Hereford (1562–1633), which Williams puts in
the category of "Mystifications: Perverse or Tolerable?": "Why Godwin adopted this pseudonym remains a mystery."[18] No one has ventured a solution. The versions of the pseudonym to survive, of which
there are four, include only names or abbreviations of names that
begin with the letters E, C, and M. These may stand for a pseudonym
that includes "*Ecce*," the possibility of which deserves a brief digression.

Godwin is remembered for *The Man in the Moone*, published in
1638, after his death. Estimates as to its date range over a fifty year
period, from 1578, when Godwin was a student at Oxford, to 1630.[19]
The book was an astounding success. Between 1638 and 1768, the
dates of the first and last London editions, it was published in four
languages and at least twenty-five printings. An account of a journey
to the moon as told in first person by a traveler called Domingo
Gonzales, it claims to be by Gonzales and to be translated from the
Spanish. It is thought to have influenced other tales of exploration
and imaginary voyages, including those of de Bergerac and Swift. An
"E. M." signs the brief preface to the English editions, and an "Edward Mahon gent" is given in the *Stationers' Register* as its translator.[20]

Godwin's Latin *Nuncius Inanimatus* (1629), that is, as the later English translation gives it, "The Mysterious Messenger," describes several projects whereby intelligence can be transmitted long distance

(by pigeons, beacons, and so on). It's a book on signaling, and has recently been described as "in fact a treatise on cryptography."[21] The note to the readers at its end is signed "Ed. M. Ch."[22] And the 1616 Latin edition of Godwin's *Catalogue of the Bishops of England*, though otherwise clearly attributed to Godwin, has a Latin dedicatory poem signed "Edw. Mahonides, *Aliàs* Christopher."[23]

There was no such person as "Edward Mahon," no Spaniard called "Domingo Gonzales," no Spanish version of the text, and the expression "a tale of a Man in the Moone" was proverbial for nonsense, as John Lyly suggests in his note to the subtitle of *Endymion* (pr. 1591).[24] Godwin was himself responsible. One may understand, as H. W. Lawton puts it, why a bishop might have "had some diffidence in signing works on subjects as far removed from faith and morals as signaling, flying, writing and deciphering codes, or discovering in the Moon new worlds which might make them suspect of heresy."[25] But why this particular pseudonym? There may, of course, be a simple solution Williams and everyone else has missed ("*Eccl*esiastical *Man*"[**cl** for **d**?] = "Church Man"?); but even if so, it may have functioned in part as cover for that of another, more daring pseudonym: "*Ecce Homo!*" *Homo* has been replaced by *Mahon*, its English equivalent rendered as the familiar (Celtic) name, and so bears a clear reference to the *Man* in the Moon. We probably have in "E. M." the simplest, earliest version of the macaronic pseudonym. In his two fantastic books Godwin extolls the extraordinary powers of a mankind that, despite serious limitations, can with mind and will master nature and put it to his service. John Anthony Butler, one of *Man*'s editors, is struck by how "often [Gonzales, the narrator] uses the term 'wonders' to describe what he sees."[26] The two books are about potentialities to be realized, prophecies thereof, complex systems of communication, flights to the moon, all of which could appropriately be introduced with "Ecce." They might well have invoked comparison with Christ the incarnate, humiliated and abused before Pilate and the people, man suffering ("Ecce Homo!"), just before His great accomplishment on the cross. "Look," the pseudonym proclaims, "what man can and will perform!"

The "Ed.," "Edw," "Edward" may reflect an intention to suggest the pronunciation of the first vowel/syllable and, along with "Ch." and "Christopher," the hard **c** (as also derived from **d**). Finding "Mahonides" where we would expect "Mahon" means simply, which Williams missed and is clear in the Latin poem it follows, that those particular verses, which are dedicated to Godwin, were written not by him at all but rather by his son—"son of *Mahon*," *Mahonides*, playing on "Behold the son of man," as often in the Bible, building, one may imagine, on the father's pseudonym. This reading of God-win's pseudonym, however, is not crucial to my case as to the way we should think about the *Calender*'s "E. K."

There can be no doubt that during this period "ecce" also func-tioned in an ironic mode, meaning its opposite. "E. K." would have been understood, certainly by anyone able to recognize that "ecce" was central to the puzzle, as a warning, a signal as to the presence of some kind of hoax. It often meant not, or not solely, "Behold" or "Look!" but rather, in effect, "Look out!" "Don't be taken in!" That is, in the case of the *Calender* and perhaps of Godwin, by this means of attribution, by these expressed accounts of composition, even, perhaps, by the implied authenticity or historicity in the texts them-selves. **Ecce**, the *Oxford Latin Dictionary* ([1968] 1.) records, "some-times for dramatic effect, refers to what is not actually present." A 1581 quotation in the *OED* is to the point: "In Distinctions, eccyties and quiddities, they [the Schoolemen] could many times easely see that thing which was no where at all." "It was not," E. M. says in the preface to *The Man in the Moone*, "the Authors intention (I pre-sume) to discourse thee into a believe [sic] of each particular circum-stance." (*Gulliver's Travels*, one Irish Bishop is reported to have said, is "full of improbable lies, and for my part, I hardly believe a word of it.") A safe course, accordingly, would be to be wary, with the *Calender* and Godwin, of conventional clues of attribution. The Latin tag could well have meant, put bluntly, "Here is a hoax!" In *Nuncius Inanimatus*, Godwin, after describing several common forms of dis-tance communication and promising to introduce a new and most wonderful one, disappoints absolutely by revealing in the end noth-ing, nothing at all.

For all that, we may yet be able, in a third reading of these initials, to proceed through "Ecce" to Spenser himself, though such will require an inference of something more than what is given in the text, a particular verbal association no longer ours. The Latin "ecce" in early English contexts usually occurs as one of two words in one of two phrases. The *OED* says as much in its brief treatment: "*Ecce*. Latin for 'lo!' or 'behold!' Used in phrases like **Ecce signum!** behold a sign! Also **Ecce Homo**, 'behold the Man' (John xix. 5) . . . ." Elizabethans who read "E. K." as "Ecce" might go on to supply, reflexively, the familiar "signum," completing what was otherwise for them half an expression, and thereby detect a second set of ini-tials—"E. S." *Ecce signum!* meant "Here is the proof," introducing for the *Calender* the evidence (in the commentary, which was not to be trusted, as being over the top, and in the poetry itself, which was) as it begins and ends an epistle proclaiming the advent of the new poet. *Ecce signum!* was of considerable currency at the time. It may be found in numerous popular plays, reduced from the apocalyptic down to the stage joke. It is with *"ecce signum!"* that Falstaff displays his hacked sword as proof of his valor on Gadshill—here is the ironic mode. It occurs in, to give a sampling, *Doctor Faustus*, Thomas Lodge and Robert Greene's *Looking Glass for England*, *Woodstock*, *The Taming of a Shrew*, John Marston's *Histrio-Mastix*, Francis Beaumont and John Fletcher's *Scornful Ladie*, and Fletcher's *Women Pleased*. It is also there, where you would expect it, in its serious mode, in a Lancelot Andrewes's Sermon of the Nativity, in elaboration of "hoc erit signum vobis."[27] *Signum* also meant "a sign in the heavens, a constellation" (*Oxford Latin Dictionary* 13), like those in each of the *Calender* wood-cuts: thus, "See the constellation(s)!" *Signum* also meant "surname" (*OLD* 3 b).

As we approach a consensus that Spenser and Harvey are more likely candidates for the commentary than is Kirke, we cannot read these initials straight. Criticism of *The Faerie Queene* has shown that it is almost impossible to over-read signals in Spenser's work—it is full of serious play, of complex significations. This reading turns up precisely the kind of thing he and his community have shown them-selves capable of elsewhere. Spenser appears to have linked himself, his name and that of surrogates for him, with "Lo!," and so, evidently, did others, when recalling him. It may have been a phonic tick whereby he eased himself, his ego, forward, self-consciously, for con-sideration. *June* opens "Lo Collin"; the envoy begins *"Loe I have made a Calender for every yeare"*; *Three Proper Letters* introduces to Harvey a sample of Spenser's hexameters with "Loe here I let you see"; *The Faerie Queene* opens "Lo I the man whose muse whilom did mask." Joseph Hall memorialized him later (*c.* 1605) with "Lo Here doth Collin ly."[28]

Looking at the first line of the envoy (*"Loe I have made a Calender for every yeare"*), we may question the assumption that Spenser is nowhere identified as author in the poem. The Latin for *"I have made (a Calendar)"* would be *dispensavi*, from the verb *dispensare*, meaning "to order, dispose, arrange, regulate" (*OLD* 2 *b*). Livy, in a passage that E. K. paraphrases in "The generall argument," employs this same verb to describe how Numa Pompilius regularized the calendar by adding months, making it useful for an extended number of years to come, that is, *"for every yeare,"* which context in Livy makes good sense of an otherwise gratuitous phrase in Spenser's envoy:

> . . . intercalariis mensibus interponendis ita dispensavit, ut vic-esimo anno ad metam eandem solis unde orsi essent, plenis omnium annorum spatiis, dies congruerent.

(He [Numa] inserted [*dispensavit*] intercalary months in such a
way that in the twentieth year the days should fall in with the
same position of the sun from which they had started, and the
period of twenty years be rounded out.

[I.19.6, Loeb])

The idea of the Latin of the one word in the first line of the envoy
(either *Ecce* or *dispensavi*) would draw notice to the Latin of the other.
Be that as it may, this line certainly adverts to Spenser's surname. In
commendatory verses to *The Faerie Queene* (1590) by "H. B.,"
Spenser is "this rare dispenser," and in a poetic tribute of 1598,
perhaps by Richard Carew, he is the *"Muses despencier."*[29]

It is through visual and aural associations of these paired characters
"E. K." that we arrive at a cluster of verbal clues one or more of
which appear to lead to the identity of the annotator(s). In the case
of "E. K.," multiple possibilities for clues may be better than just one.
Spenser and Harvey, we can easily imagine, would have delighted in
all these resonances of *eke*, *ecce*, and *ecce signum*.

University of Tennessee

NOTES

1.   Versions of this paper were presented at 2004 meetings of the Renaissance
Society of America in New York City and the Southeastern Renaissance Conference
in Durham, NC. For suggestions and encouragement I am indebted to Joe Black,
Lisa Celovsky, Rob Stillman, and David Miller. Epigraphs: *Spenser's "Shepheardes
Calender": A Study in Elizabethan Allegory* (Notre Dame, IN: University of Notre
Dame Press, 1961), 280; *The Letter-Book of Gabriel Harvey*, ed. E. J. L. Scott (1884;
repr. New York: Johnson Reprint, 1965), 82 [fol. 44]. On the meaning of the
second epigraph see Josephine Waters Bennett's comment in the next note. I have
used *The Yale Edition of the Shorter Poems of Edmund Spenser*, ed. William A. Oram
et al. (New Haven: Yale University Press, 1989).
2.   For guidance through the literature on this issue one should look backward
through the argument and references in Louise Schleiner, "Spenser's 'E. K.' as
Edmund Kent (Kenned/of Kent): Kyth (Couth), Kissed, and Kunning-Conning,"
ELR 20 (1990): 374–407 and in Louis Waldman, "Spenser's Pseudonym 'E. K.' and
Humanist Self-Naming," *Spenser Studies* 9 (1988): 21–31, noting esp. Raymond
Jenkins (1944–45), Agnes D. Kuersteiner (1935), W. H. Welply (1932, 1933, 1941),
H. O. Sommer (ed., 1890), and the summary comments in *The Works of Edmund
Spenser: The Variorum Edition*, ed. Edwin Greenlaw et al. (Baltimore: Johns Hopkins
University Press, 1932–57), vii, 645–50 and ix, 486. An impressive, full-scale argu-
ment for Harvey "hid behind the initials E. K.," which seems not to have been

available to Schleiner, is S. K. Heninger, Jr., "The Typographical Layout of Spenser's *Shepheardes Calender*," *Word and Visual Imagination*, ed. Karl Josef Hölgen et al. (Erlangen-Nürnberg: Universitätsbibliothek, 1988), 33–71. I consider the current attitude to be that in the Editors' Note to the *Calender* in *Edmund Spener's Poetry: Authoritative Texts, Criticism*, 3rd Edition, ed. Hugh Maclean and Anne Lake Prescott (New York: W. W. Norton, 1993), 542–43: "scholars nowadays prefer to believe that Spenser and Harvey collaborated in some fashion to produce these prefatory materials, or that 'the . . . initials are a cover for Spenser himself . . . .' " (quoting Lynn Staley Johnson, *"The Shepheardes Calender": An Introduction* [University Park, PA: Pennsylvania State University Press, 1990]). Anyone who doubts that Harvey was capable of such literary chicanery, and at this time ("the year between the summer of 1579 and August, 1580" [167–68]), should spend a while with Josephine Waters Bennett, "Spenser and Gabriel Harvey's *Letter-Book*," *Modern Philology* 29 (1931): 163–86. The idea for the Harvey epigraph comes from Bennett's use of it. Note her comment on one letter: "This composition is not a first draft of a real letter, but a literary hoax, intended for publication. Harvey has provided it with an editorial side-note, 'By his familiar it is most likely he menith his paper-book' (fol. 40). The 'stratagem' by which it is to appear in print without Harvey's hand being seen in the matter, is written out on the next page of the *Letter-Book* (fol. 42). Harvey, as usual, writes the Preface, which he would like some friend to write, as follows . . . " (174–75).

McLane, making the case for Fulke Greville (using the spellings *Foulk* and *Fulk)*, took the last letters of the first and last names and reversed them (288–89). The only developed nominations I find that take no account of the initials are those by Heninger and, in a case for Richard Mulcaster, by C. Margaret Greig (*Notes and Queries* 197 [1952]: 332–34). René Graziani took to be Kirke's eight lines of Latin congratulatory verses in front of a 1587 book by Everard Digby (STC 6839) by an "E. K." who was probably at Cambridge when Spenser was (other contributors were) and may have been in his set (*Notes and Queries* 214 [1969]: 21).

3.   Suggested by β (*Notes and Queries*, 5th ser., 6 [1876]: 365); Kuersteiner (E. K. is Spenser, *PMLA* 50 [1935]: 140–55); Waldman 25–26; Schleiner 378. William Nicolet found Harvey's initials disguised in EK by a shift from GH to flanking, adjoining letters, ignoring I (= J) and skipping over F and J because Gascoigne had used them already (*AN&Q* 2 (1964): 153–54). Donald Cheney speculates in the same direction, in "Afterword," *Spenser's Life and the Subject of Biography*, ed. Judith H. Anderson, Donald Cheney, and David A. Richardson (Amherst: University of Massachusetts Press, 1996), 173.

4.   Ed., *The Shepherd's Calendar* (London: Scholaris Press): 172.

5.   Ed., *Edmund Spenser's Poetry: Authoritative Texts, Criticism* (New York: Norton, 1968), 424; "On Reading *The Shepheardes Calender*," *Spenser Studies* 1 (1980): 89.

6.   *The Works of Thomas Nashe*, ed. Ronald B. McKerrow, with suppl. notes by F. P. Wilson (1904; repr. Oxford: Basil Blackwell, 1958): i, 296. A rope will do for the belt or string in *OED*'s quotation (**fast and loose** *a.*) from Halliwell (1847): "a cheating game played with a stick and a belt or string, so arranged that a spectator would think he could make the latter fast by placing a stick through its intricate folds, whereas the operator could detach it at once."

The mantelpiece from John Harvey's house illustrates that the Harveys also had something to do with beekeeping. They may have constructed hives made out of straw ropes (straw hives). The band of straw added beneath the hive to increase its capacity was also called an "eke" (*n.*¹2.b.), though *OED*'s earliest date is nineteenth century. A photo of the mantelpiece faces p. 7 in G. C. Moore Smith, ed., *Gabriel Harvey's Marginalia* (Stratford-upon-Avon: Shakespeare Head Press, 1913).

7. "Grumio's 'rope-tricks' and the Nurse's 'ropery,'" *Shakespeare Quarterly* 22 (1971): 82–85.

8. "Typographical Layout," 47n.

9. *Works*, ed. McKerrow, iii, 15, 65.

10. *A Concordance to the Poems of Edmund Spenser*, comp. and ed. Charles Grosvenor Osgood (Gloucester, MA: Peter Smith, 1963).

11. *Tempest*, III.ii.126–27 (Riverside). *Nine Daies*, ed. G. B. Harrison (New York: Dutton and Company, 1923), 32. (Is there a glance here at Spenser: [Ed]*Mundus/* Cullen [Colin]?) Neither of these two places has been thus explained before. Imprints based on this device may be misread now. *A Discoverye of a Counterfecte Conference Helde at a Counterfecte Place,* etc., e.g., of 1600, attr. to Henry Constable, has the imprint "Collen" (STC 5638.5). The speculation "[i.e., Paris?]" appears in *Dictionary of Literary Biography: Sixteenth-Century British Nondramatic Writers*, 2nd Ser., ed. David A. Richardson (Detroit: Gale Research, 1994), 136: 45. This imprint was at the time, doubtless, a misleading pointer to *Cologne* (*Köln*).

This device allows for the possibility, it should be noted, that *Kirke* is by intention in the mix (**Ed**.=**ecl**.=*ecclesia*= εκκλησια=church=*kirk*). The two references in *Three Proper Letters* (1580) to Mistress Kirke's as a place where mail should be sent by Harvey to Spenser (*Variorum Edition*, ix, 5, 12), letters that purport to have been written late in October of 1579, may have been intended to foster the notion that "E. K." was Edward Kirke, even if such a notion was an unanticipated consequence, an afterthought. With Spenser himself a "Kirke" (= **ecl**), as it were, then the London woman he would marry a few days later in October could, carrying through the jest, be called "Mistress Kirke." Alternatively, if Edward Kirke was rumored to be responsible and Spenser himself was (in part) so, then, again in jest, his wife (as she would soon be) may well be referred to as "Mistress Kirke."

12. With John Laing, New and Enlarged by James Kennedy et al. (Edinburgh: Oliver and Boyd, 1926–[62]), i, xx.

13. *Works*, ed. McKerrow, i, 267. Nashe clearly is thinking back to the *Three Proper Letters* of 1580; see, i, 296. Virginia R. Stern comments on "Harvey's use of personae to express certain aspects of his personality or interests," especially in his marginalia, in *Gabriel Harvey: His Life, Marginalia and Library* (Oxford: Clarendon Press, 1979), 136 et passim.

14. Jon A. Quitslund's translation from ll. 228–30 of "Ad Ornatissimum virum . . . G. H.," in "Questionable Evidence in the *Letters* of 1580 between Gabriel Harvey and Edmund Spenser," *Spenser's Life*, 94; the poem is in *Variorum Edition*, ix, 8–12.

15. Schleiner 382; *Harvey's Marginalia* 160–63.

16. ★3 (STC 21057); "An Initiation into Initials," *Studies in Bibliography* 9 (1957): 174; *Index of Dedications and Commendatory Verses in English Books before 1641* (London: Bibliographical Society, 1962), 109.

17. STC 4268.

18. "An Initiation," 177.

19. STC 11943. I am indebted to Grant McColley, ed., *"The Man in the Moone"* and *"Nuncius Inanimatus,"* by Bishop Francis Godwin, *Smith College Studies in Modern Languages* 19 (Northampton, MA.: Smith College, 1937); McColley, "The Pseud-onyms of Francis Godwin," *Philological Quarterly* 16 (1937): 78–80; H. W. Lawton, "Bishop Godwin's *Man in the Moone,*" *Review of English Studies* 7 (1931): 23–55; John Anthony Butler, ed., Bishop Francis Godwin, *The Man in the Moon* (Ottawa: Dovehouse, 1995).

20. *A Transcipt of the Registers . . . ,* ed. Edward Arber (London, 1877), iv, 426.

21. Butler, ed., 54.

22. P. 18 (STC 11944). The second edition (1657) was translated by Dr. Thomas Smith.

23. STC 11941.

24. *Works,* ed. R. Warwick Bond (Oxford: Clarendon Press, 1902; repr. 1967), iii, [18].

25. "Bishop Godwin's *Man in the Moone,*" 35.

26. Ed., *Man in the Moon,* 39.

27. *1 Henry IV,* II.iv.169 (Riverside); A-Text, ix.387, ed. W. W. Greg (Oxford: Clarendon Press, 1959), 234; *Looking Glass,* ed. George Alan Glugston (New York: Garland Press, 1980), G4 (p. 204), I2v (p. 225); *A Shrew: The 1594 Quarto,* iii.227, ed. Stephen Roy Miller (Cambridge: Cambridge University Press, 1998); *Thomas Woodstock,* III.iii.16–17, ed. Peter Corbin and Douglas Sedge (Manchester: Manchester University Press, 2002); VI.i, *Plays,* ed. Harvey Wood (Edinburgh: Tweedle Court, 1939), iii, 299; IV.i.9, ed. Cyrus Hoy, *Works in the Beaumont and Fletcher Canon,* gen. ed. Fredson Bowers (Cambridge: Cambridge University Press, 1970), ii, 510; III.iv.123, ed. Hans Walter Gabler, *Works* (1982), v, 491; *Works of Lancelot Andrewes* (1841; repr. New York: AMS, 1967), i, 212. Other plays are given by Morris P. Tilley, *Dictionary of the Proverbs of England in the Sixteenth and Seventeenth Centuries* (Ann Arbor: University of Michigan Press, 1950), *s.* S443.

28. R. M. Cummings, ed., *Edmund Spenser: The Critical Heritage* (London: Routledge, 1971; repr. 1995), 92.

29. Cummings, ed., 64, 95. David Lee Miller, in a remarkable discussion, "picks apart the illusion of presence . . . with Spenser's 'Loe' " that begins the envoy and helps conclude the book, sensing, as I do, a connection between this moment and Spenser's name (French *despencier*), though he does not make the link with Livy and the Latin, in "Spenser and the Gaze of Glory," *Edmund Spenser's Poetry,* 3rd Ed., 758–60. The pronoun "I" in Spenser (as also in "Lo I the man") Miller discusses in "The Earl of Cork's Lute," *Spenser's Life* 160; and "Steward" and "dispence" as references to *Spenser* in the kitchen allegory of *Faerie Queene* (II.ix.27, 29), in *The Poem's Two Bodies: The Poetics of the 1590 "Faerie Queene"* (Princeton: Princeton University Press, 1988), 176–77.

STEVEN W. MAY

Henry Gurney, A Norfolk Farmer, Reads Spenser and Others

From the leaves of Bodleian Library MS. Tanner 175 emerges a detailed portrait of a heretofore unknown and unstudied Elizabethan poet, critic, and bibliophile, Henry Gurney. From his seat at the manor of Great Ellingham, Norfolk, Gurney dispatched printed books and manuscripts to the most extensive coterie of named individuals identified to date in the Tudor and early-Stuart period. During the last decade of Queen Elizabeth's reign Gurney entered in the Tanner manuscript an inventory of his library as well as copies of more than 600 of his own poems. In several of these he explained in detail the poetic by which he judged good and bad poetry. He also transcribed his verse "censures" of more than a score of books he borrowed from the members of his circle. Among these works are titles by some of the age's most important writers including John Foxe, Robert Southwell, Richard Hakluyt, and two works by Edmund Spenser, *The Faerie Queene* and "Mother Hubberds Tale."

I. GURNEY AND TANNER MS 175

*I*N HIS FORTY-THIRD YEAR, HENRY GURNEY (1549–1616), lord of the Manor of Great Ellingham, Norfolk, began to write poetry. Over the next decade, he filled completely the blank pages of his manuscript book of estate records with his own verse, along with

Spenser Studies: A Renaissance Poetry Annual, Volume XX, Copyright © 2005 by AMS Press, Inc. All rights reserved.

detailed notes and related information about his life as a man of
letters. This volume, now Bodleian Tanner MS. 175, preserves his
poetic "censures" of more than twenty Elizabethan publications including John Foxe's *Acts and Monuments*, Robert Southwell's *St. Peters
Complaint*, Richard Hakluyt's *Voyages and Discoveries*, and John Weever's *Epigrammes*. Most interesting to readers of *Spenser Studies*, of
course, is his poetic "book review" of the *Faerie Queene*. Gurney is
among the earliest of the book's readers to record his critical reaction
to the poem, in addition to which he censured in verse a copy of
"Mother Hubberds Tale" that he may have read in manuscript. The
Tanner anthology provides us with a thorough insight into the intellectual life of this gentleman farmer and poet, for it includes family
records in prose and verse, the 1595 inventory of his library (transcribed in Appendix I), and some 628 poems, most of them by Gurney himself, on a wide variety of topics including his critical
principles for distinguishing good poetry from bad. His records also
make it possible to identify the members of Gurney's East Anglian
coterie, a group of friends, relatives, and neighbors who maintained
a lively exchange of works, primarily printed books. The story of this
remarkable interchange emerges from several types of records found
in the pages of Gurney's notebook; in aggregate, it allows us to
reconstruct the most extensive, well-defined Elizabethan literary coterie that has yet come to light.

Gurney initially organized his manuscript in commonplace fashion
to receive entries concerning the family estates under engrossed headings such as "Hingham notes" (f. 5) and "Notes of West Barsham"
(f. 7). Henry began writing in the manuscript during the 1570s,
entering at intervals in the codex copies of rentals, leases, indentures,
debts owed to him, and the like from his day-by-day business transactions. But Tanner 175 soon became a catch-all repository for other
kinds of information. Henry added to it copies of earlier family estate
records, many of them executed by his grandfather Anthony during
the reign of Henry VIII. With regard to some annotations concerning
rentals at West Barsham, for example, he observed that "the notes in
the margent were written by the same hande that first wrote this
rentall but the names that are interlined were written with a later
hand but by whome or in what yere I can not certainly saye" (f. 48).
Henry filled the notebook with such miscellaneous entries as a family
pedigree (ff. 30v-31), mercers' bills (f. 193), a list of his debts (f.
216v), and a record of burials in the church and chapel of Great
Ellingham (f. 238). From about 1592, however, the volume served
primarily as his literary notebook. In one of several autobiographical
poems, he says of himself that "till his age of forty thre a verse did

never wright" (f. 145v). Once launched on his poetic career, Henry must have devoted a good deal of his spare time to the Muses, for Tanner 175 is predominantly a collection of his own verse, much of it revised and redrafted. His datable entries in Tanner 175 continue into the early seventeenth century, the latest being 1608. He died in 1616, in his sixty-seventh year.[1]

The manuscript itself is a small folio measuring 200 x 304 mm. It consists of two contemporary preliminary leaves followed by 239 folios with folio 103 tipped in between the original folios 108 and 109. The unfoliated upper half of a leaf has also been tipped in between ff. 82 and 83. Its verso is blank, but Gurney wrote out the poem on its recto with the paper flat against the following leaf for a line of its right marginal readings trailed over onto the recto of f. 83. Aside from f. 103, little blank space remains in the codex which, except for six lines of verse added in a later hand on f. 41, is nearly all filled with Gurney's handwriting, much of it badly faded. He added rubricated titles and dates to many of his poems. On ff. 60–61v, Gurney supplied a subject index for the poems in his anthology. This he entitled "A Table for the speciall matters Conteyned in the poemes aforesaid, Directing to the page the staff, or line" (f. 60). His pagination in this listing runs as high as 488 yet this enumeration was apparently cropped during the nineteenth-century binding of the manuscript. It reveals, however, that the volume extended originally to at least 244 folios. Two of the missing leaves were lost between present ff. 71–72 where the earlier foliation skips from 75 to 78. Gurney himself explains the stub between ff. 212 and 213: "the leafe following I cutt out my self" (f. 212v). The paper of the main foliation bears the same watermark throughout, a single-handled, crowned pot design with initials E D R or E D P visible on the band, similar to Briquet 12725 (1581).[2] A parchment slip (now f. 240) was apparently cut from the volume's original binding. It is inscribed, "Edward Gurnay his booke," evidence that the manuscript was passed down to Henry's grandson Edward Gurney (1608–1641). The family's connections with Cambridge University may explain the volume's final destination in the Tanner collection, although the details of its seventeenth-century provenance are unknown. Henry's great-grandson, Henry, was admitted fellow commoner at Caius College in 1648 where he presumably studied until his admission to Lincoln's Inn in 1651. During his University career he may have given or sold the anthology to William Sancroft, then fellow of Emmanuel College, whose manuscripts eventually formed most of the Tanner collection.[3]

Much of Gurney's family history emerges from the leaves of his account book turned poetic notebook. The family had long roots in Norfolk. A Matthew de Gourney can be traced as early as the reign of Henry II.[4] In his pedigree notes, Henry records Matthew's marriage to a "daughter of Raynold fitzfhillipe" in 1183/84 (f. 30v). Henry's ancestor, Edmund Gurney (will dated 1387), acquired the important family Manor of West Barsham in the fourteenth century. The family tree on f. 68v shows Henry's descent from his grandfather, Anthony Gurney, and his father, Francis. During Henry's childhood, the Gurneys maintained viable social ties with their shire's greatest family, the Howards, who were, variously, dukes of Norfolk and earls of Surrey. Henry was sponsored at his baptism in 1549 by Lady Catherine Howard, daughter of the poet earl of Surrey. In 1547 Catherine's sister, Lady Jane Howard, stood godmother to Henry's sister, Frances, while in 1550 the widowed Lady Frances Howard, countess of Surrey, was godmother to Henry's brother, Anthony. The Howards' participation in these solemnities is all the more remarkable given the fact that the senior Anthony Gurney was foreman of the grand jury that in 1547 condemned to death Henry Howard, earl of Surrey, for high treason.[5]

Francis Gurney predeceased Anthony, who in turn died in 1557, leaving the family's male heir, Henry, an eight-year-old minor. In October, 1564, Henry matriculated pensioner from Christ's College, Cambridge but apparently did not take a degree.[6] He came of age in 1570 and settled down to manage the family estates. From his poem titled "The match & petigre of Gurnay & his wife their childrens nomber sex and age" (f. 26v) we learn that he married Helen, daughter of John Blenerhasset, and that eleven of their thirteen children were still alive when he composed these verses in 1593. Henry's prose notes on the family state that the marriage took place June 10, 1571 (f. 22).

Henry's poetry reveals much about his career as estate manager and gentleman farmer. He wrote poems in praise of dogs, geese, and properly constituted cheese. Two poems complain at some length about the damage caused to his properties by neighbors who were avid hunters:

1 My neybor goodman G B
  with two or thre of clownes
  his followers that be,
  (all following stinking howndes)
  himself vppon his Iade

& they vppon their feet
My closes do invade
& thinke yt not vnmeet
2 to breake my fence & gates
& trample on my Corne
presuming that such states
should therfore be forborne

(f. 143v)

In four passages he comments on the poetry of Thomas Tusser, who expanded his *Hundreth Points of Good Husbandry* (1561), into *Five Hundreth Points* by 1573. The book gave detailed advice in verse on proper administration of both farm and household, and was written for just such estate managers as Gurney. On ff. 82v, 186, and 187v, Henry composed verses on agricultural practices in competent imitation of Tusser's anapestic tetrameter couplets.

By 1597, Henry was growing deaf, as several of his poems on the subject testify (ff. 142, 204, 227v). He complained in verse about the kinds of problems caused by this affliction, especially when he tried to confer with his lawyers:

whileas my case wth Councellors I treate
their speech wth peyne they very lowd must sounde
wherby no less even dangers very greate
vnto my cause, do oftentimes Redound
when enimys, who standeth neere at hand
the secretes of my case may vnderstand (f. 103)

On the other hand, his deafness encouraged his writing of poetry as he explains in another poem:

Who can Inioy no company
nor be of them Inioyd
by reason of Infirmity
nor otherwise Imploid
to shorten way to wast the night
to please him self & ffrend
If honest poemes he Indite
who may it discommend

(f. 237v)

At about the same time Gurney complained that, after twenty-eight years of marriage, his wife constantly blamed him for prodigality: "Whi should his wife in teeth him daily cast/ with vayne expence & of exceeding was[t]?" Henry protests that,

> . . . he to hir, a Reconing euer streight
> did yield of all expence that he did make
> although she can no wast in him detect
> yet still much waste to him she doth obiect.

He mournfully concludes:

> for greater griefe the world can not afford
> then wiues contempt in gesture, deede & woord.
>   most rare it is for man a wife to find
>   that every wey shall well content his minde

(f. 83).

Much of Gurney's output including his magnum opus, "The Anatomy of Popery," is devoted to anti-Catholic satire. The "Anatomy" runs to more than 2000 lines of verse, not counting the multiple additions to the poem that Henry drafted in the Tanner manuscript, often with directions as to where they should be placed in the main text. His other anti-Catholic poems include translations of passages from the Latin Eclogues of Mantuan (Giovanni Baptista Spagnuoli) on ff. 137–37v, and poems with such titles as "of popish heathen Sottishnes" (f. 64v), and "Catholique popish churche" (f. 134). Gurney set forth his allegiance to the late Elizabethan regime in a number of poems that praise not only the queen (ff. 48v, 49, 83, 134, 170–72, 227v, 239) but her chief minister, Lord Burghley, as well (f. 48v). He expressed no sympathy for the Essex rebellion of 1601, but began his verse review of William Barlow's authorized account of the attempted coup with the line, "this bookes contents wch cannot be butt true" (f. 132).[7] Gurney's enthusiastic approval of Elizabeth's reign in its closing years sounds a note of caution to wide-ranging assertions that the queen's subjects had tired of her rule by the 1590s and eagerly looked forward to regime change.[8]

Most of Gurney's intellectual interests are represented among the eighty-eight titles listed in his inventory of books (including the "Bookes of myn in other mens handes") that he first set down in

1595 but augmented as he acquired new books, loaned others, and gave away still others (see Appendix I for a transcript of this list and proposed identifications of its titles). Presumably, Henry inherited from his father and grandfather a small family library as represented, for example, by the copy of de Burgo's *Pupilla oculi* (No. 62), termed by Gurney "an ould popish book" (f. 42). Sixty-six of the titles in his inventory, however, were first published after 1557 and were no doubt acquired by Gurney himself. Ten titles are marked "to Edm" or "giue Ed." apparently indicating the books Henry bestowed on his scholarly third son, Edmund. In his draft will of 1614, he left all of his Latin books to Edmund.[9] Henry's library is weighted toward religious topics, with five Bibles, three New Testaments, and more than a score of entries dealing with Reformation polemic. He owned as well books appropriate to his occupation as a rural landowner, particularly works on the law by Pulton, Lambard, Littleton, and Kitchen, plus Leonard Mascall's popular book on grafting. His interests in history and geography are represented by Grafton's *Abridgement of the Chronicles of England* and his copy of Holinshed's massive *Chronicles* in two volumes, plus Hakluyt's *Voyages and Discoveries*, and Muenster's *Cosmography*.

Gurney's book list also reveals his interest in poetry, an interest that may have been nurtured by family ties. The entry "Mirror of magistr by Tho Blenerhassit" in his library inventory refers to *The seconde part of the Mirrour for Magistrates*, a book of verse narratives published in 1578. While its author has long been identified as the son of William Blenerhasset of Norwich, evidence from the Tanner MS suggests that he was instead Henry's brother-in-law, Thomas Blenerhasset. This kinsman stood godfather to Gurney's first son, Thomas, born in 1572 (f. 22). When Henry defends certain poetic "rules" by affirming that "in all of wch Sweet Surrey, Vaux, & Mirror are precise" (f. 132), he probably refers to Blenerhasset's book rather than the original *Mirror for Magistrates* of 1559/1563. It would only be natural for Gurney to hold his brother-in-law's work in high regard rather than that of the Norwich man of the same name to whom he was very distantly related.[10] Henry may have met Thomas at Cambridge, where a Thomas Blenerhasset had enrolled at Peterhouse in 1564, the same year Gurney entered Corpus Christi.[11] A friendship between the two that began in Cambridge might also explain why Henry married a bride from Suffolk. Henry makes no mention, however, of Blenerhasset's second book of verse, *A Reuelation of the True Minerua* (1582). Other titles of literary interest in Gurney's inventory include Ascham's *Scholemaster*, Thomas Churchyard's *Lamentable, and pitifull Description of the wofull warres in Flaunders*

(1578), "livi in folio," no doubt a Latin edition of Livy, Thomas Nashe's *Pierce Penilesse*, Barnaby Riche's *Allarme to England*, Alexander Barclay's translation of Brant's *Stultifera nauis*, and Sir Philip Sidney's "book of english posy," probably *The Defence of Poesie* (STC 22535) rather than the *Apologie for Poetrie* (STC 22534), both published in 1595.

Gurney's booklist provides further and quite remarkable insight into his intellectual milieu, for ten of its entries are followed by notes indicating that he had loaned the book to a named recipient. In addition, the inventory is followed by a list of books Henry loaned to others under the title, "Bookes of myn in other mens handes at this 10 may 1595" (f. 42v). In all, Gurney recorded loaning out sixteen books between 1595 and about 1602. At that rate, however, he was a net borrower, for his twenty-one verse "censures" of books responded to titles that, with two exceptions, do not appear in his inventory.[12] Henry's subscription to his review of *The Historie of George Castriot, Svrnamed Scanderbeg* (1596, STC 15318) explains his practice of borrowing books and returning them with "book reports" in verse for the lenders:

> this Sensure I wrot on ye booke of Scanderbeges actes lent me
> by Mr Bart, wth thes verses following
> > Brief Censure of this volumes larg content
> > with my Retorne & thankes I have you sent
> > yet if your booke, or fancy yt offend
> > you may both sone & safli out it rend
>
> > > > > (f. 227v)

It is an interesting coincidence that Spenser also wrote commendatory verses for the *Scanderbeg* volume. Yet Gurney's "reviews" of Spenser's works probably indicate that he did not own copies of them, but that *The Faerie Queene* was one among a score of identifiable printed books that circulated among the members of Gurney's coterie. He responded to a copy of the first edition of *The Faerie Queene*, for he exactly describes the 1590 edition as a quarto of 589 pages (f. 135). Of his four "censures" written about books of poetry, Gurney copied samples of verse only from Spenser and from *The Passions of the Spirit* (1599), so far as I am able to determine. He began by rewording Spenser's title, "the frayr [sic] quene the first" for "The first Booke of the Faerie Queene" (sig. A2). Gurney then omitted the section title, "Canto I," at the beginning of the narrative on sig. A3 and copied out the epigraph, followed by stanzas 1–5 of the narrative. In the left margin beside stanza 1 he recorded the work's rhyme scheme with the formula "1.3/ 2.4.5.7/ 6.8.9." In fact, Gurney's interest in *The Faerie Queene* was largely technical. After describing the book's format, he observed that it was composed "alltogether of this kind of staff wherof these be the first. bearing great fame, but not in my Iudgement" (f. 135). Gurney knew that Spenser's masterpiece had been highly acclaimed, yet he expressed his skeptical disapproval of the work in a six-line verse "censure":

> ould outworne woordes, this aucthor doth observe
> And vsuall staff, or measure, doth reiect
> if praise or blame, therfor he do deserve
> I cannot Iudge, although I may suspect
>   that when a woorke is strang & new devised
>   the aucthor is Invyed, or dispised
>
> (f. 135)

Henry failed to appreciate Spenser's technical virtuosity in devising his Spenserean stanza and using it for the highly demanding purposes of *The Faerie Queene*'s narrative. Gurney's main objection, however, echoes Sir Philip Sidney's judgment of Spenser's archaic diction in *The Shepheardes Calender*: "That same framing of his style to an old rustic language I dare not allow."[13] Spenser's language and poetic form apparently kept Gurney from reading much more than the first few stanzas of Spenser's first book. This is a sad irony, for had he read on he must certainly have rejoiced in the story's allegorized glorification of Protestant England as well as its attacks on Catholicism, the pope, and Spain.

Gurney's engagement with Spenser did not end, however, with his disparaging review of the work in the stanza that he no doubt copied and included with the book when he returned it to its owner. Before he did so, he transcribed ten of Spenser's dedicatory sonnets and all but one of the commendatory verses for *The Faerie Queene* (ff. 177v-181). He copied the first eight sonnets in Spenser's initial series of dedicatory poems, those addressed to Hatton, Essex, Oxford, Northumberland, Ormond, Charles Howard, Grey of Wilton, and Ralegh. He then turned to the beginning of the series of commendatory poems that precede the sonnets in the printed book, copying out Ralegh's "A Vision" and "Another of the same." He skipped Gabriel Harvey's offering (beginning "Collyn I see by thy new taken taske" and subscribed "Hobynoll") and continued with the poems subscribed R. S. and W. L., then returned to p. 589 and H. B.'s "Graue Muses march in triumph and with prayses" that follows the commendation of R. S. He next copied "To looke upon a worke of rare deuise" by "Ignoto," then returned to the sonnets, transcribing those to Lady Carew and "To all the gracious & beatifull Ladyes in the court" (f. 181). On f. 177v Gurney added "E. S." after "&c" to the title of Hatton's dedicatory sonnet, although in this original series of dedicatory poems, only the sonnets to Lady Carey and all the ladies of the court are subscribed E. S. Overall, he followed the indentation of lines in these sonnets and their punctuation quite carefully, but he departed from the printed text by indenting the initial rhyme lines in Ralegh's "The praise of meaner wits," and the final couplets in W. L.'s sixain stanzas.

Why did Gurney find these verses peripheral to *The Faerie Queene* interesting enough to copy, and why did he decline Harvey's poem? The answer to this question may come more sharply into focus as we consider Henry's dismissal of another work by Spenser. By early 1596 he had read and composed a response to "Mother Hubberds Tale" from Spenser's *Complaints* volume published in 1591. Gurney makes no mention of the printed book or any of its other contents, however. He may have borrowed a manuscript copy of the text, several of which are extant. Presumably, many readers deemed it safest to circulate Spenser's by private transcription because of its supposed libelous allegory of Burghley and his son, Robert Cecil.[14] There is evidence, however, that in the same year that Gurney wrote his verse response to the poem, printed copies of "Mother Hubberds Tale," with its separate title page, were sold apart from the collection to which it belonged.[15] Had Gurney noted the attack on the Cecils, he would no doubt have condemned the work on that count alone, for he praised Lord Burghley in a verse riddle that includes the lines:

For lerning witt welth land & place fame princes grace & bydyng
at hyest pitch of all the wch one man hath most residyng (f. 48v)

Henry supplied the answer to his riddle in a superscript note: "hath Burley."

Yet Gurney apparently discerned in "Mother Hubberds Tale" no satire of any kind, whether aimed at Burghley or anyone else. His critique of the poem condemns it in part as a casualty of Spenser's well-established reputation:

Censure of Mother huberdes tale
No point of praise ther soundeth in myn eare
in poem wch such speciall fame doth bear
yt halteth oft aswell in Ryme as feet
hath Theame obscure & verse more harsh then sweet
myn Ignorance I rather yet Suspect
then dare avouch therin but one defect
for who that once hath gott him self a fame
his after faltes bear but reprovers blame

(f. 139v)

The poem struck Gurney not as a daring and culpable libel but one burdened with a "Theame obscure." His reaction, again, highlights the divide between the politically active class that presumably would have detected satire aimed at the Cecils in Spenser's beast fable, and the average, educated citizen of the land, who neither expected nor perceived such intentions. Whether or not the government called in the *Complaints*, Gurney's testimony suggests that its satiric intentions, if any, were too subtle to affect more than the most politically sensitive readers. So much for Spenser's debut in the provinces.

II. GURNEY'S POETIC

The theory of good and bad poetics that emerges from a cluster of poems in Tanner 175 helps to explain why Gurney disliked Spenser's poems, declined to copy Harvey's verse commendation of *The Fairie Queene*, yet took the trouble to copy out its other dedicatory and commendatory poems. Gurney set forth several poems that express both his views on poetic composition in general and the criteria by which he asks readers to judge his own poetry. He begins by defending the originality of his own verse:

The garment that is course, yet evenly match[t]
is better then with finer stuff but patcht
wch is the cause whi I so much am loath
some Silken thredes to weave in hempen cloth
And therfor will even as I have begonn
make vpp my webb wth poem my self have sponn

(f. 195)

He thus claimed independence from the content and presumably the styles of other poets, yet he tried at the same time to adhere precisely to certain technical rules of poetic composition that he discovered in the poets he admired. As he explains these principles in verses of his own, Gurney reveals his reading background in the poetry of his age and he discriminates between its talented and inept practitioners. On ff. 132 and 142, for example, he copied two drafts of a poem advocating that "accent," by which he seems to mean ceasura, must fall "on second foote" in pentameter verse, and after the third foot of such long-line meters as hexameters and heptameters. Gurney asserts that

> accordyng to best presidentes, & Rules, I so observe
> if skill afford, from perfect Ryme, nor meeter do I swerve
>
> (f. 132)

He then reveals that he derived these rules from specific authors:

> in all of wch Sweet Surrey, Vaux, & Mirror are precise
> & as especiall ornamentes even Sidney did agnize
> so Gasquoyne Goldyng Harington & Churchyardes woorkes al-
> low[ed]
> & Dannyells also but of late {have} ^{precisely have} Carefull avowd

Of these poets, Gurney's library catalogue lists only Blenerhasset's *Seconde Part of the Mirror* and Churchyard's *Lamentable, and pitifull Description of the wofull warres in Flaunders.* By the mid-1590s, Gurney could have read various published works of Sidney, Gascoigne, and Daniel. Unless he relied on manuscript sources, however, he had probably read Surrey's verse in Tottel's *Songs and Sonnets,* and Lord Vaux's in *The Paradise of Dainty Devices* (1576–1606), the only source for printed attributions to works by this poet. Before the appearance of *The Metamorphosis of Ajax* in 1596, Gurney could have known Sir John Harington's verse only from his translation of Ariosto's *Orlando Furioso* (1591), while Arthur Golding's reputation as a poet rested almost exclusively on his translation of Ovid, although he included verse in most of his other translations as well. This passage in Gurney's poem reveals, at any rate, that he was far more widely read in the poetry of his time than we could determine either from his inventory of books or his "censures" of books that he borrowed from others.

Gurney expressed his interest in the technical aspects of versification in a marginal note to his translation of a Latin passage that was rendered into English by several other Elizabethan poets:[16]

> This latine I more redily
> translate that men may know
> how english with like brevitye
> like Sence with Rome can show
> When latyn doth but only tyme
> observe & not the meeter
> the english vsing tyme & ryme
> must harder be & sweter
>
>   (f. 199v)

Gurney's fullest statement of his poetic occurs in three poems on f. 145v. The title to the second of these expresses his understanding of poetry's utilitarian function: "Of verse it is the chiefest property / to Stoare the head & helpe the memory." On that basis, he expressed in another poem his refusal to attempt the chivalric subjects of Harington's *Orlando* or Spenser's narrative in *The Faerie Queene*, or the dominant amorous themes of the Elizabethan age:

> To Sound exploites of noble feates of armes
> myne oaten pipe to Silye is & base
> of Lovers fittes therr fained Ioyes or harmes
> I skorn to wright, or tread that common trace
>
>   (f. 190v)

Henry's pastoral diction in these lines is simply a humility topos, for while his verse sometimes treats agricultural subjects, it is never pastoral in the literary sense of that term. Gurney's approval of Gascoigne, Sidney, and Daniel does not contradict the sentiments of these lines, for he referred only to their adherence to technical aspects of versification, not the subjects they treated. Similarly, he rejected *The Faerie Queene* on grounds of its poetic diction and meter although apparently aware as well that it treated "exploites of noble feates of armes," a description that could also refer to works he probably knew by Sidney, Harington, and Daniel. In the following stanza, Gurney describes the moral and practical subjects that define his own writing:

My poemes be a mix[t] variety
for matter & the sondri kindes of verse
yet most of them conteine philosophi
of eyther kinde wch here I doe Reherse
    Divine as chife, then Mathamaticall
    the morall next & last the natural

                            (f. 190)

His emphasis on variety ties in with the title of his presumably lost work, the "Medley of Conceits," which may have consisted of poems from Tanner 175 that he selected to distribute to others.

Gurney's first poem in the series on f. 145v provides us with his fullest statement of what he believed to be good poetry:

A perfect verse much matter must conteine
fit woordes & knowne, none forced nor in vayne
A word alike in meeter tyme & feete
And on the tongue Ronn Roundly smoth & sweet

To Curiously if all these props be skande
some verses be that so vpright do stand
for Poete of the greatest skill or fame
may fayle in one without a noate of blame

He next argues that a poem may survive a deficiency in one of these precepts, but a poet's failure to observe two, three, or four of them calls for extreme remedies: "if fower fayl then see for ayde you call/ to stay it vpp least hedlong it do fall." In his third poem on the subject, Henry explains that since some readers approve the contents of any verse so long as it rhymes, while others insist that poetry be extremely regular in meter, he therefore offers different versions of his works in different colored inks, in an effort to please all: "so as if that first put in black, doth not content his mind/ as Redd or greene hath altered yt, Contentment he may fynd." It should be noted that this assertion does not apply to the revised drafts of Henry's poems in Tanner 175, but must describe the fair copies he prepared for circulation among his friends.

This survey of Gurney's poetic establishes his critical priorities. Aspects of poetic language, rhythm, and rhyme trumped other aesthetic considerations such as "matter": thus his rejection of Spenser.

He apparently declined to copy Harvey's commendatory poem for similar reasons. Harvey employs only moderately archaic language, with a few "mought's" a "hight" and a "ne," but Henry also may have objected to the way Harvey eked out its meter with the forced pronunciation of "ed" endings ("chaunged" in line 9, "loued" in line 11), and the syncopated syntax that dropped adjectives before "poore pastors oaten reede" (line 23) or "thou dost vayle in Type of Faery land" (line 27). The commendatory poems he did copy, however, are couched in conventional Elizabethan forms and meters: Ralegh's English sonnet and poulter's measure couplets were stanzas Gurney would have recognized from his reading of Surrey, Gascoigne, and possibly Sidney as well. The offerings by R. S. and H. B. in combinations of cross-rhyme and couplets, and those in sixain stanzas by W. L. and "Ignoto" would likewise have passed muster by Gurney's insistence on conventional rhyme schemes. Why he copied out ten of Spenser's dedicatory sonnets is less easily explained. All are Scottish sonnets, a form Gurney might otherwise have encountered only in printed works, notably, King James's *Essayes of a Prentise, in the Diuine Art of Poesie* (1584). Nor was Gurney intrigued by the riddling nature of much lyric poetry, albeit he composed a number of verse riddles (e.g., ff. 62v, 74, 196, 200v). He could not be bothered with working out the allegory of *The Faerie Queene* after finding that its archaic diction and outlandish rhyme scheme contradicted two of his four principles of good poetry.

III. GURNEY'S COTERIE

Gurney did praise other works of verse and prose, but before glancing at some of his other "censures" I wish to define his coterie by introducing as many of its members as I have been able to identify. The task has been simplified by the fact that Henry was blessed with an orderly mind. He catalogued his books and noted their borrowers, he drew up an alphabetical list of "The Poemes dispersed in this booke" (f. 59v), followed by "A Table for the speciall matters Conteyned in the poems aforesaid" (ff. 60–61v). On ff. 146–46v he drew up a separate "Table to the treatise following," a subject index to his "Anatomy of Popery," including such headings as "Images worshipping," "Ioane the woman pope," and "Reliques popish." Page numbers in each of these lists direct us to the locations of these works and topics in the Tanner anthology. To the first of these "tables," on f. 59v, Henry appended a list of the copies of his own poems distributed to friends and family (edited below as Appendix II). Thus, his circle can be reconstructed from his lists of those to whom he loaned his books or presented copies of his poems. In all, some two dozen persons borrowed Gurney's books or received copies of his poems in manuscript, but, with three exceptions, we do not know who loaned books to him. Accordingly, we cannot identify most of the recipients of his verse "censures." The first exception can be partially reconstructed from Henry's faded, later addition to his 1595 book list: "Sidneys book of english posy lent us . . . Bailey at lon" (No. 76; hereafter, numbers in parentheses refer to the books listed in Appendix I). This apparently means that the unidentified Bailey loaned Sidney's *Defence* to Gurney, possibly in London (although "lon" could denote such neighboring Norfolk locations as Longham or Long Stratton). Regretably, no "censure" of Sidney's treatise appears in the Tanner MS. Gurney also records sending his "Censure" of a sermon by Henry Smith to "my Cosen Hasset," no doubt a Blenerhasset relative less immediate than his "brother[-in-law]" Thomas. The third loan entry concerns the "booke of Scander-beges actes lent me by Mr Bart . . . " (f. 227v). This is presumably, the same "mr Bartles" to whom Henry in turn loaned his copy of William Fulke's *Text of the New Testament* (No. 35) and sent a copy of his "Anatomy of Popery" (f. 134v). Given that only Mr. Drury among those to whom Gurney loaned books also received a copy of his poetry in manuscript, the lack of named lenders of books to him suggests that Henry's circle included more than two dozen individuals.

Gurney's coterie was centered on his friends and relatives among the landed gentry and neighboring clergymen. The Master Drury of Besthorpe who borrowed Hakluyt's *Voyages* on May 6, 1595 (No. 29) was Anthony Drury (d. 1616), whom Henry described as a "legacye grandchild" of his grandfather Anthony Gurney (f. 22v). Drury was Henry's first cousin, the son of his aunt, Ela Gurney, wife of the elder Anthony Drury (d. 1577). Anthony the younger had matriculated pensioner from Corpus Christi College, Cambridge, in Lent, 1557, about seven years before Henry's admission to the same College.[17] Like Henry, Anthony did not take a degree. Drury stood godparent to two of Gurney's sons, while his wife, Anne, was godmother to one of the daughters. Their home at Besthorpe was just two miles from Great Ellingham. Anthony is no doubt the "Mr Dr." who also received a manuscript copy of Gurney's "Medly of Conceytes" (see Appendix II). Drury had returned the *Voyages* to Henry before

Christmas, 1598, when he lent the book "to Mr Thornton of Hengham" (Hingham), about two miles north of Great Ellingham. Robert Thornton of Hingham held lands in both Norfolk and Lincolnshire as we learn from his will of 1612.[18] John Cornwallis is the "brother Cornwallys" who received "the best" copy of Gurney's "Medley" (see Appendix II). John was Henry's brother-in-law, the husband of Katherine Blenerhasset, Helen Gurney's sister. Although Cornwallis remarried sometime after Katherine died in 1584, the two kinsmen maintained their close ties. John had matriculated pensioner from Trinity College, Cambridge at Michaelmas, 1560, but, as with Gurney and Anthony Drury, took no degree.[19] His seat at Earl Soham, Suffolk, was some thirty miles southeast of Great Ellingham, making John the most distant member of Henry's coterie whom I have been able to trace. He was perhaps the most prosperous member as well, for his will refers to substantial holdings in Suffolk and Huntingdonshire, and he left Elizabeth, his second wife, "my best Coache and twoe of my Coache geldings . . ." along with other property.[20]

Gurney's coterie included five identifiable clergymen. "My Cosen furnis," who borrowed two books by Hadrianus Saravia, was probably the Ralph Furness of St. John's College, Cambridge (B.A. 1579–80; M.A. 1583; B.D. 1590) who was ordained in 1583. In that same year, Nathaniel Bacon presented him to the rectory of Merston (Merton), Norfolk, a town some eight miles northwest of Great Ellingham.[21] I have not traced Furness's relationship with Gurney. The "Mr Coppin" who received a partial manuscript of the "Medly of Conceytes" was "George Coppinge Clerke," cited in Anthony Drury's will as vicar of Besthorpe.[22] Gurney loaned his copy of the *Decretalia* of St. Gregory to "Mr Trendle the parson of ovington," a town about eight miles northwest of Great Ellingham. Bishop Redman's 1597 visitation of Norwich cited John Trendle, rector of Ovington, for failure to wear the surplice.[23] Henry recorded loans of three books to Mr. Womack (Nos. 25, 30, 44) , no doubt Henry Womack who was ordained in 1589 and presented to Fersfield Rectory in 1595 by John Cornwallis. Fersfield was some twenty miles southwest of Great Ellingham; in 1614, however, Gurney united Womack to the church at Great Ellingham.[24] The fourth cleric in Henry's circle is "mr poynton" (f. 42), who borrowed John Racster's *Booke of the Seven Planets* (No. 7), a response to William Alabaster's lost book of *Seven Motives* in defense of the Catholic faith. A John Poynton, son of Robert of Garveston, Norfolk, was admitted to Caius College, Cambridge in 1578, took his B.A. degree in 1583, was ordained in 1587 and served as Rector of Kilverstone, Norfolk from that year until his death in 1641.[25]

Gurney also loaned or gave books to other relatives, among them the "mathematicall Iuell giuen Bass throkmrt." (No. 57), no doubt his nephew Bassingbourne Throckmorton, the son of Lionel and Elizabeth Gurney Throckmorton. Lionel was Gurney's "broth Throgmor" who received a copy of the "Medly of Conceytes" (see Appendix II). Their daughter, Mary, married William Rawley of Clay, Norfolk, who is probably the "Mr. Rauly" who borrowed Gurney's copy of Thomas Playfere's sermons (No. 67). Mary, the only woman mentioned in Gurney's literary circle, likewise received a copy of the "Medley": "on[e] with my nece Mary wch is that Mr Dr. ha[d]" (see Appendix II). Family ties may also explain why "Mr Godsale" received a copy "of the Annotomy wthout the addition of Image & divers of the Chefe poemes." This was either Thomas Godsalve of Buckenham Ferry, Norfolk (matriculated pensioner from Trinity College, Cambridge at Michaelmas, 1552) or his son, Roger, who was admitted fellow commoner at Caius College, Cambridge, in 1584.[26] The Godsalves had married a Gurney relative some two generations before Henry's. This tie explains in turn the loan of "Book M," presumably a manuscript copy of Gurney's verse, to "my C[ousin]. Blondeville" (f. 89v).[27] The book Gurney loaned to "m Hobart of mor.." was an edition of the *Decretum Gratiani* that appeared in numerous fifteenth and sixteenth-century editions (No. 37). The borrower, Henry's "Cosin miles Hobert," of Plumstead, was the grandson of Ellen Gurney's great aunt. Miles's wife, Margaret, stood godmother to Gurney's daughter Elizabeth in 1573 (f. 22).[28] "My bro rich," another recipient of a copy of the "Anatomy" (see Appendix II) may be Richard Blennerhasset, the fifth son of John and Elizabeth of Barsham, born in 1566.[29]

Gurney also exchanged books and poems with other acquaintances named and unnamed. The "Mr Harris at hargham" (f. 42v) who borrowed Gurney's copy of Muenster's *Cosmographie* in 1595 may have resided at Hardingham, a village some six miles north of Great Ellingham. John Chenry, who borrowed Gurney's copy of Holinshed was presumably the "John Chynnerye" who matriculated sizar from Jesus College, Cambridge in 1585.[30] I have not identified "Tho Gh," who borrowed the second volume of Holinshed at some time after Chenry returned it. Henry's "Cosen Smith" (see Appendix II), and the Master Sundley who borrowed his copy of Hakluyt's *Voyages* in 1599, likewise remain unidentified. The "mr Bartles" (f. 42) or "Bartlet" (134v), who borrowed a New Tesatment from Henry was an important figure in the circle, for he loaned Gurney the copy of Scanderbeg's *Historie* and in return received a copy of the "Anatomy" (f. 134v). He was probably Edward Berthelet Senior of Atleburgh

Hall (d. 1605), a lawyer and justice of the peace.[31] In addition to these twenty-one named members of the coterie, four unnamed acquaintances expand the circle, barring overlap, to twenty-five. The identity of the borrower of Gurney's copy of John Jewel's *Defense of the Apologie* (No. 42) has been obscured by faded ink; we know only that the book was "Received againe." Henry also copied into the Tanner manuscript three poems sent to him by others: "A ffrendes commendation of the medly of conceyt" (ff. 39v-40), "An Invectiue against tyme sent me by a ffrend" (f. 121v), and verses "written from a frend 20 feb. 1595" (f. 181v).

The multifaceted characteristics and interactions of Gurney's coterie emerge from this reconstruction of its membership. The exchanges took place within a period of some eight years between about 1595 and 1603, and included both printed and transcribed works. Henry was not the only poet in the coterie, for, as we have seen, he preserved verse sent to him by at least one and perhaps three other friends. His circle extended as far afield as the Cornwallis estate in Suffolk, and possibly made at least one contact in London, but was centered among Henry's relatives and friends within a dozen miles of Great Ellingham. At least a third of its members had enrolled at Cambridge University, although only the clergy among them had taken degrees. Presumably, Gurney's was a strongly Protestant circle (unless we imagine him sending out the "Anatomy" to badger and insult his Catholic acquaintances). Despite his zealous opposition to the Roman Church, Gurney himself was no Puritan, for the legacies bequeathed to his younger sons in his will bore the condition that " 'none hould any fantasticall or erronious opinions, so adjudged by our bishop or civil lawes.' "[32] It may be pertinent to note here that Gurney apparently was familiar with the practice of doubling characteristic of plays performed by professional acting companies. He composed eighteen lines of verse on the theme, "This world is like a Theater or stage," in which he observes, "And wheras he whoe lately plaid ye prince/ doth sodeinly in beggers state appeare . . . " (f. 235v). As we have seen, however, Parson Trendle's refusal to wear the surplice suggests that at least one member of Henry's circle had puritanical leanings.[33]

Gurney was himself a significant publisher of manuscript verse, whether he copied all his poems personally or employed a scribe to produce fair copies for dispatch. In addition to at least twenty-one "censures" of books he borrowed from others, Henry prepared at least four copies of his "Anatomy of Popery" and at least four more of his "Medley of Conceits" (see Appendix II). It is just possible that a group of Gurney's poems, not heretofore recognized as his, in

Chetham's Library MS. Mun. A.4.15, is in fact a surviving copy of the "Medley." The Chetham MS. is a miscellany of prose and verse dating from about 1603 to 1626 or later. On pp. 111–131 of this collection the unidentified scribe copied seventeen poems for a total of some 660 lines of verse. I have located all but four of these works (totaling just fourteen lines), in the Tanner MS. The remaining texts are scattered through Henry's anthology (on ff. 49v, 50, 80, 149, 169v, 177, 194v, 195, 204–05, 208–09, 213v–14, 222v, and 228v–32), and they treat a variety—truly a medley—of subjects, from the fraud of astrologers to the value of timber holdings to wives' duties, to moral precepts. Strangely lacking are Gurney's hallmark attacks on the Catholic church. Stranger still is the fact that the Chetham anthologist chose to copy out Gurney's rather pedestrian verses at such length and in close proximity to poems by John Donne, Ben Jonson, Sir John Davies, and Sir Walter Ralegh. Whether or not Gurney's poems in this collection are a remnant of his "Medley of Conceits," their presence here is striking proof that Gurney's poems did circulate in manuscript and perhaps for some years after their creator's death.[34]

Gurney's circle of vitally active readers and writers is remarkable, especially given its location in rural Norfolk, yet its practices were not wholly unprecedented at the time. Richard Lawson, who in 1576 became rector of Letheringsett, about forty miles north of Great Ellingham, "seems to have been the instigator of a little society of the clergy in the Holt Deanery who lent books to one another."[35] This practice was continued by his son, Joseph, who became rector of North Barsham in 1614. Joseph catalogued the family's fifty-two books and recorded his father's loans of them to five named recipients. Joseph's subsequent list names nine later borrowers. While this borrowing took place over the span of a half century or longer, its general contours closely resemble those of Gurney's circle. The Lawson circle was Protestant, indeed, largely or entirely Puritan, and it included at least one woman, the "Mris. Ka. Hoe" who borrowed "A Booke on the Nature of Bees." (p. 63). The Lawsons' library included at least one transcribed work, "A Manuscript in parchment dialogue wise," and some variety of titles beyond its theological core including (in common with Gurney's list) a copy of Ascham's *Scholemaster*, plus Edmund Bolton's *Elements of Armories* (1610), George Wither's *Abuses Stript and Whipt* (1613), and a commentary on Cicero's *De Officiis*.[36] Yet there is no suggestion that the Lawsons' coterie exchanged verse in manuscript, much less the verse "censures" devised by Henry Gurney.

IV. GURNEY'S "CENSURES" AND CENSURE

Henry's remaining "censures' of the books he borrowed concern a variety of works from several sources. He no doubt gained access to John Weever's *Epigrammes in the oldest cut, and newest fashion* (1599) through his son, Edmund, rather than from interaction with his wider coterie. Edmund had been admitted to Queens' College, Cambridge on 30 October 1594, about six month's after Weever's admission there as sizar. The development of their friendship is witnessed by Edmund's contribution of commendatory verses to the *Epigrammes* (sig. A4v).[37] Weever's verse, however, with its scattering of ametrical lines and such rhymes as "counting" with "hunting" (sig. F6) and "rootes" with "bookes" (sig. G8v) was ill-designed to please Edmund's father. Henry's "Sensure of Iho wevers epigrams decemb 1599" protests that any poet who breaks the

> Rules of poesy . . .
> Can not by Iudgement good, be thought to be a perfect weaver
> whose warpe is dark, whose woofe is harsh, whose shittle,
> Rules contempt
> from iust reproof by Sensuring shall never be exempt
> Coniunctions causalls Relatiues, yea verbes you oft omitt
> as vayne, Supposing them supplide by readers only witt
>
> (f. 132)

Gurney's condemnation of Weever deals only with technical matters; it passes over in silence his epigram on the death of Edmund Spenser (sig. G3) and those in praise of other contemporary poets, including William Shakespeare.

It is tempting to suppose that family ties also explain Henry's verse review "of fugetiues vnder the king of spayne as I wrote in a voyd space of a printed book of that title sett out Ao 1595" (f. 120v). The book in question is Lewis Lewkenor's *The Estate of English Fugitiues Vnder the king of Spaine* (STC 15564), an enlarged second edition of a *Discourse of the Vsage of the English Fugitiues by the Spaniard* (STC 15563), published in the same year. Gurney's eldest son, Thomas, married Martha, daughter of Edward Lewkenor of Denham, Suffolk, on November 10, 1596 (f. 22). But Lewis Lewkenor belonged to another branch of the family, and both early editions of his work were published anonymously. Henry's eight-couplet censure echoes the main theme of Lewkenor's treatise, that Spain is not the mighty

superpower it seems to be. And this subject proved even more inspir-
ing, for on ff. 62–2v Gurney drafted a further rhymed response (with
many cross-outs and corrections), titled, "thes should follow the state
of fugetiues p. 244," referring, apparently, to his initial response to
the book on f. 120v. On f. 82v, Henry offered his "censure" of
another book about the king of Spain, but one, he complains, that
affirms Spain's wealth and military might. The poem is dated 23 June
1598, but I have not identified this work.

About half of Gurney's "censures" concern explicitly religious titles, including sermons by Henry Smith (f. 70v), John King (f. 80),
and William Barlow (f. 132). Miles Mose's *The Arraignment and Conviction of Vsuri* is likewise a collection of sermons in opposition to
usury, an attitude seconded by Henry's "censure" (f. 119v). Other
devotional works include John Northbrooke's popular *Spiritus est* (f.
188v), and Christopher Sutton's *Disce mori. Learne to Die*, which Gurney praises in this closing couplet with the date of its composition:
"vppon the foresaid godly groundes/ this Sutton heauenly descant
soundes 29 ap 1601"(f. 132). Henry's response to the Jesuit Vincenzo
Bruno's *A Short Treatise of the Sacrament of Penance* (1597) is remarkably tempered; Gurney concedes that, as a guide to penitence, "this
booke is partly fitt," yet flawed by the fact that "this aucthor doth
no scripture cite, nor Councell ould or father/ to prove the thing
he would persuade . . . " (f. 132). "Censures" of religious polemic
include Henry's denunciation of image worship (f. 67v), inspired by
Francis Bunny's refutation of Cardinal Bellarmine in his *Suruey of the
Popes Supremacie* (1595). He was equally offended by a book comprising three pro-Catholic tracts that he borrowed from an unidentified
friend. "This booke for matter or for [f]ame/ is so absurd & eke
obscuer," he begins, that while "Some good yt hath but very scant,"
he reluctantly returns it to its owner "for promise sake ells would I
not/ but would the same in fyer burn" (f. 70v). Gurney was equally
impatient with William Alabaster, the earl of Essex's chaplain who
converted to Catholicism in 1597 and then implored family and
friends in nearby Suffolk to return to the Old Faith. Henry read
Alabaster's "Motives," a lost book, as reprinted and refuted in John
Racster's *A Booke of the Seven Planets, Or, Seuen wandring Motiues, of
William Alablasters wit* (1598). Gurney's direct address to the apostate,
"What doth this late revolte Alabaster/ the Credyte of the popish
sort inhance" (f. 105v), suggests that he had some personal acquaintance with Alabaster. The only other book in his library inventory
that Gurney "censured" in Tanner 175 was Foxe's *Acts and Monuments*. Predictably, Henry heartily approved of this work. He wrote
seventy-eight lines in fourteener couplets praising "the first Tom of

ye booke of Martires," including praise of the author that implies personal knowledge of his life:

> In matters lyke besides composed his labor hath bene such
> as never yet by englishman was framed half so much
>   a fox he was by name & skill but yet a sheepe for mind
>   all fraudes he clarkely doth disclose yet was to none inclined
>
> (f. 40v)

I have not identified three of the most unexpectedly diverse publications to which Gurney responded in verse. I have already mentioned his censure of a book on the power of the king of Spain (f. 82v). Second, he describes a book in praise of women by a French author, whom he berates for failing

> . . . hir vertues to commend
> who specially doth grace ye woman kinde
> of all that are or ever yet have bene
> I meane our true & noble english quene
>
> (f. 228)

Third, on f. 106v, Gurney apparently reports on a ballad or pamphlet that described Siamese twins born in Flanders. While ballads of monstrous births were popular during the Renaissance, and at least one describes Siamese twins born in Buckinghamshire (STC 17803, 1566), I have not found a printed account of a similar instance that occurred in Flanders.

Gurney responds to Henry Lyte's *Niewe Herball* (STC 6986, from the original Dutch through the French of Charles de L'Écluse, three editions, 1578–1595) by noting that, were all its receipts (that is, medical prescriptions) efficacious, physicians "would not the same Indure," because these herbal remedies would put them out of business. Gurney interprets Hakluyt's *Voyages* as evidence that Elizabeth's prosperous reign has led to idealized colonization projects:

> Through Goverment most sage of noble queen
> such peace & welth do to hir Subiectes flowe
> as speciall meanes to noble myndes have been

Realmes most remote to serch therin to sow
    The Christian faith & Civill good behavior
    wth tradeing for ech others welth & favor

                                            (f. 83)

Explicitly poetic works account for only five of Gurney's two
dozen censures, but we should keep in mind that the sizable volumes
by Foxe, Holinshed, and Hakluyt contain substantial amounts of verse
as well.[38] Aside from Spenser's *Faerie Queene* and "Mother Hubberds
Tale," three books of religious verse round out Henry's responses to
the poetry of his age. His critique of *Saint Peters Ten Teares* is, once
more, centered on its technical attributes:

So many Rymes & feet to halt
    wch in so short a work
through aucthor or ye printers falt
    I haue not know [sic] to lurke

                                            (f. 70v)

His disapproval was probably aimed at such rhymes in this anonymous work as "name/staine" and "puts on/ mourne" (sig. A3v-4).
What Gurney perceived as halting feet are problematic, however,
for to a modern ear the poem's meter is in all-too-regular iambic
pentameter. He was more forthcoming in response to *The Passions of
the Spirit*, presumably but not certainly the work of Nicholas Breton.
Henry borrowed this book from his nephew, Bassingborne Throckmorton. In repayment, he took the liberty of rewriting "about 110
such staves as are on ye right hand of this page. all wch staves I
corrected more or less in such manner as here with redd Inke is
done" (f. 122v). And indeed, in what follows, Gurney copied out
stanzas from the *Passions*, then corrected and punctuated them in a
different ink. Yet the sentiments, phrasing, and prosody of the *Passions*
and *Saint Peters Ten Teares* are nearly identical; both poems typify a
sub-genre of late-Elizabethan devotional verse, the penitential lament
in "sixain" stanzas that rhyme ababcc.[39] Henry was confused, however, by the appearance of the *Passions*'s text on the page. The book's
octavo format caused the printer to add a decorative border around
each page and then split the pentameter lines in two so that the six-
line stanzas appear in units of twelve lines of verse. The poem's
occasional substitute feet left Henry unable to scan these half lines
with absolute regularity as alternating iambic dimeters and trimeters.
He blamed the irregularities on the printer:

Thes verses should of feete but two or thre
concist or ells they stomble or do halt
And to that tyme, the most of them agre
but many fayle, {do doub} [sic] perhapps by printers falt
   whos necligenc, with red thoug [sic] I correct
   in aucthor yet, supose then no defect

(f. 122v)

The printer, Thomas Este, filled the last two and a half leaves of the *Passions* with two verse prayers, one of which was much more to Gurney's liking. He copied out the first two stanzas of the poem beginning, "O heavenly God, O Father dear," after drawing this contrast with the preceding work:

the verses wch do here Insue
although of lower stile & phrase
yet pithy, easy, smoth, & true
do all delight, & none amase
   but former ragged, & obscure
   small profite, & delight, procure

(f. 122v)

Gurney is here entirely in step with the taste of his times, for "O heavenly God" was one of the most admired and widely distributed lyrics of the Elizabethan age. First printed in the *Paradise of Dainty Devices* of 1576, it was reprinted in all later editions plus two other books before 1603, while texts survive in fourteen contemporary manuscripts, not counting incipits to musical settings of the poem.[40] In summary, Gurney responded to the *Passions* by copying out a number of its stanzas only for the sake of correcting their meters. He then transcribed "O heavenly God," and this text with his excerpts from the *Faerie Queene*, including its dedicatory and commendatory poems, appear to be the only verses from books that came his way that he judged fit to copy into his anthology.

Of all the poetry Gurney responded to in the Tanner MS, he reserved his highest praise for Robert Southwell's *Mœoniæ. Or, Certaine excellent Poems and spirituall Hymnes*. The book was published under the initials "R. S." shortly after Southwell's execution in February, 1595. Someone lent Henry a copy within a year of its publication, for he dated one of his responses to it "23 Ia. 1595 El. 38" (1596 by modern reckoning). Southwell's anthology saw at least nine

editions by 1602. Its contents sidestepped controversial religious doc-
trines and expressed devotional sentiments that both Catholics and
Protestants could accept. Gurney was well aware that a Jesuit wrote
these poems, and he countered any praise of the work that implied
more than poetic fame for its author. Papists, he argued, cannot
" . . . shew other worke, their Iudgement so to grounde/ save only
thes few poemes wch, no controversies sound." To attribute any
other preeminence to Southwell would be as absurd, he affirmed, as
to do the same for earlier Catholic poets: "So Chaucer, Lydgate,
Surrey, Vaux, no less in those their tymes/ in other artes should be
preferrd, as in their verse or rymes" (f. 139v).

Gurney clearly spent some time reading and enjoying *Mœoniæ*. He
expressed admiration for the content as well as the style of Southwell's poems:

> For matter form Choise woordes and fittest phrase
> Deepe Style or arte, or godly meditation
> as presidentes thes poemes may we blase
> & compt for woorkes of speciall estimation
> my Censure saith to truth or Conscience debtor
> for all respectes scarse redd I ever better

(f. 139v)

Henry must have found it easy to approve Southwell's style because
of its reliance on conventional Elizabethan meters and stanzas, especially its repeated use of the "sixain" stanza and a smattering of fourteener couplets plus "ballad" stanzas and other simple cross-rhyme
schemes in short-line meters. Southwell's style was made all the more
familiar by his practice of adapting well-known secular lyrics to religious purposes.[41] Gurney qualified his praise of Southwell's verse only
with regard to the poetic diction of "Saint Peters Complaint," the
centerpiece of this collection of his poetry. The "Complaint," in
sixain stanzas, was perhaps the archetypal influence on the spate of
similar pentitential works that appeared in England over the next
decade or so. Henry noted, however, that its often elegant expression
seemed out of character for the blunt, unsophisticated disciple, Peter.
He returned to Southwell's volume on 24 January 1596 to comment,

> If that ther may a fault espied be
> it is in that Decorum is not kept
> sith youthfull phrase & arte do disagree

from fisher man, that into age was stept
    whose Stile appostolique was grave & plaine
    as that wch doth worldes Curiousnes disdeyne

                        (f. 139v)

He then stepped in to give Southwell this excuse for his lack of decorum:

the aucthor thus may hervnto replye
sith verses now so comonly be demde
no better then for foolish poetry
& therfor but of yonger sort estemd
    he tempered arte with pietye & truth
    as best might treine, Content, & Season youth

                        (f. 139v)

Given his radical anti-Catholicism, it is remarkable and much to Gurney's credit that he was able to show so much forbearance toward a fellow poet who was also a Jesuit.

Criticizing others' verses, Gurney discovered, was a two-way street. His acquaintances seem not to have shared with him their sentiments regarding any of the books they borrowed from him, but they did respond to the poetry of his own that he sent them in manuscript. By early 1596 he had obtained feedback on his "Anatomy of Popery" "from a frend" who praised him for employing " . . . your golden penn/ that truth may stand by god his woord/ the praise of all good men" (f. 181v). Henry replied to these verses in kind, one of the few examples of the exchange of original verse within the coterie. Yet other readers of his poetry were less charitable in criticizing his work, as his poem "an vnhappy descent" laments in some detail (f. 83). In this much corrected draft, he complains that these critics, his "nerest frendes," derided his works "before his wife, child, servant, foe, or ffrend" (f. 83). They attacked, he continues, "Such poemes as to please them he did write/ & straungers do even very much applaude." Gurney then protests that their condemnation was unfair because they failed to enumerate his faults:

Yet if they could by aucthor, Rule, or reason,
Avouche & prove, how his conceytes do fayle
for matter, forme, Condition, Cense, or season

in stead of grief they should him muich avayle
>   who soner would to servantes will dissend
>   then twhart [sic] the truth, against his meanest frend

(f. 83)

Much worse lay ahead, however, for Henry must have winced at
the very negative response to his poetry expressed in verse by his
learned son, Edmund. In "of Poesy rules" (f. 84v), Gurney had attacked modern poets for abandoning what he considered the "Aun-
cient Rules" that governed good poetry. It must have been with
a very reluctant hand indeed that he copied as the next entry in
his anthology,

> Ed: G his Censure of ye verses prec[eding].
> >   thes verses may I not dissemble
> >   except in ryming pros resemble
> of this your Censuring no Sense I find
> to shew your lyking or dislyking mynde
> in Imitating those you most commend
> no better then for prose, you yet disende.

Edmund no doubt resented his father's failure to appreciate John
Weever's *Epigrammes*. In rataliation, he ironically deprecates Henry's
own prosody on grounds that it violates the very rules he is defining,
the same rules Gurney used to condemn Weever. Edmund stresses
as well the prosaic nature of his father's verse. His worst condemnation of Henry's talent occurs in the couplet, "much better wert, you
made no verse at all/ then from ye Rules therof so much to fall"
(f. 84v).

The "rules," of course, were the least of Henry's deficiencies as a
poet. Edmund's critique of his father's prosaic versification defines
the problem all too well. Henry never grasped the essence of his art,
the imaginative, suggestive, aesthetic qualities that differentiate the
creative art of poetry from expository prose. Yet contemporary writers had recognized and publicly analyzed that distinction by the time
he turned to writing verse in the early 1590s. If Gurney read Sidney's
Defence, he made no connection between his own writing and the
"golden world" of creative writing described there. Sidney, however, defined poetry's potential for moral didacticism in a way that
should have appealed to the author of the "Anatomy of Popery."
Even more to the point, Sir John Harington avowed in his "Apologie

for Poetry" (1591) that he could not himself claim "the glorious name of Poet" because his original verse lacked creativity.[42] Gurney's poems are less satiric, overall, than Harington's epigrams, yet they cover an even broader range of subjects and they resemble Harington's work in treating real rather than imaginary subjects. For Harington, the poet was a *creative* artist who devised fictions, while he and other versifiers put the substance of expository prose into rhyme and meter. For Gurney, likewise, the poet treated everyday themes in colloquial English differentiated from prose only by its expression in rhyme and meter. If Henry ever recognized poetry's more sophisticated capabilities, he applied them neither to his own verse nor to his criteria for judging the poetry of others.

IV. CONCLUSION

Henry Gurney's anthology provides a detailed look in cross section at the backbone of the Elizabethan regime. It reveals the most heartfelt attitudes, interests, and commitments of a middle-class landowner loyally devoted to the queen, her ministers, and to the Church of which she was the Supreme Governor. We learn as well of his vehement opposition to his nation's enemies, Spain, and Catholicism. In doing so, Gurney's anthology demonstrates the importance of manuscript evidence toward constructing a balanced understanding of the Elizabethan age. While we may reasonably question the sincerity of printed endorsements of Elizabeth's reign simply because they are set forth in this public medium, Gurney's multiple encomia of the queen in his private collection of verse confirm his genuine devotion to her to the very end of the reign. Some courtiers and members of the politically active class in Parliament and at the Inns of Court, for example, eagerly anticipated the queen's death. Yet on this subject Gurney's poetry and prose in Tanner 175 remain silent; he wrote nothing about the succession, the king of Scotland, or any other candidate for the post-Elizabethan throne. Nor was Henry's devotion to church and crown an aberrant commitment. He may well represent mainstream attitudes among his countrymen—not an overwhelming majority, perhaps, but still the dominant outlook among English men and women throughout the Queen's reign. Her successors eventually paid the price for a style of sovereignty that discouraged and finally snuffed out this broad-based support.

The testimony of Gurney's verse as it relates to the poetry of his age is equally instructive. Once Sidney and Spenser had begun to

influence Elizabethan poetry, our literary history effectively ignores
the continuation of the mid-century tradition. We are prone to believe that the new, "golden" poetic achieved widespread if not universal acceptance and imitation after 1590, if not before. By then it
had rendered passé the mid-century tradition with its long-line meters, heavy alliteration, and allusion piled upon allusion. This out-
worn poetic enjoyed, however, a vigorous afterlife that stretched well
into the next century.[43] Gurney's verse is a telling example of its
influence upon a thoughtful and well-educated middle-class reader
of the time. He never acknowledged the centrality of imagination
to the finest poetry and its most pleasing, uplifting effects. Although
he was quite familiar with both the old and new modes, he rejected
innovative techniques in favor of the overly regular meters, limited
stanza forms, and clichéd rhetoric of the mid-century tradition. As a
result, it is tempting to dismiss Gurney as a Norfolk bumpkin who
preferred Tusser's jigging vein to Spenser's supple and infinitely var-
ied prosody, yet Gurney also exercised enough poetic sensitivity and
forbearance of Catholicism to praise Robert Southwell's verse. And
again, in both judgments he is fully representative of his age if we
consider the contemporary popularity of these three poets. For it is
also easy to forget that after the augmented reprint of *The Faerie
Queene* in 1596, it waited until 1609 for a third edition. In sharp
contrast, Tusser's work on husbandry saw a total of seventeen Elizabethan editions, while Southwell's poetry went through twelve editions
in the time it took *The Faerie Queene* to reach four. Gurney's preference for these poets over Spenser simply reflects the taste of the age as
measured by the relative popularity of the three books in question.[44]

Tanner 175 is perhaps the least representative of its time in its
detailed revelation of the workings of a rural coterie of late Elizabethan readers. Henry's library list and censures of the books loaned to
him by his friends create a fascinating record of the actual titles
exchanged within this circle of rural Norfolk readers. Oddly, however, Gurney's anthology offers no absolute evidence that his circle
was connected with any of the age's widespread networks of manuscript circulation. Aside from Gurney's own poetry, copied and dis-
seminated among his friends, and a few responses to it, it is not
clear that this coterie exchanged manuscript texts. Yet we know
that transcribed texts of all kinds were widely dispersed throughout
England at this very level of society. As Henry Woudhuysen has
shown, even so considerable a work as Sidney's *Old Arcadia* took
only three or four years to spread across the country in manuscript.
Moreover, this dissemination was accomplished by collectors of
about the same social and economic standing as Gurney.[45] Perhaps

Henry's well-developed sense of organization caused him to reserve Tanner 175 primarily for his own verse. He may have copied works that reached him in manuscript into a separate collection. If so, he would have preserved manuscript works sent to him by other writers in his coterie, along with his responses to them, in another volume. Speculation aside, it seems safe to conclude that Henry's dedication to writing poetry was unusual for Elizabethans of his social and educational standing. His political and religious attitudes place him in the mainstream of his society, however, while his personal anthology reveals in detail his individuality as a husband, parent, estate manager, and man of letters.

Georgetown College

NOTES

1.   Henry's birth and death dates are cited in his brief biographical notice under his son, Edmund Gurnay, in the *Oxford Dictionary of National Biography* (2004). Henry's will was not proved until 1623 (M. A. Farrow and T. F. Barton, *Index of Wills Proved in the Consistory Court of Norwich and now preserved in the District Probate Registry at Norwich 1604–1686*, Norfolk Record Soc. 28 [1958], 96).
2.   C. M. Briquet, *Les Filigranes*, ed. Allan Stevenson (Amsterdam: Paper Publications Soc. 1958), vol. 4.
3.   John Venn and J. A.Venn, *Alumnae Cantabrigienses*, Pt. 1, vol. 2.276; *DNB* 17.731.
4.   Francis Blomefield, *An Essay Towards A Topographical History of the County of Norfolk* (London, 1807), vol. 7.45.
5.   Daniel Gurney, *The Record of the House of Gournay* (London, 1848), part 2, p. 419.
6.   Venn and Venn, pt. 1, 2.276.
7.   STC 1454, *A Sermon Preached at Paules Crosse . . . With a short discourse of the late earle of Essex his confession, and penitence.* Gurney wrote six couplets that reveal his full agreement with the official government interpretation of the earl's crimes.
8.   Bishop Godfrey Goodman affirmed that late in Elizabeth's reign "the people were very generally weary of an old woman's government" (*The Court of King James the First* [London, 1839], 1.97), a view echoed by many modern historians. The sentiment, I believe, was held more widely among the genteel politically active class than by the populace at large.
9.   Gurney, *Record*, part 2, p. 456. Edmund (1577–1648) matriculated from Queens' College Cambridge in 1594 (B.A. 1600), M.A. and B.D. from Corpus Christi College, rector of Endgefield, and later Harpley, Norfolk. He published five works on religious subjects, primarily attacking the Catholic Church (*DNB*).
10.   Venn and Venn base their identification of the Thomas Blenerhasset who studied at Trinity Hall in 1564 on the *DNB* identification of the *Mirrour's* author as

Thomas, son of William Blenerhasset of Norwich. But *DNB* (and STC) surely conflate two Thomas Blenerhassets when they equate the poet of 1578 who published another book of verse in 1582, *A Reuelation of the True Minerua*, with the author of *A Direction for the Plantation in Ulster* (STC 3130, 1610). In his dedication to Prince Henry, the Blenerhasset responsible for this tract refers to himself as "a playne Country man" (sig. A2v), while author of the *Mirrour* refers to "Souldiers, of whiche I am one by profession" (sig. *iii verso). The identification is complicated, moreover, by the fact that Blenerhasset was often abbreviated to "Hasset" by contemporaries (see Lily Bess Campbell, *Later Additions to the Mirror for Magistrates* [Cambridge: Cambridge Univ. Press, 1946], 370). The Cambridge records fail to identify the families or residences of any of the three Thomas Blenerhasset/Hassets who studied at the university in the 1560s and 1570s, but one of them is surely the author of *The Seconde part of the Mirrour*, for in his "Epistle vnto his friende," this Thomas Blenerhasset reminds the addressee that "I once translated for you, Ouid, De remedio Amoris, as you said, to your contentation, we beyng then in Cambridge, . . . " (sig. *iii recto). I think it most likely that the poet is the same Thomas Blenerhasset recorded at Trinity Hall in 1564, the same year that Gurney enrolled at Corpus Christi, whether or not Thomas addressed his "Epistle" to Gurney. Their acquaintance at the University might well explain both Henry's marriage into the Suffolk family and the copy of the *Second Part of the Mirror* in his library. Campbell argues that the Thomas Hasset who matriculated from St. John's College, Cambridge, in 1571 is the poet, soldier, and Irish freeholder who died in 1624 (pp. 370–76).

11.   Venn and Venn, pt. 1, 1.166.

12.   Henry perhaps acquired his own copy of Foxe's *Acts and Monuments* after composing his seventy-eight line poem "On the first Tom of ye booke of Martires" (ff. 40v-41).

13.   *Miscellaneous Prose of Sir Philip Sidney*, ed. Katherine Duncan-Jones and Jan Van Dorsten (Oxford: Clarendon Press, 1973), 112.

14.   Steven W. May and William A. Ringler, Jr., *Elizabethan Poetry: A Bibliography and First-Line Index of English Verse 1559–1603* (London: Continuum, 2004), EV 12867. Partial transcriptions from the *Complaints* survive in at least three Elizabethan manuscripts. For allegorical interpretations of the Fox and Ape in the *Tale* see Brice Harris, "The Ape in *Mother Hubberds Tale*," *HLQ* 4 (1941), 191–203; A. C. Judson, "Mother Hubberd's Ape," *MLN* 63 (1948), 145–49; Anthony G. Petti, "The Fox, the Ape, the Humble-Bee," *Neophilologus* 44 (1960), 208–15; Richard S. Peterson, "Laurel Crown and Ape's Tail: New Light on Spenser's Career from Sir Thomas Tresham," *Spenser Studies* 12 (1998), 1–35.

15.   In "A Bibliographical Note on *Mother Hubberds Tale*," *ELH* 4 (1937), 60–61, Josephine Waters Bennett cites a list of books purchased 20 October 1596 by Anthony Bacon, secretary to the earl of Essex. There, "Mother Hubberds Tale" is recorded at the exorbitant price of five shillings, further evidence that this text was considered dangerous to circulate by any means.

16.   Two different translations of the Latin, beginning "Pastor, arator, equibus . . . " occur, one in Bodleian Library MS. Rawl. poet. 112, f. 73, and a second in Bodleian MS. Rawl. poet. 85, f. 83v (with another copy in Marsh's Library, Dublin, MS. Z 3.5.21). British Library Harl. MS. 7392 (2) preserves both versions of the poem (f.

61) which, unlike Gurney's translation, can be read as in the Latin from top to bottom as well as from left to right. For details of the poem's popularity see H. R. Woudhuysen, *Sir Philip Sidney and the Circulation of Manuscripts 1558–1640* (Oxford: Clarendon Press, 1996), 285 and note.

17.   Gurney, *Record*, part 2, p. 449; Venn, Pt. 1, vol. 2.68.

18.   Public Record Office, PROB 11/126, 72 Rudd.

19.   Venn and Venn, Pt. 1, vol. 1.399.

20.   Public Record Office, PROB 11/126, 85 Rudd, proved October 20, 1615.

21.   Venn and Venn, Pt. 1, vol. 2.186. See Appendix I, "Bookes of myn in other mens handes," Nos. 3 and 4). John Nurse Chadwick, *Index nominum; being an index of Christian and surnames (with arms,) mentioned in Blomefield's History of Norfolk* (King's Lynn, 1862), vol. 9.428. I am grateful to W. H. Kelliher for supplying me with this reference.

22.   Public Record Office, PROB 11/128, 109 Cope. Joel Coppin, son of George, rector of Besthorpe, was admitted sizar at Caius College, Cambridge 20 February 1595/96 (Venn and Venn, Pt. 1, vol. 1.395.).

23.   *Diocese of Norwich Bishop Redman's Visitation 1597*, ed. J. F. Williams, Norfolk Record Soc., 18 (1946), 70.

24.   Venn and Venn, Part 1, vol. 4.450.

25.   Venn and Venn, Pt. 1, vol. 3.390. In 1581 Robert owned lands valued at twenty-five shillings in Garveston, a town about eight miles north of Great Ellingham according to the "Lay Subsidy, 1581 Assessors' Certificates for Certain Norfolk Hundreds," in *A Miscellany*, Norfolk Record Soc. 17 (1944), ed. E.D. Stone, 115.

26.   Venn and Venn, Part 1, vol. 2.228; Rye, *Visitation of Norfolk*, 40–41.

27.   Thomas Godsalve's daughter, Elizabeth, married Edward Blundeville (d. 1568), son of Rafe Blundeville and his wife, Constance, the daughter of Henry's grandfather, William Gurney. Henry's cousin Blondeville was probably Thomas, the son of Rafe and Constance or Thomas's son, Anthony. Walter Rye, *Norfolk Families* (Norwich: Goose and Son, 1913), vol. 1.261; Gurney, *Record*, part 2, 425.

28.   *Visitation of Norfolk*, 2 vols., ed. A. W. Hughes Clarke and Arthur Campling (London, 1933, 1934), vol. 1.165. Ellen Blenerhassett, the daughter of John Blenerhasset of Frenze, Norfolk, married Miles Hobart of Plumstead who drew up his will 6 August 1557 (Dashwood, 2.61). The younger Miles was their grandson, who married Margaret, daughter of Thomas Woodhouse.

29.   Joan Corder, *The Visitation of Suffolk* (London, 1984), part 2, 360–61.

30.   Venn and Venn, Part 1, vol. 1.328.

31.   Chadwick, vol. 1.533; Gurney controlled the advowson of a third part of Atleburgh (vol. 1.484). I am grateful to W. H. Kelliher for providing me with this identification.

32.   Daniel Gurney, *Supplement to the Record of the House of Gournay* (King's Lynn, 1858), 876.

33.   A. Hassell Smith terms Trendle a "puritan minister" in *County and Court: Government and Politics in Norfolk, 1558–1603* (Oxford, CP, 1974), 185.

34.   Alexander B. Grosart edited the Chetham anthology as *The Dr. Farmer Chetham MS.*, 2 vols. (Manchester: for the Chetham Society, 1873).

35.   Charles Linnell, *Some East Anglian Clergy* (London: Faith Press, 1961), 45.

36. Linnell, 61–64.

37. *Oxford DNB*, "Edmund Gurnay," "John Weever."

38. Elizabethan editions of Foxe's book included from thirty-five to fifty-two poems, while Hakluyt's *Principall Navigations* printed nine poems in 1589 but twenty-four in the full editions of 1598–1600, one to a length of more than a thousand lines.

39. Breton wrote several canonical works in this mode including "A Solemne Passion of the Soules Loue" (STC 3665, 1595; expanded and reissued in STC 3696, 1598). For similar poems in the same six-line stanza, see Robert Tofte's "Deo, Optimo, Maximo" (STC 24096, 1598), *Marie Magdalens Lamentations for the Losse of Her Master Iesvs* (STC 17569, 1601), and *The Passion of a Discontented Minde* (STC 3679.5, 3680, 1601–02), composed by Robert Devereux, earl of Essex, while imprisoned in the Tower of London before his execution in 1601.

40. The *Paradise* text was attributed to "F. K." (Francis Kinwelmarsh), in that anthology's first six editions. The rival authorial claim of Walter Devereux, first earl of Essex, is refuted by Hyder E. Rollins in his notes to his edition, *The Paradise of Dainty Devices (1576–1606)* (Cambridge: Harvard University Press, 1927), 251–52. In *Nicholas Breton, Poems not Hitherto Reprinted* (Liverpool: Liverpool University Press, 1967), Jean Robertson concludes that "it is almost certain that Breton wrote these prayers" (p. lix), on the basis of their appearance in the same volume as the *Passions*.

41. Southwell's "Phansie turned to a sinners complaint," for example, is a couplet-by-couplet imitation of Sir Edward Dyer's popular lament in poulter's measure beginning "He that his mirth hath lost." "Content and rich" is based on the well-known song, "My mind to me a kingdom is," and "What joy to live" is a religious parody of Petrarch's *Rime* 134. See *The Poems of Robert Southwell, S. J.*, ed. James H. McDonald and Nancy Pollard Brown (Oxford: Clarendon Press, 1967), 36–40, 53–54, 67–69 and notes.

42. Prefaced to Harington's translation of Ludovico Ariosto's *Orlando Furioso*, ed. Robert McNulty (Oxford: Clarendon Press, 1972), 5.

43. Their survival goes virtually unstudied because the new poets are so much more accomplished and interesting. During the 1590s, however, while Shakespeare, Drayton, and Daniel were publishing their works and John Donne's verse circulated in manuscript, practitioners of the "drab" style rivaled them in popularity. Among the most prominent examples, William Warner's lengthy narrative in fourteener couplets, *Albions England*, saw seven editions between 1586 and 1612; Arthur Golding's translation of the *Metamorphoses* reached an eighth edition in 1612, and that model mid-century anthology, the *Paradise of Dainty Devices*, saw at least eleven editions between 1576 and 1606. Moreover, George Chapman's renderings of the *Iliad* (1598) and Odyssey (1614?) owe much in both language and technical form to the earlier tradition.

44. Jean R. Brink makes this point in passing in *Michael Drayton Revisted* (Boston: Twayne, 1990), p. ix. I am grateful to Professor Brink for elaborating on the idea in private conversation.

45. Woudhuysen, 317. Woudhuysen shows that within a few years during the 1580s, manuscript copies of the work had spread as far afield as north Wales, and Suffolk through agency of such local families as Thelwall (Denbighshire) and Tollemache (Helmingham Hall) pp. 319–24.

APPENDIX I: GURNEY'S INVENTORY OF HIS BOOKS, 10
MAY 1595

The initial listing of books is followed by his record of "Bookes of myn in other mens handes at this 10 may 1595." The entries have been numbered for greater clarity and are followed by tentative identifications of each entry set off in brackets and a different font.

[f. 42] Inventory taken of my bookes 10 may 1595
1. Augustine 4 Tom giue Ed.
2. Allens appol. of eng. Cath. [STC 373, Cardinal William Allen, *A True Sincere and Modest Defence of English Catholiqves*, (Rouen, 1584)]
3. Abstract Answered by Cosons [STC 5819.5–19.7, Richard Cosin, *An Abstract, of Certaine Acts of Parlement*, 1584.]
4. Actuarus de vrinis [*Actuarius De Vrinis, libri spetem*, tr. A. Leo. Paris, 1522; another edition (with other works), Paris, 1548].
5. Ascham his scholemaster [STC 832–36, Roger Ascham, *The Scholemaster*, 1570–89.]
6. abbregment greatest of states bought 1597 [Possibly STC 9531.5, *An abstract of all the penall Statutes which be general*, 1596 (Ferdinand Pulton's abridgement of the statutes, but see Gurney's No. 62)].
7. Alablasters motiues answ by Rackster [William Alabaster, "Seven motives" (No copy known). Answered by STC 20601, *A Booke of the Seven Planets, Or, Seuen wandring Motiues, of William Alablasters wit . . . .by Iohn Racster*, 1598.]
   lent mr poynton 11 Iuly 1600 [diff. ink] restored
8. Bible great in english at hirgha [STC 2068–76, 2079, 2081, 2089, 2091, 2094, 2096, 2098–98.5, 2102–2104, 21 eds., 1539–1569? *The Bible in Englishe* (the "Great Bible")].
9. Bible great in english at Hargha
10. Bible great in lat. of hent. edition [*Biblia, Ad vetustissima exemplaria nunc recens castigata* (Edited by Johannes Henten). Antwerp, 1563, 1572; Lyons, 1569, Venice, 1583, and many other continental editions.]
11. Bible ye first of vatab. editio in latine giue Ed. [*Biblia Vtriusque Testamenti* (with annotations by Franciscus Vatablus). Geneva, 1557; Basel, 1564; Salamanca, 1584–85.]
12. Bilson against ye Jesuites [STC 3071, Thomas Bilson, *The Trve Difference Betweene Christian Svbiection and Vnchristian Rebellion - . . . defended against the Popes censures and the Iesuits sophismes*, 1585.]

13. Bible english bought Ao 96
14. Caranza abridgmet of Councells [diff. ink] to Edm [Bartholomaeo Carranza/Caranza, *Summa Conciliorum A S. Petro Vsqve Ad Jvlivm III*. Salamanca, 1549, 1551; Lyons, 1570, 1587. Many continental editions]
15. Ceremoniarum eccle. Rom. [Rudolf Hospinian, *Oratio de origine et progressu rituum et ceremoniarum ecclesiasticarum Rodolphi Hospiniani*. Tiguri, 1585. 1586, 1587, 1588.]
16. Concordans to ye vulgar tranla. [STC 13228b-28b.16, Robert Herrey, *Two right profitable and fruitfull Concordances*, 1580–1600.]
17. Cartwright his last booke [STC 4715. Thomas Cartwright, *The Rest of the Second Replie Agaynst Master Vuhitgifts second ansvuer*, 1577.]
18. Charke answer to Campion [STC 5005–06, William Charke, *An Answere to a seditious Pamphlet lately cast abroade by a jesuit*, 1580–81.]
19. his reply to ye Censurer [STC 5007, William Charke, *A replie to a Censure written against the two answers to a jesuites seditious pamphlet*, 1581.]
20. Caius de antiq. Cantabrigie [STC 4344, Joannes Caius, *De Antiguitate Cantabrigiensis adademiae libri duo*, 1568.]
21. Carion abridgment [Johann Carion, *Chronicon Carionis Philippicvm in Enchiridii Formam Redactvm*. Rostochii, 1596.]
22. Calapine [Ambrosius Calepinus, *Dictionarium* octo linguarum. Basel, 1584, 1590.]
23. Cronicon Croni. [STC 3593, Florentius Bravonius, *Chronicon ex Chronicis ab initio mundi vsque ad annum Domini*. 1592]
24. Churchyard his description of flader [sic] [diff. ink] lost [STC 5239, Thomas Churchyard, *A Lamentable, and pitifull Description of the wofull warres in Flaunders*, 1578.]
25. [diff. ink] Ceremoniarum eccl. Rom. in octav. lent Mr womact 17 Apl. 1600 [Christophorus Marcellus, *Sacrarum Caeremoniarum, sive Rituum Ecclesiasticorum S. Rom. Ecclesiae*. Venice, 1582. Many continental editions, 1516+]
26. Decretalia Grego [Pope Gregory IX, *Decretales D. Gregorii Papae IX suae integitati vna cum glossis restitutae, cum priuilegio Gregorii XIII*. Rome 1584. Numerous continental editions. Many continental editions, 1472+]
27. Dering his answ to hard. Reionyder [STC 6725, Edward Dering, *A Sparing Restraint, of many lauishe vntruthes, which M. doctor harding dothe chalenge. With an answere*, 1568.]

28. Digges pantenometria [STC 6858–59, Leonard Digges the Elder, *A Geometrical Practise, named Pantometria,* 1571, 1591.]
29. discovery of viages . . . [diff. ink] look next p. 1 [diff. ink] Mr Sundley apl. 99 [STC 12625–26a, Richard Hakluyt, *Principall Navigations, Voiages and Discoueries of the English Nation,* 1589, 1598, 1599.]
30. Esebius wth Mr womact at this 10 Feb. 97 to Ed [STC 10572–73, Eusebius, Bishop Pamphili, *The Ancient Ecclesiasticall histories,* 1579–85.]
31. Farnilia opera in ij bookes in octa. [diff. ink] exchange
32. fox his actes & monumentes whereof on at Mr Risley church cost 40 s [STC 11224– 26, John Foxe, *Actes and Monuments,* 1576–96.]
33. [diff. ink] king through cop t sh at 60 [unidentified; very faded]
34. fulkr. defenc of tranla [STC 11430–30.5, Wiliam Fulke, *A Defense of the sincere and true Translations of the holie Scriptures into the English tong, against . . . Gregorie Martin,* 1583.]
35. his answer to Rhei: Test [diff. ink] lost [diff. ink] for wch kinges liues in fol lent mr Bartles [STC 2888, William Fulke, *The Text of the New Testament . . . With a Confutation of all such Arguments, glosses . . . manifest impietie.* 1589?]
36. {Grafton his} [STC 12147–61, Richard Grafton, *Chronicle,* or *An Abridgement of the Chronicles of England,* 1569–1595]
37. Gratiani Decretum [diff. ink] lent m hobart of mor [faded] [Gratian, *Decretum Gratiani emendatvm, et notationibvs illvstratvm.* Turin, 1588. Many continental editions, 1472+.]
38. Graftons abridg. of cron. [STC 12148–61, Richard Grafton, *Chronicle, or An Abridgement of the Chronicles of England,* 1563–1595.]
39. graffing & plant. by maskall [STC 17573.5–78, Leonard Mascall, *A Booke of the Art and Maner, Howe to plante and graffe all sortes of Trees,* 1569–92.] and at barsham
40. Hollingsett his Cron. ij vol. [diff. ink] lent Ion chenry to [diff. ink] restored ye seco'd vol lent Tho Gh. 21 mar. 1600 [STC 13569–69.5, Raphael Holinshed, *The First and Second Volumes of Chronicles,* 1587.]
41. [diff. ink] hackettes wick life herisy & end [STC 5823, Richard Cosin, *Conspiracie . . . A treatise discouering the late designments . . . by William Hacket,* 1592.]
42. Iuelles defence of ye appol [STC 14601, John Jewel, *A Defense of the Apologie of the Churche of Englande . . . By Iohn Iewel, Bishop of Sarisburie* [sic], 1570.]

43. [diff. ink] nterchange able conesv. folio x 2s 6 by . . . his servant..
    [diff. ink] Received againe to Ed [faded ink; unidentified]
44. Kempnitias confuting the Councel of trent[diff. ink] lent mr
    womack 12 Nov 1602 [Possibly STC 5116, Martinus Chem-
    nitius, *A discouerie and batterie of the great fort of vnwritten tradi-
    tions: otherwise, an examination of the Counsell of Trent*, 1592.]
45. Knewstius against popish positions [STC 15037.5, John Knews-
    tub, *An Aunsweare vnto certaine assertions tending to maintaine the
    Churche of Rome*, 1579.]
46. against h. N. of ye fam. of love [STC 15040, John Knewstub,
    A Confutation of monstrous and horrible heresies taught by H. N.,
    1579.]
47. kitchinge of keeping of courtes [STC 15017–22, John Kitchen,
    Le court leete, 1583–98.]
48. Lyra. iij volumes of iiij to Edmd [Possibly an edition of Nicolaus
    de Lyra, *Biblia sacra, cum glossis . . . Nicolai Lyrani postilla*. A
    six-volume edition was published at Venice in 1588.]
49. linwood de Constitu. provinc. to ednd. [STC 17102–13, Bishop
    William Lyndewode, *Constitutiones provinciales*, 1483–1557.]
50. lambor his Iust. of peac [STC 15163–69, William Lambarde,
    Eirenarcha: or Of the office of the Iustices of Peace, 1581–99.]
51. litleton his tennure [STC15719–53, Sir Thomas Littleton, *Lyttyl-
    ton's Tenures*, 1482–1599.]
52. livi in folio [diff. ink] to Ednd [Titus Livius (Livy), *Historiarum
    ab urbe condita libri, quae extant xxxv*, folio editions e.g., Venice,
    1555, 1572; Paris 1552, 1573.]
53. Marbeck his comonplaces [STC 17299, John Marbecke, *A booke
    of Notes and Common places*, 1581.]
54. Musculus comon places belong to ye church [STC 18308–09,
    Wolfgang Musculus, *Common places of Christian Religion*,
    1563–78.]
55. Mirror of magistr by Tho Blenerhassit [STC 3131, Thomas
    Blenerhasset, *The seconde part of the Mirrour for Magistrates*, 1578]
56. Munstres Cosmography look next pa. 2 at Barsh [STC
    18242–43.5, Sebastian Muenster, *Briefe Collection . . . oute of
    the Cosmographye of S. Munster*, 1572–91, or Muenster, *La cos-
    mographie vniuerselle*, 2 vols. Paris, 1575; Antwerp, 1584; Basel,
    1550, 1572, and many other continental edtions.]
57. [diff. ink] mathematicall Iuell giuen Bass throkmrt. [STC 3119,
    John Blagrave, *The Mathematical Iewell*, 1585.]
58. Nowell against dorman & sanders [STC 18739, Alexander No-
    well, *A Confutation, as wel of M. Dormans last Boke . . . as also
    of D. Sander*, 1567.]

59. Nicholls Recantation [STC 18533–33.5, John Nichols, *A declaration of the recantation of Iohn Nichols*, 1581.]

60. Nash his piers peniles [STC 18371–75, Thomas Nashe, *Pierce Penilesse his Supplication to the diuell*, 1592–95.]

61. Quenes mati speeches at ye parliament [STC 6052, *The Copie of a Letter to the Earle of Leycester . . . with a Report of Certain Petitions . . . .and Her Majesty's Answers thereunto*, 1586 (includes Elizabeth's two speeches to Parliament on the execution of Mary, Queen of Scots]

62. Pupillus oculi an ould popish book [Johannes de Burgo, *Pupilla oculi De Septem Sacramentorum administratione*, Strasbourg, 1514, 1517; Paris, 1518, 1527.]

63. parochial Sacerd. [unidentified]

64. perkins cases lost [STC 19634–41, John Perkins, *A Profitable booke of Maister Iohn Perkins . . . treating of the lawes of Englande*, 1560?-1601.]

65. Poultons abrid of statutes at hargha. [STC 9526.7–31.5, Ferdinando Pulton, *Abstract of all the Penall Statutes . . .* 1577–96.]

66. platina de vitis pontifi [Bartholomaeus Sacchi de Platina, *B. Platinae Historia de uitis pontificum Romanorum*, Venice, 1562]

67. playforde sermon of weepe not lent Mr Rauly. [STC 20014, Thomas Playfere, *A Most Excellent and Heavenly Sermon . . . Weepe not for me*, 1595.]

68. Rastall his abridg of statutes abridgemen greatest & last [STC 9516–26, John Rastell, *The newe great abredgement brefly conteynynge, all thactes and statutes of this Realme*, 1521–51.]

69. Rich Barnaby his alarm to warr [STC 20978–79, Barnaby Rich, *Allarme to England*, 1578]

70. Sacerdotale Tridentum [*Sacerdotale ad consuetudinem S. Romanae Ecclesiae . . . Summa nuper cura iuxta S. Tridentini Consilij Sanctiones emendatum, & auctum*, Venice, 1576, 1585, 1587.]

71. Suma Angelica [*Summa angelica de casibus conscientialibus / R.P.F. Angeli de Clauasio ordinis minor. obser. reg. Cum additionibus quam commodis R.P.F. Iacobi Vngarelli Patauini . Venice*, 1569.]

72. Sutclif against precisians [STC 23450, Mathew Sutcliffe, *An answere to a certaine libel supplicatorie, or rather diffamatory, and also to certaine calumnious articles, and interrogatories, both printed and scattered in secret corners, to the slaunder of the ecclesiasticall state*, 1592]

73. Statutes at larg all that ever were print till 29 El. in on volume. [STC 9487, Statutes, *Anno xxix. Reginae Elizabethae. At this present Session of Parliament*, 1587]

74. Stultifera navis by Alex Barkley [STC 3546, Sebastian Brant, *Stultifera Nauis*, tr. Alexander Barclay, 1570]
75. Schardius de Imperiali et pontif. potestate to Edm [Simon Schardius, *De Jurisdictione, Auctoritate, et Praeeminentia Imperiali, ac Potestate Ecclesiastica*, Basle, 1566]
76. [diff. ink] Sidneys book of english posy lent us Bailey at lon [faded] [STC 22535, Sir Philip Sidney, *The Defence of Poesie*, 1595.]
77. Test novum vulgat edit. in octavo et aliud in decimo sext [STC 2800–01, 2803, 2804? *Testamentum nouum*, 1568–76.]
78. testament gallice in decimosexto [*Le Nouueau Testament*, tr. P. R. Olivetan, Lyon, 1545, 1553–54, 1558, 1563; Paris, 1567; Rouen, 1581.]
79. testament in english with beza his notes in iiij^{to} an other in decimo sexto [STC 2808 (4o); 2805, 2809, 2810a.3–10a.7 (16mo), *Nouum Testamentum, T. Beza interprete*, 1577–1599]
80. Travers of church discipline [STC 24180.7–85 (various ecclesiastical works of Walter Travers), 1574–88.]
81. Valerius maximus in secundo cum comendt [Valerius Maximus, *Valerii Maximi dictorum factorumque memorabilium libri IX*, Antwerp 1567; cum notis H. L. Glareani, Basel, 1577; *commentariis enarrati cum duplici indicem*, Venice, 1564; Corrected and annotated by S. Pighius, Antwerp, 1585. Many other continental editions.]
82. Whitacr against bellarmine [STC 25366, William Whitaker, *Disputatio de sacra Scriptura, contra R. Bellarminum & T. Stapletonum*, 1588]
83. Wright against sleepers [STC 26033.5–35, Leonard Wright, *A Summons for Sleepers*, 1589–96.]

(f. 42v) Bookes of myn in other mens handes at this 10 may 1595 [Gurney numbered the first five entries 1–5]

1 Discovery of viages [No. 29] lent Mr Drury of besthope & sent by Turnor his man 6 may 1595
2 Munsters Cosmography [No. 56] lent Mr Harris at hargham 19 Apll. 95
3 Saravia in latyne mayteyning the english church governmet lent my Cosen furnis A 94 [No. 84: STC 21746, Adrien Saravia, *De Diversis Ministrorvm Evangelii Gradibvs, Sicvt A Domino fuerunt instituti*, 1590.]
4 Saravia answering Beza lent my sayd Cosen furnis [No. 85: STC 21748, Saravia, *Defensio Tractationis de diuersis ministrorum . . . contra Responsionem T. Bezae*, 1594.]

5 Decretalia Gregor [No. 26] a great booke & on of the partes of
   the Canon law lent Mr Trendle the parson of ovington above
   iij yeares sent sent him by his boye
[diff. ink] all the bookes aboue said I receyved againe except the
   two Sarauaes [above the line] I haue agay [sic]
[6] I have iiij bookes of Aeani plines all in octavo vidz lemnius de
   mirracules ocultis [No. 86: Lemnius Levinus, De miraculis
   occultis naturae libri IIII. Books 1–2 first published in 1559;
   octavo editions of all four volumes at Antwerp, 1574, 1581.]
   ree rustiae auctho Conrado heresbacho [No. 87: Conrad He-
   resbach, Rei rusticae libri quatuor. Octavo editions published
   at Cologne in 1570, 1573.]
   Lycosthenis facetiae Naturae brevum of the first editio [No. 88:
   Conrad Lycosthenes, Julii Obsequentis prodigiorum liber . . .
   per C. Lycosthenem . . . integritati suae restitutus. Octavo
   edition published at Basel, 1552.]
   all wth bookes beneath on the [faded] Closet to be borrowed and
   lye togither in my Closet vppon [faded]
[7] Discovery of viages [No. 29] lent to Mr Thornton of Hengham
   a week befor Christmes Ao 1598 Eliz. 41 Deliuerd to him self
   being then heare sent home againe by phillip Turnor. 17 mar
   Ao Eliz. 41 Dmi 98

APPENDIX II: GURNEY'S LIST OF COPIES OF HIS POEMS
SENT TO OTHERS

(f. 59v) Mem[orandum] exscriptes of thes poems at this 24 Iun
on with Mr Godsale of the Annotomy (wthout the addition of Images) & divers of the Chiefe poemes
an other Annotomy with poems with my bro rich
an other with my br throg [diff. ink] brought home 17 apr. 1597
An other Anotomy wth the additio[n] of Images & other poemes
   with Aliot being the best [diff. ink] wch my broth. L. hath
The medly of Conceytes on with my nece Mary wch is that Mr
   Dr. hau
an other with my broth Throgmor [diff. ink] comm hom 17 ap 97
an other with my Cosen Smith ye sam my Cos h had
an other ye best with my brother Cornwallys [diff. ink] It I hav
part of on wth Mr Coppin

TAMARA A. GOEGLEIN

Reading English Ramist Logic Books as Early Modern Emblem Books: The Case of Abraham Fraunce

Historians of dialectical studies have long dismissed Ramist dialectic as rhetoricized logic in large measure because Ramist logic books exemplify logical principles with passages from oratory, poetry, and the Bible. These rhetorical illustrations consistently figure the logical abstractions in highly visual, concrete, and ekphrastic images and, thus, they often serve as "speaking pictures" for the Aristotelian taxonomies and nomenclature. The Ramist logic book might profitably be understood as bimedial, much like an emblem book, and its *modus legendi* a dynamic act whose end is acquiring conceptual knowledge. Focusing on the dialectical and emblematic writings of the Ramist Abraham Fraunce, this essay explores the extent to which Ramist habits of mind move between verbal thinking and visual thinking—move between words and word-pictures—to grasp the logical concepts printed on the pages of the popular dialectics.

1.

DURING THE LATE SIXTEENTH century and early seventeenth century, England witnessed a groundswell of vernacular dialectical handbooks that were modeled after the Latin *Dialectica* of Peter Ramus (Pierre de la Ramée, 1515–1572). Ramus defied scholasticism and Catholicism and, for this, the French Huguenot suffered a grisly death in the St. Bartholomew's Day Massacre (August 24, 1572). His defiance in France, however, would elevate him in an England fearful of Catholic France and Spain. Just two months before the Protestant massacre, Queen Elizabeth sent a diplomatic entourage that included a young Philip Sidney to Paris to ratify a defensive pact known as the Treaty of Blois—Sidney remained in Paris during the politically hot summer of 1572, meeting literary and intellectual figures that included none other than Peter Ramus whose friendship he enjoyed, though not for long.[1] Christopher Marlowe's *Massacre at Paris* dramatized the murder of Ramus as a martyr's death, and English Ramists declared it such in the titles and front matter of their bestselling logic books. Historians of dialectical studies have described these handbooks as logically inspired rhetorics rather than legitimate dialectical manuals because, among other things, they incorporate citations from poetry and oratory to illustrate the abstract principles of logical analysis. The Ramists were not the first dialecticians to pair logical definitions with exemplary quotations in their manuals—both Rudolph Agricola and Lorenzo Valla did so before Ramus—but the Ramists did so with such copiousness and relish that their manuals have attracted the most attention of historians.[2] William and Martha Kneale offer a fairly canonical interpretation of Ramist logic within the context of dialectical studies:

> From [Cicero and Quintilian] the men of the Renaissance acquired the Roman attitude to scholarship, with the result that *genuine logic* was neglected for rhetoric and books which purported to be on logic quoted Cicero as often as Aristotle . . . . The most famous logician of this tendency was Petrus Ramus.[3]

Since humanist dialectic violates Aristotelian semantics, it is not "genuine logic" but rather rhetoric in disguise. That the Ramist dialectical treatises share qualities associated with Renaissance rhetorical manuals is indisputable, but what this means is not.

We all agree that, because of the numerous exemplary quotations, Ramist manuals resemble rhetorical treatises or anthologies of poetry or commonplace books.[4] Our understanding of Ramist logic, however, is not adequately served by assuming a binary opposition between the dialectical and rhetorical arts. I have elsewhere analyzed the poetic illustrations in Ramist dialectics and suggested that the semiotics of Ramist method is basically figurative—the claims articulated in Ramist discourse become truth-statements through a series of semantic associations forged between the poetic examples and the entities they logically represent.[5] The Ramist dialectical handbook, in sum, is bimedial. In this essay, I investigate further the interplay between the language of the logical apparatus (dialectical discourse) and the language of the illustrative example (rhetorical discourse). I will be less concerned with evaluating Ramist logical philosophy per se and more concerned with discovering how the poetic insertions made sense to Ramist readers, especially in the light of other contemporary reading practices.

The bimedial form of the Ramist manual exerted interpretive pressure on its readers not unlike the popular emblem book, another bimedial form of exemplary literature. The logic books and the emblem books elicit dynamic responses from their readers as their eyes move between two kinds of media presented on a single page. What, if any, cross-fertilization or spillover might have occurred betwixt and between these two genres and the experiences of reading them? The poetic illustrations in Ramist handbooks are so notably ekphrastic that they share not only a discursive fraternity with emblem books but an aesthetic fraternity as well. To what extent was the art of reading a logic book shaped by the verbal artistry in the logic book?

One English humanist whose published and unpublished writings describe strategies for reading emblems was Abraham Fraunce.[6] Fraunce enjoyed the friendship and patronage of the Sidney family and was drawn into literary circles that included Gabriel Harvey and Edmund Spenser, whose poetry illustrates Ramist principles in Fraunce's logical writings. In 1588, Fraunce published three books: a Ramist dialectic entitled *The Lawiers Logike*, a Ramist rhetoric entitled *The Arcadian Rhetorike* (modeled after Omer Talon's *Rhetorica*), and an emblem treatise entitled *Insignium, Armorum, Emblematum, Hieroglyphicorum, et Symbolum, quae ab Italis Imprese nominantur, Explicatio (A plain exposition of ensigns, arms, emblems, hieroglyphs, and the symbols, which are called imprese by the Italians).*[7] The emblem treatise is divided into three books, the third of which offers a theory of symbolic forms that centers on the *impresa* and the emblem. The relationship among Fraunce's logic book, rhetoric book, and emblem book is "unclear," as Michael Bath says, but "it makes some sense to see all three works as part of a concerted attempt to lay the basis for an English theory of the arts of language, logic, and sign."[8] Fraunce takes after leading sixteenth-century continental emblem theorists who, as Robert Klein has suggested, understood the *impresa* as a symbolic vehicle to express thought itself and thus understood it as belonging "to the order of logic."[9] Fraunce's treatise can be considered an elegant amalgam of those theoreticians he mentions

specifically at its outset (Paolo Giovio, Luca Contile, Scipione Bargagli, Hieronimo Ruscelli, and Alessandro Farra), and, when set beside his *Lawiers Logike,* it lets us glimpse his awareness that the poetic
illustrations were integral, not secondary or accidental, to the logical
habits of mind deployed by the Ramists.[10] His emblem treatise and
logical handbook virtually speak to one another and, together, they
bespeak an emblematic impulse in Ramist reading strategies.[11]

Early modern emblem theorists, who were wont to discuss the
word-picture relationship in terms of a soul-body relationship, were
adamant that the word and the picture were to be mutually interde-
pendent rather than redundant. The experience of reading the early
modern emblem book amounts to moving between a word and a
picture which, together, animate the idea presented. According to
Fraunce, the emblematic idea "derived from that third source which
is already constituted by the soul and the body" ("ab eo tertio deriuata, quod iam ex anima et Corpore constitutum est."[12] Fraunce's
"third source" ("tertio deriuata") is a conceptual middle term engendered by readers as they cognitively move between the soul and
body, between the text and figure, to recover the emblematic idea.
They shift their attention between two representational modes, and
this cross-reading leads them to apprehend conceptual knowledge in
a third, dramatic dimension. Such a volatile reading experience requires readers to translate the one medium in terms of the second,
not unlike the experience today of reading a multimedia display of
text and video where the visual elements often appear as insertions
or emblems.

Alastair Fowler and others have pointed out that "emblem" (Greek
emblem and Latin *emblema*) refers to "mosaic, appliqué, or inlaid ornament—as in Milton's paradise, 'the ground more coloured than with
stone/Of costliest emblem.' "[13] Thomas Thomas's *Dictionarium Lin-
guarium Linguae Latinae et Anglicanae* (1587) defines "emblem" as a
"Picture worke of wood, stone, or mettall, finelie set or painted in
divers coloures, as in chesse-bourdes and tables: small images, flowers,
or like ornamentes set on plate, or other thing by a vice, to take off,
and put on when we will." Much like these decorative insertions,
the poetic illustrations in Ramist dialectics transform the one-dimen-
sional peripatetic discourse into multidimensional logical mosaics, a
process that aptly characterizes Fraunce's *Lawiers Logike.*

Throughout this manual, Fraunce inserts passages from Edmund
Spenser's *Shepheardes Calender,* that collection of emblematic eclogues
in which each month's pastoral begins with woodcuts picturing the
shepherds and concludes with their mottos.[14] Ruth Samson Luborsky
has argued that each "eclogue unit" in *The Shepheardes Calender* is

"so printed as to resemble the individual emblematic unit in the popular annotated emblem book."[15] This choice of exemplary verse transforms Fraunce's handbook into a discourse comprising logical emblems, underscoring Fraunce's interest in the theoretical connections among logical and visually symbolic languages and in the modes of thought they create. That *The Shepheardes Calender* models the bookish elements of humanist scholarship is not insignificant either, for the logical habits of mind born of the emblematic insertions into Fraunce's manual are bookish.

Let us look at an instance in *The Lawiers Logike* where the insertion from Spenser's *Shepheardes Calender* suggests a deliberate fashioning of an emblematic aesthetic. To illustrate the principle of the formal cause, Fraunce inserts a portion of the August eclogue that is actually pictured in the accompanying woodcut to Spenser's poem. Before Fraunce quotes Spenser's poetry, however, he defines the formal cause in the language of Aristotelian logic: "The forme is a cause by the which a thing is that which it is, and therefore by the forme thynges bæ distinguished" (G.y.v). Fraunce then exemplifies the definition with the poetic passage in which Willy describes the mazer—the wooden drinking bowl depicted in the woodcut—that he pledges in his verse-capping contest with Perigot:

A Mazer ywrought of the maple warre,
Wherein is enchased many a faire sight
Of Beares, and Tygers that maken fierce warre.
And ouer them spread a goodly wilde Vyne
Entrayled with a wanton yuy twyne.
There by is a lambe in the Wolues iawes:
But see how fast runneth the shepheardes swayne
To saue the innocent from the beastes pawes,
And here with a sheephooke hath him slayne.
Tell me, such a cup hast thou euer seene?
Well mought it beseeme any haruest queene.

(G.iy.r)

Not unlike Keats's Grecian urn, Willy's mazer depicts a moment that only his words, his poetry, can create. Willy brings the "many a faire sight" to life, places them in a temporal sequence—"see how fast runneth the shepheardes swayne"—and gives voice to the moral lesson they picture but cannot tell. Still, and this is important in the poetics of ekphrasis, Willy's words depend on the thingness of the mazer, and this snippet underscores the mazer's materiality: the maple wood engraved with animals and vines and a shepherd with his crook.

Spenser too calls particular attention to Willy's poetic ekphrasis, and not coincidentally to his own, when Willy asks Perigot, "Tell me, such a cup hast thou euer seene?" Perigot might well answer "no," or "yes," but his reasoning in either case would be far different from ours since he lives within the fiction—and on the pages—of *The Shepheardes Calender*. Willy's question really asks Perigot to acknowledge the uniqueness of the mazer and thus its high value as a prize, but it asks us to acknowledge the emblematic aesthetic of *The Shepheardes Calender*, for, if we look closely at the August woodcut, we indeed can "see" the mazer Willy's poetry describes, although in which sense(s) we see becomes the next question (fig. 1).[16]

Our answer to Willy's question ("Tell me, such a cup hast thou euer seene?") depends on one's own reading of the semiotic relationship between the visual, woodcut image of the mazer and Willy's verbal, ekphrastic image of it. Is it the selfsame "cup"? Fraunce is tacitly posing a version of this question in his logic manual when the "form" of Willy's mazer is inserted to illustrate the abstract language of the "formal cause." There is no accompanying visual picture in the logic manual, but the ekphrastic insertion and the Aristotelian nomenclature both ostensibly describe the same "thing," namely the formal cause. Or do they? Do we "see" them with the same set of eyes? How do we read the symbolic language and the logical language in tandem? Which mode of language has priority? How do we get from image to cup? The image of the cup is more sensible, more capacious and the definition more intelligible, more abstract. Does the visual orchestrate the verbal, or vice versa? These were fundamental questions for early modern emblematics, and Fraunce's selecting Willy's mazer from Spenser's *Shepheardes Calender* exploits the logical complexities in the emblematic aesthetic and provides some clues about how emblem books and Ramist logic manuals were read.

Michael Bath has surveyed the generic contours of early modern emblem books both in practice and in theory, and he warns against our anachronistic impulse to codify the emblem book rigidly; it displayed variation and was subject to the joint efforts—but not necessarily collaborations—of epigram writers, printers, and theorists. The tidy tripartite unit associated with Andrea Alciati—the motto, the icon, and the epigram—should not be taken as the normative emblem format. Hessel Miedema, trying to separate the modern terminology used in emblem studies today from that used by sixteenth-century

Auguſt.

Ægloga Octaua.

Argument.

IN this *Aeglogue is ſet forth a delectable controuerſie, made in imita-tion of that in Theocritus: whereto alſo Uirgil faſhioned his third and ſeuenth Aeglogue.* They chooſe for vmpere of their ſtrife, Cuddie a neat-heards boye, Who hauing ended their cauſe reciteth alſo himſelſe a proper ſonge, Whereof Colin hee ſayth Was Author.

Willie,   Perigot.   Cuddie.

Tell meͤ Perigot, what ſhalbe the game,
    Wherefoͥe with mine thou dare thy muſick matche?
    Oͥ bene thy Bagpypes renne farre out of frame?
Oͥ hath the Crampe thy ioynts benomb with ache?

Perigot.

Ah Willie, when the hart is ill aſſayde,
How can Bagpipe, oͥ ioyntes be well apayde?

Willie.

What the foule euill hath thee ſo beſtad?
Whilom thou was peregall to the beſt,
And wont to make the iollͦ ſhepheards glad
With pyping and dauncing, didſt paſſe the reſt.

                    P 3.   Perigot.

Fig. 1. "August," *The Shepheardes Calendar.* STC 23091. By permis-sion of The Folger Shakespeare Library.

emblematists, has shown that in a 1522 letter to the publisher Francesco Calvo Alciati in fact understood an emblem as "an epigram which describes something, so that it signifies something else."[17] Alciati writes:

> I give in each separate epigram a description of something, such that it signifies something pleasant taken from history or from nature, after which painters, goldsmiths and founders can fashion objects which we call badges and which we fasten on our hats, or else bear as trade-marks.

> Singulis enim epigrammatibus aliquid des scribo, quod ex hixtoria [sic], vel ex rebunaturalibus aliquid elegans significet, unde pictores, aurifices, fusores, id genus conficere possint, quae scuta appellamus et petasis figimus, vel pro insignibus gestamus.[18]

These "badges" refer to the popular *imprese*, and Alciati's mention of them here serves to distinguish his own view of the emblem as ekphrastic poetry from what his emblems were to become in the next decade.

The famous 1531 edition of Alciati's *Emblematum liber* was "probably invented by accident" when the Augsburg printer, Heinrich Steyner, supplemented Alciati's Latin epigrams with woodcuts.[19] And, according to Bernhard F. Scholz, it is not until

> The 1534 Paris edition of the *Emblemata*, [. . .], the edition by Christian Wechel of which Alciato appears to have approved, that perceptual gestalt is indeed realized: every three-part combination of motto, icon, and epigram occupies one single type page, thus allowing for a reading/viewing of the illustrated *Emblemata* in which those combinations of word and image are not only held together linguistically and by means of co-reference, but also by what the gestalt psychologists would call a "good gestalt."[20]

If we adapt this notion of a bimedial textual coherence between word and image, which Scholz calls "perceptual gestalt," to Ramist logic books, we may gain insight into the Ramist *modus legendi*, the way that the Ramist dialectical manual might have been perceived and read by its practitioners.[21] The writings of Abraham Fraunce indeed suggest the likelihood of the dialectical definition being read as a motto—the dialectical text—and the rhetorical example as the icon—the illustrative picture in the sense of Alciati's ekphrastic epigram.

A considerable part of the following argument will be that the exemplary passages invite the reader to visualize the conceptual principles articulated in the logical passages: the poetic imagery is remarkably concrete and functions by picturing the logical axioms at hand. A comparison between logic books and emblem books will thus illuminate Ramist reading strategies for understanding the dense, abstract Aristotelian taxonomies and nomenclature, strategies that are implied by the ways the logical passages and illustrative passages interact on the pages of the manuals. It may be impossible to discern precisely how Peter Ramus imagined his reformed logic books to be interpreted by their readers—in fact, it may be impossible to discern how Peter Ramus himself interpreted his logical enterprise, given his continual textual revisions and thus the plethora of textual variants diligent Ramist bibliographers offer up to us—but it is possible to draw some conclusions about how Ramists such as Abraham Fraunce read the logical tradition they had inherited.[22]

2.

While there is no consensus among historians of dialectical studies about just how influential Ramist dialectical manuals actually were in the early modern English university curriculum, all agree that they were bestsellers among Protestant intellectuals and that they were avowedly designed to help their readers better comprehend logical analysis.[23] It is unlikely that all English translators and adapters of Ramist logic were as theoretically self-conscious as Abraham Fraunce about the poetics of ekphrasis, but they all seem utterly aware of the heuristic potential of ekphrasis in the poetic illustrations. R(obert) F(age)'s catechetical *Dialectica* (London, 1632) nicely dramatizes this. His description of a "logical subject," for instance, moves between the technical, abstract language associated with dialectical discourse and the figurative, belletristic language associated with rhetorical discourse:

Q. *What is the Subiect?*
A. The Subiect is that to which any thing is adioined.
Q. *Make this playner by examples?*
A. The minde is the Subiect of science, ignorance, vertue, vice, because these happen beside the being. The body, of health, sicknesse, strength, weaknesse, beauty, deformity. Man is the Subiect of riches, poverty, honour, infamy, apparrell, company. The place is the Subiect of the thing placed.

[....]

Q. *Giue example out of some Poet.*
A. So Virgill in his Georgicks admonisheth that the place bee diligently sought out for things proposed: as corne, trees, plants pastures.

> *Before we passe into a sea unknowne,*
> *Know we the wind and various maner of heauen,*
> *Our native soyle and every habitation,*
> *What will refuse or grow in any nation:*
> *Some beareth corn, th'other with grapes doth passe*
> *Some with tall trees, the rest with unsowne grasse*[24]

The reader is here challenged with the pedagogical puzzle of figuring out how the Virgilian stanza exemplifies the logical subject. The Aristotelian definition seems to function much like a terse, enigmatic Alciatan motto that is brought to life by a Virgilian speaking picture. There was apparently no consensus among emblem theorists about which of the two media, the word or the image, accomplishes the "bringing to life" of the emblem, nor was there consensus about their priority. The etymology of "illustration" (*illustrare*) is visual (to light up, to illuminate), yet, according to Michael Bath, "emblem writers use the term 'illustration' to refer to the verse epigram rather than, as we might expect, the woodcut or engraved picture." Similarly, although we might be inclined to think just the opposite, the title page of George Wither's *A Collection of Emblemes* (1635) announces that his emblems are "quickened" with "Metricall illustrations."[25]

F[age] too "quickens" the dense concept of logical subjectivity with Virgilian "metrical illustrations," though his down-to-earth poetic image acts more as an embodiment, a visual anchor, for the ephemeral, abstract logical concept. We can see the conceptual opacity of the definition ("The Subiect is that to which any thing is adioined") visualized in Virgilian imagery: agricultural produce (the adjoints) grow out of the "soyle and every habitation" (the subject) and, thereby, their regional variety (corn, grapes, trees, and grass) "make playner" the logical domain of the subject. The ratio is unmistakable: just as a landscape is known by its fruit, so is a subject known by its adjoints. We might say that F[age]'s poetic insertion has given this basic logical entity—the logical subject—a "local habitation and a name." It supplements the logical language in the way that the emblematic word and image supplement one another to create Scholz's "perceptual gestalt." F[age]'s emblematic puzzle, however, is not entirely resolved once the reader discovers the ratio established between the logical subject and the Virgilian landscape, because this elementary analogy gives rise to the problem of how the subject is actually made "playner" by perceiving it as a fertile place. How, we might ask, is a logical subject equivalent to some thing or place that can be "plainly" visualized? How do the visual images work to clarify, explain, complicate, and, ultimately, supplement the Aristotelian logical principles set forth in the Ramist manuals?

Let us look more closely at this interactive play by examining a couple of passages from Roland MacIlmaine's *Logike of the Moste Excellent Philosopher P. Ramus Martyr*, which was the first English translation and adaptation of Peter Ramus's *Dialectica*. MacIlmaine's *Logike* was published by Thomas Vautrollier in 1574 and faithfully follows the 1569 edition of Ramus's *Dialectica*. MacIlmaine uses many of the same illustrative examples as does Ramus himself, and he follows the order of logical topics arranged by Ramus. MacIlmaine opens book one with the fairly standard Aristotelian definition of the formal cause: "The formall cause is that by the which the thing hathe his name and beyng. And therfore euery thing is distingued from another by his forme."[26] MacIlmaine then introduces emblematic play into his manual by "quickening" the technical definition of the formal cause with a series of lengthy illustrations whose imagery elaborately pictures the formal cause. Again, the textual interplay between dialectical axiom and verbal image is remarkably similar to the strategy used in emblem books for understanding the interplay between didactic motto and graphic image. MacIlmaine begins his illustrations with a description from Caesar's *Commentarii de Bello Gallico* that "settethe forthe the forme of the walles of Fraunce." The passage from Caesar goes on for quite a stretch and urges a figurative resemblance between the formal cause and the battlements encircling cities in Gaul:

The walles of Fraunce are almost buylded after this forme: The beames of one peece direct in longitude, euery one being

equally distante from another, are sett on their two endes in
the earthe, hard bounde within, and couered with a greate
countermure. The places betwixt the beames are stuffed vp before with great stones: Thiese beyng so placed and sett togeather, there is added, to ouer aboue the same another ranke,
so that the same space and distance is alwayes kept, that none
of the beames do touche another, but eche beame being distant
from the other by an equall space, is fast ioyned togeather with
stones, sett in betwixt beame and beame . . . . [This kind of
wall] is muche conuenient for the profitte and the defence of
cities [. . .].

(B.5v–B6r)

The exacting realism of this image of Gallic walls (the horizontal and
vertical coordinates of the beames and their scrupulous ranking and
placement) represents in spatial terms the logic of the formal cause:
the physical structure of the walls, by separating a town from what
it is not, exemplifies the logical structure of the formal cause, which
is a principle of distinction. The walls are a visual metaphor of the
formal cause because they enable a city to maintain its formal integrity, its form. The reader is urged to move between, on the one
hand, the walls figured as material objects keeping an urban space
safe from the incursion of hostile "otherness" and, on the other hand,
the logical principle of separation articulated in the philosophical
realism of Aristotelian language. What marks the emblematic significance here is the dynamic juxtaposition of visual thinking to verbal
thinking and of thingness to abstraction that directs the reader to
conceive the ideas of form and formal causality.

MacIlmaine's text continues with a long citation from the first
book of *The Aeneid* that describes a seascape. Here the formal cause
is imagined as a narrow piece of land—a cape—that distinguishes
the high seas from the quiet harbor:

There is with in this long place solitare,
    An Ile extending out two poyntes right farre.
Makyng a rode, where bankes on euery syde,
    From the deepe sea the waters do deuyde.

(B.6r)

The "Ile" makes a "rode" that traces the boundary of the harbor and
thus gives the harbor its unique form by "dividing" it from what it

is not, namely the ocean: "Within this hauen, when wearye Shippes do lande,/They haue no neade of cable nor of bande." The image of this Virgilian harbor, like Caesar's battlements, doubles back to explicate MacIlmaine's technical definition by forging an analogue of physical resemblance to it. The material, concrete, and visual images of the battlements and of the harbor trope into imaginative existence the formal cause, but the formal cause cannot be theoretically equated with the images, for the images are metaphorical. The image figuratively resembles the formal cause, but it cannot completely capture the concept since formal causality has no singular reality in the material world: the formal cause is an intellectual abstraction, a rational calculator that distinguishes logical entities one from another. The dialectical definition is not fixed by the material images, but, together, the logical motto and its picture give rise to an emblematic understanding of formal causality: The attention of MacIlmaine's readers shifts between visual analysis and textual analysis until they finally grasp the conceptual. Formal causality, and every other logical concept for that matter, has no fixed location, not in language alone or in things alone or in metaphorical representations of matter. This is where the Ramist dialectical manuals reveal what G. A. Padley calls a "mixed approach" to language, because, while the manuals do not explicitly reject the Aristotelian "order of things," the logical mosaics undercut the referential semantics of scholastic logic.[27] They use figurative language and figurative habits of mind to keep their dialectical entities in conceptual play, even while anchoring the conceptual play to a word-picture of concrete and objective thingness.

Thingness has preoccupied literary scholars of Ramist dialectic at least since Walter J. Ong argued that the visual and impersonal tendencies in Ramist habits of thought silenced interpersonal communication between logical disputants as well as silenced the inner voice of the logician himself.[28] For Ong, the spoken word of scholastic dialectical disputation becomes the Ramist printed word, which was now fixed firmly in the space of the mind and in the space of those famous dichotomous diagrams (fig. 2).[29]

With the advent of Ramism, moreover, the word loses its effervescent sonority and becomes a moveable object in space. At the very heart of Ong's extensive thesis is the notion that Ramus (and Rudolph Agricola before him) confuses the dialectical commonplace (or *loci* or *topoi*) with Aristotle's categories. He writes:

The manner of conceptualizing is different for the categories [of predication] and the places: relation (*relatio*) is a category,

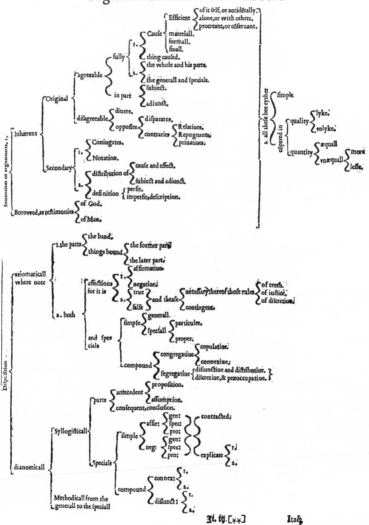

Fig. 2. *The Lawiers Logike*, sig Ii.ii[**]. STC 11344. By permission of The Folger Shakespeare Library.

related items (*relata*) a place: likeness (*similitudo*) falls under the
categories, like items or like things (*similia*) are among the places.
The topics [i.e., places] are thus more concrete conceptualiza-
tions than the categories.

(104–05)

In essence, Ong claims that Ramus (and other followers of Agricolan
logic) substituted topical logic for predicational logic and that Ramist
method thus vitiated dialectical thought by reducing the word to a
thing: "reduction to spatial form fixes everything, even sound. *Verba
volant, script manent*" (109).

I agree with Ong's thesis to the extent that Ramist place-logic
readily encodes a spatial metaphoricity in the language and thus in
the figurative order of the handbooks, yet the visual mind set he
ascribes to Ramism needs to be nuanced and modified to acknowledge a volatility still inherent in the Ramist modes of thought and
analysis.[30] If we accept Ong's alignment of impersonal-visual-space,
on the one hand, and personal-verbal-sound, on the other, then the
almost universal presence of the poetic, oratorical passages in the
Ramist manuals argues not for a Ramist impulse to supplant the
fleeting voice with those stationary, objectified words skewered on
the tines of the Ramist brackets. Rather, the verbal insertions argue
for the need to supplement vision with voice, to supplement the
fixed word with "speaking pictures." The intellectual conduct neces-
sitated by the Ramist handbooks is a "quickening," to borrow from
the title page of George Withers's emblem book. And the act of
reading a Ramist manual is not static but volatile, requiring a cognitive activity that flutters between the logical axiom and its belletristic
example, between a verbalized medium and a visualized medium,
between a word and a word-picture.

3.

More than R(obert) F(age) and Roland MacIlmaine, Abraham
Fraunce self-consciously recognized the Ramist *modus legendi* as
bimedial, intertextual, and emblematic. In the prefatory letter to *The
Lawiers Logike*, Fraunce defends the intellectual legitimacy of his
multi-discursive project in an imaginary, Chaucerian conversation
between himself and a resistant, curmudgeonly lawyer. Lawyers have
been the butt of jokes for quite a while, and here we witness Fraunce

having great fun at his interlocutor's expense. The lawyer objects to
the possibility of a "reasonable" practice of law: "It cannot bee that
a good Scholler should euer prooue [a] good Lawyer" (¶2r). And he
goes on to equate scholarly, university training with a feminized
learning that ironically implicates Fraunce himself:

> Mary, quoth hee, thease fine Vniuersity men haue beene trained
> vp in such easie, elegant, conceipted, nice, and delicate learning,
> that they can better make new-found verses of Amyntas death,
> and popular discourses of Ensignes, Armory, Emblemes, Hiero-
> glyphikes, and Italian Impreses, than apply their heads to the
> study of the Law, which is hard, harsh, vnpleasant, vnsauory,
> rude and barbarous.
>
> (¶2r–v)

The joke is that Fraunce published a verse translation, *The Lamentations of Amyntas* (1587), not to mention his *Insignium, Armorum, Emblematum, Hieroglyphicorum, et Symbolum, quae ab Italis Imprese
nominantur, Explicatio*. Here, the lawyer is distinguishing between the
"easie" learning of the university and the "hard" learning of Inns of
Court, between elegant, conceited academic discourse and harsh,
unpleasant legal discourse. Fraunce's deliberate oppositions lampoon
lawyers who take an obvious pride in the barbarities of their tribe,
but, more to my point, the irony of Fraunce's imagined dialogue
undercuts discursive stereotyping and asserts a similarity between the
"popular discourses" of emblems and the analytical discourses of
logical and legal practice. *The Lawiers Logike* encourages a cross-reading of logical, legal, and poetic writings, but the juxtaposition between the logical and poetic languages is the transactional heart of
each chapter while the legal materials stand as virtual appendices.
The practice of cross-reading dramatized in *The Lawiers Logike* is the
enterprise of Fraunce's emblem treatise, in which he theorizes how
one entity, a symbol, can stand for another and thus, by extension, he
teaches his readers how one discourse can likewise stand for another.

Let us turn to Fraunce's definition of a symbol in the opening line
of his emblem treatise:

> The Symbol: that is the means by which we infer and know
> something. It denotes a watchword or signal given in war, a
> sign, and even money, as in Terence: *He paid his money; he dined.*

Symbolum. id est quo aliquid coniectamus et cognoscimus. sig-
nificat tesseram vel signum bellicum, notam quin et pecuniam
vt apud *Terentium*. Symbolum dedit, cænauit.

(2–3)

Interpreting a symbol is an act of cognition requiring inference.
In the example from Terence, we must bridge the gap between
money and dining by inferring what is left unstated, namely that
dining costs money. Our puzzling to find this unspoken middle term
constitutes symbolic thinking. For Fraunce, to read *imprese* and emblems is thus to determine the unspoken link, or middle term, that
binds the image and the word into a semantic or "symbolic" unit.
Fraunce's definitions of *imprese* and emblems tend to be tangled and
confusing, initially because of problems with terminology: in Latin
and in theory, *simbolum* appears to be the genus of which the *emblema*
and the *impresa* are species, but Fraunce, like other continental theorists, was in the habit of referring to the Italian *impresa* alone by the
term *simbolum*. Here, however, Fraunce seems to articulate some
"rule of thumb" distinctions:

The emblem is founded upon the basic principle that its intention and meaning may have general application. Now an *impresa*
has its own peculiar character and is adapted to set forth the
intention of some individual, but I will not deny that the same
imprese can suit very many people.

Emblema ita constituitur vt generalis sit illius præceptio et doctrina. Simbolum autem proprium est et ad vnius alicuius hominis institutum indicandum accomodatum nec tamen inficias
inero, eadem Simbola pluribus convenire posse.

(14–15)

The meaning of an *impresa* commonly refers to an individual—his
sentiments, his virtues, his class standing—whereas the meaning of
an emblem commonly makes a universal claim about morality and
wisdom, though this theoretical division between *impresa* and emblem is not hard and fast. To my mind, this division does not alter
Fraunce's point that reading and creating a bimedial symbol, whether
an *impresa* or an emblem, is centered in formulating the missing
middle term between word and image.

Fraunce speaks of the word as the "soul" and the image as the
"body," and he writes, following Paolo Giovio, that the first rule of

a "perfect and complete *impresa*" is a "just proportion and agreement between soul and body" ("Quinque mihi necessario requiri videntur ad perfectam Simboli naturam absoluendam. Primum id est vt inter animam et corpus iusta quædam intercedat proportio et analogia," 1–2).[31] This notion of "just proportion" is repeatedly mentioned throughout the treatise, in terms of a "true symmetry" ("Symetria," 6–7) or a "composition" between body and soul ("Compositionem," 24–25), to underscore the semantic cohesion that must be achieved between the word and the image to create a symbol. Fraunce cautions his reader, and would-be emblem maker, to avoid redundancy:

> One must be careful here that the words do not simply describe the image nor, in themselves, make the full and complete meaning, as we have already frequently said. But if they are removed from their position and separated from the image, they should leave a certain sense of imperfection and incomprehensibility.

> Cavendum hic est ne verba figuram declarent, neve sola per se sensum efficiant plenum et perfectum, quod iam sæpe diximus. sed si loco moueantur et a figura seiungantur, imperfectum nescio quid relinquant et tale quod non intelligas.

> (18–19)

Fraunce articulates two important rules here: first, the motto ought not describe the image, and second, the motto is incomplete without its image. The words and image are not to duplicate but to supplement one another, for without the image the words are incomprehensible. The hint or suggestion of a hidden middle term, that which gives the emblematic symbol its enigmatic, heuristic quality, is crucial to the perfecting of body and soul.

This emblematic middle term is hidden, as it were, in the white space of the page that separates the motto from the picture. The *mise-en-page* of the emblem book has come to express the aesthetic Fraunce is describing: the blank, empty space is to be inscribed by the reader, who, in an act of cognition, goes back and forth between the words on the page and the image on the page until he comprehends their semantic link—their "just proportion"—and thereby discovers the full, perfected meaning of the emblem. The *mise-en-page* of the Ramist logic books evokes the *mise-en-page* of the emblem book, where the white space between the logical language (the motto) and the poetic insertion (the image) materially represents this hidden third term. Page layout and typography can provide what Jerome McGann calls "bibliographic clues," which are those material aspects of a book that contribute to the meaning of a text, "whether we are aware of such matters when we make our meanings or whether we are not."[32] Examining the page design of *The Lawiers Logike*, while it may or may not signal Fraunce's authorial intention, does nonetheless provide us with clues for how his readership may have received it and how his publishers and/or printers may have conceived it. The material presentation of *The Lawiers Logike* can be a rich source for our understanding how the rhetorical insertions and the logical text interact, and to it I now turn in order to suggest how its *mise-en-page* encourages reading strategies that are consonant with Fraunce's theory for reading a bimedial symbol. In essence, reading an emblem book is similar to reading an English Ramist logic book.

On sigs. C2v-C3r, Fraunce is discussing the doctrine and techniques of inventing syllogistic arguments. Here, he illustrates the syllogistic work of the middle term with verse from Spenser's July eclogue (Fig. 3). A noteworthy aspect of this page design is its typography: Fraunce's logical language is printed in black letter and the illustrations in roman and italic. This typographic pattern continues throughout the entire *Lawiers Logike* making it what Johanna Drucker calls "a marked text," a text whose typography deliberately and aggressively manipulates how it is to be read.[33] For Fraunce's sixteenth-century English reader, the alternation between the two main typefaces of the time—black letter and roman—amounts to an alternation between the *gravitas* of authority and the elegance of antiquity. The gothic black letter typeface, which dominated sixteenth-century printed books in England, was associated with tradition, custom, and familiarity, for it was the typeface of most Bibles, primers, prayer books, psalm books, hornbooks, ABCs, and reading manuals.[34] Roman and italic typefaces, the *littera antiqua*, were typefaces for the transmission of Latin literary texts, in large measure because of the practice of Aldus Manutius and the Florentine humanists.[35] The visual effect of this alternating typographic pattern is to provoke the reader into an emblematic habit of mind that searches for semantic coherence, a "just proportion" if you will, between the two (logical and poetic) discourses. Before actually reading the words on the page, the reader sees the words on the page and is given cues about which word-groupings belong to one another and about how these word-groupings are "marked" with cultural significance: the visual dynamic of the page inflects how the text is to be read and eventually

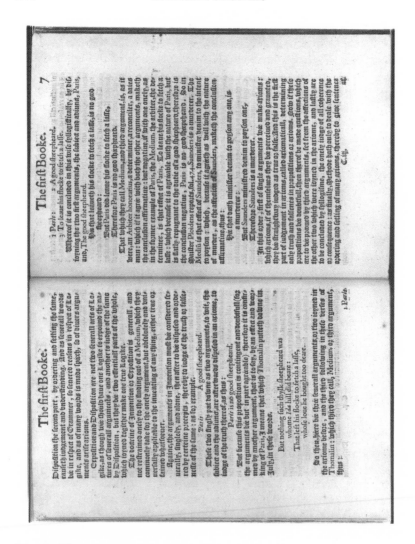

Fig. 3. *The Lawiers Logike*, C2v–C3r. STC 11344. By permission of The Folger Shakespeare Library.

how it is to be understood. In this section of *The Lawiers Logike* (fig. 2), the authoritative *gravitas* of the gothic typeface accrues to the logical discourse even as the rhetorical eloquence of the *littera antiqua* accrues to the pastoral poetry. In emblematic terms, the gothic seems to be "quickened" by the *littera antiqua* just as the rhetorical examples "bring to life" the moribund nomenclature of Aristotelian logic. The white space between them, the middle ground, is just as important as the blackened, typed spaces, for across this blank space the reader must cognitively inscribe how the logical discourse and the poetic discourse emblematically interact.

This emblematic *mise-en-page* also occurs in other sixteenth-century English language Ramist logic books: in Roland MacIlmaine's two English editions of Ramist *Logike* (1574 and 1581), both printed by Thomas Vautrollier, but, interestingly enough, not in MacIlmaine's Latin editions (1574 and 1576), also both printed by Vautrollier. In MacIlmaine's Latin editions, the logical discourse is printed in roman typeface whereas the rhetorical discourse is printed in either a smaller roman font or a roman typeface with quotation marks in the left margin, neither of which creates an emblematic effect though they do "mark" the discourses as distinct.[36] What is most important for my argument is that Fraunce's logic book adumbrates the typographical aesthetics of the emblem book just as Fraunce makes the connection between reading logic books and reading emblem books. And he seems to be doing just this in his definition of the syllogistic middle term (fig. 2). In this section of *The Lawiers Logike*, he offers useful advice for inferring the missing link between two stated premises—as one may expect—but he likewise appears, remarkably, to offer up useful advice for reading across two media.

In terms of logical matter, this section on the middle term is common fare in Ramist manuals, but Fraunce's rendition of the matter echoes his emblem treatise. Fraunce is here explaining that in the process of logical invention the logician must create a proposition or an "axiome" ("Paris is no good sheepheard") from the two "arguments," the subject and the adjunct ("Paris" and "A good sheepheard"). But before its truth may be judged, the proposition must be confirmed by another proposition, which is what Fraunce calls the "Medium, and third argument [. . .], as it were, an Arbiter honorarius, a determiner, a reconciler, a daies man." This is none other than that basic, critical middle term in an Aristotelian syllogism, but Fraunce's series of fanciful names for the middle term works to personify the logical operation and thereby to draw our attention to the logical operation. The names call to mind a day laborer, an honorable judge, a mediator, all going about their work of plowing, adjudicating, and negotiating. Such an imaginative description of the middle term appears to be unique to Fraunce and thus calls to mind the work of the emblematic middle term as it "works the ground" between the motto and picture, adjudicating and negotiating the semantic space between them. It is as if Fraunce is thinking about the construction of a perfect emblem rather than a syllogism in this section of his logic book.

I would suggest that the concept of a middle term serves as a common point between Fraunce's logic book and his emblem book, for readers of both genres need to cultivate a habit of mind that traverses two media (or two arguments) and formulates the middle term between them. Discovering it amounts to comprehending the ethical, spiritual, or dialectical lesson. And this is what we are being enjoined to do on these very pages of Fraunce's logic manual as we puzzle through the typographic cues, the logical instructions, and the poetic images, to which I now turn. The roman-typed Spenserian verse is inset and framed by black letter text—this page design and typography highlight the verse as an insertion. At first glance, the verse presents Thomalin's "axiome" that Paris is not a good shepherd because he leaves his "place" on "Ida hill" to follow his desire. The full effect of Fraunce's illustration, however, depends on a reader aware of several allusions implied in the Spenserian example, an allusiveness quite typical of an emblem book. Fraunce's reader would know, first, that the July eclogue offers a debate between the shepherds Thomalin and Morrell over the "place" virtuous shepherds should occupy, and, second, that the woodcut accompanying the July eclogue depicts Morrell atop a hill, inviting Thomalin to join him. Ruth Samson Luborsky underscores the importance that "place" plays in the July eclogue by pointing out that its woodcut adopts a "mode of illustration" that is "attributive," by which she means that the shepherds can be identified "by where they sit or stand."[37] Thus, we know that Morrell is sitting on the hill and Thomalin is standing at its bottom. Morrell's emblem at the end of the eclogue, "*In summo foelicitas*" (felicity is at the height), moralizes the woodcut picture of him atop his hill within a platonic concept of the good, whereas Thomalin's emblem, "*In medio virtus*" (virtue is in the middle), adapts the Aristotelian notion of "the golden mean" to personal virtue.[38] Thomalin's indictment of Paris's flight from "Ida hill" stems from his own ethical stance of the "virtuous middle":

But nothing such thylk sheepheard was
   whome Ida hill did beare:
That left his flocke to fetch a lasse,
   whose loue he bought too deare.

"Thylk sheepheard" Paris is "nothing" good for having left his place, and thus the "medium"—the middle term in the syllogism—is Paris's moving away: "To leaue his flocke to fetch a lasse: which because it is agreeable with the nature of Paris, but is flatly repugnant to the dutie of a good sheepheard." The first two arguments, "1 Paris 2 A good sheepheard" are mediated by this third, "3 To leaue his flocke to fetch a lasse," which leads to a negative conclusion, namely that "Paris is no good sheepeheard." Thomalin will not accept Morrell's invitation to come up the hill and, in Thomalin's view, Paris should not have come down off "Ida hill."

The climax of emblematic exegesis arrives when the symmetry, composition, or "just proportion" between the verbal and visual is comprehended, which involves wrapping one's mind around the verbal and visual wit at the core of the emblem. Within Fraunce's logical emblem, the logical language describes the function of the middle term and the poetic language illustrates it by dramatizing Thomalin's motto "*In medio virtus*" (virtue is in the middle). What is so witty about Fraunce's logical emblem is that the hidden middle term between the dialectical words and the poetic picture is precisely the notion of the middle or "the golden mean." The "just proportion" of the logical emblem is the "logic of the middle," for it is both the subject of Fraunce's dialectical discussion and the center of Thomalin's virtue.

While there is a certain "thingness" to the ekphrastic illustrations in Fraunce's *Lawiers Logike*, the interaction between the illustration and the logical definition points not to rational arguments as objects but to rational arguments as conceptions, notions, and ideas. Ultimately, the logical emblem refers to a *res*, not as an "object" but as a "matter," and thereby encourages us to glimpse the intelligible in the sensible. As Fraunce writes in his emblem treatise, following Scipione Bargagli, the perfect emblem is "an expression [of an idea conceived within the mind] achieved by means of a certain resemblance, together with an image of some object—either natural [. . .] or artificial, with the addition of a motto which is clear, concise, to the point and witty" ("expressio singularis alicuius animi notionis per similitudinem quandam confecta cum figura alicuius rei naturalis [. . .] vel artificialis, et voce arguta, breui acuta, lepida, adiuncta,"

28–29). Fraunce is saying that the image and the motto, together, express "an idea conceived in the mind" ("animi notionis") that resembles some thing or matter ("rei"). Again, Fraunce writes:

> The motto does not describe the image nor the image the motto, but the image together with the motto convey an idea conceived within the mind.
>
> Non vox figuram nec figura vocem, sed figura cum voce animi notionem explicat.
>
> (14–15)

Emblems do not refer to things but to ideas. In like fashion, the Aristotelian "logic of the middle"—an "idea conceived within the mind" ("animi notionem")—is represented by the "certain resemblance" achieved between Fraunce's logical discourse and Spenser's eclogue. *Pace* Walter J. Ong, Ramism did not utterly objectify dialectical habits of mind because the reading strategies cultivated by Ramist logic books are figurative, volatile, and emblematic. Like emblem books, Ramist logic books refer to lively ideas, not to dead things.

4.

Early modern emblematists cultivated a kind of reading that is best described as a succession of cognitive activities that relate language to things, things to patterns of thought, and thought to spiritual and moral dispositions. Ramist logic books cultivate this kind of reading too, though we might more accurately say they elicit cognitive activities that relate abstract language to ekphrastic images, these images to patterns of thought, and this mode of thought to conceptual knowledge. The logical message arises from its medium or rather its media, for it is the bimedial format of these early modern printed dialectics that gives rise to emblematic habits of mind. Books can shape readers, but readers, such as Abraham Fraunce, can shape books too. Historians of early modern dialectical studies tend to overlook the role the history of the book can play in interpreting the *corpus aristotelicum*, especially during the Renaissance, when the printed codex plays a significant role in reforming the content of Aristotelian dialectic. The important and ongoing questions posed to Ramist dialectic about its legitimacy and about its influence and about its originality need to acknowledge both mutability in the material shape of logic books and creativity in their readers. D. F. McKenzie has argued that "new readers [. . .] make new texts, and [. . .] their new meanings are a function of their new forms."[39] The emblematic aesthetic of the Ramist logic books enabled a new way to comprehend Aristotelian dialectic by fashioning a logical mindset that moves between a word and an image to grasp the conceptual.

Franklin & Marshall College

NOTES

I am grateful to Franklin & Marshall College for a grant that enabled me to research this essay, and I warmly thank Judith H. Anderson for her helpful commentary on it.

1. James M. Osborn notes that the "best evidence" of Sidney's friendship with Ramus is that Ramus's former student Théophile de Banos dedicated his *Petri Rami Commentariorum de Religione Christiana Libri Quatuor* (Frankfurt, 1576) to Sidney with these words: " 'You not only entertained the tenderest love for our writer [i.e., Ramus] when alive, but now that he is dead, esteem and reverence him' ": *Young Philip Sidney* (New Haven: Yale University Press, 1972), 50.

2. Peter Mack notes that literary examples increase over time in the Ramist manuals: "In the September 1543 edition, there is more explanation than examples. By the 1550s examples almost exclude explanations": "Agricola and the Early Versions of Ramist Dialectic," *Autour de Ramus. Texte, Théorie, Commentaire*, eds. Kees Meerhoff and Jean-Claude Moisan (Québec: Nuit Blanche Éditeur, 1997), 27, note 33.

3. *The Development of Logic* (Oxford: Clarendon Press, 1962), 300 (my emphasis). For a more recent formulation of this view, see Mordechai Feingold, "English Ramism: A Reinterpretation," *The Influence of Petrus Ramus*, eds. Mordechai Feingold, Joseph S. Freedman, and Wolfgang Rother (Basel: Schwabe, 2001), 127–76.

4. Ann Moss notes that "Ramus belonged to a generation reared on the commonplace-book, with its stock of short excerpts at the ready to provide model formulae for all the figures of rhetoric, and examples of dialectical procedures at work": *Printed Commonplace-Books and the Structuring of Renaissance Thought* (Oxford: Clarendon Press, 1996), 156. Mary Thomas Crane likewise argues that the Ramist dialectic is indebted to the commonplace book, particularly to the basic commonplace techniques of gathering and framing passages: *Framing Authority. Sayings, Self, and Society in Sixteenth-Century England* (Princeton: Princeton University Press, 1993).

5. " 'Wherein hath Ramus been so offensious?': Poetic Examples in the English Ramist Logic Manuals (1574–1672)," *Rhetorica* 14 (1996): 73–101.

6. An unpublished manuscript by Fraunce in the Bodleian Library (MS Rawlinson D 345) contains both a Ramist treatise and a selection of Paolo Giovio's *imprese* that

is dedicated to Philip Sidney: Peter M. Daly and Mary V. Silcox, *The Modern Critical Reception of the English Emblem* (New York: K. G. Saur, 1991), 169–70.

7. *Insignium, Armorum, Emblematum, Hieroglyphicorum, et Symbolum, quae ab Italis Imprese nominantur, Explicatio* (London: Thomas Orwin, 1588), *The Arcadian Rhetorike* (London: Thomas Orwin, 1588), and *The Lawiers Logike* (London: Thomas Orwin, 1588). Subsequent reference to *The Lawiers Logike* is parenthetical.

8. *Speaking Pictures. English Emblem Books and Renaissance Culture* (London: Longman, 1994), 143. These other three treatises were also published in England at this time, but Fraunce alone seems interested in tracing out the connections among language, logic, and symbols: *The Worthy Tract of Paulus Iovius* (1585), translated by Samuel Daniel; *The Heroicall Devises of M. Claudivs Paradin* (1591), translated by the anonymous P.S.; the chapter on *imprese* in *Remains Concerning Britain* by William Camden (1604/05).

9. "The Theory of Figurative Expression in Italian Treatises on the *Impresa*," *Form and Meaning*, trans. Madeline Jay and Leon Wieseltier (New York: Viking, 1979), 14. Klein argues that the *impresa* treatises of sixteenth-century Italy reveal a deliberate interest in establishing an epistemological connection between the concept expressed in and by the *impresa*. The discussions were indebted primarily to Aristotelian traditions, but Klein also detects the introduction of mystical, neoplatonic attributions to their *impresa*-conceiving intellect (23).

10. For a survey of *impresa* literature, see Mario Praz, *Studies in Seventeenth-Century Imagery* (Rome: Edizioni di Storia e Letteratura, 1964), chap. 2.

11. The French Ramist Claude Mignault (Claudius Minos, 1536–1606), to whom Fraunce's emblem treatise and rhetorical manual are indebted, seems likewise to have apprehended the semantic link between the word and the image in Ramist habits of thought, but the clustered publication of Fraunce's three theoretical treatises makes him the ideal candidate for my study. We know that Mignault provided notes to a 1571 Paris edition of Alciati's emblems: by 1577, his notes had flourished into a meticulous, and well known, commentary in and on Alciati's *Emblematum liber* (Antwerp, Plantin), entitled "Syntagma de symbolis, stemmatum et schematum."

12. All references to Fraunce's emblem theory will be to his manuscript, *Symbolicæ-philosophiæ liber quartus et ultimus*, ed. John Manning, trans. Estelle Haan (New York: AMS, 1991), 8–9. Subsequent reference is parenthetical. I refer to Fraunce's manuscript rather than to his book, *Insignium, Armorum, Emblematum, Hieroglyphicorum, et Symbolum, quae ab Italis Imprese nominantur, Explicatio*, because the manuscript probably represents Fraunce's mature thoughts on emblem theory (for more on this, see *Symbolicæ philosophiæ*, xiii-xxxi).

13. "The Emblem as a Literary Genre," *Deviceful Settings: The English Renaissance Emblem and its Contexts*, eds. Michael Bath and Daniel Russell (New York: AMS, 1999), 7.

14. In the early 1580s, Fraunce wrote the unpublished precursor to *The Lawiers Logike* entitled *The Sheapheardes Logike*, which exists as a unique manuscript in the British Museum (Additional MSS 34361).

15. "The Illustrations to *The Shepeardes Calender*," *Spenser Studies* 2 (1981), 3.

16. Edmund Spenser, *The Shepheardes Calender* (London: John Wolfe, 1586), 7.

17. "The Term *Emblema* in Alciati," *Journal of the Warburg and Courtauld Institutes* 31 (1968), 238.

18. Miedema, 236. Miedema's interpretation of Alciati's definition is as follows: "an emblem is an epigram in which something specific is described in such a way as to give additional meaning ("significet") to a pleasant, but fortuitous fact or phenomenon; or: in such a way that what is described comes to indicate something else and thereby itself acquires a pleasing moral" (241).

19. Bath, 1.

20. "From Illustrated Epigram to Emblem: The Canonization of a Typographical Arrangement," *New Ways of Looking at Old Texts*, ed. W. Speed Hill (Binghamton: Medieval & Renaissance Texts & Studies, 1993), 152.

21. Scholz, 152.

22. See Walter J. Ong, *Ramus and Talon Inventory* (Cambridge: Harvard University Press, 1958); Joseph S. Freedman, "The Diffusion of the Writings of Petrus Ramus in Central Europe, c. 1570–1630," *Renaissance Quarterly* 46 (1993): 98–152. The textual scholarship of Nelly Bruyère-Robinet is quite useful as well: *Méthode et dialectique dans l'oeuvre de La Ramée: Renaissance et age classique* (Paris: Vrin, 1984) and *Dialectique 1555: un Manifeste de la Pléiade* (Paris: Vrin, 1996). Peter Sharratt mentions the formation of the international project, *Réseau International d'Etudes Ramistes* (RIER), one of whose aims is to analyze variants in Ramus's major texts: "Ramus 2000," *Rhetorica* 18 (2000), 454.

23. See Anthony Grafton and Lisa Jardine, *From Humanism to the Humanities: Education and the Liberal Arts in Fifteenth—and Sixteenth-Century Europe* (Cambridge: Harvard University Press, 1986); Wilbur S. Howell, *Logic and Rhetoric in England, 1500–1700* (Princeton: Princeton University Press, 1956). Grafton, Jardine, and Howell argue for Ramus's considerable influence in England, while Mordechai Feingold argues that Ramist logic is popular among "Puritans" only during that period immediately following Ramus's death in the St. Bartholomew's Day Massacre in 1572 (138).

24. *Peter Ramus of Vermandois [. . .] His Dialectica* (London: W. J.[ones], 1632), Cr-v.

25. Bath, 54.

26. *Logike of the Moste Excellent Philosopher P. Ramus Martyr* (London: Thomas Vautrollier, 1574), B5r. Subsequent reference is parenthetical. For more on MacIlmaine and the textual history of his Ramist manuals, see Goeglein, "Roland MacIlmaine," *Dictionary of Literary Biography*, ed. Edward Malone, vol. 281 (Detroit: Gale Research, 2003), 173–77.

27. See G. A. Padley, *Grammatical Theory in Western Europe, 1500–1700: The Latin Tradition* (Cambridge: Cambridge University Press, 1976), 30. Padley describes theoretical oscillations in Ramist grammar (77–96).

28. I refer to Ong's thesis about thingness because Anglo-American literary critics mostly know Ramist logic through Ong's *Ramus, Method, and the Decay of Dialogue* (Cambridge: Harvard University Press, 1958). Subsequent reference to *Ramus, Method, and the Decay of Dialogue* is parenthetical.

29. *The Lawiers Logike*, Ii.ii[**]. Fraunce inserts this Ramist diagram to map the contents of *The Lawiers Logike*.

30. Ong mentions the *Mnemonic Logic* of Thomas Murner (1475–1537), which was a card game inscribed with mnemonic illustrations of Aristotelian logical terms and

operations, but he dismisses a tie between this game and Ramist textbooks: "Murner's use of allegorical figures relates him to the emblem books which the new inventions [of printing] also popularized and thus marks a divergence from tendencies leading into Ramism. For at the heart of the Ramist enterprise is the drive to tie down words themselves, rather than other representations, in simple geometric patterns" (89).

31.   As John Manning points out in his "Introduction" to *Symbolicæ philosophiæ liber quartus et ultimus*, to distinguish between Fraunce's own ideas and the ideas of those emblem theorists he is quoting or paraphrasing is often impossible (xvii-xviii). For example, in this phrase "it seems to me" ("mihi . . . videntur"), the "me" could refer either to Fraunce or Giovio. Unless Fraunce explicitly refutes the ideas of others, I assume he shares their beliefs.

32.   *The Textual Condition* (Princeton: Princeton University Press, 1991), 12.

33.   *The Visible Word. Experimental Typography and Modern Art, 1909–1923* (Chicago: University of Chicago Press, 1994), 94–95. While Drucker argues that the "marked text" had "its most vibrant spurt of development" in late-nineteenth-century advertising, she maintains that the practice of "marking" texts was present from the beginning of the printed word—Gutenberg's printed Indulgences are quintessentially "marked texts" (95–96). For Gérard Genette, typography is a basic paratextual device, and he writes that "typographical choices may provide indirect commentary on the texts they affect": *Paratexts: Thresholds of Interpretation*, trans. Jane E. Lewin (Cambridge: Cambridge University Press, 1991), 34.

34.   Sabrina Alcorn Baron, "Red Ink and Black Letter: Reading Early Modern Authority," *The Reader Revealed*, ed. and comp. Sabrina Alcorn Baron (Washington, D.C.: The Folger Shakespeare Library, 2001), 25.

35.   Martin Lowry, *The World of Aldus Manutius*, (Ithaca: Cornell University Press, 1979), 136–42.

36.   In Dudley Fenner's *Artes of Logike and Rhetorike* (Middelburg: R. Schilders, 1584), the emblematic effect is created by the logical discourse being set in roman typeface and the rhetorical discourse set in italic typeface, although this effect is less pronounced.

37.   Luborsky, 35.

38.   Spenser, 129.

39.   *Bibliography and the Sociology of Texts* (Cambridge: Cambridge University Press, 1999), 29.

GLEANINGS

ANTHONY MILLER

Red Crosse's Imprisonment and Foxe's Inquisition

In Spenser's historical or prophetic allegory in *The Faerie Queene*, Book I, Orgoglio and Duessa are associated with the menace of Spain and Rome, and their prison with the horrors of the Spanish Inquistion as documented in John Foxe's *Acts and Monuments*. Correspondences include: the darkness and solitude of Red Crosse's prison; the despair bred by these conditions in the Christian not yet "thoroughly instructed in holy doctrine"; the combination of "ceremonial pomp" with "barbarous abuse and cruelty" that marks his captors; the secrecy, ignorance, and suppression of speech of the Inquisition, enancted in the figure of Ignaro. As in Foxe, this silence is answered in Spenser by the reports and appeals of Una and the Dwarf and by the witness of writings such as *The Farie Queene* itself.

*T*HE IMPRISONMENT OF RED CROSSE Knight in *The Faerie Queene*, I.vii–viii, signifies as theological allegory human frailty: it is the bands of sinfulness, "his owne foolish pride,"[1] that imprison Red Crosse, a condition from which he is saved only by God's grace, in the person of Arthur. As historical allegory, the imprisonment enacts the Protestant church history propagated by John Bale and John Foxe, in which England was imprisoned by the whorish papacy (Duessa), who enfeebled her subjects by the potions of Romish superstition (viii.14), and who allied herself to the kings of the earth (Orgoglio), who himself was both fathered and served by ignorance (Ignaro).[2] To these well-known allegorical senses should be added a more specific association of Orgoglio and Duessa with the menace of Spain, and

Spenser Studies: A Renaissance Poetry Annual, Volume XX, Copyright © 2005 by AMS Press, Inc. All rights reserved.

of their prison with the horrors of the Spanish Inquisition as documented by Foxe. These senses are not mutually exclusive but mutually reinforcing, since all apply to different areas of experience in the grand Christian narrative of captivity and release. The association of Red Crosse's imprisonment with the Inquisition warns the Elizabethan reader that, though the Reformation may have delivered England from the Babylonian captivity of papistry, a revival of that captivity remained a real and present danger. Nevertheless, it reassures faithful Protestants of their eventual success, due partly to writings like Foxe's *Actes and Monuments* and *The Faerie Queene* itself.

Especially in the aftermath of 1588, Protestant Englishmen saw the Spanish nation and its king, Philip II, as the principal secular arm of the Roman religion, a role that Philip himself devoutly embraced. English Armada writings insistently link the two powers: "our Italian *Lamec* and Spanish *Nimrod,* the pope I meane and the Spanishe king"; "when *Balaam* of *Rome* hath cursed, yet hast thou blessed us. When *Balaac* of Spaine hath practised mischiefe against vs, then hast thou discouered and disapointed it."[3] In this context, Orgoglio, "An hideous Geant horrible and hye,/That with his talnesse seemd to threat the skye" (vii.8), represents allegorically the formidable power of Spain, which was associated both with a puffed-up pride and with the towering ships of the Armada.[4] Orgoglio's "arrogant delight" in his parentage possibly puns on Philip's kingdom of Aragon, which in turn recalls the parentage of the papist persecutor Mary Tudor (vii.10; the word does not appear elsewhere in Spenser), and the eventual fall of Orgoglio, like the collapse of a "Castle reared high and round" (viii.23) probably puns on the Philip's kingdom of Castile and on the heraldic emblem of that kingdom, a castle.[5] The contrast between Orgoglio's gigantic stature and his deflation into an "emptie bladder" (viii.24) recalls English accounts of the Armada, with its huge ships and their miraculous dispersal: "Thus the magnificent, huge, and mighty fleet of the Spaniards (which themselves termed in all places invincible) . . . in the yeere 1588 vanished into smoake."[6]

More specifically again, the imprisonment of Red Crosse re-enacts Foxe's dreadful account of the Spanish Inquisition as the persecutor of reformed religion. Englishmen believed that Philip's conquest of England would impose the Inquisition on their own nation, as it had been imposed in the Spanish realms of Naples, Sicily, and the Netherlands, and on Englishmen in Spain.[7] Such an intention was announced in a series of distichs allegedly written in Lisbon and reprinted in England, with much triumphant scorn, after the defeat of the Armada. These distichs again make Spain the instrument of Roman tyranny:

Tu, quae Romanas uoluisti spernere leges,
   Disces Hispano subdere colla iugo.

(Thou England which the Romish lawes, long time hast now
reiected,
      Shalt learne ere long to Spanish yoke, thy necke shalbe
subiected.)[8]

Foxe describes the conditions of imprisonment under the Inquisition in these terms: "neither is it permitted to any person to enter
in to the prisoner; but there he is alone, in a place where he cannot
see so much as the ground where he is; . . . but there endureth in
darkness palpable, in horrors infinite, in fear miserable, wrestling with
the assaults of death. By this it may be esteemed what trouble and
sorrow, what pensive sighs and cogitations they sustain, who are not
thoroughly instructed in holy doctrine."[9] The Spanish martyr whose
story Foxe relates most fully, Franciscus San Romanus, was "detained
in a deep cave or dungeon, with much misery, the space of eight
months" near Antwerp, and then in Spain "he was delivered to the
inquisitors; by whom he was laid in a dark prison under the ground"
(pp. 448, 449). Red Crosse's companions, the Dwarf and Una, lament
his fate in terms similar to Foxe's description. The Dwarf tells how
Orgoglio has shut him away in darkness and solitude: "And now in
darkesome dungeon, wretched thrall,/Remedilesse, for aie he doth
him hold" (vii.51). Una emphasizes the role of Duessa and the prisoner's "fear miserable":

      For she it is, that did my Lord bethrall,
      My dearest Lord, and deepe in dongeon lay,
      Where he his better dayes hath wasted all.
   O heare, how piteous he to you for ayd does call.
                                                    (viii.28)

The dual attribution of responsibility in these speeches may refer to
the fact that "The cruel and barbarous inquisition of Spain first began
by king Ferdinand and Isabella his wife," or to the cooperation of
secular and religious arms, which Foxe carefully emphasizes.[10] When
eventually Arthur arrives to rescue Red Crosse, he too finds it not
"permitted . . . to enter in to the prisoner": "Whose gates he found
fast shut, ne liuing wight/To ward the same, nor answere commers
call" (viii.3). After Arthur forces his way into the prison he encounters the full horror of an underground darkness "where he cannot

see so much as the ground where he is": "Where entred in, his foot could find no flore,/But all a deepe descent, as darke as hell" (viii.39).

By the time this rescue finally arrives, Red Crosse has succumbed to the condition of Foxe's prisoner, re-appearing pathetically as "The chearelesse man, whom sorrow did dismay" (viii.43). Because he is not yet "thoroughly instructed in holy doctrine," as will happen in the House of Holiness, he has succumbed in particular to suicidal "trouble and sorrow, . . . pensive sighs and cogitations" before "the assaults of death":

Therewith an hollow, dreary, murmuring voyce
   These piteous plaints and dolours did resound;
   O who is that, which brings me happy choyce
   Of death, that here lye dying euery stound,
   Yet liue perforce in balefull darkenesse bound?
   For now three Moones haue changed thrice their hew,
   And haue beene thrice hid vnderneath the ground,
   Since I the heauens chearefull face did vew,
  O welcome thou, that doest of death bring tydings trew.
                          (viii.38)[11]

The triumphal displays of Orgoglio and Duessa after their capture of Red Crosse manifest the simultaneous display of "ceremonial pomp" along with "barbarous abuse and cruelty" by which Foxe characterizes the Inquisition (p. 451). The wedding of these two characteristics is written insistently into Spenser's narrative. Orgoglio adorns Duessa in "gold and purple pall" and a "triple crowne," but he also sets her on a seven-headed beast, "for to make her dreaded more of men,/And peoples harts with awfull terrour tye" (vii.16). The combination recurs in viii.6,[12] and most dreadfully inside Orgoglio's prison:

There all within full rich arayd he found,
   With royall arras and resplendent gold.
   And did with store of euery thing abound,
   That greatest Princes presence might behold.
   But all the floore (too filthy to be told)
   With bloud of guiltlesse babes, and innocents trew,
   Which there were slaine, as sheepe out of the fold,
   Defiled was, that dreadfull was to vew,
  And sacred ashes ouer it was strowed new.
                          (viii.35)

Foxe relates how the "sacred ashes" of the innocent Franciscus San Romanus were revered: "certain of the emperor's soldiers gathered of his ashes; also the English ambassador procured a portion of his bones" (p. 450). The disrobing and flight of Duessa, as well as revealing the ugliness of error that lies beneath the meretricious beauties of the Roman church, demonstrates its literally "barbarous" quality, as Duessa flees the world of men to "wander wayes vnknowne":

> She flying fast from heauens hated face,
>   And from the world that her discouered wide,
>   Fled to the wastfull wildernesse apace,
>   From liuing eyes her open shame to hide,
>   And lurkt in rocks and caues long vnespide.
>
> (viii.50)

The mechanics of the Inquisition are characterized for Foxe by secrecy and ignorance:

> During all this time, what is done in the process, no person knoweth, but only the holy fathers and the tormentors, who are sworn to execute the torments. All this is done in secret, and (as great mysteries) pass not the hands of these holy ones. And after all these torments so many years endured in the prison, if any man shall be saved, it must be by guessing; for all the proceedings of the court of that execrable inquisition are open to no man, but all is done in hugger-mugger and in close corners, by ambages, by covert ways, and secret counsels. The accuser is secret, the crime secret, the witness secret, whatsoever is done is secret, neither is the poor prisoner ever advertised of any thing.
>
> (p. 452)

The inability or refusal of Spenser's Ignaro to convey information represents the tenacious secrecy of the Inquisition. Like Foxe with his "holy fathers" and "holy ones," Spenser accords Ignaro an ironical reverence. Like the victims of the Inquisition and their friends, Arthur elicits no information from Ignaro but must guess at his true nature and guess at how to rescue Red Crosse. The remorseless repetition of the word "secret" in Foxe is mirrored, more mildly but no less injuriously, in Ignaro's rote disavowals:

His reuerend haires and holy grauitie
  The knight much honord, as beseemed well,
  And gently askt, where all the people bee,
  Which in that stately building wont to dwell.
  Who answerd him full soft, he could not tell.
  Againe he askt, where that same knight was layd,
            . . . againe he sayde,
He could not tell: ne euer other answere made.

Then asked he, which way he in might pas:
  He could not tell, againe he answered.
  Thereat the curteous knight displeased was,
  And said, . . .
Aread in grauer wise, what I demaund of thee.

His answere likewise was, he could not tell.

(viii.32–34)[13]

An extension of secrecy and ignorance is the manifold abuse of
speech and silence by Foxe's Inquisition. Whether by words or by
silence, one is equally at risk of being found guilty: "If any word
shall pass out of the mouth of any, which may be taken in evil part;
yea, though no word be spoken, yet if they bear any grudge or evil
will against the party, incontinent they command him to be taken,
and put in a horrible prison" (p. 451). Foxe gives several examples
of believers who are forbidden to speak at their trials or executions.[14]
Once the prisoner is shut away, there follows a silence of enforced
assent from his family and friends: "in the mean time no man living
is so hardy as once to open his mouth for him. If the father speak
one word for his child, he is also taken and cast into prison as a
favourer of heretics" (pp. 451–52). When Arthur first enters Orgoglio's castle, he meets an eerie silence that gathers up these associations
of the Inquisition with the suppression of speech:

Then gan he lowdly through the house to call:
  But no man car'd to answere to his crye.
  There raignd a solemne silence ouer all,
Nor voice was heard, nor wight was seene in bowre or hall.

(viii.29)

As was proved by the coming of the Reformation, and by Foxe's own book commemorating its heroic martyrs, this situation cannot however prevail. True speech and writing will fill the void created by their papist suppression. Red Crosse's friends are able to "tell his great distresse" (vii.19; cf. vii.21–27) and thus win the aid of Arthur. It is a blast from the horn of Arthur's Squire that eventually throws open Orgoglio's prison: "No gate so strong, no locke so firme and fast,/But with the percing noise flew open quite, or brast" (viii.4).[15]

This sound, piercing perfidious silence, represents both the eventual apocalyptic overthrow of Satan's realm and also the trumpet blast of the Reformation. This blast was sounded in large part through the medium of books, as Foxe famously declared: "How many presses there be in the world, so many block-houses there be against the high castel of St. Angelo, so that either the pope must abolish knowledge and printing or printing must at length root him out."[16] Though the prisoner of Foxe's Inquisition "is not suffered either to read or write," Foxe is able to expose the Spanish Inquisition by obtaining reliable written documentation and then circulating it in print, "according as we have faithful records of such as have come to our hands by writing" (p. 452). Spenser's poetic revelation of the reality of Orgoglio's prison is designed to serve the same purpose, as witnessed by Arthur, who compares his experience of the prison to a reading experience, and whose ethical moralisation includes the recognition that Spenser's book, like Foxe's, will teach contempt for the world, in contrast to the worldly irreligion of Rome and Spain:

> This dayes ensample hath this lesson deare
> Deepe written in my heart with yron pen,
> That blisse may not abide in state of mortall men.
>
> (viii.44)

University of Sydney

NOTES

1.   Quotation from Edmund Spenser, *The Faerie Queene*, ed. A. C. Hamilton (London: Longman, 1977), I.viii.1. All references to *The Faerie Queene* incorporated in the text are to Book I. The fullest treatment of these cantos is D. Douglas Waters, *Duessa as Theological Satire* (Columbia: University of Missouri Press, 1970). Waters proposes a specifically eucharistic allegory, in which Duessa is "the Roman Mass

personified as a witch and whore" (p. 79), Orgoglio "the proud, gigantic Mass-priest" (p. 71), and Arthur the "Christian magnanimity" (p. 85) which assists Red Crosse to recognize his theological and ethical error in embracing the Mass.

2.   The classic modern restatement of the historical allegory is Frank Kermode, "*The Faerie Queene,* I and V," *Bulletin of the John Rylands Library* 47 (1964), 123–50, rpt. in *Shakespeare, Spenser, Donne: Renaissance Essays* (London: Routledge and Kegan Paul, and New York: Viking, 1971), pp. 33–59. Both theological and historical allegories derive from Spenser's use of the biblical Book of Revelation; the definitive modern discussion is John E. Hankins, "Spenser and the Revelation of St John," *PMLA* 60 (1945), 364–81, rpt. in *Source and Meaning in Spenser's Allegory* (Oxford: Clarendon Press, 1971), pp. 99–119.

3.   Daniel Archdeacon, trans., *A True discourse of the Armie which the King of Spaine caused to bee assembled in the Haven of Lisbon* (1588), sig. A4v, cf. sig. A6; R. H[umston], *A Sermon Preached at Reysham . . . the 22. of September, An. Do.* 1588 (1589), sig. D1v, cf. sig. C8v. In Foxe, allegiance to the Pope is the paramount concern of the Inquisition: "The friars could suffer him meanly well to speak, till he came to the pope, and began to speak against his dignity, and their profit; then could they abide no longer, but thundered against him words full of cruelty and terror" (*The Acts and Monuments of John Foxe,* ed. George Townsend, 8 vols. [London: Seeley, Burnside and Seeley, 1843–49], vol. 4, p. 448). All references to *The Acts and Monuments* incorporated in the text are to vol. 4.

4.   "But the Almightie God, who alwayes . . . bringeth downe his enemies that exalt them selues with pride to the heauens, ordred the winds, to be so violently contrarious to this proud Nauie, as it was with force disseuered," *The Copie of a Letter sent out of England to Don Bernadin Mendoza Ambassadour in France for the King of Spaine* (1588), sig. F1–F1v. (The letter was actually a propaganda document composed by Burleigh.) "Quam bene, te ambitio mersit vanissima, ventus:/Et tumidos tumidae, vos superastis aquae!" Théodore Beza, *Ad Serenissimam Elisabetham,* in Richard Hakluyt, *The Principal Navigations . . . of the English Nation,* 12 vols. (Glasgow: James MacLehose, 1903–5), vol. 4, p. 235.

5.   Cf. the similar and definite allusion, III.iii.49.

6.   Hakluyt, *Navigations,* vol. 4, p. 234. For the castle simile, cf. "for ships they haue built them like Castels: . . . for munition, they haue much and maruellous", Archdeacon, trans., *A True discourse,* sig. A6. The emphasis on the formidable cannon of the Armada here and elsewhere in the Armada writings may also account for Spenser's epic simile of cannon, vii.13; cf. viii.9. See, e.g., the broadside *A ioyful new Ballad* (1588): "Stronge was she stuft,/with Cannons great and small: . . . In her was placed,/an hundreth Cannons great."

7.   Foxe, *Acts and Monuments,* vol. 4, pp. 458, 447–48, 457.

8.   *The Holy Bull, And Crusado of Rome* (1588), sig. A4. The Latin texts are printed also in Archdeacon, trans., *A True discourse,* and "N. Eleutherius," ed., *Triumphalia de uictoriis Elisabethae* (1588).

9.   *Acts and Monuments,* vol. 4, p. 452.

10.   *Acts and Monuments,* vol. 4, pp. 451, 453.

11.   Red Crosse's complaint has been compared to Psalm 107:10–14 and Romans 7:24 (Hamilton, ed., *Faerie Queene,* p. 115). Anne Lake Prescott points out to me

that Red Crosse's "piteous plaints," his comparison of himself to the dead, and his physical debility also echo Psalm 88:4–5: "I am counted among them that go downe vnto the pit, and am as a man without strength: Free among the dead, like the slaine lying in the graue, whome thou remembrest no more, and they are cut off from thine hand" (Geneva). The heading to this Psalm in the Geneva Bible also glosses Red Crosse's condition: "A grieuous complaint of the faithfull, sore afflicted by sicknes, persecutions and aduersitie . . . Being as it were left of God without any consolation."

12.   The topicality of "late cruell feast" (viii.6) and of Duessa's beast, "swolne with bloud of late" (viii.12), has been related to the widespread executions of the *Conseil des Troubles* imposed by the Spanish governor-general Alva after the Protestant revolt of 1566–67 in the Netherlands (Hamilton, ed., *Faerie Queene*, p. 109). The beast's "heads like flaming brands" strengthen this connection with the burnings that were the usual form of execution for heresy. For the *Conseil des Troubles* and the exiles who carried news of it to Protestant lands, see Jonathan Israel, *The Dutch Republic* (Oxford: Clarendon Press, 1995), pp. 155–68.

13.   Ignaro recalls another model for Spenser's episode, Christ's Harrowing of Hell. The *Golden Legend,* citing "Gregorye Niceus and saynt Austyn/lyke as is founde in some bokes," tells how Hell's "porter blacke and horryble amonge them in scylence began to murmure" ([1527], sig. c8v, contractions expanded).

14.   Alphonso Perez, vol. 4, p. 455; Anthony de Herezuelo, vol. 4, pp. 456, 457.

15.   This detail also derives from the Harrowing of Hell: "at the commaundement of our lorde all the lockes all the barres and shyttynges ben broken and to frusshed. And loo the people of sayntes that come knelynge tofore hym/in cryenge with piteous voice" (sig. c7v).

16.   Cited by Elizabeth Eisenstein, *The Printing Press as an Agent of Change,* 2 vols. (Cambridge: Cambridge University Press, 1979), vol .1, p. 306; cf. Eisenstein's provocative discussion, pp. 303–13, 367–78. Like many of Foxes's Protestants, Franciscus San Romanus was converted by preaching and by the diligent study of books. He himself sought to disseminate truth by writing letters and a catechism, while the friars of the Inquisition "burnt his books before his face" (vol. 4, p. 448).

JASON LAWRENCE

Calidore fra i pastori: Spenser's return to Tasso in *The Faerie Queene*, Book VI

This essay focuses on Spenser's allusions to Tasso's episode *Erminia fra i pastori* from Canto VII of *Gerusalemme liberata*, to elucidate Calidore's increasing ambivalence towards his epic task in the final cantos of the last completed book of *The Faerie Queene*. I argue that a previously unacknowledged allusion to Tasso's dedicatory stanza to Alfonso II of Ferrara, in which the poet is described as a wanderer lost at sea until offered literary protection, as Calidore converses with Meliboe in Canto IX, demonstrates a sense of growing uncertainty in the figure of the poet himself. The latter part of the essay considers how Spenser's sustained reworking of the Petrarchan image of the lover as an endangered ship in the *Amoretti* offers an alternative passage for the ship conceits of *The Faerie Queene*, signalling a marked shift in the trajectory of Spenser's later poetic career.

SPENSER'S PRINCIPAL NARRATIVE debt to Tasso in *The Faerie Queene* is the account of Guyon's arrival at the Bowre of Blisse in the final canto of Book II, which contains the first examples of direct translation from *Gerusalemme liberata* in the poem: the description of the "due donzellette garrule" playing in the fountain [XV. lviii–lx] at II. xii. 63–65, and his version of the celebrated *canto della rosa* [XVI. xiv–xv] in stanzas 74 and 75 of the same canto. According to Donald Cheney, this episode is "Spenser's most famous single borrowing from the *Gerusalemme liberata*," and the considerable and increasingly detailed body of criticism on the respective treatments bears this out.[1]

Spenser Studies: A Renaissance Poetry Annual, Volume XX, Copyright © 2005 by AMS Press, Inc. All rights reserved.

   This criticism has gradually come to emphasise the important differences in Spenser's rendering from the Italian original, prompting
John Watkins to argue that in *The Faerie Queene* "episodes like the
Bower of Bliss inculcate Virgilian self-denial on both a fictional and
a metafictional level. Spenser not only applauds Guyon's resistance
to Acrasia but upholds his own resistance to Tassean romance as
a lesson in temperance."[2] The ability ultimately to withstand the
temptation to abandon the epic quest, which Tasso's Armida embodies, becomes the principal structural device of Spenser's Book II.
From the opening tale of Mortdant and Acrasia, which Amavia relates
to Guyon in Canto I, through Cymochles's self-abandonment to the
sensual delights of Phaedria in Canto VI (in contrast to Guyon's
ability to withstand the same temptation), the narrative moves relentlessly towards Guyon's release of Verdant, and his complete destruction of Acrasia's Bowre in the final canto. Yet, if both Spenser and
Sir Guyon are able to resist the distracting influence of Tasso's eroticism in the 1590 edition of *The Faerie Queene*, in the second edition
of 1596 Spenser and one of his titular knights, Sir Calidore, demonstrate a rather more ambivalent attitude to the question of withdrawal
from the epic task, when the poet turns again to *Gerusalemme liberata*
in his final completed book of the poem.
   Cheney registers the similarity of Calidore's pastoral retreat in
Canto IX of Book VI to the episode of *Erminia fra i pastori* in Canto
VII of Tasso's poem, noting that the old shepherd Meliboe's account
of his ten-year sojourn at court is written "in language so close to
the original that the passage might for all practical purposes be taken
as an allusion to Tasso."[3] In contrast to the conscious echoes of, and
alterations to, Tasso's epic in Book II, however, Spenser's use of
Gerusalemme liberata in the second part of his poem has received scant
attention. Even where the allusion is quite deliberate and sustained,
as in the conversation between Meliboe and Calidore in Canto IX,
the critical focus has tended to be on a less specific consideration of
pastoral convention: thus, Patricia Parker suggests of Book VI that
"the Legend is even generically in touch with its origins, in its return
to pastoral, a traditional and, for Spenser, actual early mode."[4] I want
to concentrate on these allusions to Tasso's shepherd as part of Spenser's reconsideration of his own epic task as he approaches the nominal
half-way point of *The Faerie Queene*, taking into account Parker's
contention that "Calidore's 'delay' among the shepherds . . . is here
virtually indistinguishable from the author's own kind of 'straying'."[5]
   Cheney details Spenser's alterations to Tasso's account of Erminia's
dialogue with the old shepherd in order to stress Calidore's "ulterior
intent" in wishing to remain in the pastoral world: his desire to court

Meliboe's supposed daughter Pastorella, adding what Paul Alpers describes as a "pastoral erotics" to the episode.[6] Calidore's response to the shepherd's wisdom initially echoes that of Erminia closely, and it is only in the second half of Spenser's stanza that his dual focus of attention becomes apparent:

> Mentre ei cosí ragiona, Erminia pende
> de la soave bocca intenta e cheta;
> e quel saggio parlar, ch' al cor le scende,
> de' sensi in parte le procelle acqueta.
>
> [VII. xiv. 1–4]

(While he reasoned thus, Erminia hung on his gentle mouth intently and silently; and that wise speech, which descended into her heart, calmed in part the storms of her passions.)

> Whylest thus he talkt, the knight with greedy eare
> Hong still vpon his melting mouth attent;
> Whose sensefull words empierst his hart so neare,
> That he was rapt with double rauishment,
> Both of his speach that wrought him great content,
> And also of the obiect of his vew,
> On which his hungry eye was alwayes bent.
>
> [VI. ix. 26. 1–7][7]

Spenser replaces the calming effect of the shepherd's wise words on Erminia's storms of passion ("le procelle . . . de' sensi") in line 4 with Calidore's "double rauishment" for both Meliboe and Pastorella; significantly, however, he will return to Tasso's image later in their exchange. Erminia's decision to remain among the shepherds is predicated on her hope that the pastoral setting may help to disburden her heart of its cares ("Forse fia che' l mio core infra quest' ombre / del suo peso mortal parte disgombre" [VII. xv. 7–8]), caused by her deep love for the Christian (and thus hostile) knight Tancredi. That the motivation for the pastoral retreat in Tasso is predominantly amorous in nature suggests a continuity in Spenser's rendering, rather than a conscious alteration which would serve to stress "the duplicity that characterizes his [Calidore's] conduct among the shepherds" in his pursuit of Pastorella's affections.[8]

Spenser continues to follow the exact pattern of Erminia's response in his rendering: Calidore, like Erminia, ill-advisedly offers gold in recompense for the pastoral hospitality he receives, and also clothes himself "in shepheards weed" to tend Pastorella's flock.[9] The most striking change in the two episodes, however, is the image with which Spenser chooses to convey Calidore's decision to stay, at least temporarily, with the shepherds. Calidore initiates the conversation on the advantages of the pastoral life with the image of protection from the storms of life ("Leading a life so free and fortunate / From all the tempests of these worldly seas / Which tosse the rest in dangerous disease" [VI. ix. 19. 3–5]), and Tasso's "procelle" recur later in Spenser's account:

> Since then in each mans self (said *Calidore*)
> It is, to fashion his owne lyfes estate,
> Giue leaue awhyle, good father, in this shore
> To rest my barcke, which hath bene beaten late
> With stormes of fortune and tempestuous fate,
> In seas of troubles and of toylesome paine,
> That whether quite from them for to retrate
> I shall resolue, or backe to turne againe,
> I may here with your selfe some small repose obtaine.
>
> [VI. ix. 31]

Calidore may choose wilfully to misunderstand the implications of Meliboe's contention that "It is the mynd, that maketh good or ill" [VI. ix. 30. 1] in defining his doctrine of self-fashioning, but his appeal to the shepherd for temporary shelter from the "stormes of fortune" immediately qualifies the apparent self-reliance of the opening two lines. The image of the endangered ship approaching, but never quite reaching, the haven of the port is a common one in *The Faerie Queene*, as Jerome Dees has noted,[10] and it occurs again in the poet's description of Calidore's desire to

> set his rest amongst the rusticke sort,
> Rather then hunt still after shadowes vaine
> Of courtly fauour, fed with light report
> Of euery blaste, and sayling alwaies on the port.
>
> [VI. x. 2. 6–9][11]

In this instance, the inability of the ship to reach port is linked specifically with the vain pursuit of "courtly fauour," and so Calidore's decision to remain in the pastoral world, where he may achieve "some small repose," can be seen as a rejection of the "sacred noursery" [VI. Proem. 3. 1–2] that fosters his virtue of Courtesy. The virtue is directly associated with the poet's "soueraine Lady Queene" at the start of Book VI [Proem. 6], and Calidore's rejection of the court of Faerie at this point seems also to imply a significant change of emphasis within the figure of the poet himself, with regard to both the public world of the Elizabethan court, and perhaps even the dedicatee of his poem.

I want to suggest that Calidore's response to Meliboe does not derive solely from Tasso's own pastoral interlude; Spenser uses the knight's words in stanza 31 to allude to another part of *Gerusalemme liberata*. The "ship conceit" occurs frequently in Italian epic, although, surprisingly, it is not one of the "conspicuous allusions" identified by Dees. The most significant example of Tasso's use of the image of the stricken ship is in the dedication of the poem to Alfonso II; this is the stanza to which Spenser is alluding:

> Tu, magnanimo Alfonso, il qual ritogli
> al furor di fortuna e guidi in porto
> me peregrino errante, e fra gli scogli
> e fra l'onde agitato e quasi absorto,
> queste mie carte in lieta fronte accogli,
> che quasi in voto a te sacrate i' porto.
>
> [I. iv. 1–6]

(You, magnanimous Alfonso, who rescued me from the storms of fortune and guided this wandering traveller, perturbed and almost drowned amidst the rocks and the waves, into the port, accept in good faith these lines of mine, that I dedicate to you as an almost sacred offering.)

Tasso addresses his patron, the duke of Ferrara, as the person who enables the poet to fulfil his epic task successfully, by offering both physical and literary protection to the "peregrino errante," who then offers the completed poem in return.[12] In 1595, Samuel Daniel dedicates the first edition of his epic poem *The Civill Warres* to his patron Charles Blount by paraphrasing closely Tasso's dedicatory stanza:

And thou *Charles Montioy* borne the worldes delight
That hast receiu'd into thy quiet shore
Me tempest-driuen fortune-tossed wight
Tir'd with expecting, and could hope no more:
And cheerest on my better yeares to write
A sadder Subject then I tooke before,
Receiue the worke I consecrate to thee,
Borne of that rest which thou dost give to me.

[I. v. 1–8 (1595)]

Mountjoy's role in the development of Daniel's verse corresponds exactly to that of Alfonso II at the opening of Tasso's poem; in around 1594 Blount provides Daniel with a room in his house on the Strand ("thy quiet shore"), which allows the poet to continue work on his epic, in the same way that the duke of Ferrara had offered Tasso protection at his court during the early 1570s in order to complete *Gerusalemme liberata*. The deliberate echo is intended as a generous compliment to a patron who would be fully able to appreciate the Italian allusion:[13] in return for the room Blount has provided for the poet, Daniel offers his patron a *stanza* (with the secondary sense of "room" in Italian) from Tasso's poem. The pun in Italian is made explicit in Daniel's final revisions for the 1609 edition of *The Civill Warres*, printed after Mountjoy's death, in which the stanza is offered as a lasting memorial of Blount's generosity to the poet during his life:

Beholde: my gratitude makes good my word
Ingag'd to thee (although thou be no more)
That I, who heretofore haue liv'd by thee,
Doo giue thee now a roome to liue with me.

[I. v. 5–8 (1609)][14]

It is striking, however, that Spenser transfers the words from Tasso's figure of the poet to one of his principal characters in the pastoral context of Book VI. Despite the high regard that his sovereign has for both the duke of Ferrara and this Italian poem in particular,[15] Spenser consciously alludes to Tasso's dedication *not* to compliment Queen Elizabeth's analogous role in the composition of his own epic poem, but rather to stress the withdrawal of one of his knights from his royally-appointed task.[16] Calidore instead seeks his "repose" with a simple shepherd and his daughter, and his retreat privileges private and emotional motives over the public and political.

Spenser's use of Italian materials in his later poetry seems to mirror this movement away from epic endeavor. His indebtedness to both Ariosto and Tasso is considerably reduced in the second volume of *The Faerie Queene*, and, when the poet does turn again to the *Gerusalemme liberata* in Book VI, he deliberately chooses and adapts Tasso's pastoral interlude to highlight both Calidore's and his own growing uncertainty about the continuation of their respective epic tasks. At exactly the same time (or so the poet would have us believe), Spenser switches his attention to a sequence of love sonnets, the *Amoretti*, printed in 1595; it is significant that this change of focus is registered, at least partly, by a concomitant shift in the *type* of Italian sources that he draws upon. The *Amoretti* are both generically, and specifically, Petrarchan in many of the sonnets, and Spenser's use of Petrarch is frequently filtered through his knowledge of later Italian sonneteers, particularly the lyric poems of Tasso.[17]

An examination of Spenser's use in the *Amoretti* of a celebrated Petrarchan conceit, that of the poet-lover as a ship lost at sea in a storm ("Passa la nave mia colmo d'oblio" [sonnet 189]), demonstrates this increasing tension between the epic and lyric modes in his later poetry. In his first allusion to Petrarch's sonnet in the sequence, Spenser borrows and develops the image of the beloved's eyes as guiding stars, hidden from view in the mist and rain, from the final tercet ("Celansi i duo mei dolci usati segni" [12]),[18] as the controlling conceit for the octave of sonnet XXXIIII:

> Lyke as a ship that through the Ocean wyde
> by conduct of some star doth make her way,
> whenas a storme hath dimd her trusty guyde,
> out of her course doth wander far astray:
> So I whose star, that wont with her bright ray
> me to direct, with cloudes is overcast,
> doe wander now in darkness and dismay,
> through hidden perils round about me plast.
>
> [XXXIIII. 1–8][19]

Spenser initially uses the Italian sonnet to suggest a moment of crisis in the relationship between the poet and the beloved, but where Petrarch concludes with unrelieved despair ("tal ch' i' 'ncomincio a desperar del porto" [14]), the English poem offers in the sestet the slight hope that "my *Helice* the lodestar of my lyfe / will shine again" [10–11], in which the beloved's name Elizabeth is figured metaphorically as the constellation Ursa Major. The guidance that the poet-lover seeks from his beloved is demonstrated in sonnet LIX, where

Spenser reworks Petrarch's ship conceit to stress the steadiness of the female pilot, in contrast to the uncertainty of the male figures in the Italian original, and his own earlier sonnet. The positive transformation of Petrarch's poem in the *Amoretti* culminates in sonnet LXIII, marking a significant movement towards reciprocity in the relationship between the poet and his beloved in the final part of the sequence:

> After long stormes and tempests sad assay,
> Which hardly I endured heretofore:
> in dread of death and dangerous dismay,
> with which my silly barke was tossed so sore,
> I doe at length descry the happy shore,
> in which I hope ere long for to arryve.

> [LXIII. 1–6]

The moment of crisis to which Spenser alludes through Petrarch's ship conceit in sonnet XXXIIII follows on immediately from the first reference to *The Faerie Queene* in the sequence. In the preceding sonnet the poet expresses his anxiety to Lodowick Bryskett about completing his unfinished epic poem, caused by the mental distraction of his unrequited love. In the couplet of sonnet XXXIII the poet longs for the "rest" from his torment which sonnet LXIII will finally offer, but it is clear that at this point Spenser's uncertainty is both amorous and poetic. The perceived connection between the *Amoretti* and *The Faerie Queene* in sonnets XXXIII and XXXIIII can be illustrated in two ways: in the first volume of the epic Spenser includes an extended paraphrase of Petrarch's sonnet 189 in Britomart's passionate love lament on the seashore [III. iv. 8–10].[20] The link is clearer still in Book VI, where the opening stanza of the final canto shares the first line from sonnet XXXIIII of the *Amoretti*.

There is, however, a different Italian source for the line, and the stanza it introduces, in the final completed book of *The Faerie Queene*. If the line in the sonnet sequence alludes to the familiar Petrarchan conceit, in the epic poem it echoes instead an image from the start of the last canto of *Orlando Furioso*:

> Like as a ship, that through the Ocean wyde
> Directs her course vnto one certaine cost,
> Is met of many a counter winde and tyde,
> With which her winged speed is let and crost,

And she her selfe in stormie surges tost;
Yet, making many a borde, and many a bay,
Still winneth way, ne hath her compasse lost:
Right so it fares with me in this long way,
Whose course is often stayd, yet neuer is astray.

[VI. xii. 1]

Or, se mi mostra la mia carta il vero,
non è lontano a discoprirsi il porto; [. . .]
ove, o di non tornar col legno intero,
o d' errar sempre, ebbi già il viso smorto.
Ma mi par di veder, ma veggo certo,
veggo la terra, e veggo il lito aperto.

[XLVI. i. 1–2 /5–8]

(Now if my chart tells me true, the harbour will soon be in sight. [. . .] Oh, how I had paled at the prospect of returning with but a crippled ship, or perhaps of wandering forever! But I think I see . . . yes, I do see land, I see the welcoming shore).[21]

In Ariosto's poem the image of the ship is associated with the figure of the narrator as pilot, and it becomes a kind of "formal analogue for the poetic process,"[22] by which the poem is eventually brought home to port after the constant strayings of its journey. Spenser has already alluded to Ariosto's image twice in the final canto of Book I ("Behold I see the hauen nigh at hand / To which I meane my wearie course to bend" [I. xii. 1. 1–2], and I. xii. 42), to convey a sense of resolution to the self-contained narrative of that book. The reappearance of the conceit of the narrator guiding his ship towards port at the end of the final printed book of the poem suggests a similar motion towards completion.

The keen reader of Spenser's poetry in 1596 could be forgiven for believing that the poet was hinting strongly that he had gone as far as he was able to with the composition of *The Faerie Queene*. Despite the hope expressed in sonnet LXXX of the *Amoretti* that he will soon return refreshed to his epic task ("give leave to rest me being halfe fordonne, / and gather to my selfe new breath awhile" [3–4]), Spenser's own increasing ambivalence is recorded in the same sonnet by the temporary focus on his private love ("the handmayd of the Faery Queene" [14]) rather than his public poetic duty. Sonnet LXXX anticipates Colin Clout's beatific vision of his beloved in the final book printed in 1596 [VI. x. 12–16], while Spenser's positive recon-figuration of the Petrarchan conceit of the ship from sonnet XXXIIII through sonnet LXIII both alerts the reader to, and offers an alterna-tive passage for, the ship derived from Italian epic poetry in the concluding cantos of *The Faerie Queene*. Calidore appropriates Tasso's opening image of the epic poet as a wanderer lost at sea until rescued by his patron, in order to stay and pursue his private affections for Pastorella in the pastoral retreat, which also has its principal source in *Gerusalemme liberata*. The allusion to Ariosto's ship in the last canto suggests a sense of finality, and thus the privileging of the image in its transfer into the lyric mode of the *Amoretti*. Spenser's simultaneous use of the same conceit from two distinct Italian modes seems finally to confirm an important adjustment in the trajectory of his literary career, away from the quest for public influence and political patron-age through poetry, towards a private, emotional fulfilment in his later epic and lyric verse.

University of Hull

NOTES

1.   Donald Cheney, *Spenser's Image of Nature: Wild Man and Shepherd in the Faerie Queene* (Yale University Press, New Haven, 1966), 93. Guyon and the Palmer's rescue of Verdant from Acrasia's Bowre is heavily indebted to Tasso's account of Carlo and Ubaldo's recovery of Rinaldo from Armida's island in Cantos XIV–XVI. See C. S. Lewis, *The Allegory of Love* (Oxford University Press, Oxford, 1936), 324–40; Robert M. Durling, "The Bower of Bliss and Armida's palace", *Comparative Literature* 6 (1954), 335–47; Stephen J. Greenblatt, "To fashion a Gentleman: Spenser and the destruction of the Bower of Bliss" in *Renaissance Self-Fashioning: From More to Shakespeare* (University of Chicago Press, Chicago, 1980), 157–92; Judith A. Kates, *Tasso and Milton: The Problem of Christian Epic* (Bucknell University Press, Lewisburg, 1983), 136–44 and appendix; Alistair Fox, *The English Renaissance: Identity and Repre-sentation in Elizabethan England* (Blackwell, Oxford, 1997), 162–74.

2.   John Watkins, *The Specter of Dido: Spenser and Virgilian Epic* (Yale University Press, New Haven, 1995), 4.

3.   Cheney, *Spenser's Image of Nature*, 220; Castelli is more direct in referring to part of Meliboe's speech [VI. ix. 24–25] as "la seconda traduzione letteraria" in the poem, from stanzas xii and xiii in Canto VII of Tasso's poem: Alberto Castelli, *La Gerusalemme liberata nella Inghilterra di Spenser* (Vita e Pensiero, Milan, 1936), 33. Spenser also uses significant elements of Tasso's stanzas x and xi in his preceding stanza 23.

4.   Patricia Parker, *Inescapable Romance* (Princeton University Press, Princeton, 1979), 107. Anderson says of Meliboe's idyllic stanzas that "much as they bear a

general resemblance to Marlowe's 'Passionate Shepherd' and to Tasso's treatment of the old shepherd who comforts Erminia, their honeyed indulgence is distinctively Spenser's, or rather, Melibee's own": Judith H. Anderson, "Prudence and her silence: Spenser's use of Chaucer's *Melibee*," *ELH* 62 (1995), 29–46; 39.

5. Parker, *Inescapable Romance*, 63. Bernard also alludes to the association of Calidore and Spenser by suggesting that "the poet's vindication of his hero hints at a deeper identification of the two than has generally been granted": John Bernard, *Ceremonies of Innocence: Pastoralism in the Poetry of Edmund Spenser* (Cambridge University Press, Cambridge, 1989), 147.

6. Cheney, *Spenser's Image of Nature*, 219; Paul Alpers, "Spenser's late pastorals," *ELH* 56 (1989), 797–817; 802.

7. All references to Tasso are from ed. Lanfranco Caretti, *Gerusalemme liberata* (Einaudi, Turin, 1971); 199. All references to *The Faerie Queene* are from eds. Edwin Greenlaw et al., *The Faerie Queene: Books VI and VII* (Johns Hopkins Press, Baltimore, 1938); 108.

8. Richard Neuse, "Book VI as conclusion to *The Faerie Queene*," *ELH* 35 (1968), 329–53; 345.

9. See Harold H. Blanchard, "Imitations from Tasso in *The Faerie Queene*," *Studies in Philology* 22 (1925), 198–221; 219.

10. Dees records that the "image of the ship" occurs more than thirty times in the poem: Jerome S. Dees, "The ship conceit in *The Faerie Queene*: 'conspicuous allusion' and poetic structure," *Studies in Philology* 72 (1975), 208–25; 213. See also his entry on "ship imagery" in ed. A. C. Hamilton, *The Spenser Encyclopedia* (University of Toronto Press, Toronto, 1990), 655–6.

11. In the 1609 folio edition of the poem, the final line reads "in the port," rather than "on the port," which suggests the eventual arrival there more strongly than the 1596 reading.

12. The association between the pastoral episode and the stanza to Alfonso may have been triggered by the phrase "il furor di peregrine spade" [VII. ix. 5], where the old shepherd describes his pastoral world's immunity to the fury of invading armies. The Italian word "peregrine" clearly makes an impression on Spenser, who chooses it as the name for his son by his second wife Elizabeth Boyle, whom he marries in the summer of 1594.

13. Mountjoy's love of the Italian language and culture is praised by Iacopo Castelvetro in the dedication to "Signor Carlo Blunt" of his edition of Guarini's *Il Pastor fido* and Tasso's *Aminta*, printed by John Wolfe, in 1591:

> Subitamente a lei si voltò, come ad amatrice e ardente seguitatrice d'ogni bella scienza, e sopra ogni altra della nostra favella, e de gli scritti de suoi poeti.

> (Straightaway he turned to you, as to a lover and ardent follower of every beautiful science, and above all else of our language, and of the works of our poets.)

14. Ed. Laurence Michel, *Samuel Daniel: The Civil Wars* (Yale University Press, New Haven, 1958), 72.

15.   See Iacopo Castelvetro's letter to Lodovico Tassoni, Alfonso II's secretary in the Ferrarese fiefdom of Modena, written in June 1584, printed in Angelo Solerti, *La Vita di Torquato Tasso* (Turin and Rome, 1895), ii, 204–05.

16.   Cain points out that Book VI is the only one in the poem that contains no direct praise of Queen Elizabeth: Thomas H. Cain, *Praise in the Faerie Queene* (University of Nebraska Press, Lincoln, 1978), 155–80.

17.   Brand claims that "at least twelve sonnets show textual reminiscences of Tasso's *Rime* and three could be considered translations of Tasso's originals." The three "translations" are sonnets LXXII, LXXIII, and LXXXI: C. P. Brand, *Torquato Tasso* (Cambridge University Press, Cambridge, 1965), 290. See Janet G. Scott, *Les sonnets élisabéthains* (Honoré Champion, Paris, 1929), 159–77 and 319–20, and also Veselin Kostic, *Spenser's Sources in Italian Poetry* (Belgrade, 1969), 38–75, for the sources of *Amoretti*. Scott points out, with reference to Tasso, that "son influence est manifeste dans la seconde moitié des *Amoretti*" [163], and suggests that the following sonnets are indebted to his poetry: LXVII, LXXII, LXXIII, LXXVI, LXXVII, LXXIX, LXXXI, LXXXIV, and LXXXIX. Sonnet LXVII best demonstrates Spenser's simultaneous engagement with Petrarch and Tasso, where the latter's sonnet "Al signor Cesare Pavese" provides a direct model for reconfiguring positively the relationship between poet and unattainable lady figured as a deer in Petrarch's celebrated "Una candida cerva" [sonnet 190].

18.   Ed. Robert M. Durling, *Petrarch's Lyric Poems* (Harvard University Press, Cambridge, 1976), 335.

19.   All references to *Amoretti* are from eds. William Oram et al., *The Yale Edition of the Shorter Poems of Edmund Spenser* (Yale University Press, New Haven, 1989); 621–22.

20.   This is the only Italian analogue for the "ship conceit" in Spenser's poem that Dees cites: Dees, "Ship conceit," 220. Britomart concludes by expressing a similar hope of relief from torment as the poet-lover in *Amoretti* LXIII:

> At last blow vp some gentle gale of ease,
> The which may bring my ship, ere it be rent,
> Vnto the gladsome port of her intent.

> [III. iv. 10. 3–5]

21.   Ed. Lanfranco Caretti, *Orlando furioso* (Einaudi, Turin, 1966), 1380. Translation by Guido Waldman, *Orlando Furioso* (Oxford University Press, Oxford, 1983), 557.

22.   Dees, "Ship conceit," 212, though the phrase refers to Spenser rather than Ariosto in this instance.

JAMES SCHIAVONE

Spenser's Augustine

A manuscript at Pembroke College, called *Wren's Catalogue of the Library, Its Donors and Benefactors,* contains a handwritten note about a library fine levied in 1545. This note proves that alumnus Thomas Pattenson had donated a complete ten-volume set of Augustine's *Opera* (Erasmus's edition) to Pembroke Library by that year. The presence of Erasmus's Augustine as part of Spenser's intellectual milieu has implications, especially as to the competing and nuanced interpretations of Augustine's theology available at Pembroke during the 1570s. Erasmus's arrangement and interpretation of Augustine's theological works highlights the shift from moral and sacramental theology in the anti-Donatist works (A.D. 393–411) to predestinarianism in the anti-Pelagian works (A.D. 412–30), making it possible that Spenser would have distinguished between the early and the late theology of Augustine. This distinction may shed light on the coexistence of predestinarian and free will statements and images in Book 1 of *The Faerie Queene.*

*I*N THE COURSE OF EXPLORING the influence of Augustinian theology on *The Faerie Queene,* I visited Pembroke College Library to determine what works of Augustine had been accessible to Spenser in the 1570s, since I did not want to quote from any work of Augustine unavailable to Spenser. The library possesses a set of Erasmus's magnificent ten-volume edition of Augustine's works, printed by Johan Froben at Basle in 1527–29, but that does not prove that Pembroke College had acquired the set by 1570. However, a handwritten inscription, "Thomas Pattenson/to Pembrokhall, Cambridg," appears on the title page of each volume. The *Alumni Cantabrigienses* records this information about Thomas "Patinson": "B.A. 1492–93. Of Northumberland. M.A. 1496; B.D. 1503–04; D.D. 1522–3. Fellow of Pembroke, 1494, Proctor, 1500–1. Repeatedly employed on University business, Ord. deacon (Ely) Sept. 24 (described as of Durham diocese); priest, Dec. 17, 1496. V. of Bures, Suffolk. Probably V. of Albury, Herts. Perhaps R. of Bishop Wearmouth, 1548–60. Founded a scholarship of God's House. Will of one of these names proved 1546."[1]

This skeleton biography suggests that Pattenson, ordained a Catholic priest under Henry VII, left the Roman church during the Henrician Reformation, since he continued to hold offices in the English Church. We can only guess what intellectual rationale accompanied this change of loyalties. His ownership of Augustine's collected works is suggestive. Both Luther and Calvin attributed their understanding of grace and predestination to their reading of Augustine, and saw his conversion as a model of their own. But was Pattenson's interest in Augustine a cause or a consequence of his convictions? We do not know, but his biography makes it almost certain that Pattenson has donated the set of books before Spenser arrived at Cambridge, since he would have been over 90 years old in 1570.

Another reference clinches the case: Wren's *Catalogue of the Library, its History and Benefactors,* a manuscript from 1617, lists Thomas Pattenson as the donor of the ten volumes, followed by this notation in Latin: "Quic quid rei erat, solvunt pro siccatione/Librorum Doctoris Patenson A.D. 1545—4d." Elizabeth Leedham Green interprets this strange note as a record of a library fine: "If anything was damaged, [then] corrected by drying . . . [the fine is] 4 denarii [pence]." Probably some of the books got wet and were set out to dry in 1545. It is noteworthy in this regard that volumes one and nine of the set are later replacements, lacking Pattenson's usual dedicatory note. Whatever the meaning of the strange first line, the phrasing clearly indicates that the books were donated by 1545. This date also matches up with the will of 1546. These volumes appear to be included in item #2157 in H. M. Adams.[2]

Erasmus produced editions of several different Church Fathers. The publisher Johan Froben recruited Erasmus to the Augustine project in 1517 or 1518. Erasmus worked slowly and intermittently, daunted by the scope of the task and diverted by other projects, and he even sought help, persuading the Spanish humanist Juan Luis Vives to edit and annotate *The City of God,* which was the first volume of the set to come out, in 1522. The massive and expensive volume did not sell very well, so Erasmus abandoned the work for a time, but Froben pestered him to finish the project. Erasmus eventually complied, completing two volumes in 1527 and the other seven by 1529.[3]

The ten-volume *Opera* is a monument to humanist scholarship. Although it contains errors, it was the most accurate text of Augustine in its time, and a great advance over the Amerbach *Opera omnia* of 1506. Many colleges at Cambridge must have possessed a copy of Erasmus's edition. Queen's, Christ, Gonville and Caius, Trinity, St. John's, St. Catherine's, and Corpus Christi all currently have copies,[4] probably acquired during the Reformation. Erasmus's edition includes a selection of Augustine's letters and sermons, and all of the major theological works except the unfinished work *Contra Julian* and the *Deeds of Pelagius (de gestis Pelagii)*. Thus we can be sure that Spenser and his fellow scholars at Pembroke had access to nearly all the works of Augustine.

My argument does not stand on a literal claim that Spenser handled this particular edition, although I think it likely that he did. Even if he did not, the very presence of Erasmus's work shows one of the competing and nuanced interpretations of Augustine available at Pembroke in the 1570s. Augustine's influence on Reformation and Counter-Reformation theology was pervasive and inescapable. Among all the Church Fathers he, by the time of the Reformation, had achieved nearly a mythical stature and an authority second only to that of scripture. This status made disputants on all sides eager to appropriate his authority. His works being copious, unsystematic, addressed to the needs of the moment and to the most contemporary heresy requiring refutation, they lent themselves to widely (I almost wrote "wildly") divergent interpretations, while also furnishing Reformation polemicists with models of doctrinal argument. His works were a field little less fertile than scripture itself for the doctrinal battles which raged in sixteenth-century Christendom. Erasmus, for example, in *De libero arbitrio* argues for the ability of the will to cooperate with grace, emphasizing the change in Augustine's thought on this topic over the years. He explains that Augustine reacted—indeed, overreacted—to the changing circumstances: "After his battle with Pelagius, Augustine became much less just toward free choice than he had been before."[5] Again, he attributes Augustine's position on the lack of merit in good deeds of pagans to the rhetorical situation in which Augustine wrote:

What, then, is free choice worth in us after sin and before grace? About this point ancient and modern writers differ amazingly, as each is concerned with a different aspect of the problem. Those who would avoid despair and complacency, but who would inspire men to hope and endeavor, attributed more to free choice . . . St. Augustine and those who follow him, considering how harmful to true godliness it is for a man to trust in his own powers, are more inclined to favor grace, which Paul everywhere stresses.[6]

This curiously "modern" method of interpreting Augustine's words according to his rhetorical purposes does not accord with the methods of interpretation of the Reformers. In the words of Martin Luther: "To say that Augustine exaggerates in speaking against heretics is to say that Augustine tells lies almost everywhere. This is contrary to common knowledge."[7] In their effort to strip man completely of pride, Luther and Calvin offer an interpretation of Augustine which discounts any human free choice contributing to salvation. In this battle, it was important to have a mastery of Augustine's corpus of works, so that one could not be out-quoted or contradicted. Although Calvin leans heavily on the anti-Pelagian works, he seems to have all of Augustine's writings at his fingertips: he quotes, for example, from Augustine's letters to prove God's righteousness in predestination (III.xxiii.11).[8] As Calvin says: "If I were inclined to compile a whole volume from Augustine, I could easily show my readers that I need no words but his" to explain these high matters (III.xxii.8).[9] Almost the greatest argumentative point that one could score in the debates of sixteenth-century soteriology was to show that Augustine lined up on your side, and against your opponent's position, so that Heinrich Bullinger, in a typical gesture, could trumpet: "I have cited the very words of St. Augustine" on sin, law, and grace.[10]

All of this raises the question: So what? I want to suggest one way in which the availability of Erasmus's Augustine might affect our reading of Spenser. For years, I have been arguing that the first book of *The Faerie Queene* reflects an Augustinian paradox of free will coexisting with predestination. In her book on *Spenser and Biblical Poetics,* Carol Kaske has replied that, although Spenser may have read Augustine in this way, this is not a paradox at all, but a distinction between the early Augustine and the later Augustine, who retracted his former belief in free will, and emphasized God's sovereignty and human helplessness, under pressure of refuting the Pelagian heresy in the last two decades of his life.[11] I used to think this was too sophisticated a way for Spenser to have read Augustine, but a reexamination of the Erasmus edition and of his comments in *De libero arbitrio* has made me think that Spenser may have distinguished, in the same way that Erasmus and Kaske do, the early from the later Augustine. Erasmus's more or less chronological arrangement of Augustine's works, especially the organization of volume seven, would make clear, even to a Cambridge undergraduate, the trajectory of Augustine's thought, from the anti-Donatist works of A.D. 393–411, with their emphasis on sacramental efficacy, to the anti-Pelagian works of 412–430, with their emphasis on predestination. A closer look at the *Opera*'s notes and commentary would help us understand how a reader like Spenser would have understood Augustine, filtered through the lens of Erasmus's editorship.

Tennessee Wesleyan College

NOTES

1   John Venn and J.A. Venn, *Alumni Cantabrigienses, Part I: From the Earliest Times to 1751*, vol. 3 (Cambridge: Cambridge UP, 1924), 319.

2   H.M. Adams, *A Catalogue of Books Printed on the Continent of Europe 1501–1600, in Cambridge Libraries* (London: Cambridge UP, 1967), 78.

3   The information in this paragraph comes from John C. Olin, *Six Essays on Erasmus and a Translation of Erasmus' Letter to Carondelet, 1523* (New York: Forham University Press, 1979) 36–40.

4   Adams, 78.

5   Erasmus, *De libero arbitrio* in *Luther and Erasmus: Free Will and Salvation*, tr. E. Gordon Rupp and Philip S. Watson (Philadelphia: The Westminister Press, 1969), 90.

6   Erasmus, 51–52.

7   Martin Luther, *Disputation against Scholastic Theology* in *Luther's Works*, vol. 31, ed. Harold J. Grimm (Philadelphia: Muhlenberg Press, 1957), 9.

8   John Calvin, *Institutes of the Christian Religion*, tr. John Allen (Philadelphia: Presbyterian Board of Christian Education, 1936, 211.

9   Calvin, 193.

10   Heinrich Bullinger, *The Decades* (London: The Parker Society, 1849–52, 402.

11   Carol V. Kaske, *Spenser and Biblical Poetics* (Ithaca: Cornell University Press, 1999), pp. 144–45.

Appendix: Contents of Erasmus's Agustine

For scholars interested in the works of Augustine available in six-teenth-century Cambridge, the following is a transcription of the table of contents of Erasmus's *Opera*. (There is actually a comprehensive table of contents in volume one, and an individual table in each volume. They differ only in minor matters of abbreviation and capitalization.) I have sometimes transposed u and v for clarity, and have added m when represented by a tilde (~) in the original.

In regard to volume 2 (selected letters of Augustine), it is no use to give the numbering of the letters, since Erasmus's numbering system does not correspond to any modern edition's, as far as I know. Erasmus's titles for the letters should help.

Volume 1

Retratationum
Confessionum
De grammatica
Principia dialectiæ
Categoriæ decem
Principia Rhetorices
De musica
Contra Academicos
De ordine
De vita beata
Soliloquiorum
De magistro
De immortaliate animæ
De quantitate animæ
De libero arbitrio
De vera religione
De moribus ecclesiæ catholicæ, & de moribus Manichæorum
De Genesis contra Manichæos
Regulæ Augustini
Posidonius de vita Augustini

Volume II

Compleatens illius epistolas, non mediocri cura

Consolatio super obitu mariti
De Petro reprehenso a Paulo
De bene vivendo
De baptisom parvulorum
De origine animarum
Quæstio ex epistola Iacobi
De contemptu mundi
Execratio idolatriæ
Paganismi irrisio
De contemptu mundi perfecto
De libero arbitrio
De vi corrigendis hæreticis contra Donatistas
Sex quæstiones contra Paganos expositæ
De correctione Donatistarum, & de moderate cohercendis hæreticis
De vera felicitate
Pro reis quomodo intercedendum
De curiosis quæstionibus
De præsentia dei, & quomodo deus ubiq
De varijs scripturæ locis explicandis
Ad quæstiones novem Paulini
De cohercendis hæreticis
De cohercenda temulentia & contentione
De trinitate unius dei
De immanitate Circumcellionum
Quatenus mali tolerandi
De contemptu mundi, & potestate humana quomodo utendum
De phantasijs intellectus ac memoriæ
De ornatu Christiano
De blasphemijs Manichæorum
Ad ob unius peccatum, alius possit excommunicati
De monachis apostatis
De tempori secundi adventus incerto
De die secundi adventus
De supremo mundi die
De ocio monachorum
Consolatio in adversis
De trinitate incorporea
De ieiunijs priscorum
Contra Pelagianos & Manichæos

Contra Pelagionos
Damnatio Pelagionorum
De Pelagio
De evangelio mortuis prædicato
De anima incorporea
De actu animæ fine corpore
De inquisitione rerum divinarum
Ad Petrus fuerit baptizatus
Regula monachorum
De electione Eradij
De vivendo deo
De tranquillitate animi
De consuetudinibus varijs regionum
Ad inquisitiones Ianuarij
De ritibus ecclesiæ ibidem
De gratio novi testamenti
De orando deum
De afflictione piorum
Consolation super morte uxoris
De corrigendis hæreticis
Exhortatio ad paim vitam
De catholicæ ecclesiæ incremento
De disciplinis liberalibus
De officio doctoris ecclesiastici
De perpetiendis malis spe vitæ coelestis
Quomodo laudari possit Christianus
De afflictionibus patienter ferendis
De non temere iudicando
Exhortatio ad amorem charitatis
De pia tristitia quam boni ferunt ex impietate malorum
De corporum resurrectione
De schismate finiendo
Institutio episcopi
De toleranda adversa valetudine, & cohibenda ira
De ineffabili trinitate
De vera beatitudine
Contra Donatistas
De iureiurando, Idolothytis, & uim ui repellendo
De vera amicitia
De malis huius mundi tolerandis
De origine animarum & Pelagianis
De peccato originali parvulorum
De corrigendis hæreticis citra mortis œnam

De mansuetudine ecclesiastica
De ecclesia catholica contra Donatistas
Contra Donatistarum pertinacium
    Et de innocentia Cæciliani, ibidem
De concorda sarcienda
De schismate Donatistarum
De dessidio Donatistarum
Exhortatio ad concordiam ecclesiæ
De Donatistis vi cohercendis
De parricida Donatista rebaptizato
De immani licentia Donatistarum
Contra Arianos
De deo non triformi, sed uno
Altercatio inter Augustinum & Pascentium, de trinitate
De fuga in persectutione
Epistolæ Bonifacij ad Augustinum, Augustini ad Bonifacium
Votum continentiæ non suscipiendum nisi ex coniugum consensu
De Iudaismo, & vocabulo Iudæ
De moderando supplicio nocentum
Quomodo etiam cogendi sint homnies ad bona

Volume III

De doctrina Christiana
Locutionum
De fide & Symbolo
Enchiridion ad Laurentium
De ecclesiasticis dogmatibus
De fide ad Petrum diaconum
De trinitate
De Genesi ad litteram imperfectus
De mirabilibus sacræ scripturæ
De agone Christiano
De opere monachorum
De spiritu & literra ad Marcellinum
De divinatione dæmonum
De spiritu & anima
Speculum [de praeceptis dominicis]
Quæstiunculæ de trinitate
De benedictionilus Jacob patriarchæ
Sententiæ [ex Augustini & aliorum libris deceptæ]

Volume IV

De mendacio ad Consentium
Contra mendacium ad eundem
De fide & operibus
Quæstionum [Exudum?]
Quæstionum evagelicarum
Quæstionum evang. secundum Matthæum
De consensu Evangelistarum
Octogin tatrium quæstionum
Vigintiunius sententiarum
De diversis quæstionibus ad Simplicianum
De octo Dulcitti quæstionib.
Quæstionum LXV dialogus
Quæstionum ueteris & novi testamenti
De cura pro mortuis gerenda ad Paulinum
De catechizandis rudibus
De incarnatione verbi
De trinitate & unitate dei
De essentia divinitatis
De fide rerum invisibilium
De substantia dilectionis
De continentia
De patientia
De bono viduitatis
De vera & falsa poenitentia
De salutaribus documentis
De amicitia
De sermone domini in monte
Expositionis epist. Pauli ad Rom. inchoate
Expositionis quarundam propositiorum ex epist. ad Rom.
Expositionis epistolae Pauli ad Galatas
Annotationum in Iob

Volume V

De Civitate Dei

Volume VI

De hæresibus ad Quoduultdeum
De quinq hæresibus oratio
De altercatione ecclesiæ & synagogæ, dialogus

De utilitate credendi ad Honoratum
Contra epistolam Manichæi, quam vocant Fundamenti
De duabus animabus contra Manichæos
Contra Fortunatum quendam Manichæorum presbyterum
Contra Adimantum Manichæum
De actis cum Felice Manichæ
Contra Secundinum Manichæum
De natura boni contra Manichæos
De fide contra Manichæos
Contra adversarium legis, & prophetarum
Contra Priscillianistas, & Origenistas ad Orosium
Contra sermonem Arianorum
Contra Maximinum Arianorum episcopum
Contra Felicianum Arianum de unitate trinit. ad Optatum
De bono coniugali contra Iovinianum
De sancta virginitate
De adulterinis coniugiis ad Pollentium

Volume VII

Divi Augustini contra partem Donati, Psalmus
Contra epistolam Parmeniani
Contra litteras Petiliani Cirthensis episcopi Doinatistæ
Contra Cresconium Donatistum grammaticum
Contra Gaudentii Donatistarum episcopi epistolam
De baptismo contra Donatistas
De unico baptismo contra Petilianum
De unitate ecclesiae contra Petiliani Donatistae episolam
Opus breviculi collationum cum Donatistas
Post collationem contra Donatistas
Super gestis cum Emerito Donatistarum episcop, sermo
De gestis cum Emerito Donatistarum episcopo
Contra Fulgentium Donatistam
De peccatorum meritis & remissione, ac de baptismo parvulorum,
ad Marcellino
De natura & gratia contra Pelagianos
De gratio Christi et de Peccato originali, contra Pelagium &
Cælestium
De nuptiis & concupiscentia ad Valerium comitem
Contra duas epistolas Pelagianorum ad Bonifacium
Contra Iulianum Pelagianum
De anima & eius origine
De prædestinatione & gratia

Prosperi epistola ad Augustinum de reliquiis Pelagianæ hæreseos
Hilarij epistola ad eundem de eadem materia
De prædestinatione sanctorum
De bono perseverantiæ
De prædestinatione dei
De gratia & libero arbitrio ad Valentinum
Ad eundem de correptione & gratia
Ad articulos sibi falso impositos, Augustini responsio
Contra Pelagianos hypognosticon
De perfectine iusticiæ Hominis contra Cælestium

Volume VIII

Enarrationes in Psalmos mysticos

Volume IX

In Evangelium Ioannis expositio
In epistolam Ioannis expositio
In Apocalypsim Ioannis ad Parthos expositio
Meditationum
De diligendo deo liber alius, qui & Meditationum inscribitur
Soliloquiorum animæ ad deum
Manuale [ad Laurentium]
De triplici habitaculo
Scalæ Paradisi
De duodecium abusionum gradibus
De contritione cordis
De cognitione veræ vitæ
De speculo
De vita Christiana
De assumptione beatæ Mariæ virginis
De disciplina Christiana
De decem chordis
De cantico novo
De contemptu mundi
De vanitate seculi
De obedientia & humilitate sermo
De bono disciplinæ sermo
De visitatione infirmorum
De consolatione mortuorum sermones duo
De quarta feria, sive cultura agri dominici sermo
De cataclysmo sermo

De tempore Barbarico sermo
De sobrietate & virginitate sermo
Speculum peccatoris tractatus
De pœnitentiæ medicina
De utilitate pænitentiæ tractatus
De conflicto vitiorum & virtutum
De quatuor virtubibus charitatis tractatus
De laudibus charitatis tractatus
De honestate mulierum
De pastoribus
De ovibus liber sive homilia
De symbolo fidei ad catechumenos
De convenientia decem præceptorum & decem plagarum
De rectitudine catholicæ conversationis tracta
De utilitate ieiunij tractatus
De urbis excidio tractatus
De creatione primi hominis tractatus
De arbore scientiæ boni & mali tractatus
De pugna animæ tractatus
De antichristo tractatus
Psalterium quod matri suæ composuit
Super Magnificant expositio
Super Magnificant expositio

Volume X

Sermones habet
De verbis domini
Deverbis Apostoli
Homiliæ L.
Homiliæ de tempore
Homiliæ de sanctis
Ad Fratres in Eremo

Index

291